$13.50

TEXTBOOK OF DENDROLOGY

THE AMERICAN FORESTRY SERIES

Henry J. Vaux, consulting editor

Allen and Sharpe · An Introduction to American Forestry
Avery · Forest Measurements
Baker · Principles of Silviculture
Boyce · Forest Pathology
Brockman · Recreational Use of Wild Lands
Brown, Panshin, and Forsaith · Textbook of Wood Technology
    Volume II—The Physical, Mechanical, and Chemical Properties of the Commercial Woods of the United States
Bruce and Schumacher · Forest Mensuration
Chapman and Meyer · Forest Mensuration
Chapman and Meyer · Forest Valuation
Dana · Forest and Range Policy
Davis · American Forest Management
Davis · Forest Fire: Control and Use
Duerr · Fundamentals of Forestry Economics
Graham and Knight · Principles of Forest Entomology
Guise · The Management of Farm Woodlands
Harlow and Harrar · Textbook of Dendrology
Hunt and Garratt · Wood Preservation
Panshin and de Zeeuw · Textbook of Wood Technology
    Volume I—Structure, Identification, Uses, and Properties of the Commercial Woods of the United States
Panshin, Harrar, Bethel, and Baker · Forest Products
Shirley · Forestry and Its Career Opportunities
Stoddart and Smith · Range Management
Trippensee · Wildlife Management
    Volume I—Upland Game and General Principles
    Volume II—Fur Bearers, Waterfowl, and Fish
Wackerman · Harvesting Timber Crops

Walter Mulford was consulting editor of this series from its inception in 1931 until January 1, 1952.

Opening buds of sugar maple ×12.

TEXTBOOK OF DENDROLOGY

Covering the Important Forest Trees
of the United States and Canada

WILLIAM M. HARLOW, Ph.D.
*Emeritus Professor of Wood Technology, State University
of New York, College of Forestry*

ELLWOOD S. HARRAR, Ph.D., Sc.D.
*James B. Duke Professor of Wood Science
School of Forestry, Duke University*

Fifth Edition

McGRAW-HILL BOOK COMPANY

New York   St. Louis   San Francisco   Toronto   London   Sydney

TEXTBOOK OF DENDROLOGY

Library of Congress Catalog Card Number 68-17188

ISBN 07-026569-0

101112131415 HDMB 79876543

In memory of HARRY PHILIP BROWN
whose zeal we admired and whose friendship we prized

Preface

Most tree books featuring North American trees are either (1) encyclopedic, such as Sargent's monumental "Silva of North America," later condensed into one volume, which has been adapted by nearly every writer of tree books since it first appeared, or (2) local, as exemplified by the many excellent state and regional manuals.

Nearly all these publications have been written from the botanical or taxonomic standpoint and in general treat each species in the same detail. It is obviously impossible for a beginning student in forestry to gain an adequate knowledge of more than a few of the nearly one thousand tree species native to this country. Rather, it is desirable only to cover as many groups (genera) as possible, and to illustrate these with the species of greatest importance to forestry.

The native coniferous genera have all been included because of their relative importance and fewer numbers; but several families, and many genera and species of the broad-leaved trees, have been omitted. It is felt that students of forestry should first know well the commercial species of North America, and then become familiar with the other important trees and shrubs of the locality where they may find themselves practicing forestry. The latter must usually be done by the student himself with the aid of a local tree manual. If he has mastered generic characters during his course in dendrology, discovering the identity of previously unknown local species should be a pleasurable experience.

The nomenclature, with but few exceptions, conforms to that of the latest U.S. Forest Service Check List (212). Where the common names in that publication depart from those in "Standardized Plant Names" (197), the SPN name is also given. Several species of trees used by the lumber and woodworking industries have still other names that do not appear in either of these two publications. These trade names are also listed and are indicated by the symbol (Tr) which appears immediately after each of them.

In the fourth and fifth editions, there have also been some changes in the spelling of certain scientific names. Certain specific epithets formerly ending in a single *i* are now written with a double *ii*, for example, *michauxii, engelmannii, kelloggii,* or *sargentii.* A single *i* is still used, however, when it follows a vowel or *-er* or *y,* as in such names as *catesbaei, coulteri,* and *jeffreyi.* The "International Rules" insist that scientific names must follow the exact spelling of their authors unless, of course, such names were obviously misspelled. Even though it seems incongruous to use a single *n* in *Prunus pensylvanica* and a double *nn* in *Fraxinus pennsylvanica,* we have done so rather than violate the "Rules."

Several illustrations have been borrowed, and the source is gratefully indicated in each case, with the exception of a few which first appeared over the name of one of the authors in *American Forests Magazine,* to whom acknowledgment is now made.

The plates in the Introduction were prepared by Mr. L. E. Partelow, State University College of Forestry, Syracuse, N.Y. Several of them are adapted from similar illustrations in "Trees of New York State," by permission of the author, Dr. H. P. Brown.

Although by definition botanists no longer consider the reproductive organs of the conifers as "flowers," we have retained this designation for convenience. Statistics concerning the number of seeds per pound are from the "Woody Plant Seed Manual" (358), an excellent reference book that every forestry student should own.

During the infinitesimally short passage of geological time since this text first appeared in 1937, the identifying features of the woody plants described have changed but little, if at all. However, information about them, particularly that under the heading of General Description, continues to accumulate.

The literature on dendrology and allied subjects is expanding on a vast scale. As examples, C. E. Wood, Jr. (387) in preparing a paper on the genera of woody Ranales in the southeastern United States mentions that one and one-half years were spent checking through some 50,000 references on the seed plants of this area, and Bakuzis and Hansen (22) in their monograph on a single species, balsam fir, consulted some 2,300 references.

We can only hope that we have not overlooked too many significant contributions to the dendrology of the United States (exclusive of Hawaii) and Canada, and shall be glad to have such oversights as well as those of fact called to our attention. In any case, the Selected References can be only suggestive and not exhaustive.

The range maps in this fifth edition are adapted from those of Little

(127) and Critchfield and Little (80) with other sources also consulted. For beginning students it is believed best to present only a general pattern of the distribution of each species. No attempt is made to include far outlying stations; these can be found in the two references cited. Also, within the patterns shown, there may be sizable areas where a species is not found. In the mountainous western United States, especially, this is correlated with elevation.

To draw absolutely accurate maps showing the distribution of species covering thousands of square miles is virtually impossible. Published maps are always subject to revision as more knowledge becomes available.

Because this book does not cover all the woody species for any one portion of the country, detailed keys are omitted. Instead, tables covering family, generic, and specific features are provided. Our experience shows that basic information is more readily assimilated in this form. This does not mean that keys are not of primary importance, and considerable time should be spent with them in identifying local material.

We are grateful to our many friends who have made helpful suggestions during the preparation of the original manuscript and the four subsequent revisions.

In this, the fifth edition, we are happy to include the following: Bryant Bannister, R. W. Becking, E. L. Core, J. E. Ericson, P. W. Fletcher, Emanuel Fritz, R. S. Goodrich, Fay Hyland, E. H. Ketchledge, E. L. Little, Jr., W. E. McQuilkin, F. A. Meyer, J. L. Morrison, G. L. Partain, T. O. Perry, J. C. Sammi, D. M. Schmitt, A. J. Sharp, R. B. Smith, A. E. Squillace, G. R. Stairs, Arthur Stupka, G. H. Vincent, D. B. Ward, F. M. White, H. V. Wiant, Jr., and P. J. Zinke. Grateful acknowledgement is made to Luise E. Walker for the proofreading of this fifth edition.

William M. Harlow
Ellwood S. Harrar

Contents

List of Primary Species

The following list gives the one hundred primary species found in this book.

Pines. Eastern white, western white, sugar; red, pitch, jack, longleaf, shortleaf, loblolly, slash, Virginia, ponderosa, Jeffrey, lodgepole.
Larches. Tamarack, western.
Spruces. Red, black, white, Sitka, Englemann.
Douglas-fir.
Hemlocks. Eastern, western.
Firs. Balsam, Pacific silver, California red, noble, grand, white.
Redwood, and giant sequoia.
Baldcypress.
"Cedars." Incense, northern white, western red, Atlantic white, Port-Orford, Alaska, eastern red.
Black willow.
Poplars. Quaking aspen, balsam poplar, eastern cottonwood, black cottonwood.
Black walnut and butternut.
Hickories. Shagbark, shellbark, mockernut, red, pignut, pecan, bitternut.

Birches. Yellow, sweet, paper.
Red alder.
American beech.
American chestnut.
Oaks. White, bur, overcup, post, Oregon white; northern red, black, Shumard, southern red, cherrybark, scarlet, pin, Nuttall, willow, water, laurel, live.
Elms. American, rock, slippery.
Hackberry.
Magnolias. Cucumbertree, southern.
Yellow-poplar.
Sweetgum.
American sycamore.
Black cherry.
Locusts. Honey, black.
Maples. Sugar, black, red, silver, boxelder, bigleaf.
Basswood.
Tupelos. Water, black.
Ashes. White, green.

Additional species important to forestry listed in "Silvics of Forest Trees of the United States" (127) are:

Pinyon, pond, sand, and Monterey pines; mountain hemlock; subalpine fir; Rocky Mountain and western junipers; bigtooth aspen; swamp cottonwood; tanoak; swamp white and chinkapin oaks; water and nutmeg hickories; winged elm; sugarberry; sassafras; California-laurel; white basswood; Pacific madrone; Ohio and yellow buckeyes; and flowering dogwood.

These as well as many others are included in "Textbook of Dendrology," but in smaller type than the primary species. Cucumbertree and boxelder are not listed in "Silvics of Forest Trees."

Introduction

A knowledge of the names of trees, their habits, and principal botanical features is basic to advanced studies in forestry. Literally, dendrology means "the study of trees," but through common usage it has come to signify the taxonomy of woody plants [1] including trees, shrubs, and vines. Taxonomy is concerned with the classification, nomenclature, and identification of natural objects whether these are insects, reptiles, trees, birds, or others of the host of living things found on the earth.[2] Besides the taxonomy of woody plants, dendrology as here defined includes tree habits and ranges, since these seem to be most easily learned when first contact is made with the various species covered in both the field and the classroom.[3]

To most of us a tree may be a rather definite thing; yet the line of demarcation between trees and shrubs is by no means clear-cut. A given species may be shrubby near the extremities of its range, or at or near timberline, and still attain large proportions elsewhere. For example, the Alaska-cedar is ordinarily a moderately large tree, but in exposed situations at timberline it is often reduced to a dwarfed or even heathlike shrub; and white spruce, an important pulpwood tree of eastern Canada, is shrubby in habit in the far north. Similarly, the distinction between shrubs and vines is often poorly defined since several native species of woody plants are at first vinelike, and then become shrubby as they approach maturity.

For the sake of convenience, a tree may be defined as a woody plant

[1] Woody plants differ from herbaceous plants in having an aerial stem which persists for more than one season, and in most cases a cambium layer for periodic growth in diameter.
[2] Also including extinct forms through fossils or other remains, and even inanimate objects.
[3] For a historical discussion of the meaning of the word "dendrology" see W. A. Dayton (93).

1

which at maturity is 20 ft or more in height,[1] with a single trunk, un-branched for at least several feet above the ground, and having a more or less definite crown. Shrubs, in contrast, are smaller and usually exhibit several erect, spreading, or prostrate stems and a general bushy appearance. Lianas are climbing vines; plants of this sort are extremely numerous in the rain-drenched forests of the tropics, although a few species such as the wild grape, the moonseed, and the Virginia creeper are indigenous to temperate regions.

A knowledge of the fundamentals of *classification, nomenclature,* and *identification* is requisite to all work in dendrology. Accordingly, each of these taxonomic phases will be discussed.

CLASSIFICATION

The classification of plants dates back to ancient Greek civilization, when Theophrastus (372–287 B.C.), a student of Aristotle's, and by many considered to be the father of botanical science, described and classified about 480 kinds of plants. He differentiated between woody and herbaceous forms but did not recognize any botanical relationships.

In the sixteenth century, Caesalpino (1519–1603), an Italian physician, published a classification of a large number of plants based upon the nature and structure of their seeds.

Carolus Linnaeus, or Carl Von Linné (1707–1778), the great Swedish botanist, has been called the founder of modern plant classification through his extensive works "Genera Plantarum" and "Species Plantarum." He arranged plants by a "sexual system," using the number and placement of stamens and pistils to separate the various kinds into workable groups. He never claimed that this was a "natural" system, but only a very convenient one for arranging and identifying plants. It should be remembered that in his day it was thought that every plant and animal was a separate creation which had existed from the "beginning," some 4,000 years B.C. Few if any scientists could visualize the development of present-day plants from primitive ones, through vast stretches of hundreds of millions of years. The concept of evolution had yet to be established.

The modern age in biology began in 1859 when Charles Darwin published his "Origin of Species"—revolutionizing scientific thinking and provoking almost unending controversy. At last, man began to look upon all of life from an entirely new viewpoint. Instead of grouping plants merely for convenience, that is, *artificially,* the aim was to construct *natural* or *phylogenetic* [2] arrangements of related groups, with the most primitive or

[1] Sudworth (341) proposed a minimum height of 8 ft and a diameter of 2 in.
[2] The noun phylogeny signifies genealogy (race or family history).

oldest coming first, followed in order by the others, and terminating with the most recent ones resulting from the processes of evolution. The construction of a phylogenetic system has proved to be an enormously difficult task. It is one thing to place all plants with 5 stamens in a single group (artificial), and quite another to decide whether the presence of 5 stamens means that the plants are *related* to each other. The fossil record (paleontology) may show that certain of these plants are millions of years older, or younger, than the others. However, flower structure when viewed in perspective has proved extremely valuable in building natural systems. To the fossil record, and the classic features of flowers, fruit, seeds, leaves, and other plant parts, there can now be added such things as wood anatomy, cytology, genetics, pollen morphology, and biochemistry (2, 303, 328, 350). Plants with flowers of simple structure are usually regarded as primitive or of great antiquity, while those with structurally complex flowers are ordinarily conceded to be of much more recent origin. If this were invariably true, the taxonomist should experience little difficulty in arranging trees and other seed-bearing plants in the order of their apparent descent, listing those of greatest age first and those of most recent origin last. However, the phylogenetic positions of several plant families have never been accurately determined because of conflicting evidence. It is often extremely difficult to ascertain whether a certain plant (or group of plants) is inherently simple structurally, or whether it is simple through extensive evolutionary modification. Plants of the latter sort are said to be *reduced* or simplified through *reduction*. Such plants are the subjects of much taxonomic disagreement among systematists. One group of investigators may assert that a given family is inherently primitive and classify it accordingly, while another group of equally well-qualified botanists may insist that the same family is a reduced type, and subsequently assign it to an advanced position in their own classification.

The difficulties involved in constructing a natural system can be demonstrated graphically by sketching a tree with its trunk, limbs, and many small branchlets or twigs. One may allow certain present-day groups, e.g., the birches, alders, oaks, beeches, and chestnuts, to represent the twigs or branch ends, and it can then be seen that each of these joins, or is related to, the larger branches which eventually pass into the main trunk. These larger limbs represent extinct forms from which it is presumed the modern species have evolved. Now if one erases all of the tree except the branch tips, or, in other words, the various species as they are known at present, the problem of the taxonomist will instantly be appreciated, namely, that of reconstructing the original tree, or at least the arranging of the branch tips in proper relation to each other.

Since the problems are so extremely complex, it is not surprising that no one system of classification is universally accepted.[1]

The monumental "Genera Plantarum" (1862–1883) developed by George Bentham and Sir Joseph Dalton Hooker at the Royal Botanic Gardens, Kew, England, using their extensive collections, has been called "the greatest taxonomic work ever produced in Great Britain." It is interesting that although this work was published during the turmoil resulting from the publication of Darwin's "Origin of Species," and Hooker supplied Darwin with certain collections, no claim was ever made that "Genera Plantarum" comprised a natural or phylogenetic system. However, later taxonomists were to find that it is closer to a natural system than some others that have been proposed. Bentham and Hooker were remarkable men, who complemented each other in background and experience. Bentham was an herbarium man with a legal education, while Hooker, at home in forest and jungle, roamed the earth collecting plants on every one of the major land masses; eventually, he followed his illustrious father as director of the world-famous Kew Gardens.

The system proposed by Bentham and Hooker was favored by Great Britain and the Commonwealth, and was recently followed by Hutchinson in his "Genera of Flowering Plants" (182).

The United States and other countries have preferred the system developed by the great German taxonomists Adolf Engler and Karl Prantl in "Die natürlichen Pflanzenfamilien" (1887–1909) and continued by Engler with other authors in more recent works (117). As far as the families in "Textbook of Dendrology" are concerned, perhaps the most obvious difference between the Bentham-Hooker and the Engler-Prantl systems lies in the position of the Amentiferae (see page 215). Engler and Prantl considered these families as most primitive, while Bentham and Hooker began their system with the Magnoliales and thought the Amentiferae to be more recent, their floral structures simplified by reduction. While it is recognized that the Engler-Prantl system may not include the most recent concepts of natural classification, it is used in this text for convenience in the presentation and arrangement of the various families. A system initiated by Charles E. Bessey (1845–1915), an American botanist, has found much favor with taxonomists both in this country and abroad.

DEFINITION OF A SPECIES. Since a species is but a biological concept, its limits are largely a matter of individual interpretation. The French taxonomist de Jussieu defined a species as "the perennial succession of similar individuals perpetuated by generation." Perhaps a simpler way of

---

[1] For an excellent account of the precursors of some of our modern trees, see "Tree Ancestors" by Berry (33).

saying the same thing is that a *species* is a collection of individuals so similar that they suggest common parentage and produce like offspring.

According to Gleason (138),

A proper concept of a classificatory group, no matter what its rank or extent, is always reached by a process of synthesis rather than analysis. Our ideas of a species, so far as we develop them from personal experience, are derived entirely from the specimens which we see. From the visible concrete morphological characters of each specimen we abstract the common features which we then regard as the general characters of the species, and at the same time we assume that there exist in nature other individuals of like character which we have not seen. In general this assumption is true, since new collections of material are usually referable to known species without necessitating any revision of our previous concepts. Many species are first brought to the attention of botanists by a single specimen, so that the concept of the species is no broader than the single plant affords. The collection of further material almost invariably leads to the merging of one species with another. How broad a specific concept may be, how great a variation in structure may be permitted within the confines of one species, are matters of personal opinion. Most of the differences in classification are caused not by different bodies of facts available to the disagreeing botanists, but to different values or interpretations given to these facts.

Even though a species is thought of as a group of individuals, it is commonly founded upon a single specimen, the "type" which was first described, named, and published by its author. The location and availability for reference of this specimen (*holotype*) is of the greatest importance to future workers.

For an excellent, perceptive discussion of the species problem, see also "Biosystematy" by W. H. Camp (60).

Minor differences, such as those of needle length or color of foliage, may give to certain individuals of a given species the status of a *variety* (*varietas*).

At the World Botanical Congress of 1950, in Stockholm, the idea of "typical varieties" was adopted. A species is considered as the sum of its varieties. Therefore, when a first variety in a species is named, there is automatically created another variety, the *typical variety* which comprises the type species as first described. In the case of ponderosa pine (typical) the name is written *Pinus ponderosa* var. *ponderosa* without any author's name following it. In this text there seems to be no possibility of mistaken identity, and so for the sake of simplicity this practice is not followed.

A *hybrid* is a plant produced by crossing two species, or geographic races within a species. Hybrids may be either natural or artificial. The symbol $\times$ is placed before the species names of hybrid plants. For instance, *Quercus* $\times$ *jackiana* Schneid. is thought to be a hybrid between *Q*.

alba L. and *Q. bicolor* Willd. This also could be written *Q. alba* × *Q. bicolor*. (See 213, 307.)

Better trees for the future are being developed by controlled hybridization (see chestnut, page 286). Certain hybrid crosses may yield progeny of great promise. Similar progenies can then be produced by repeating the successful crosses in seed orchards established for this purpose. If the hybrid progeny shows too much variation, a single outstanding tree can be propagated vegetatively. The population developed from a single tree, the *ortet*, is called a *clone*. The cuttings, root sprouts, or scions are *ramets*.

To bring order out of the chaos of "varietal" names, there was published in 1958 the "International Code of Nomenclature for Cultivated Plants." Article 5 states "the term cultivar (variety) denotes an assemblage of cultivated individuals which are distinguished by any characters (morphological, physiological, cytological, chemical or others) significant for the purposes of agriculture, forestry, or horticulture, and which, when reproduced (sexually or asexually), retain their distinguishing features." cv or cultivar names must not be written in Latin, and are enclosed by single quotation marks. As an example there is *Gleditsia triacanthos* L. 'Calhoun' (Sunnyridge Nursery, Swarthmore, Pa., catalogue, 1948). This was selected for its heavy production of fruits to be used as fodder.

Although the terms cultivar and "variety" are exact equivalents, it should be noted that *variety* (*varietas*), as already mentioned, is a botanical category intermediate between *species* and *forma*.

DEFINITIONS OF LARGER UNITS. A *genus* is a collection of closely related species, and in like manner a *family* is composed of related genera; the larger groups may be defined similarly. When any one of these groups, except the species, contains only one of the next smaller units, it may be called *monotypic* or a *monotype*.[1] This situation commonly results when a certain plant is so different from all others that it will not fit into an already described group. An extreme case is the Oriental ginkgo tree, which is monotypic as to order, family, and genus.

SAMPLE CLASSIFICATION. To illustrate the relative positions of the various groups, one of the varieties of limber pine may be classified as follows:

KINGDOM	Plant
DIVISION	Spermatophyta
SUBDIVISION	Gymnospermae
ORDER	Coniferales
FAMILY	Pinaceae
GENUS	*Pinus*
SPECIES	*Pinus flexilis* James
VARIETY	*Pinus flexilis* var. *reflexa* Engelm.

[1] Strictly speaking, monotypic is applied only to a genus with but a single species.

The word *taxon* (plural *taxa*) is an abbreviation of the words "taxonomic group," and may be applied to any of the above groups (order, family, genus, etc.).

NOMENCLATURE

COMMON NAMES. How trees acquire names is an interesting chapter not only in dendrology but also in the social development of a people in relation to their use and enjoyment of the forest.

The chief characteristics of trees usually influence the selection of their common names, although the names of many botanists or their friends have also been commemorated in this way. A few examples are: (1) *Habitat:* swamp white oak, sandbar willow, subalpine fir, river birch, mountain hemlock. (2) *Some distinctive feature:* weeping willow, bigleaf maple, whitebark pine, bitternut hickory, cutleaf birch, quaking aspen, overcup oak. (3) *Locality or region:* Pacific yew, Idaho white pine, southern red oak, Ohio buckeye, Virginia pine. (4) *Use:* canoe birch, sugar maple, tanoak, paper-mulberry. (5) *In commemoration:* Nuttall oak, Engelmann spruce, Sargent cypress, Douglas-fir. (6) *Adaptation of names from other languages* (e.g., Indian, Latin, Spanish): chinkapin, arborvitae, and frijolito.

Unfortunately for the beginner, the application of common names is not regulated by any constituted authority, and one may encounter two or more totally unrelated species with identical common names, as illustrated by the use of the term "larch." Botanically the larches comprise a group of deciduous conifers belonging to the genus *Larix*. However, lumbermen along the lower Columbia River apply the term larch to noble fir, and in some instances even to Pacific silver fir. Furthermore, the lodgepole pine of the West may be called "tamarack" or "larch." The term "larch" as applied to these three species is inaccurate and misleading. Another example is the lumberman's use of the name "pine." The only true pines belong to the genus *Pinus*, but the Australian *Araucarias* and members of several other unrelated genera of the Southern Hemisphere are also marketed under the name of pine. Similarly, Douglas-fir timber has been exported as "Oregon pine" to England, Japan, Australia, and other timber markets of the world.

Conversely, as might be expected, many trees have from 10 to 30 different local or trade names, and often there has been no general agreement in applying a single name to a given species over its entire range; this can be strikingly demonstrated by traveling from one community to another and cataloguing the different local names applied to the same set of species. During his lifetime, G. B. Sudworth of the U.S. Forest Service kept such records, and these are incorporated in the 1927 Check

List (341), which is a tabulation of our native trees, their names and ranges. Altogether, more than one thousand different trees are listed; but the total number of names applied is about 9,000, or approximately an average of eight for each.[1] Sudworth's 1927 Check List is especially valuable to the forester because it lists a large number of common names for the various species, especially the important ones. As an example, 30 names are given for longleaf pine, together with the regions or states where these names are used.

The American Joint Committee on Horticultural Nomenclature has attempted to adopt a single acceptable common name for each species, and the results of their labors are to be found in "Standardized Plant Names" (197), a catalogue of names both common and scientific. In this book, whenever a species is not what its common name seems to indicate, the two words of the name are compounded or at least hyphenated, thus, pineapple, osageorange, and white-cedar. Using this system, the student knows at a glance that the first species is not an apple, the second is not an orange, and the third is not a cedar. This is a very useful principle and has been followed extensively, but not wholly, by the 1953 Check List of the U.S. Forest Service (212). Some of the SPN "combinations" were thought to be just too much for the eye to follow, or too remote from common usage, e.g., whitecedar, falsecypress, mountainlaurel, and fish-fuddletree. The nomenclature of this fifth edition of "Textbook of Dendrology" is that of the Check List with the additions mentioned in the Preface, page ix.

Finally, common names are restricted in use to people of one language. For example, the maple in Spain is known as *acre*, in Germany as *Ahorn*, and in France as *érable*.

SCIENTIFIC NAMES. Because of the great confusion in common names, it is necessary to have some universal system which can be used not only within the boundaries of a single country but throughout the world. Such a system has been developed through the use of Latin names, many of which were first applied when this language was used by scientists of all countries. This practice has been continued, and even now not only are technical names written in Latin but also the initial descriptions of new species. These are then followed by translations into whatever language is used by the journal in which the descriptions appear. Since Latin is a dead language, the laws governing its syntax remain unchanged with the passing of time.

Scientific names have been in common use since the middle of the eighteenth century when Linnaeus published his monumental "Species

---

[1] According to the 1953 Check List (212), there are in North America, exclusive of Mexico, 77 families of trees (or containing trees), 252 genera, 865 species, 61 varieties, and 101 hybrids.

Plantarum" (1753). In this book, Linnaeus gave the generic or group name, the species designation, which usually consists of a short descriptive phrase, and finally in the otherwise blank margin of the page a single name set in italics. He called this the "trivial" name and used it as an indexing device. His students and followers soon found it convenient to write the generic name followed by the "trivial" name. This practice gives a generic name followed by a species name for each plant, the combination constituting *binomial nomenclature*. This system has been credited to Linnaeus, even though it seems doubtful that he originally intended to promote it, and rarely used it himself until late in life. Furthermore, other botanists, among them Gaspard Bauhin, had used binomials more than a century earlier, but they were not consistent in the practice.

The complete designation for a tree or other plant consists of three parts, viz., a generic name, a specific name, and the full or abbreviated name of the person, or persons, responsible for the original published plant description. Thus in the scientific name *Quercus imbricaria* Michaux, *Quercus* is the generic or group name, *imbricaria* is the specific or species name, and Michaux is the person who named and described the tree. Generic names always appear first and are always capitalized, while specific names begin with small letters.[1] In common practice, the author's name is omitted except in scientific writing, where it is used at least once when a species is first mentioned, to dispel any doubt as to its identity. It is customary to underline technical names in written or typewritten work, and to set them in italics in printed manuscripts; but the authors' name, when it appears, should never be designated in either of these two ways.

Since *Quercus imbricaria* is the scientific name of the shingle oak, it follows that no other species may be so designated. Other oaks will have, of course, the same generic name, but it will always be in combination with other specific epithets. For example, the scientific name of black oak is *Quercus velutina* Lam., while that of coast live oak is *Quercus agrifolia* Née, and that of pin oak is *Quercus palustris* Muenchh. The varietal name, if any, follows the specific name. For example, cherrybark oak, which is considered to be a variety of the southern red oak, is technically known as *Quercus falcata* var. *pagodaefolia* Ell. In some books, such as Sudworth's Check List (341), the "var." is omitted.

One frequently encounters scientific names followed by the names of two authors, the first of which appears in parentheses. *Taxodium distichum* (L.) Rich. was originally *Cupressus disticha* L. Linnaeus included baldcypress in the same genus with the true cypresses. Later,

---

[1] Some authors capitalize species names if named after a person, or if derived from an old generic or classical name. The "Rules" allow this usage but advise against it.

Richard recognized the baldcypresses as a distinct group, gave them a separate, new generic name, *Taxodium* Rich., and transferred this species under the new combination, *Taxodium distichum* (L.) Rich. When a scientific name is followed by the names of two authors, e.g., *Pinus jeffreyi* Grev. & Balf., it means that both authors were responsible for the original description.

The use of scientific names and the coinage of new ones are governed by a botanical code of nomenclature. The first code of this sort was outlined at the Paris International Botanical Congress in 1867 and provided (1) that a plant could have but one valid scientific name; (2) that the name should be the oldest usable one beginning with Linnaeus' "Species Plantarum," published in 1753; (3) that two different species or two different genera could not bear the same name; (4) that the generic and specific combinations should be succeeded by the name or names of their authors. In 1905, almost forty years later, the third International Botanical Congress was held in Vienna, Austria. It was generally agreed that the Paris code had been satisfactory, and with a few minor changes it was readopted for permanent use. At this congress a group of American taxonomists submitted a code which was rejected by the general assembly in favor of the revised Paris code, now commonly referred to as the Vienna code. It is perhaps unfortunate that this body of Americans decided to use their own code in spite of its reception in Vienna. Thus, while the Vienna code became the accepted one for the botanical world at large, both the Vienna and the American codes were used in the United States for a number of years.

So far as the species included in this book are concerned, there are only a few which do not have the same name in both codes. The rules were revised at the Fifth International Botanical Congress at Cambridge in 1930, agreement was reached, and the best features of both codes were combined. The concept of types, including type specimens, type species, etc., was adopted from the American code. [For a good summary of the history of the codes of nomenclature, see C. A. Weatherby, "Botanical Nomenclature since 1867" (368).]

The student should consult a copy of the "International Code of Botanical Nomenclature" (207) and see for himself the legalistic framework under which proposed changes in names must be justified: "This Code aims at the provision of a stable method of naming taxonomic groups, avoiding and rejecting the use of names which may cause error or ambiguity or throw science into confusion."

In view of the above quotation, and the "rule of priority" that the oldest "usable" name must be applied, it would seem that scientific names should be unchanging, and for the most part they are. However, in a few cases the common name for a tree may have been stable for 50 years or more while the scientific name has changed three or four times! During the last century or two when many explorer-botanists were searching the world for new plants, two or more of these workers often published different names for the same species at different times. Perhaps one of the names received immediate acceptance, while another published earlier lay hidden in some obscure journal. In Darwin's day this multiplicity of scientific names was most annoying. He said "What miserable work again it is searching for priority of names. I have just finished two species which possess seven generic and 24 specific names." Although much of the sifting has now been done and the scientific names of most of our trees are established "forever," an occasional change may still be made. As an example, Franco found in 1950 that *Pseudotsuga taxifolia* (Poir.) Britton for Douglas-fir is based upon an earlier name which lacks priority, and that the correct name is *Pseudotsuga menziesii* (Mirb.) Franco. The 1953 Check List may be studied to learn the exact reasons for this change. Another good example of a taxonomic snarl to be untangled is that of the correct binomial to apply to the water tupelo [R. H. Eyde (120)].

Before leaving this subject, it should be indicated that the factors which influence the original choice of common names (page 7) often apply as well to scientific names.

IDENTIFICATION

The identification of a tree may be accomplished in one of a number of ways. The most popular and least scientific method is to compare the plant in question with illustrations from tree manuals. This, however, is not only very time-consuming but also discouraging on account of the large number of species encountered. Comparison with herbarium specimens of known origin, if available, is more practical provided one knows approximately the group in which to look. Although the quickest and easiest method is to go into the field with someone who is thoroughly familiar with the various species, no course in dendrology is complete without considerable practice in the use of keys, which furnish the best means for relocating forgotten forms or discovering the identity of new ones. Keys are found in most of the more important tree manuals and, when the necessary taxonomic terminology has been learned, are not difficult to use. Since this book is not a manual and includes descriptions of only the more important trees of North America (excluding Mexico), it has not seemed advisable to prepare keys for the limited number of species described.

Before attempting to understand keys, or the descriptions of species in this or other tree books, one should become familiar with the character and variation in form and size exhibited by the leaves, flowers, fruits, twigs, and bark of woody plants.

General features. Leaves are temporary organs which are concerned chiefly with the manufacture (photosynthesis) of plant food, respiration, and transpiration. Since they display certain characteristic patterns, they are of considerable value in taxonomy. The expanded portion of the leaf is the *lamina* or *blade,* and the stem or supporting stalk is the *petiole.* This may be either short or long, slender or stout, terete, angular, grooved, or laterally compressed, and sometimes it bears small glands. The petioles of certain leaves are swollen at the base and encase the next season's bud. In some cases the petiole is lacking and the blade is attached directly to the twig; such leaves are said to be *sessile.* Some leaves are accompanied by a pair of small scaly or leaflike organs known as *stipules* which are attached to the twig on either side of the petiole. Plants having stipules are *stipulate,* those without them *estipulate.*

Leaf arrangement (phyllotaxy). Upon careful observation of normal twigs it will be noticed that leaves are usually arranged in one of three definite ways: (1) if they are paired at the same height, one on each side of the twig, they are *opposite;* (2) when more than two are found at the same node, they are *whorled* or *verticillate;* [1] and (3) where only a single leaf is attached at each node, close inspection will show that the leaves are arranged in spirals about the twig and are in this case *alternate.* A modification of this condition arises when the leaves are arranged in such a manner that they appear nearly opposite. This is characteristic of a few trees such as buckthorn or cascara and is termed *subopposite.* With the alternate arrangement the determination of the number of leaves in each complete turn of the spiral is important since it is often the same throughout a genus and sometimes applies to all the members of the same family. In determining spiral phyllotaxy, the twig is held in a vertical position and two leaves are chosen, one of which is directly above the other; twisted, deformed, or very slow growth twigs should not be used, and the inspection should be confined to a single season's growth. Neglecting to count the lower leaf of the two chosen, ascend the spiral and count the number of leaves passed, up to and including the upper leaf, and also note the number of complete turns made around the twig. A fraction may then be formed, using the number of turns as the numera-

[1] In a few instances, the opposite and whorled arrangements intergrade, usually as a result of abnormal growth. For example, fast-growth maple may show whorled leaves, although normally they are paired (opposite), and catalpa, where they are often whorled, may show opposite arrangement on slow-growing twigs.

tor and the number of leaves as the denominator. If this is done, it will be found that one of the following fractions has resulted: ½, ⅓, ⅖, ⅜, ⁵⁄₁₃, ⁸⁄₂₁ . . . (Only the first three are common in broad-leaved trees, although the higher fractions occur in some of the conifers.)

Several peculiar relationships are immediately evident in this series. If the numerators and denominators, respectively, of the first two fractions are added, the result is the next higher fraction of the series, and this rule applies to all the rest of the members as one ascends the scale; also, the numerator of the third term is the same as the denominator of the first, that of the fourth the same as the denominator of the second, etc.

The Italian mathematician Leonardo Fibonacci (circa 1170–1230) proposed the summation series 0, 1, 1, 2, 3, 5, 8, 13. . . . The numerators of the leaf arrangement series fit this pattern. Schimper (1829), Braun (1831), and other early botanists seeking to understand spiral phyllotaxy used this sequence and the principles of spirals of Archimedes to form what may be called a fractional Fibonacci series. Even though the leaves of some plants show considerable deviation from the theoretical arrangement (86), they certainly do not occur in a haphazard fashion, but rather with almost mathematical precision.

The ½ phyllotaxy typical of elm and birch is the simplest arrangement and results in a so-called "two-ranked" placement of the leaves. The ⅓ type is characteristic of the alders, while the ⅖ is found in many trees including the oaks and poplars.

Leaf composition.   A leaf with a single blade is a *simple leaf,* but the leaves of some trees consist of three or more blades attached to a common stalk. Leaves of this type are *compound,* and the individual blades are *leaflets* or *pinnae.*[1] The stalk supporting the leaflets is the *rachis.*

When leaflets are attached laterally along the rachis, the leaf is *pinnately* compound (Fig. 184, 4). Leaflets may be sessile on the rachis, or stalked. The stalk or stem of a leaflet is a *petiolule. Odd* or *even* pinnate are terms applied to compound leaves having odd or even numbers of leaflets respectively. Leaves of this sort may be divided further to form *bipinnately* compound leaves; that is, the leaflets may be again compounded into *pinnules* (Fig. 184, 3). A further division of the pinnules would result in a *tripinnately* compound leaf.

If, on the other hand, several leaflets radiate from the end of the rachis, the leaf is *palmately* compound (Fig. 201).

Leaf shapes.   The shape of a leaf or leaflet is usually characteristic of a species. Since terminal leaflets may differ in outline from lateral ones in compound leaves, it is sometimes necessary to describe both types. The

---

[1] To determine whether a leaf is simple or compound, follow it toward the woody stem until a bud is reached. Separate the leaf from the stem at that point. This is the complete leaf.

shape of lobed leaves conforms to the outline produced by running an imaginary line around the tips of the lobes. For example, maple leaves are usually orbicular in outline, and the leaves of many oaks are considered to be more or less oblong. The most common shapes of tree leaves are illustrated in Fig. 1.

Leaf shapes (Fig. 1)

1. *Acicular*—needlelike; very slender, long, and pointed. (Example: pine needle.)
2. *Scalelike*—small, short, sharp-pointed, broadened at the base.
3. *Linear*—a number of times longer than wide; narrow, with approximately parallel sides.
4. *Oblong*—longer than broad, and with sides nearly parallel.
5. *Lanceolate*—lance-shaped; several times longer than broad, widest at a point about one-third of the distance from the base; narrowed at the ends.
6. *Oblanceolate*—inversely lanceolate.
7. *Ovate*—egg-shaped, with the broadest part near the base.
8. *Obovate*—inversely ovate.
9. *Elliptical*—shaped like an ellipse with sloping ends.
10. *Oval*—broadly elliptical, with the width greater than one-half the length.
11. *Orbicular*—circular in outline or nearly so.
12. *Reniform*—kidney-shaped.
13. *Cordate*—heart-shaped.
14. *Deltoid*—shaped like the Greek letter delta; triangular.
15. *Rhomboid*—similar to a rhombus; with equal sides but unequal angles; diamond-shaped.
16. *Spatulate*—narrower than obovate, shaped something like a spatula.

Leaf margins. The edge of a leaf blade is called the *margin*. Figure 2 depicts a number of margins characteristic of tree leaves.

Leaf margins (Fig. 2)

1. *Revolute*—rolled backward, or underneath.
2. *Entire*—smooth, without lobes or teeth.
3. *Repand*—slightly wavy.
4. *Sinuate*—deeply or strongly wavy.
5. *Crenate*—with rounded to blunt teeth.
6. *Serrate*—with sharp teeth pointing toward the apex.

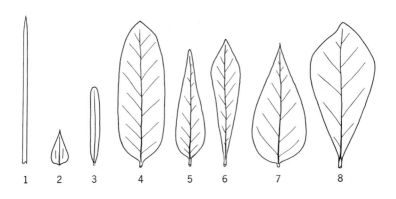

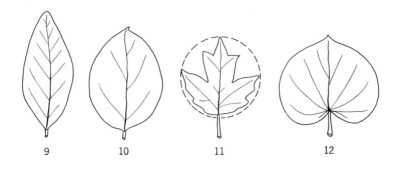

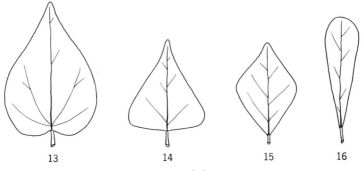

Fig. 1. Leaf shapes.

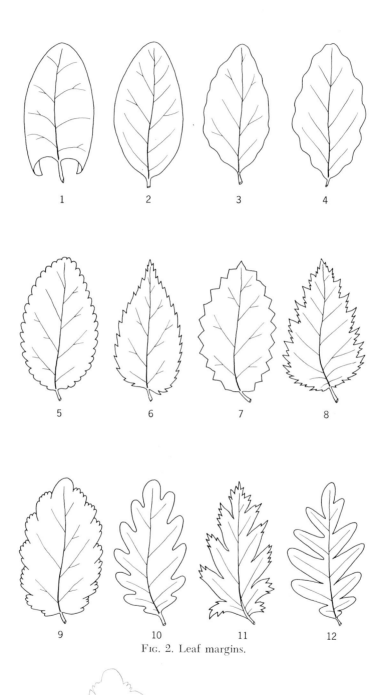

FIG. 2. Leaf margins.

7. *Dentate*—with sharp teeth pointing outward.
8. *Doubly serrate*—coarsely serrate, the teeth margins again serrated.
9. *Doubly crenate*—coarsely crenate, the teeth margins again crenated.
10. *Lobed*—divided into lobes separated by rounded sinuses which extend from one-third to one-half of the distance between margin and midrib.
11. *Cleft* [1]—divided into lobes separated by narrow or acute sinuses which extend more than halfway to the midrib.
12. *Parted* [1]—divided by sinuses which extend nearly to the midrib.

Leaf apices and bases. The tip of a leaf or that portion of the blade farthest removed from the petiole is termed the *apex*. That portion nearest to the petiole is the *base* of the blade. Some common types are illustrated in Fig. 3.

Apices (Fig. 3)

1. *Acuminate*—shaped like an acute angle with a long attenuated point.
2. *Acute*—shaped like an acute angle (less than 90 deg.) but not attenuated.
3. *Mucronate*—abruptly tipped with a hairlike or bristly mucro.
4. *Cuspidate*—tipped with a sharp, rigid point.
5. *Obtuse*—blunt, the sides forming an angle of more than 90 deg.
6. *Rounded*—a full sweeping arc.
7. *Truncate*—as though abruptly cut off transversely and forming an angle of about 180 deg.
8. *Emarginate*—with a shallow notch.

Bases

9. *Cuneate*—wedge-shaped, tapering evenly to a narrow, acute base.
10. *Acute*—shaped like an acute angle but not attenuated.
11. *Cordate*—heart-shaped.
12. *Inequilateral*—asymmetrical.
13. *Obtuse*—blunt, the sides forming an angle of more than 90 deg.
14. *Rounded*—a full sweeping arc.
15. *Truncate*—as though abruptly cut off transversely and forming an angle of approximately 180 deg.
16. *Auriculate*—with earlike appendages.

[1] In common practice, 10, 11, and 12 are all referred to as "lobed."

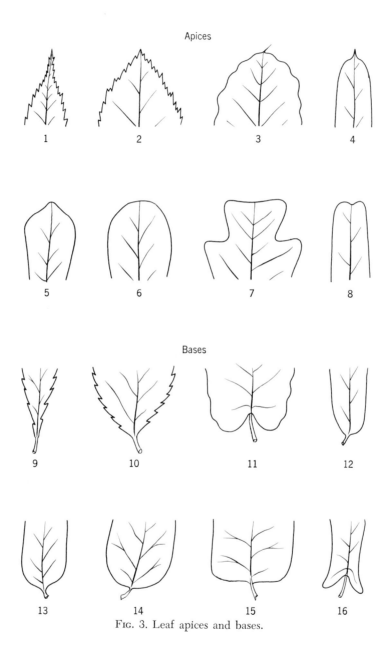

FIG. 3. Leaf apices and bases.

18

Leaf venation. There are two general types of leaf venation, the *parallel* or *closed*, which is found in the monocotyledons (Fig. 4, *1*), and the *netted* or *open*, characteristic of the dicotyledons (Fig. 4, *2, 3, 4*). In the first, the veins run nearly parallel to each other from the base to the apex of the leaf and are connected by transverse veinlets, thus giving a "closed" system. Netted venation, in contrast, is featured by a branching system of anastomosing veins, some of which run out and end blindly in the leaf tissue, hence the term "open." There are three kinds of netted venation in the leaves of forest trees. When three or more secondary veins branch radially from the base of the leaf (apex of the petiole), the

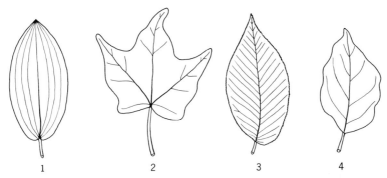

1   2   3   4

Fig. 4. Leaf venation.

leaf is *palmately* veined (Fig. 4, *2*). If a midrib (primary vein) is present, extending the length of the leaf, with secondary veins branching off at intervals, the leaf is *pinnately* veined (Fig. 4, *3*); and a modification of this is the *arcuate* type in which the secondary veins curve and run almost parallel to the leaf margin for some distance (Fig. 4, *4*). A rare type of venation characteristic of the ginkgo tree of the Orient is featured by a two-way branching, known as *dichotomous* (Fig. 14).

Surface features. The following terms are used to describe the surfaces of leaves:

1. *Glabrous*—without hair of any sort, smooth.
2. *Pubescent*—with fine, soft, short hairs.
3. *Villous*—with long, silky, straight hairs.
4. *Tomentose*—with curled, matted, wooly hairs.
5. *Scabrous*—with short bristly hairs; "sandpapery."
6. *Glaucous*—with a white to bluish waxy bloom.
7. *Rugose*—wrinkled, owing to a sunken condition of the veins.
8. *Glandular*—with numerous superficial or embedded oil or resin glands.

Finally, leaves may be *coriaceous* (thick and leathery), or at the other extreme *membranous* (thin, often translucent).

Crown and foliage features. An excellent introduction to species identification from large-scale panchromatic and color aerial photographs is provided by Heller, Doverspike, and Aldrich (170) and by Zsilinszky (394). The human eye can separate only about 200 tones of gray (white to black), but with colors it can distinguish some 20,000 hues and chromas.

FLOWERS

Flowers may be considered to be modified branches whose leaves have undergone such change that they have become, or support, the reproductive organs of the plant. Flowers of woody plants are ordinarily in blossom for so short a time that, during the greater part of the year, they are of little value for practical purposes of identification. However, since all natural classifications of seed plants are based upon flower structure, it is essential to have a basic knowledge of tree flowers.

Flower parts. A flower having a *calyx* (sepals), a *corolla* (petals), *stamens,* and one or more *pistils* is said to be *complete*. Figure 5 illustrates in detail a flower of this type. The omission of one or more of these parts, that is, the lack of either calyx, corolla, stamens, or pistil results in an *incomplete* flower. A *perfect* flower includes actively functioning organs of both sexes, but the *accessory* parts (calyx and corolla) may or may not be present. It follows, therefore, that a perfect flower may be either complete or incomplete. A flower lacking either functioning stamens or functioning pistils is *imperfect.* Imperfect flowers are also known as *unisexual* flowers, while perfect flowers are called either *bisexual* or *hermaphroditic.* Careful examination reveals that some flowers

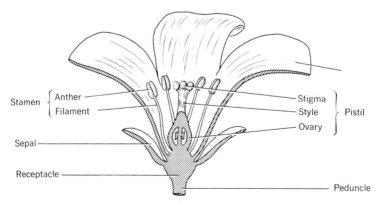

Fig. 5. Flower structure.

which appear to be perfect, at least superficially, are in reality imperfect, since one of the sex organs is abortive or degenerate, and hence sterile. Such flowers are called imperfect on this account. An imperfect flower in which the only functioning sex organs present are stamens is a *staminate* flower, while one in which the pistil is the only active organ is *pistillate.* A species in which these separate staminate and pistillate flowers are both borne on the same tree, although frequently on different branches, is termed *monoecious,* from the Greek "one house." When the staminate flowers are borne on one tree, and the pistillate on another ("two houses"), the species is *dioecious.* In some instances both perfect and unisexual flowers occur on the same tree. Species exhibiting this condition are termed *polygamous.* If perfect flowers, together with unisexual flowers of both sexes, are present on a single individual, the species is *polygamo-monoecious,* but if the perfect flowers are accompanied by one sex on some individuals and with the opposite sex on others it is *polygamo-dioecious.*

When both calyx and corolla are wanting, a flower is *naked.* If only the corolla is omitted, however, the flower is *apetalous.* When the corolla is composed of separate petals, the flower is classified as a *polypetalous* type; but when the petals are partially or wholly fused with one another it is *sympetalous.* The fusion of like floral parts is called *cohesion,* while the union of unlike structures is known as *adhesion.* The table below, adapted from Pool's "Flowers and Flowering Plants" (285), summarizes the organization of flowers.

The parts of some flowers are so arranged that a number of planes passed through their central axis invariably produce symmetrical halves. Flowers of this type are *regular* or *actinomorphic.* In other flowers this symmetrical arrangement of parts is wanting, and they can only be divided into two equal portions by one axillary plane or in some instances not at all. These flowers are *irregular* or *zygomorphic.* Flowers obviously dependent on wind for pollination are *anemophilous,* while those relying on insects for pollination are *entomophilous.*

Flower arrangement. Flowers may arise from separate buds, or they may appear in the same bud with the leaves. When they appear in the axil of a leaf, they are *axillary,* and when they terminate the growth of the season, they are *terminal.* In some cases flowers appear singly, but usually they are borne in clusters of several to many. A cluster of flowers or the mode of floral arrangement is an *inflorescence.* When the central stalk or *rachis* of an inflorescence terminates in a flower which blooms slightly in advance of its nearest associates, the inflorescence is *determinate.* (The illustrations in Fig. 6, *1a* and *1b,* are examples of this type.) If, on the other hand, the flowers open progressively from the base to the apex, or from the outside toward the center in flat-topped clusters, the inflo-

Organization of flowers

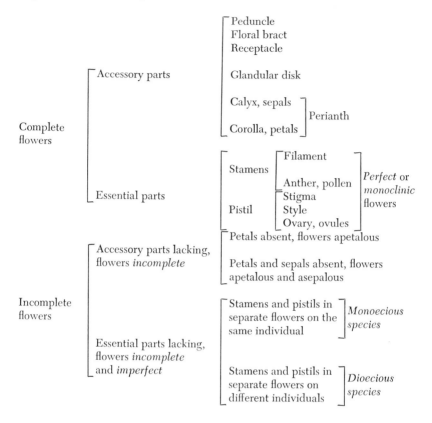

rescence is *indeterminate*. A number of inflorescences common to woody plants are described below and are illustrated in Fig. 6.

Flower arrangement (Fig. 6)

DETERMINATE

1. *Cyme*—an inflorescence consisting of a central rachis bearing a number of pedicelled flowers: (*a*) *cylindrical*—the pedicels of nearly equal length at maturity; (*b*) *flat-topped*—the pedicels of unequal length.

INDETERMINATE

2. *Spike*—an inflorescence consisting of a central rachis bearing a number of sessile flowers.

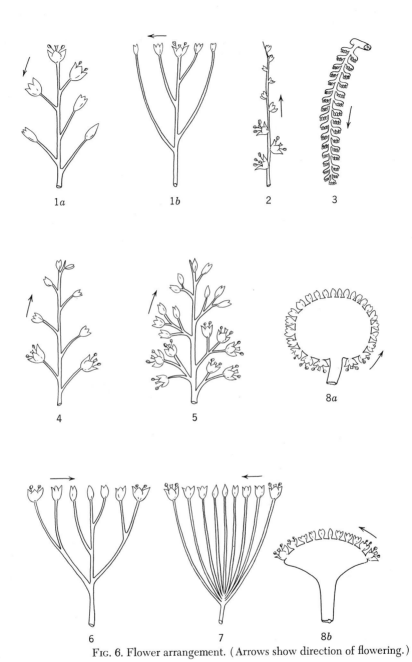

FIG. 6. Flower arrangement. (Arrows show direction of flowering.)

3. *Catkin* or *ament*—a flexible, usually inverted, scaly spike bearing apetalous unisexual flowers.
4. *Raceme*—an inflorescence consisting of a central rachis bearing a number of pedicelled flowers; the pedicels of nearly equal length at maturity.
5. *Panicle*—a compound or branched raceme.
6. *Corymb*—an inflorescence consisting of a central rachis bearing a number of branched pedicels; the lower ones much longer than the upper, resulting in a flat or more or less round-topped cluster of flowers. (Simple corymbs, i.e., corymbs with unbranched pedicels, are rare in woody plants.)
7. *Umbel*—an inflorescence consisting of several pedicelled flowers with a common point of attachment.
8. *Head*—an inflorescence consisting of a number of sessile flowers clustered on a common receptacle: (*a*) *globose;* (*b*) *flat-topped.*

FRUIT

A fruit may be defined as the seed-bearing organ of a plant. Since the fruits of conifers are quite different in structure from those of the angiosperms (broad-leaved trees), each group is considered separately.

Coniferous fruits. The fruits of many conifers are obtainable at any time of the year, either attached to the branches or scattered on the ground under the tree. Therefore they are often very useful in identification; in fact, in western forests which are largely coniferous, the use of cones in distinguishing between closely related species is not infrequently the most reliable means of separation in the field.

Coniferous fruits may be either dry or fleshy. In the majority of cases they ripen during the first season, although in several genera, two and occasionally three years are necessary for their maturation. Morphologically, the fruits of American conifers fall into one of two classes: (1) those which consist of a single seed, partially or wholly surrounded by a fleshy *aril* (Fig. 91), and (2) those which are composed of a number of woody, leathery, or fleshy scales, each with one or more seeds, and characteristically arranged about a central axis to form a *cone.* The fruit of yew illustrates the first type, while those of the pines, spruces, and redwood are examples of the latter.

The principal unit of the cone is the *cone scale* (carpel). The scales are attached to a central woody axis and may be spirally borne (Pinaceae and Taxodiaceae) or *decussate* (Cupressaceae). They may be either thin or thick, flexible or rigid, broader than long (some species of fir), narrow-oblong (some pines), or *peltate* (shield-shaped) in a few groups such as baldcypress, and some "cedars," and cypresses.

The exposed portion of the cone scale in a mature unopened cone is known as the *apophysis.* The apophysis is usually lighter in color than the remaining portion of the scale, although this is not always the case. In some species the apophysis is smooth, in others it is wrinkled; also it may be grooved or ridged. In a few species the cone margins are slightly reflexed or revolute, while in others they appear to be eroded (*erose*).

In pine cones, which mature at the end of two or rarely three seasons, the apophysis terminates in a small protuberance called the *umbo.* When the umbo is found at the tip of the scale, it is *terminal,* but if it appears on the back or raised portion, it is *dorsal.* Umbos are often wartlike, or they may terminate in a prickle, spine, or claw.

Seeds are borne at the base of the cone scales. In several species depressions in the scales denote their original position, while in others minute scars are left after seed dispersal. The number of seeds per cone scale varies with the species, as will be shown later. Seeds are terminally winged in most of the Pinaceae (wingless in a few species), and laterally winged in the Taxodiaceae and Cupressaceae (some species wingless).

The ovuliferous bracts are prominent features of some cones, but very inconspicuous in others. These bracts subtend the cone scales in the Pinaceae, are partially fused with those of the Taxodiaceae, and wholly fused in those of the Cupressaceae. Hence they are of little diagnostic value in the last two groups.

Angiospermous fruits.   The fruit of an angiosperm is generally described as a ripened ovary, although in some fruits various accessory parts such as the receptacle, involucre, calyx, and style are also included.

These fruits may be classified in a number of ways. If their origin is traceable to a single pistil,[1] they are *simple fruits,* but when two or more pistils on the same receptacle are involved in their formation, they are *compound.* Both types of fruits may be either *dry* or *fleshy.* Dry fruits may be papery, leathery, or woody. The mature dry fruits of some species split along definite lines of suture to release their seeds, while those of other species lack this feature. A fruit releasing its seed in this manner is said to be *dehiscent,* while one lacking sutures is *indehiscent.*

I. Simple fruits (See Fig. 7)

A. DRY INDEHISCENT FRUITS

1. *Achene*—a small, one-celled, one-seeded, unwinged but often plumose fruit.
2. *Samara*—a winged achenelike fruit.
3. *Nut*—usually a one-celled, one-seeded fruit with a bony, woody,

[1] This may itself be either simple or compound.

leathery, or papery wall, and usually partially or wholly encased in an involucre,[1] or husk.

1. *Legume*—the product of a simple pistil splitting along two lines of suture.
2. *Follicle*—the product of a simple pistil splitting along a single line of suture.
3. *Capsule*—the product of a compound pistil splitting along two or more sutures.

C. FLESHY FRUITS

1. *Pome*—the product of a compound pistil; the outer ovary wall fleshy, the inner wall papery or cartilaginous, and encasing numerous seeds. The enlarged receptacle, without, constitutes most of the fruit.
2. *Drupe*—a usually one-seeded fleshy fruit, usually the product of a simple pistil; the outer wall fleshy, the inner wall bony.
3. *Berry*—a several-seeded fruit (rarely one-seeded), the outer and inner walls of which are fleshy, with the seeds embedded in the pulpy mass. In practice it may not always be easy to distinguish between the pit of a drupe and a seed with heavy coats from a berry. In the drupe, the bony structure surrounding the seed is the *inner ovary wall*. In the berry, the inner ovary wall is fleshy, and any hard coats around the seed are a part of it and do not belong to the ovary.

II. Compound fruits

A. AGGREGATE FRUIT.   A compact cluster of simple fruits traceable to separate pistils of the *same flower* and inserted on a common receptacle (Fig. 169, page 358).
B. MULTIPLE FRUIT.   A compact cluster of simple fruits traceable to the pistils of *separate flowers* and often borne in a head (Fig. 179, page 377).

[1] In certain of the Juglandaceae, a portion of the ovary wall, or exocarp, becomes the husk.

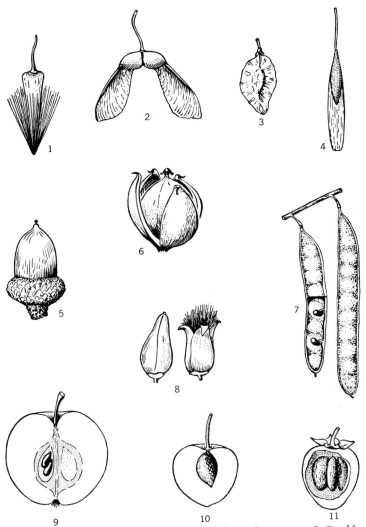

F<small>IG</small>. 7. Some angiosperm fruits. *1. Achene* of sycamore. *2. Double samara* of maple. *3. Single samara* of elm. *4. Single samara* of ash. *5. Acorn (nut)* of oak. *6. Nut* of hickory. *7. Legume* of black locust. *8. Capsule* of poplar. *9. Pome* of apple. *10. Drupe* of cherry. *11. Berry* of persimmon.

TWIGS

Twigs offer an excellent means of identifying trees and shrubs throughout the year, except for a short time during the spring when the buds formed the previous season are opening and those for the current season have not yet appeared. The most conspicuous features of twigs are their buds, leaf scars, stipule scars, and pith, although their color, taste, odor, and the presence or absence of cork, spur shoots, spines, thorns, glaucous bloom, or pubescence are also valuable characters for purposes of identification. Figure 8, *1*, illustrates a typical butternut twig, while part *2* depicts the features of a slippery elm twig.

Buds. These are conspicuous on most twigs and may be of two sorts. Those borne along the twig in the axils of the previous season's leaves are termed *laterals,* while the one appearing at the apex is usually larger and is called the *terminal.* In the latter instance, the bud thus limits further growth in length for the season. In certain groups, however, a true terminal is not formed and growth continues until checked by external factors. When this occurs, the tender leading shoot dies and finally sloughs off at the last formed mature lateral bud below. This bud then *appears* to be apical, is called *pseudoterminal,* and is distinguished from the true terminal by its smaller size (it is really a lateral) and the presence of a minute *twig scar* which shows, with a hand lens, concentric rings of bark and wood. Occasionally, the withered twig tip is persistent.

If more than one bud appears at a node, the bud directly above the leaf scar is considered to be the true lateral bud and the others are designated as *accessory buds.* If the accessory buds are arranged on either side of the lateral buds, they are said to be *collateral,* while if they appear above the lateral bud, they are called *superposed.*

Buds are either *scaly* or *naked.* Bud scales are actually modified leaves or stipules and serve to protect the enclosed embryonic axis and its appendages. In some buds the scales are often rather numerous and overlap one another in a shinglelike fashion. Bud scales so arranged are *imbricate.* When the buds are covered with two or three scales which do not overlap, they are described as *valvate.* In a few genera the buds are covered by a single caplike scale. When the terminal bud opens with the renewal of growth in the spring, the scales slough off, leaving *bud-scale scars.* *Naked buds* lack scaly coverings and are common to certain trees of tropical climates, but are relatively rare elsewhere. *Submerged buds,* that is, buds embedded in the callous layer of leaf scars, are featured by a few species. When two sizes of lateral buds occur on the same twig, the larger usually contain the rudiments of flowers and are called *flower buds.* *Mixed buds* containing embryonic leaves and flowers are characteristic of some species, in contrast to those enclosing leaves only (*leaf buds*).

Leaf scars. When a leaf falls from a twig, there remains at the point of attachment a *leaf scar.* Leaf scars vary in size and shape with different species and hence are usually diagnostic. On the surface of each leaf scar are found one or more minute dots or patches which show where the now ruptured strands of vascular tissue passed from the twig into the leaf.

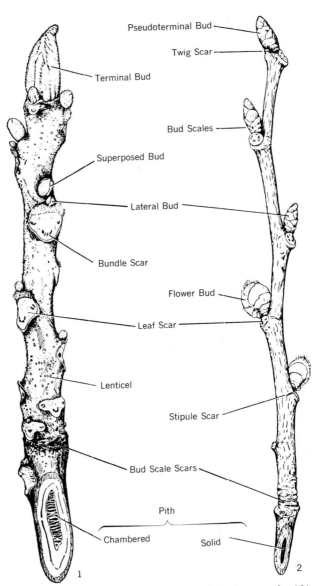

FIG. 8. Twig features. Butternut (*1*); slippery elm (*2*).

The size, number, and arrangement of these so-called *vascular bundle scars* are often helpful in identification.

Stipule scars. Stipule scars are not found on all twigs since many species are *estipulate*. When present, they occur in pairs, one on either side at the top of the leaf scar. As a rule, they are slitlike in shape, and in most instances they are inconspicuous without a hand lens. In a few species they completely encircle the twig.

Lenticels. Lenticels are small, usually lens-shaped patches, sometimes wartlike, consisting of loosely organized tissue, which provide aeration. As a rule, they are of little value in identification.

Pith. *Form.* The medial or central portion of a twig is composed of *pith.* Pith is usually lighter or darker in color than the wood which surrounds it; hence it is readily discernible in transverse sections of twigs. The shape of the pith when viewed in this section usually conforms to one of several patterns. For example, it is *stellate* (star-shaped) or *pentagonal* in oaks and cottonwoods, *triangular* in alders, and *terete* in ash and elms. Pith not infrequently varies in color through shades of pink, yellow, brown, or green to black or white.

Composition. To determine the composition of the pith, a smooth longitudinal cut should be made through the center of the twig. In most native trees, the pith is *solid* or *continuous,* and *homogeneous.* A distinct modification of this type is the *diaphragmed* pith, which is featured by more or less regularly spaced disks of horizontally elongated cells with thickened walls. In longitudinal section, these appear as bars across the pith and are often readily visible to the naked eye. Yellow-poplar and black tupelo are common examples of this type. In a few trees, such as the walnut, the pith is divided into empty horizontal chambers by cross partitions and is termed *chambered.* The chambering in certain species does not take place until the fall of the year, and the season's growth is homogeneous until that time. A small portion at the end of each season's growth apparently remains unchambered, and therefore the age of a twig with this kind of pith may be estimated by sectioning it and counting the number of yearly "plugs" present. *Hollow* pith and *spongy* pith are characteristic, respectively, of some species of woody plants.

Types of pith

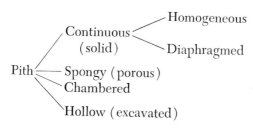

Lammas shoots. It will be observed that a new shoot or sprout usually consists of a single stem bearing a number of characteristically arranged leaves. Soon after twig elongation and leaf enlargement have ceased, minute buds appear in the leaf axils. These buds continue to enlarge and by midsummer have attained their full growth. Normally they then re-

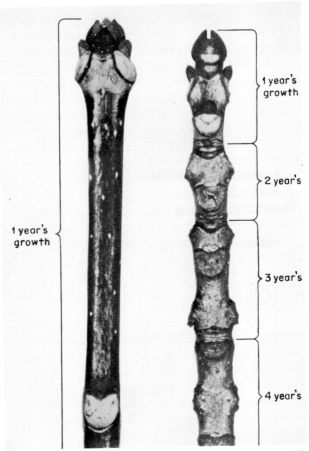

FIG. 9. Twigs of white ash from the same tree, showing difference in rate of growth.

main dormant until the following spring. However, in some species such as yellow-poplar, sweetgum, cascara, beech, sassafras, and water tupelo, these newly formed lateral buds often exhibit renewed growth activity. Within a few days after their maturation they become swollen, open, and then produce a second shoot subtended by its own leaves and axillary buds. These second or midseason twigs are known as *lammas*[1] *shoots*, and while rarely diagnostic, they do occur much more frequently on some species than on others. Lammas shoots are most easily recognized in the late summer or early fall when they still may be seen in the axils of leaves.

[1] Lammas Day, featuring a harvest festival, was celebrated in England on Aug. 1. The use of the word for these shoots indicates their appearance late in the growing season.

Spurs. Spur growth is characteristic of a few genera, and the presence of these structures is often useful in identification. Spurs are in reality dwarfed twigs and differ essentially from the more normal structures only in that little or no internodal development and elongation ever occur. Because of this, alternate leaves are so crowded that they may appear opposite or whorled. Spurs may continue to grow for several years and bear a new complement of leaves each season (ginkgo, larch, birch), or in a few instances flowers (pear).

Thorns, spines, and prickles. The presence of these pointed structures is often important in identifying certain species or genera.

Thorns (honeylocust, hawthorn) are modified twigs and as such usually bear minute leaf scars and buds. Thorns may be single or branched.

Spines (black locust) are modified stipules, or in certain plants (barberry) they may derive from other leaf parts such as the apex or margin.

Prickles (rose) emerge from the superficial tissues of the twig (cortex, epidermis) and, having no connection with the vascular system, are easily dislodged.

BARK

Bark is one of the most important features in the identification of large trees, particularly when leaves and twigs are inaccessible, or during the winter months when the former may be lacking. The average timber cruiser relies almost wholly upon bark in tallying species, and log scalers of necessity use bark features since crown parts of the tree are left behind in the slash after logging. Bark characteristics are best learned by actual observation, since it is very difficult to describe them satisfactorily. Beginning students in dendrology often underestimate the value of these features in the identification of trees, but a few field trips usually suffice to change this attitude appreciably.

The dead outer bark protects the inner living bark and cambium. Periderm on twigs usually has its origin in the superficial layers of the primary cortex. Periderm arises in mature parenchyma and forms an impervious sheath around young stems and branches; it is ordinarily smooth, or broken only by lenticels. On older trees cork cambiums originate in phloem parenchyma. This is generally described as deep cork formation, and when once these layers are formed, the tissues on the outside die, and the bark ultimately becomes more or less scaly, or furrowed. Deep cork formation commonly shows first at the base of a tree, so that while the surface there may be quite rough, that along the bole is still relatively smooth. Another place where early roughening may be expected is below the branch insertions in such groups of species as the poplars and birches.

FIG. 10. Douglas-fir, Sitka spruce, western hemlock, and western redcedar (left to right) on the Olympic Peninsula near Willapa Harbor, Washington. (*Photograph by Asahel Curtis, Seattle.*)

The color, together with the shape and prominence of lenticels, is the most important feature of the bark on young stems. On old trunks the configuration, texture, thickness, and color are features to be observed. In some species, such as persimmon, alligator juniper, flowering dogwood, and black tupelo, the bark is divided into small rectangular plates having the general appearance of alligator leather. In others, such as the cherries, most birches, and some of the alders, it is very smooth and peels readily into thin horizontal sheets (ring-barked). Bark of this sort is often marked by elongated horizontal lenticels. Small, rounded, loosely appressed scales feature the bark of most spruces; and broad exfoliating plates are characteristic of several hickories. The bark of Port-Orford-cedar, redwood, baldcypress, and several junipers is extremely fibrous, while in others, such as Douglas-fir, hemlock, and some pines, it is deeply furrowed but nonfibrous. Deeply furrowed bark is also characteristic of certain hardwoods. The trunks of ponderosa pine and Jeffrey pine are plated, while that of the hophornbeam is very shreddy. The bark of white fir is quite horny on old trunks, while that of the sequoias is soft and spongy, and that of corkbark fir is corky.

Bark varies greatly in thickness within a species as well as between species. It is quite thin in most of the spruces, maples, and birches, but is often as much as 12 to 24 in. thick on old trunks of such species as Douglas-fir and the giant sequoia.

The color of bark varies with age, site, and even light conditions. As an example of the first factor, the bark of young ponderosa pine is often dark brown to nearly black, while that on old trunks is usually yellowish brown to cinnamon-red. A bronze or reddish-brown bark features young trees of paper birch, but on older stems it is creamy white, and finally black at the base of the bole. The color of the freshly cut inner bark is often characteristic. In Douglas-fir and American elm, for example, it is brown streaked with white, while in hemlock a reddish-purple hue is typical. The inner bark of black oak is yellow to bright orange, that of the western balsam firs brown, reddish brown, or beef-red, and in red alder, orange-red.

Economically, bark is also important. Hog fuels,[1] containing appreciable amounts of bark, have a much higher calorific value (up to 15 percent) than fuels in which bark has not been included. Dyes, tannins, alkaloids, and other pharmaceutical compounds are extracted from the bark of certain species, and cordage and paper fibers are obtained from others.

---

[1] Term commonly applied to mixture of wood chips and sawdust.

VARIATION

The most important principle to keep in mind when commencing the study of trees or other natural objects is that of *variation*. It is a common observation that no two persons are identical in either physical proportions or mental capability. In the former instance, the same is true of trees, and although the leaves of a given species may always follow a certain recognizable pattern, no two leaves have yet been found one of which could be exactly superimposed upon the other.

Variation is responsible for the feeling of uncertainty, characteristic of beginners in taxonomy, and often leads to the unfortunate habit of "guessing" rather than weighing the evidence presented by a particular plant which does not look exactly like one of the same species previously observed. This bias can be corrected only gradually by observing many dozens, if not hundreds, of individuals of each species. Only then does one begin to acquire a background and an appreciation of the *range in variation* to be expected. This is most important and varies in itself from one species or group to the next; for instance, the leaves of a given tree may vary in length from 2 to 4 in., while in another this dimension varies from 2 to 6 in. Obviously, in the latter instance, the range in length variation is greater. This principle applies to all portions of tree morphology, such as leaf shapes, flower parts, fruits, twigs, and especially bark, which is probably the most variable feature of all.

Although variation creates problems for beginning students, it is the chief reason why one's interest in the forest is never dulled even after spending several decades in the same locality; it is almost certain that some queer prank of nature will have resulted in an abnormality never before seen on previous field trips.

The ability to recognize a large number of trees or other plants can be gained only through continued observation, preferably in the field, over a considerable period of time.

DESCRIPTIONS OF SPECIES

Before considering the various genera and species in detail, a brief analysis of the form of presentation may prove helpful.

DISTINGUISHING CHARACTERISTICS. Although there are frequently many features by which a given species may be recognized, it is best at first to select only a few of the most striking characters and to learn the variation to be expected in them; this is especially true when attempting to cover a relatively large number of species in a short time. Other important characters can be more gradually absorbed, since, as already indicated, real familiarity with the trees and shrubs of one's locality cannot be gained except by constant observation over a period of at least several years.

It is preferable to use this tabulated section as a summary; it should be read once before considering the more complete botanical description and the illustrations, when present, then several times thereafter until the various features are firmly in mind.

BOTANICAL FEATURES. The principal characteristics of leaves, flowers, fruits, twigs, and bark are included here, but lack of space prevents more detailed descriptions, which are available in many of the local flora or reference works listed among the selected references.

GENERAL DESCRIPTION. Under this heading have been included a number of features largely concerned with silvics, or the relation of a tree to its environment. Silvical features are not only of great importance in the practice of forestry, they are often useful as well in conjunction with botanical characters for species identification. Having made this commitment, it should be added that this is in no sense a book on silvics, and that in most cases only those features are presented which serve to characterize a given species from its associates. For detailed information, the student should own the 762-page "Silvics of Forest Trees of the United States," which also includes range maps for the various species (127).

A few comments need to be made on the evaluation of specific information under the subheads which follow.

1. *Sizes of mature trees.* These are very variable and are influenced by local conditions of site or by geographical distribution, especially with boreal species which may become shrubby or prostrate at the northern limits of their range. Maximum sizes are often from old-growth trees which are no longer standing, and in some instances it is not certain whether actual measurements were made or whether sizes were merely estimated. Maximum heights and diameters as given are usually not from the same tree.

The American Forestry Association is continuing a survey to locate the largest trees of each species still standing (284). Starred (*) tree heights or diameters in this text are taken from the AFA surveys, and are always larger than figures obtained from Sargent (313) or other early writers. The purpose of the AFA is to list the largest standing tree of each species; ours is to give the largest dimensions ever attained by the species, based upon reliable reports from any and all sources. From time to time new lists are published by the AFA in which maximum sizes may be increased or decreased, and species may be added or dropped. The starred dimensions in this text are the maxima which have appeared at any time in the several AFA surveys, and the latest one should be consulted for the current measurements of the largest standing trees. Whenever a diameter is starred (*) in the following tree descriptions, it is calculated to the nearest foot less than that obtained by dividing the AFA reported cir-

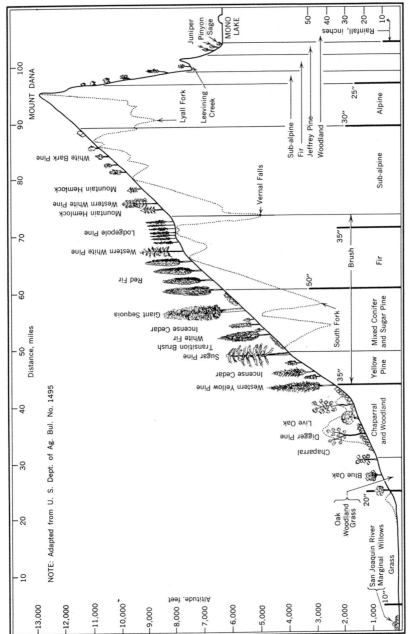

FIG. 11. Profile of the Sierra Nevada showing the effect of elevation and rainfall upon forest distribution.

FIG. 12. Topography of North America. (*Courtesy U.S. Geological Survey.*)

1. Olympic Peninsula
2. Cascade Mountains
3. Inland Empire
4. Coast Ranges
5. Sierra Nevada
6. Great Basin

7. Rocky Mountains
8. Black Hills
9. Ozark Mountains
10. Gulf Coastal Plain
11. Atlantic Coastal Plain
12. Piedmont Plateau

13. Appalachian
    Mountains
14. Adirondack Mountains
15. Green Mountains
16. White Mountains
17. Laurentian Plateau

cumference by π. AFA heights may be estimated in one of several ways. Cooperators may get directions from them on how to proceed.

Foresters commonly measure tree diameter at 4½ ft above the ground (diameter breast high). Diameter at this height is usually above the flaring base of the tree, and is a measure of trunk size. On very large trees where butt swell and flaring may extend six feet or more upward, d.b.h. exaggerates actual trunk size.

2. *Form.* Trees when grown in the open tend to develop characteristic shapes which may be typical of individual species or groups of species (genera); this is well illustrated in such trees as American elm, white oak, Lombardy poplar, or eastern white pine. In general, open-grown specimens have large crowns, which may reach nearly to the ground, and the clear trunk is short, with considerable taper.[1] Under forest competition, the form is very different: the bole is long, more cylindrical, often clear of branches for one half or more of its length, and the crown small. Certain species, especially those which are extremely tolerant, resist crown restriction, but it may be said that most trees develop typical shapes only in the open; such individuals, of course, are usually unfit for lumber because of the short clear length and many side branches which would appear as knots in the finished boards.

3. *Site.* Although many trees are cosmopolitan in this respect, others are invariably associated with certain combinations of soil and moisture. Thus it is as futile to look for a black ash on a high, excessively dry hillside as to expect ponderosa pine to inhabit a permanent swamp. Site relationships are frequently very complicated, and the absence of a certain species may not be due to its inability to grow in a given situation, but merely because other forms can compete more advantageously there.

The effect of latitude on site is also pronounced, since trees of the North when found at the southern limit of their range often grow only in cool bogs, even though farther north they are found on dry ground.

4. *Associates.* When left unhampered, trees as well as other plants tend to group themselves on the basis of soil and climatic factors and their ability to compete with their neighbors. In this way fairly definite plant associations, which may be semipermanent or only temporary in nature, come into being. Logging and fire usually destroy the primeval or "climax" forest society, and so alter the environment that a totally different set of species preempts the area. This occurrence is of the greatest significance to foresters and illustrates the importance of ecological studies. Since a large portion of the forests of this country have been devastated, and the new growth springing up is often so different from that which preceded it, lists of associated tree species lose much of their

[1] In a few intolerant species, the open-grown form is more like that developed in the forest.

value unless one knows the recent history of the particular forest in question; for example, quaking aspen originally occurred as a scattered tree in the spruce-hardwoods of the Northeast, but following logging and fire, this species has now spread in nearly pure stands over wide areas. Such stands, unless managed, are temporary and are eventually replaced by shade-enduring species that grow beneath them.

5. *Tolerance.* It has been known for a considerable time that certain species will grow under varying densities of forest cover, while others exist only in the open. For many years this was interpreted as a reaction to light, and hence an intolerant tree was one which could bear little or no shade. However, in 1907, Zon (393) reported the results of root-cutting experiments by Fricke, in Germany, which seemed to show that the inability of certain species to prosper under old-growth forest was due in large part to excessive root competition, since trenched plots under heavy cover, formerly bare of young growth, soon showed vegetation of various sorts, including tree seedlings, the next season after the roots of neighboring trees had been severed. Considerable discussion followed, and in the United States Toumey, Korstian, and others later obtained similar results. Without accepting either extreme, it seems best at present to consider tolerance as the ability of a plant to complete its life history from seedling to adult, under the cover of a dense forest, regardless of the specific factors involved. Or, put more simply, a tolerant tree is one which can exist, if not prosper, under forest [1] competition; when this is removed or lessened, the rate of growth usually shows a marked increase. For a more recent discussion of tolerance see Decker (97).

Tolerance is influenced by site (soil, exposure, climate, etc.) so that the best comparisons are made only between trees growing together under the same set of external conditions. Little is gained in attempting to compare two species of widely separated ranges, growing on different soils and with dissimilar associates.

6. *Seed production and germination.* These are very variable, the former depending on many factors, including temperature extremes, condition of the tree, the presence or absence of competition, and the time elapsed since the last heavy crop was borne. The germination percentages vary exceedingly, being influenced by a large number of factors, such as storage (temperature, moisture, and stratifying media, if any) and conditions surrounding actual germination (81).

7. *Growth.* It is difficult to make general statements of any value, unless they are accompanied by such facts as the age of the tree, the density of the stand, and the quality of the site.

From the preceding discussion, it should be clear that the silvical features given are suggestive rather than comprehensive and have been

[1] Including, in the case of small trees, weed competition [Baker (21)].

included only for the purpose of giving further individuality to the various species. A detailed consideration of the intricate relationships and interplay of forces which go into the development of a forest society is the province of silviculture and ecology, not dendrology, as it is here defined.

RANGE. The known geographical distribution of a plant is ascertained from reports of many observers, usually over a long period of time. A few comments on certain qualifying factors will lead to a better understanding of written ranges and plotted range maps as seen in this and other publications.

1. *Ranges not fixed.* Although this may not be immediately apparent, it should be remembered that we are now in a postglacial period and that certain species are still slowly creeping northward following the retreat of the last ice sheet.

A much more revolutionary change, however, has been effected by man in the wholesale devastation of forests, which often introduces factors not present in nature, and by the introduction of foreign species, or the planting of native forms in parts of the country outside their natural range. When species foreign to a certain locality grow and reproduce there, maintaining themselves without any further aid by man, they are said to be "naturalized"; Scotch pine is an example of such a species, brought over from Europe and now established in the northeastern United States. The natural range, then, may be greatly extended, or more rarely reduced to the point of extinction by human efforts.

2. *Commercial range.* This is almost without exception smaller than the botanical range and is often restricted to scattered areas with certain combinations of soil and moisture, though it may be more extensive; in any event, quantity and best development influence the importance of a species in a particular locality.

3. *Altitudinal distribution.* Especially in the West, altitude is a limiting factor, and over wide areas certain species are commonly found only in horizontal belts which conform to more or less specific elevations. The relation between latitude and elevation is also important, and species which occur at sea level in the North are found progressively higher toward the South, until a height of 10,000 to 11,500 ft may be reached at the southern limit of distribution.

4. *Range maps.* It should not be supposed that the various species are evenly distributed as shown by the range-map patterns which follow. The scale of the maps is too small to show local distribution even if sufficient knowledge were available to make this possible (see remarks in Preface).

DENDROCHRONOLOGY

Although the study and interpretation of tree-ring patterns is not included in dendrology as previously defined, it seems appropriate at this point to say something about this fascinating and now well-established science which correlates with climatology and archaeology (25, 168, 244).

Tree rings as seen on a stump or the end of a log have always intrigued man, and they are of course studied by foresters as indicators of growth. But it was A. E. Douglass (108), an astronomer, who in the early 1900s worked with ring patterns from trees of the arid Southwest and saw that so-called "sensitive" ring series provide a veritable calendar into the past. In this region and others like it throughout the world, isolated trees may grow on dry rocky slopes where annual precipitation is minimal. The rings of such drought-resisting trees may reflect directly the amount of precipitation received each year. If one fells such a living tree, a calendar can be started stretching from the present back to the date of the tree's center.

Before continuing this discussion, the difference between a "sensitive" ring series and a "complacent" one should be understood.[1] Complacent ring series are typical of trees growing in an equable climate where there is ample ground water, and no competition for light, or for soil nutrients. Also the trees must be free from diseases or insect attacks that might cause defoliation. Ring patterns of such trees are usually uniform; in youth growth is rapid, gradually diminishing as the tree ages. Such patterns are generally useless as calendars.

Where sensitive ring series are found, many trees in a given locality show a similar pattern. Starting at the outside, the first few rings may not be noteworthy, but then there may be a group of three very narrow rings. Several other rings are counted before coming to a single narrow one, and so on to the center of the tree. Perhaps near the center, the ring formed in 1904 is very narrow, that for 1903 is normal to wide, and the one for 1902 is again very narrow. These three rings form an identifiable triad which may then be matched in the *outer* rings of a standing but long dead tree nearby. If so, the calendar can be extended to the center (presuming no decay) of the dead tree. Perhaps near its center is a significant group of rings which match the pattern of rings from a timber used in an ancient Pueblo structure. The timber can now be dated, and after careful assessment (including possible re-use of the timber in later structures) the date can be used by archaeologists in the reconstruction of prehistory.

---

[1] Many common English words are given specific and different meanings in science. Trees are not actually "sensitive" or "complacent" in the sense used, they only reflect in their growth layers the total environment, and in arid regions the most important variable is the annual precipitation.

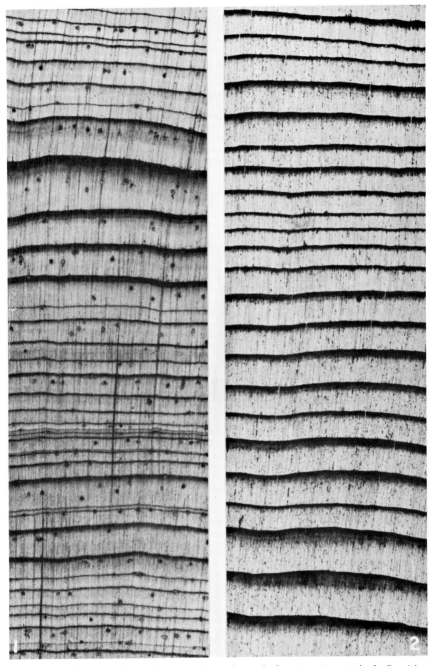

Fɪɢ. 13. Dendrochronology. Cross sections of wood showing rings × 4. *1*. Sensitive series in ponderosa pine; widest ring formed in 1767. *2*. Complacent series in eastern hemlock. (*Dating in No. 1 by Laboratory of Tree-Ring Research, Univ. of Arizona.*)

Many thousands of precise tree-ring dates provide Southwestern archaeologists with excellent prehistoric reference points.

The center for this kind of exploration is the Laboratory of Tree-Ring Research at the University of Arizona, Tucson. Beginning in 1934 they have published the *Tree-Ring Bulletin,* numbers of which may be consulted for papers and references in this interesting field. It should not be supposed that the interpretation of tree-ring data is as simple as the illustration given might indicate. In Alaska, for instance, temperature may be more important than precipitation; also, some workers have been critical of conclusions drawn by others. Nevertheless, dendrochronology is proving to be extremely valuable in studying the climate of past ages, and the dating of ancient wooden structures or portions of them.

GYMNOSPERMS

Gymnospermae

This group includes many of the world's most interesting and useful trees whose importance, especially in the temperate forests of both Northern and Southern Hemispheres, can hardly be overemphasized.

Historically, the gymnosperms have received much attention because of their very ancient lineage which extends backward to the mid-Paleozoic era (the Devonian period [1]). A number of them were contemporaries of that large flora which was responsible for the formation of the extensive coal beds of that period. It is still conceded that the gymnosperms antedate the angiosperms, even though the latter have now been found as far back as the Jurassic [2] [Chamberlain (63)]. Any direct evolutionary link between these two great groups of plants through fossil forms has yet to be found, and at present they seem to extend in parallel lines into the distant past.

The criterion most frequently used for separating them is the presence in the angiosperms of an ovary which encloses the ovules. The gymnosperms, in contrast, exhibit a naked seed which is commonly subtended by a scale. By definition, the pollen- and ovule-bearing structures in the gymnosperms are not considered to be "flowers," but for convenience they are so called in the descriptions which follow.

According to Engler (115), modern gymnosperms are divided into 4 orders, 12 families, about 63 genera, and 675 species. Commercially, the conifers are most important. The others have greater scientific than economic interest, and for convenience will be considered first, even though one of them is probably more advanced phylogenetically.

---

[1] About 400 million years ago.
[2] At least 160 million years ago.

CYCADALES   Cycads

These are tropical plants which mostly resemble the palms or tree ferns. The trunk is unbranched, often tall (20 to 60 ft), and bears at the top a cluster of large pinnate leaves; in contrast certain forms are tuberous with partly submerged stems. In the columnar type, an age of nearly 1,000 years may be attained, and the persistent leaf bases along the trunk furnish an armorlike layer which is very characteristic. The cycads are dioecious, and the strobiles mostly terminal; the staminate vary greatly in size but may be very large (in one species about 3 ft long). Ovulate cones may weigh up to 100 lb.

One family, the Cycadaceae, is recognized. It comprises 9 genera and about 100 species. The largest genus, *Zamia*, with 28 species, ranges from southern Florida to Chile. Several other genera with fewer species are found in Cuba and Mexico, and the remaining groups are endemic to southeastern Africa and Asia.

The cycads may be considered as the most primitive of present gymnosperms, but not necessarily the oldest.

GINKGOALES   Ginkgo

Although once represented by a number of species, this order is now restricted to a single form, *Ginkgo biloba* L., the ginkgo or maidenhair

FIG. 14. *Ginkgo biloba*. Ginkgo. *1.* Staminate flowers × ¾. *2.* Ovulate flowers × ¾. *3.* Seed × ¾. *4.* Pit × ¾. *5.* Leaf × ½. *6.* Twig × ¼.

tree of China and Japan. It has been cultivated for centuries in the temple gardens of these two countries, but trees growing in the wild state have rarely if ever been found. A ginkgo tree in Sendai, Japan, is reported to have a height of 97 ft, a circumference of 27 ft, and an estimated age of 1,200 years. This species is a common ornamental in the United States. It does not appear to have any fungous or insect enemies, and has been considered resistant to smoke and drought. However, see R. T. Major (228a) for a recent resume of this species, including the chemistry of leaf extracts.

The leaves are fan-shaped, with or without one or more sinuses, and show dichotomous venation. On young twigs they are borne in spirals but on older growth recur only upon short spur shoots; the flowers are of special interest because of the free-swimming antherozoids found in the pollen tubes. This feature is also characteristic of the cycads, but not of the Gnetales or Coniferales. The seed resembles a plum in shape and size, and possesses a fleshy outer layer which upon ripening is exceedingly malodorous owing to the formation of a substance similar to butyric acid or its derivatives (odor of rancid butter). The pit is large, of a silvery color,[1] and when roasted is considered a delicacy by Orientals. Like the cycads, *Ginkgo* is also dioecious.

GNETALES

This order is probably the most recent, geologically. Fossil forms have not been found below the Tertiary,[2] and the origin of these plants in relation to other gymnosperms is obscure (64). They are of considerable interest because of their intermediate position in structure between the gymnosperms and the angiosperms. The secondary wood of the Gnetales, in addition to tracheids, exhibits vessels, a feature not found in other gymnosperms, but characteristic of the angiosperms. The flowers are also advanced and show indications of a perianth.[3] These similarities, however, can hardly be interpreted to mean that the angiosperms have evolved from the Gnetales, but rather that the latter have advanced along parallel lines to a similar stage in development.

The Gnetales are mostly dioecious, and their leaves opposite or whorled. Three families may be recognized, the Welwitschiaceae, the Ephedraceae, and the Gnetaceae.

The first is a monotype found only in the deserts of western South Africa. This plant, *Welwitschia mirabilis* Hook., presents an exceedingly

[1] The Chinese name signifies "white nut" or "silver apricot."
[2] About 60 million years ago.
[3] Often not distinguishable, however, from the bracts surrounding the flowers in certain of the Coniferales.

bizarre appearance. The large bulbous body is like a gigantic turnip, and from each side of the elliptical exposed top, which may be upward of 4 ft in diameter, is borne a broad, flat leaf which often extends outward to a distance of 6 or 8 ft. These are the only leaves developed during the life of the plant (which may embrace nearly a century), and as the ends become frayed, growth at the base continually lengthens them.

The Ephedraceae, with one genus *Ephedra*, comprise about 42 species of desert plants found mostly in the warmer parts of southern Europe and Asia and in North and South America. They are shrubby with jointed or fluted stems and scalelike leaves; in some species they develop prostrate, sometimes underground, stems. Ephedrine, an alkaloid used as a substitute for adrenalin, and in the treatment of hay fever and asthma, is obtained from several Asiatic species of this genus.

The Gnetaceae, with the single genus *Gnetum*, include about 30 species of small trees or woody climbers (lianas), found in tropical forests. The leaves are broad, sometimes trifoliate, with netted veins, and are very similar in appearance to those of the dicotyledons.

CONIFERALES   Conifers

These are by far the most important of the modern gymnosperms and are of primary value for forest products. In the Northern Hemisphere the Pinaceae comprise the most noteworthy family, followed by the Taxodiaceae and Cupressaceae. South of the equator, the Podocarpaceae and Araucariaceae are preeminent, and in the latter is found one of the world's most massive trees, the kauri-pine *Agathis australis* Salisb. of New Zealand. Although the maximum height may not exceed 150 ft, large old-growth trees were reported to attain a diameter of some 20 ft. Below a bushy crown, the nearly cylindrical trunk free of branches yields a remarkable amount of high-quality wood (293, 354).

Besides the large amounts of timber produced, the conifers furnish such products as turpentine and rosin (naval stores), and also serve to control erosion on the steep slopes of mountains. In the latter instance, especially in the cooler portions of the North Temperate Zone, vast, nearly pure forests of coniferous species are typical and greatly enhance the value of these regions for recreational purposes.

The various members of this group are known as "conifers," "evergreens," or "softwoods." In the first instance, the common name has reference to the fruit which in four families is a cone. The name "evergreen" is less satisfactory since at least four genera (*Larix, Pseudolarix, Taxodium,* and *Glyptostrobus*) have deciduous leaves, while in some species of broad-leaved trees (dicotyledons) the leaves are persistent. The term "softwood" is clearly of lumbermen's origin and is commonly

Family[a]	Leaves	Flowers	Fruit
1. Pinaceae	persistent or deciduous, spirally arranged (fascicled in one genus), acicular or linear	bract and ovuliferous scale distinct; ovules inverted, 2 on each scale	a woody cone maturing in 1, 2, or rarely 3 seasons; seeds terminally winged or wingless
2. Taxodiaceae	persistent or deciduous, spirally arranged, linear, or less commonly ovate	bract and ovuliferous scale partially fused; ovules erect (in native genera), 2 to 9 on each scale	a woody cone (in native genera), with peltate scales maturing in 1 or 2 seasons; seeds laterally winged
3. Cupressaceae	persistent, scalelike or awl-shaped, decussate, or the latter sometimes ternate	bract and ovuliferous scale wholly fused; ovules erect, 2 to many on each scale	a woody, leathery, or fleshy cone maturing in 1 to 3 seasons; seeds laterally winged or wingless
4. Taxaceae	persistent, spirally arranged, mostly linear	ovulate flower comprising a single erect ovule	a single seed surrounded by a fleshy aril; or drupelike

[a] Formerly, 1, 2, and 3 were included under one family, the Pinaceae.

used in distinguishing between the conifers and the broad-leaved trees or "hardwoods." It often happens, however, that the wood of a "softwood" (conifer) is harder than that of a "hardwood" (broad-leaved tree); for example, wood of longleaf pine is harder than that of basswood. Even though most of these terms are none too satisfactory, they are all useful provided their limitations are understood.

The leaves of the conifers are acicular (needlelike), scalelike, awl-shaped, or linear, in the last instance with veins running parallel but not connected by cross veinlets, as in the monocotyledons. In most cases, they are persistent but may be deciduous; they are borne singly or in fascicles and may be spirally arranged, opposite, whorled, or on short spur shoots. The great majority of the coniferous species are monoecious. The fruit is commonly a woody cone (rarely fleshy), or merely a single seed, with a fleshy seed coat, or surrounded by an open fleshy aril.

The order comprises 7 families, with about 51 genera, and some 520 species. The families and genera represented in this country are indicated in the following list:

1. PINACEAE:
   Pinus, Larix, Picea, Pseudotsuga, Tsuga, Abies.
2. TAXODIACEAE:
   Sequoia, Taxodium.
3. CUPRESSACEAE:
   Libocedrus, Thuja, Cupressus, Chamaecyparis, Juniperus.
4. TAXACEAE:
   Taxus, Torreya.

The distinguishing features of the coniferous families with indigenous North American species are outlined in the table on page 49.

Pinaceae: The pine family

This is the largest and most important family of the Coniferales. It includes 9 genera and about 210 species, mostly distributed through the Northern Hemisphere from the forests of the tropics to the northern limits of tree growth beyond the Arctic Circle. *Pinus, Larix, Picea, Pseudotsuga, Tsuga,* and *Abies,* each represented in the United States by two or more species, are described in subsequent paragraphs.

Two of the three remaining genera are restricted to China. One of these, *Pseudolarix,* is a monotype; the single species, *P. amabilis* Rehd.,[1] golden larch, is found only in the eastern provinces of Kiangsu and Chekiang, and differs from the true larches in that the cones disintegrate upon ripening. *Keteleeria* includes three species scattered through southeastern and western China and Formosa. Superficially, these resemble the balsam firs, but unlike that group, their cone scales are not deciduous at maturity.

The remaining genus, *Cedrus,* comprises four species. The Atlas cedar, *C. atlantica* Mane., is native to the Atlas Mountains in northern Africa; while the deodar cedar, *C. deodara* (Roxb.) Loud., is a commercially important tree in the western Himalaya. In Lebanon, the cedar of Biblical times, *C. libani* A. Rich. still thrives, although it is now largely of historical interest. *C. brevifolia* Henry is a little-known species native to the island of Cyprus. All of these, together with numerous horticultural varieties, are used as ornamentals in cities along the Pacific slope, and to a lesser degree in milder portions of eastern United States. The leaves of this genus are linear and similar in arrangement to those of *Larix* or *Pseudolarix,* but persistent; the cones resemble those of *Abies* but require two or three years to mature.

[1] *P. fortunei* Mayr., also *P. kaempferi* Fort.

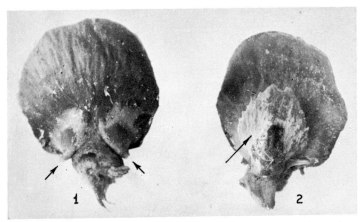

Fig. 15. Ovulate scales of a spruce flower × 10. *1.* Upper or inner face of scale. (Arrows show inverted ovules.) *2.* Lower or outer face of the same scale. (Arrow shows bract or cover scale.)

BOTANICAL FEATURES OF THE FAMILY

Leaves deciduous or persistent; spirally arranged, in certain genera recurring in false whorls on spur shoots developed on older growth; solitary or in fascicles (*Pinus*); needlelike or linear.

Flowers with bract and ovuliferous (seed) scale distinct; ovules inverted, 2 at the base of each cone scale (Fig. 15); all species monoecious.

Cones woody, stalked or sessile, pendent or upright, maturing in 1, 2, or rarely 3 seasons, in some groups, disintegrating at maturity; seeds terminally winged, or wingless.

PINUS L.   Pine

This genus, the largest and most important of the conifers, includes some 90 species widely scattered through the Northern Hemisphere from near the northern limits of tree growth in North America, Europe, and Asia southward to northern Africa, Asia Minor, Malaysia and Sumatra [here one species crosses the Equator (80)]. In the New World, pines are found as far south as the West Indies and Nicaragua. The pines are of primary importance in the production of timber, although the wood of nearly all of them is also suitable for pulp and paper manufacture. Turpentine, pine-wood oils, wood tars, and rosin, collectively known as "naval stores," are obtained from the wood of several species, notably *P. palustris* Mill. and *P. elliottii* Engelm. of North America, *P. pinaster* Ait. of the Mediterranean basin, and *P. longifolia* Roxb. of India. The leaf oils of several species are used in the manufacture of medicines, and

Genus	Leaves	Cones
Pinus (pine)	persistent; acicular; mostly in fascicles of 2 to 5	pendent; bracts, shorter than the seed scales; maturing in 2 (rarely 3) seasons
Larix (larch)	deciduous; linear; triangular or 4-sided; on the growth of the season borne singly in remote spirals, on older growth recurring only in clusters on short spur shoots	upright; bracts shorter or longer than the seed scales; maturing in 1 season
Picea (spruce)	persistent; linear; usually 4-sided (in certain species flattened); sessile, borne on conspicuous peglike projections from the twig	pendent; bracts shorter than the seed scales; maturing in 1 season
Pseudotsuga (Douglas-fir)	persistent; linear; flattened; petioled; borne on moderately raised leaf cushions	pendent, bracts 2-lobed with a central spine, and longer than the seed scales; maturing in 1 season
Tsuga (hemlock)	persistent; linear; flattened; petiole more conspicuous than in *Pseudotsuga*; more often 2-ranked; borne on short peglike projections from the twig	same as *Picea,* but mostly smaller
Abies (fir)	persistent; linear; flattened (2 species 4-sided), sessile; may or may not appear 2-ranked	upright; scales and bracts deciduous from the cone axis; bracts longer or shorter than the seed scales; maturing in 1 season

the seeds of several others are suitable for food. These so-called "pine nuts" are commonly offered for sale in many cities in this country.

Natural enemies of the pines are very numerous. Because of the resinous nature of the foliage, bark, and wood, fire is always a serious menace, while sawflies, weevils, bark beetles, and tip moths cause considerable damage. White pine blister rust, a fungous disease, not only destroys true white pines but other five-needle soft pines as well.

About 35 species of *Pinus* are native to the United States, and nearly all the principal timber-producing regions contain one or more important pines. Thirteen species are native to the East and South, and the remaining ones are found in the West.

Leaves of two sorts: (1) primary (juvenile) leaves, scalelike, solitary, spirally arranged, usually deciduous within a few weeks after their appearance, bearing in their axils (2) the acicular, secondary or adult fascicled leaves (needles).[1] *Needles* triangular, semicircular, or rarely circular in transverse section, borne in fascicles of 2 to 5 (rarely as many as 8, or solitary) usually with several lines of stomata on each surface; *apex* acute; *margin* often sharply serrulate; *basal sheath* deciduous or persistent, composed of 6 to 12 bud scales; *vascular bundles,* 1 or 2; *resin canals,* 2 to many (rarely obscure); needles persistent for 2 to several (exceptionally 17) years, exhaling a pungent aroma when bruised.

Fig. 16. Three stages in the development of a pine seedling, showing cotyledons and first juvenile leaves. (*Photograph by B. O. Longyear.*)

Flowers unisexual, *staminate* strobili axillary, red, orange, or yellow, in clusters of few to many at the base of the season's growth, consisting of a number of spirally arranged, two-celled, sessile anthers; *ovulate* cones subterminal or lateral, erect, composed of several to many spirally arranged bracts, each subtending an ovuliferous scale bearing 2 inverted basal ovules; all species monoecious.

Fruit a woody cone maturing in 2 (rarely 3) growing seasons; *cone scales* armed or unarmed; *seeds* obovoid, with terminal wings or rarely wingless; *cotyledons* 3 to 18. The rather remarkable opening mechanism of pine-cone scales has been investigated by Harlow, Côté, and Day (160).

[1] In seedlings, the first foliage to appear consists of a whorl of cotyledons (seed leaves); the growing shoot then develops linear, spirally arranged, serrulate juvenile leaves the first season, and in certain species for several seasons before the adult fascicled needles ultimately develop.

Buds scaly, the scales appressed, or free at the ends and then fringed; extremely variable in size, shape, and color, resinous or nonresinous. **Growth habit.** Although the growth of a terminal leader and a "whorl" of side branches each year is a feature of several coniferous genera, it is especially typical of the pines. Certain species usually produce a single set of side branches each year, while others are multinodal and develop 2 or 3 such arrangements on the elongating leader during the season. Since the leaf arrangement in *Pinus* is alternate (spiral), so too is that of the branches, and the term *false whorl* should be used for these arrangements.

The pines may be readily separated into two groups, namely, (1) the "soft" pines, and (2) the "hard" pines.[1]

DIFFERENCES BETWEEN SOFT PINES AND HARD PINES

Feature	Soft Pines	Hard Pines
Needles	in fascicles of 2 to 5,[a] usually 5; cross section of needle shows 1 fibrovascular bundle	in fascicles of 2 to 3 (rarely 5 to 8); cross section of needle shows 2 fibrovascular bundles
Fascicle sheath	deciduous	persistent
Cone scales	usually thin at the apex; mostly unarmed	usually thick at the apex; mostly armed
Wood	soft; transition from spring to summer wood gradual	hard (with few exceptions); transition from spring to summer wood abrupt

[a] In one form, solitary (*P. monophylla*).

SOFT PINE GROUP   (Subgenus Haploxylon)

The soft or white pines may be further divided as indicated below:

CONSPECTUS OF THE SOFT PINE GROUPS

Subdivision	Needles	Cones
White pines	5 in a fascicle; 2″ to 6″ long (in native species)	long-stalked; cone scales thin, umbo terminal and unarmed; wing longer than seed

[1] Since the wood of one or more of the "hard" pines is nearly as soft as that of the "soft" pines, these terms are used only for convenience.

Subdivision	Needles	Cones
Stone pines	5 in a fascicle; 3½" long, or less; clustered at the ends of the branches	short-stalked; scales thick, umbo terminal, usually unarmed; wing shorter than seed or lacking
Pinyons or nut-pines	2 to 4 in a fascicle; [a] 2" long, or less; incurved	short-stalked; scales thick, umbo dorsal; wing rudimentary or absent
Foxtail pines	5 in a fascicle; less than 2" long, incurved; borne in close spirals and persistent for a number of years, thus giving a brushlike appearance to the branch	same, except umbo armed, and wing longer than seed

[a] In one form, solitary (*P. monophylla*).

THE WHITE PINES

DISTINGUISHING CHARACTERISTICS

Species	Needles	Cones
P. strobus, eastern white pine	straight, slender, and flexible	about 5" long
P. monticola, western white pine	same	about 8" long
P. lambertiana, sugar pine	often twisted, relatively stiff	about 16" long, often thicker-scaled than those of the other two species

Pinus strobus L.   Eastern white pine; northern white pine

BOTANICAL FEATURES

Needles 3" to 5" long, in 5's, dark bluish green, slender and flexible, marked ventrally by 3 to 5 rows of stomates appearing as whitish lines; persistent until the end of the 2d season or the following spring; *resin canals* 2 (rarely 1 or 3), dorsal and external.[1] **Cones** 4" to 8" long, narrowly oblong-conic, often slightly curved, stalked, with thin scales; usually falling from the tree during the winter or following spring; *apophysis* nearly smooth or slightly lined; *umbo* terminal, unarmed; *seeds* ¼" long, ovoid, red-

[1] *External,* touching the epidermis or hypoderm; *medial,* entirely surrounded by green tissue (mesophyll); *internal,* touching the endodermis.

dish or grayish brown, mottled with dark spots, wings ¾" long, lined; about 27,000 (20,000–53,000) seeds to the pound.[1]

Twigs orange-brown, glabrous or sparingly puberulent; *buds* covered with thin reddish or orange-brown scales.

Bark on young stems thin and smooth, dark green, soon furrowed; on old trees 1" to 2" thick, deeply and closely fissured into narrow, roughly rectangular blocks, minutely scaly on the surface.[2]

GENERAL DESCRIPTION

Eastern white pine is the largest of northeastern conifers, and from the beginning of logging in this country it has been a most valuable species; first in New England, then in Pennsylvania and New York, and finally in the Lake states where magnificent stands once covered large areas.

This species commonly varies from 80 to 100 ft in height and 2 to 3½ ft in diameter (max. 220 by 6 ft or more). In the open, young trees produce broadly conical crowns with living branches persisting nearly to the ground; but under forest competition, especially that of hardwoods, a tall cylindrical bole is developed which is often clear, on older trees, for two-thirds of its length. The crown of middle-aged and old trees is composed of several nearly horizontal or ascending branches, gracefully plumelike in outline and very distinctive in comparison with those of other associated conifers. The root system is wide-spreading and moderately deep with only the vestige of a taproot; with age, root development nearer the surface may occur.

Eastern white pine is found on many different sites, even including such extremes as dry rocky ridges and wet sphagnum bogs. Best development, however, is made on moist sandy loam soils, or those with a small proportion of clay.

Especially in the Lake states, moderately moist soils supported extensive pure forests, while on drier areas, mixtures with red pine or even jack pine were quite common. On heavier soils the hardwoods could compete more successfully, and this pine occurred only as a scattered tree, often reaching, however, large proportions and excellent form in such mixtures.

[1] These and subsequent figures on number of cleaned dewinged seeds per pound are taken from the Woody Plant Seed Manual of the U.S. Forest Service (358). The figure given is the average number per pound, and the numbers in parentheses represent the "low" and "high," respectively.

[2] Sometimes almost corky in appearance, hence locally "cork pine."

FIG. 17. *Pinus strobus.* Eastern white pine. *1.* First year's cone × ¾. *2.* Mature cones and foliage × ⅓. *3.* Opened cone × ¾. *4.* Seed × 1. *5.* Fascicle of needles × ¾. *6.* Cross section of needle × 35. *7.* Bark of young tree. *8.* Bark of old tree.

Fig. 18. Old-growth eastern white pine.

In Canada, pure stands, or mixtures with red pine and red spruce, frequently occur, while in the northeastern United States, in addition to limited pure groups, eastern white pine occurs on sandy loams with the northern hardwoods, red spruce, and eastern hemlock; here the scattered pines usually tower 40 to 50 ft above the crowns of their associates. Farther south, although reaching large size, it is not so abundant and is found in company with many of the central hardwoods and eastern hemlock.

Although extensive logging has destroyed most of the original pine forests, this species has always been aggressive in reproducing itself. When the exodus from eastern farms began in the late 1860s many abandoned fields quickly seeded in with this tree, and nearly pure stands have since developed. This process has been continuous and has earned for this species the local name of "old field pine." [1]

[1] See also loblolly pine.

Eastern white pine may be classified as intermediate in tolerance. It is more tolerant than such species as paper birch, the aspens, red pine and jack pine, but less so than sugar maple, American beech, and hemlock.

This pine begins to produce cones at an early age, sometimes when not more than 10 ft high, but good seed production can rarely be expected until the trees are 20 to 30 years old, and under forest conditions from one to two decades later. Large crops usually occur at three- to five-year intervals, but a few cones may be produced nearly every year. Germination varies from 70 to 90 percent; and although some seeds retain their viability after several years in storage, a practical limit seems to be from two to three years.

After the first two seasons, the rate of growth of young trees increases, and when once established, this species makes rapid growth. On the best sites and during favorable seasons, young white pine may grow nearly 4 ft in height and 1 in. in diameter per year. This, however, is exceptional, and average trees usually attain not more than one-half this rate of increase. Between the ages of 50 and 100 years, height growth, especially, decreases but maturity is not reached for another 100 years, and very old trees have been reported which showed at least 450 annual rings.

This pine develops one horizontal false whorl of side branches each year, a useful feature in estimating the age of the tree.[1] In contrast, the pitch and jack pines, as well as some of the southern species, often produce two or three such whorls in a single growing season.

Because of the demand for the wood, the ease in handling of nursery stock, and the high percentage of survival when properly planted, this tree has been established by the millions throughout the Northeast; in fact, it has been the principal species used in reforestation for many years. Two serious enemies threaten it, however, especially in pure stands: (1) the white pine blister rust caused by a fungus, and (2) the white pine weevil. The former is a bark disease which eventually kills the tree, and the latter deforms the trunk by killing, often repeatedly, the terminal shoots. Open-grown, scattered pasture trees are sometimes successively weeviled to such an extent that they become bushy and totally unfit for good lumber,[2] and even trees in denser stands are badly deformed. Control measures have been applied to each of these enemies, and planting plans modified in an endeavor to lessen the amount of damage incurred.

[1] To the count of whorls should be added two or three, since as seedlings, side branches are not at first developed; this method obviously cannot be used on old trees where the bark has completely obliterated the branch scars.

[2] Such trees are often called "cabbage pines."

Although eastern white pine shows certain geographical variations, these are not sufficient to warrant the recognition of races, with one possible exception (251).

This pine was first introduced into England about 1705 by Lord Weymouth, after whom it is often called, and soon after it was taken to Germany, where it has become naturalized (184). It is valued for planting in certain situations.

RANGE

Southern Canada, Lake states, the Northeast, and the Appalachian Mountains (map, Plate 1). Also occurring in southern Mexico and Guatemala, unless one chooses to call this taxon *Pinus chiapensis* (Mart.) Andresen (7).

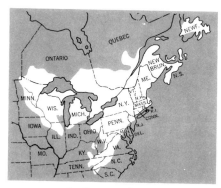

1. *Pinus strobus.*   2. *Pinus monticola.*

PLATE 1

Pinus monticola Dougl.   Western white pine; Idaho white pine

BOTANICAL FEATURES

Needles 2″ to 4″ long, in 5's, blue-green, glaucous, with 2 to 6 rows of stomata on the ventral surfaces, slender, flexible, persistent until the 3d and 4th seasons; *resin canals* 2 (occasionally 1 or 3) dorsal and external.

Cones 5″ to 15″ long,[1] narrowly cylindrical, often curved, stalked, *apophysis* yellowish brown to reddish brown, inner surface of scale deep red; *umbo* terminal, unarmed; *seeds* ⅓″ long, reddish brown, frequently mottled with black, with a terminal wing about 1″ in length; about 27,000 (14,000–32,000) seeds to the pound.

Twigs moderately slender, often clothed with orange-brown pubescence during the

[1] Most writers state that western white pine cones vary between 5 and 11 in. in length. Cones collected from trees growing on the Columbia National Forest in western Washington during the fall of 1935 varied in length between the limits noted above, but the largest one observed measured 14.3 in. exclusive of the stalk.

first season but ultimately becoming dark reddish brown to purplish brown and glabrous; *buds* about ½" long, cylindrical, blunt, covered by several closely appressed, imbricated scales.

Bark smooth, gray-green to light gray on young trees, thin even on old trunks where it breaks up into nearly square or rectangular, dark-gray or purplish-gray blocks separated by deep fissures.

GENERAL DESCRIPTION

Western white pine was first observed along the banks of the Columbia and Spokane Rivers in 1831 by the Scottish botanist David Douglas. Reaching a height of 150 to 180 ft, and a d.b.h. of 2½ to 3½ ft at maturity (max. 219° by 8 ft), this tree develops a long, slightly tapered shaft, often clear for 70 to 100 ft or more of its length and a usually short, symmetrical and somewhat open crown. Seedlings produce a prodigious taproot which is supplemented in later life by a deep, widespreading system of lateral roots which makes the trees unusually windfirm.

Except in the Puget Sound basin, on the Olympic Peninsula of western Washington, and on Vancouver Island, where it not infrequently occurs at or near sea level, this species is typically a mountain form. Best development is attained in northern Idaho on rich, porous soils in moist valleys and on middle and upper slopes and flats of northerly exposure. Here, where nearly 80 percent of the commercial timber of the species is found, it is very common and occasionally forms nearly pure stands, the best of which contain from 50,000 to 60,000 ft B.M. to the acre. Elsewhere, western white pine occurs largely on poorer and drier soils as an occasional tree or in small groves in mixture with other softwoods, and on such sites it rarely constitutes more than 5 percent of the stand. Its chief associates in the Rocky Mountain region include western larch, Engelmann spruce, lodgepole pine, grand and subalpine firs, and occasionally western redcedar. In Washington and Oregon, western white pine is frequently found with Douglas-fir, western hemlock, and grand, noble, and Pacific silver firs; and in California with red and Shasta red firs, Douglas-fir, and lodgepole pine.

This species rarely produces large seed crops; but as a rule some seed is released at intervals of two or three years after the fortieth to sixtieth year. Reproduction is best on a fresh mineral soil, although seeds lodging in humus often germinate and the young trees continue to develop provided they are amply supplied with moisture during the growing season. Rated as intermediate in tolerance, young trees are shade-enduring, but full light is required in later life and mature trees usually dominate mixed stands. Growth is moderately fast but decreases noticeably after the 125th to 150th year, and maturity is attained in about 200 to 350

FIG. 19. *Pinus monticola*. Western white pine. *1*. Closed cone and foliage ×
¾. *2*. Seeds × 1. *3*. Bark. (*Photograph by British Columbia Forest Service.*)

years. Jepson (189) states, "Its extreme age is about 400 years," while Sudworth (344) indicates that the five-century mark may be reached. The oldest recorded western white pine is a tree in British Columbia, with an age of 615 years (127).

This pine is one of the first tree species to inhabit the peat bogs of the Puget Sound basin. Here the young trees develop with such rapidity that they not infrequently outstrip those standing on firmer, drier soils nearby.

Western white pine has a number of natural enemies. The bark, even of mature trees, is extremely thin (rarely more than $1\frac{1}{4}$ in. thick), and in consequence the trees are easily damaged by even a light ground fire. White pine blister rust and bark beetles also take a heavy annual toll.

RANGE

Inland Empire, Pacific Northwest, and Sierra Nevada Mountains of California (map, Plate 1). *Altitudinal distribution:* sea level to 3,000 ft west of the summit of the Cascade Mountains in British Columbia, Washington, and Oregon; 2,000 to 7,000 ft east of the summit of the Cascade Mountains in Washington and Oregon and in Idaho and Montana; 5,000 to 10,000 ft in California.

Pinus lambertiana Dougl.   Sugar pine

BOTANICAL FEATURES

Needles 2" to 4" long; spirally twisted, in fascicles of 5, blue-green to gray-green, often silvery; with 2 to 6 lines of stomata on all three surfaces; persistent until the 2d and 3d seasons; *resin canals* usually 2, dorsal.

Cones 10" to 26" long, 4" to 5" in diameter when open, cylindrical, stalked; *apophysis* somewhat thickened, yellowish brown, inner surface of scale brown or reddish brown; *umbo* terminal, unarmed; *seeds* $\frac{1}{2}$" to $\frac{5}{8}$" long, dark brown to nearly black, lustrous, with a dark brown or black terminal wing about 1" to $1\frac{1}{2}$" in length; about 2,100 (1,500–3,200) seeds to the pound.

Twigs rather stout, at first covered with glandular pubescence but at length becoming orange-brown to purplish brown and glabrous; *buds* about $\frac{1}{3}$" long, ovoid, sharp-pointed, clothed with several closely appressed, chestnut-brown imbricated scales.

Bark dark green, thin, and smooth on young stems, grayish brown to purplish brown on old trunks, $1\frac{1}{2}$" to 4" or more in thickness, and broken into regular, superficially scaly ridges separated by deep fissures.

GENERAL DESCRIPTION

Sugar pine, another of David Douglas' discoveries, derives its name from a sweet resinous substance, pinite, found in the canals of both bark and

Fɪɢ. 20. *Pinus lambertiana*. Sugar pine. *1*. Closed cone × ½. *2*. Open cone × ⅓. *3*. Seeds × 1. *4*. Transverse section of needle × 35.

wood. It is the largest member of the genus *Pinus,* and 300-year-old trees on good sites commonly vary from 170 to 180 ft in height, and from 30 to 42 in. or more in diameter (max. 250 x 10* ft). The boles of forest trees are usually long, clear, and cylindrical, and support short crowns composed of several massive, horizontal or occasionally contorted branches. The root system is similar to that of western white pine.

Sugar pine never forms pure stands, except in small scattered areas, and while it may occasionally comprise up to 75 percent of a mixed stand, throughout most of its range it seldom occupies more than 25 percent of a forested area. It attains its best development on the granitic and andesitic soils of the west slopes of the Sierra Nevada between the San Joaquin and Feather Rivers between elevations of 4,500 and 5,500 ft. Forest associates within these limits include ponderosa and Jeffrey pines, Douglas-fir, California red, Shasta, and white firs, giant sequoia, and incense-cedar. In southern Oregon and northern California, sugar pine is often found with digger and ponderosa pines, Douglas-fir, tanoak, California black oak, bigleaf maple, and Pacific dogwood, usually at elevations of less than 4,000 ft. Toward the southern limit of its range, this species invades alpine forests, and has been found at elevations of 10,000 ft. This pine is usually found on somewhat cooler and wetter sites than those occupied by most other pines, and to the east of the Sierran crest, where drought and extreme fluctuations in temperature not infrequently occur, it is very limited.

Sugar pine is not a prolific seeder. Small amounts of seed are usually produced annually, but large crops are normally released only at irregular intervals of from two to seven years after the eightieth to hundredth year. The percentage of germination varies from 40 to 70 percent. A moist mineral soil covered by a thin layer of humus makes a good seedbed. Pine seeds are eaten by squirrels and other rodents, making natural reproduction in some sections very sparse. Although sunlight is beneficial to the seedlings, protection from extremes of temperature is needed for continued growth, and the most vigorous young trees are usually found under partial shade. The tolerance of this species is intermediate.

PLATE 2. *Pinus lambertiana.*

FIG. 21. Bark of mature sugar pine.

Sugar pine is the most rapidly growing tree in the Sierra (with the exception of the giant sequoia), and on good sites trees 100 years old may be 140 ft tall and nearly 30 in. in diameter. It is long-lived and occasionally attains an age of 500 to 600 years.[1]

Sugar pine is unusually windfirm and is reasonably free from fungous diseases and insect pests, although the white pine blister rust and the mountain pine beetle sometimes cause serious losses. Mistletoe and fire cause considerable damage to young trees, and fire scars are a major source of culls in mature timber.

RANGE

Central Oregon to southern California (map, Plate 2). *Altitudinal distribution:* 1,000 to 4,000 ft in the North; 4,000 to 7,000 ft through northern and central California; 7,000 to 10,000 ft in the South.

THE STONE PINES

DISTINGUISHING CHARACTERISTICS

Species	Cones
P. flexilis, limber pine	cylindrical, mostly about 5" long, opening at maturity; their seeds each with a very short terminal wing, or wingless
P. albicaulis, whitebark pine	ovoid, about 2½" long, remaining closed at maturity; their seeds wingless

Pinus flexilis James   Limber pine

Distinguishing characteristics. *Needles* in 5's about 2½" in. long, clustered near the branch ends, dark green, stout, rigid, stomatiferous on all surfaces; resin canals dorsal. *Cones* 3 to 10 in. long, cylindrical, the scales thickened, and slightly reflexed at the apex; *seeds* large, with rudimentary wings or wingless. *Bark* on young stems smooth, silvery white to light gray or greenish gray; that on old trunks dark brown to nearly black, separated by deep fissures into rectangular to nearly square, superficially scaly plates or blocks.

General description. Limber pine was first observed near Pike's Peak by Dr. Edwin James, an army surgeon attached to Long's Mountain Expedition of 1820. Like other relatively inaccessible trees of high altitudes, limber pine is primarily of importance in the protection of valuable watersheds. Ordinarily the tree attains but small proportions, varying from 30 to 50 ft in height and from 15 to 24 in. d.b.h. (max. 85 by 7° ft). The bole is stout, noticeably tapered, and supports a number of large plumelike often drooping branches. The result is an extensive crown which not infrequently

[1] The oldest tree recorded by the Forest Service was 623 years. Its records also include 17 trees over 500 years of age.

reaches to within a few feet of the ground. Young trees develop a long, sparsely branched taproot which is later supplemented by several laterals.

Range. East slopes of the Rocky Mountains in southern British Columbia and southern Alberta, south along the mountains to Arizona and New Mexico; west to the mountains of southern California, and north along the Sierra Nevada to northern California; east through Nevada and Idaho (one outpost is found in the Black Hills of South Dakota). *Altitudinal distribution:* 4,000- to 10,000-ft elevation in Montana, Wyoming, and Idaho; 4,500 to 11,500 ft in Colorado; 8,000 to 11,800 ft in southern California.

FIG. 22. Stone pines. *1.* Open cone, *Pinus flexilis* × ¾. *2.* Seeds × 1. *3.* Fascicle of needles, *Pinus albicaulis* × ¾. *4.* Cone × ¾. *5.* Seeds × 1.

Pinus albicaulis Engelm.   Whitebark pine

Distinguishing characteristics. *Needles* in 5's similar to those of limber pine, clustered toward the ends of the branchlets; resin canals dorsal, with an additional ventral one usually present (118). *Cones* about 2½ in. long, ovoid, purplish brown, with thickened apophyses and terminally armed umbos. *Bark* on immature trees brownish white to creamy white, smooth or superficially scaly at the base, rarely more than ½ in. thick. (Similar in general appearance to the preceding species.)

General description. This is a small alpine tree which rarely attains a height of more than 30 to 50 ft or a diameter of 12 to 24 in. (max. 85° by 6° ft). In sheltered places whitebark pine produces an erect, rapidly tapering bole which supports a crown of long, willowy-appearing limbs; these are extremely tough and are rarely damaged by heavy snow or even by the cyclonic winds characteristic of alpine sites. Trees on exposed areas are usually sprawling, or even prostrate and fail to develop anything remotely resembling a central stem.

Range. Western British Columbia in the vicinity of Lake Whitesail south along the Olympic and Cascade Mountains of Washington, the Siskiyou, and Blue Mountains of Oregon, to the Sierra Nevada of California; south through Alberta and eastern British Columbia to northern Montana, northwestern Wyoming and the Bitterroot Mountains of Idaho. *Altitudinal distribution:* 5,000 to 6,000 ft in British Columbia and Washington; 5,500 to 9,000 ft in Oregon; 5,000 to 10,000 ft in Idaho, Montana, and Wyoming; and 7,000 to 11,000 ft in California.

THE PINYONS OR NUT PINES

DISTINGUISHING CHARACTERISTICS

Species	Leaves
P. cembroides, Mexican pinyon	in fascicles of 2 and 3, margins serrulate
P. monophylla, singleleaf pinyon	solitary or occasionally in fascicles of 2, margins entire
P. quadrifolia, Parry pinyon	in fascicles of 4 (rarely 1 to 5), margins entire or remotely serrulate
P. edulis, pinyon	in fascicles of 2 (rarely 3), margins entire

(Cones of all species 1″ to 2″ long, few-scaled, ovoid, globose.)

This group of pines is widely distributed through the semiarid regions of the West; all are small trees rarely attaining heights of more than 20 to 40 ft or diameters of 12 to 24 in. Trees growing in protected situations usually develop a fairly straight, moderately tapering bole and a short rounded crown. On the other hand, those in the open are commonly shrubby, often contorted, and in some instances actually sprawling. Excellent anchorage is afforded by moderately deep and widespreading root systems. As a group the nut pines are usually encountered on dry, comparatively shallow, gravelly, or rocky soils of mesas, benches, and canyon walls.

Pinus cembroides Zucc., the Mexican pinyon, occurs as a scattered tree in the mountains of southern and central Arizona, western Texas, northern Mexico, and Lower California between elevations of 4,500 and 7,500 ft.

Singleleaf pinyon, *P. monophylla* Torr. and Frém., not infrequently forms extensive pure, open forests. It ranges from southeastern Idaho to the eastern foothills of the Sierra Nevada Mountains, then south along their east slopes and the more western San Bernardino Mountains to northern Lower California. To the east it reappears in the mountains of central and northeastern Arizona and in Utah west of the Wasatch range. Altitudinally, singleleaf pinyon occurs at elevations of from 2,000 ft in the North to 7,000 ft in the South.

The Parry pinyon, *P. quadrifolia* Parl., and the pinyon, *P. edulis* Engelm., like the Mexican pinyon, occur as scattered trees or in small groves in association with scrub oaks and junipers. The former is found only in the mountains of southern Cali-

Fig. 23. Cone and foliage of singleleaf pinyon × ½.

fornia and northern Lower California between 3,500 and 6,000 ft in elevation. The range of nut pine, however, is much more extensive, and the tree is found from north-central Colorado and eastern Utah south through western Oklahoma, western Texas, central and southern Arizona to northern Mexico. Its altitudinal limits range from 5,000 to 9,000 ft.

THE FOXTAIL PINES

DISTINGUISHING CHARACTERISTICS

Species	Leaves	Cones
P. balfouriana, foxtail pine	in 5's, bright blue-green, persistent for 10 to 12 years	about 4″ long, ovoid to cylindrical, the umbo armed with a minute incurved, deciduous prickle
P. aristata, bristlecone pine	in 5's, bright blue-green, persistent for 14 to 17 years, commonly dotted with white resin flecks	about 3″ long, subcylindrical, the umbo armed with a long, stiff incurved prickle, often covered with shiny resin droplets

The foxtail pines, so-called because of the bushy nature of the foliage on young branches, comprise a small group of alpine trees, two of which are found in the western United States. They are quite similar in habit to the stone pines, but in contrast they retain their foliage for many years. Furthermore, the cone scales are dorsally armed and the seeds have long terminal wings. The trees are very small, rarely attaining a height of more than 30 to 40 ft or a diameter of 12 to 24 in. (max. 60 by 3 ft). They develop a short, stocky, often malformed trunk which is commonly clothed for the greater part of its length in a dense, narrow irregular crown. Owing to their inaccessibility they contribute little or nothing to the nation's timber supply; nevertheless, they provide valuable cover on many of our high western watersheds.

   P. balfouriana Grev. and Balf. is restricted to high peaks of the Coast ranges and Sierra Nevada Mountains in California between 5,000 and 12,000 ft.

Fig. 24. Foxtail pines. *1.* Open cone, *Pinus balfouriana*, × ¾. *2.* Fascicle of needles × ¾. *3.* Open cone, *Pinus aristata*, × ¾. *4.* Seed × 1.

   P. aristata Engelm., in contrast, ranges from the mountains along the Nevada-California border east through the highlands of Nevada, Utah, Colorado, northern Arizona, and northern New Mexico. Schulman (314) indicated that in the White mountains of the Inyo National Forest in east-central California near the Nevada border, bristlecone pine at elevations of about 10,000 ft attains the greatest age of any living thing. Seventeen trees over 4,000 years old were found, and the patriarch showed 4,600 growth rings. Growing conditions are most rigorous and trees may attain only an inch in diameter in a century. Such trees are often valuable for studying the climate of past millennia (244). Currey (83a) reports a 4,900-year-old tree in eastern Nevada.

HARD PINE GROUP   (Subgenus Diploxylon)

THE NORTHEASTERN YELLOW PINES

Species	Needles	Cones
P. resinosa, red pine	in fascicles of 2, about 5″ long, flexible, brittle	about 2″ long, ovoid, umbo unarmed; cones deciduous the following season
P. banksiana, jack pine	in fascicles of 2, about 1¼″ long, divergent, often twisted	about 1¾″ long, oblong-conic, often incurved, umbo armed with a minute prickle; cones persistent for many years
P. rigida, pitch pine	in fascicles of 3, about 3½″ long, stiff, twisted	about 3″ long, ovoid, umbo armed with a conspicuous rigid prickle; cones often persistent for many years

Pinus resinosa Ait.   Red pine [1]

BOTANICAL FEATURES

Needles 4″ to 6″ long, in fascicles of 2,[2] serrulate, dark yellow-green, flexible, straight, breaking off cleanly when doubled between the fingers,[3] persistent until 4th or 5th season; *resin canals* 2 to 6; 2 always present, external on the flat surface, the others when present either external or medial.
Cones 1½″ to 2¼″ long, ovoid-conic, subsessile; *apophysis* chestnut-brown, rounded; umbo dorsal and unarmed; *seeds* ³⁄₁₆″ long, somewhat mottled, with wings ½″ to ⅔″ long, oblique, chestnut-brown; about 52,000 (30,000–71,000) seeds to the pound.
Twigs orange-brown, lustrous; *buds* covered with thin, ragged orange-brown or reddish-brown scales, often grayish on the margin.
Bark on young trees flaky, orange-red; eventually breaking up into large, flat, reddish-brown, superficially scaly plates irregularly diamond-shaped in outline.

GENERAL DESCRIPTION

Red pine is one of the most distinctive of northern conifers. Even at a considerable distance, the symmetrically oval crown with its tufted

[1] Through the Lake states, red pine is widely known as "Norway pine." The term "Norway" as applied to this tree is unfortunate, since it is a native American species. It is said that early explorers mistook it for Norway spruce, and also that it grew in abundance near the town of Norway, Maine.
[2] Rarely also in 3's on tip-moth-infested shoots, or on young trees (373).
[3] This feature will in most cases separate red pine from other associated or commonly planted long-leaved two-needle pines, with the exception of the Japanese and Chinese red pines, *P. densiflora* Sieb. and Zucc. and *P. tabulaeformis* Carr., respectively, both of which also have somewhat brittle needles.

Fig. 25. *Pinus resinosa.* Red pine. *1.* Fascicle of needles × ¾. *2.* Cross section of needle × 35. *3.* Open cone × ¾. *4.* Closed cone × ½. *5.* Seed × 1. *6.* Bark of old tree.

dark-green foliage appears very different from that of the ragged, unkempt jack pines or the plumelike tops of the eastern white pine. The bole of red pine is well formed, long and cylindrical and is supported by a spreading root system and poorly developed taproot (89). Although attaining a maximum size of 125* by 5 ft, most trees vary from 50 to 80 ft in height and 2 to 3 ft in diameter.

Best development in the United States was made in the upper Great Lakes region where magnificent pure and mixed stands of this species occurred. On light acid sandy soils too poor for white pine, red pine grew in abundance, and on the better sites was mixed with the former species; occasional trees, often of large size, were found in hardwood mixtures on heavier soils. Following logging and fire, much of the land which had supported red pine became too poor for anything but jack pine, which over large areas established itself as a pioneer tree. In a similar way, red pine occupied former eastern white pine land.

In its soil and moisture requirements and ability to grow under forest competition, red pine is intermediate between jack pine and eastern white pine. Arranged in order of tolerance, eastern white pine is first and jack pine third, while in adaptability to dry sandy soils, this order is reversed. On cutover land, red pine appears to follow jack pine and is

FIG. 26. Old-growth red pine left after logging.

often found in mixture with it. Both trees experience great variations in seasonal temperatures, with extremes of 40 to 60°F below zero in winter to 90 to 105°F in summer. The growing season for red pine is from 80 to 160 days.

Seeds may be produced in small quantities each year, but good crops occur only at intervals of from three to seven years. Under the best conditions, germination varies from 80 to 90 percent, but the seeds need a mineral soil, and little reproduction takes place on areas covered by sod or brush. Growth of established unshaded young trees is fast, and during the first two decades they will often outstrip the eastern white pine. Some 30-year plantations of red pine in New England contain trees with a height of 35 ft and a diameter of 6 in. The maximum age for the species is about 350 years.

Red pine is grown in large numbers for reforestation purposes and also has its place in ornamental plantings, particularly on light sandy soils.

This species is sometimes attacked by the Nantucket pine moth, and also the European pine-shoot moth, both of which locally may cause considerable damage.

RANGE

Southern Canada, Lake states, and the Northeast (map, Plate 3).

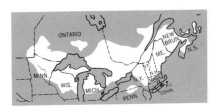

PLATE 3. *Pinus resinosa.*

Pinus banksiana Lamb.   Jack pine

BOTANICAL FEATURES

Needles ¾" to 1½" long,[1] in fascicles of 2 [also 3 near the tip of the leader on young trees], yellow-green, flat or slightly concave on the inner surface, divergent, stout, often twisted; persistent for 2 or 3 years; *resin canals* 2, medial; epidermal cells rectangular in cross section.

Cones 1½" to 2" long, oblong-conic, sessile, light brown, usually pointing forward, often strongly incurved, with the scales well developed only on the outer face; opening tardily and often persistent for many years; *apophysis* rounded, smooth; *umbo* dorsal, armed with a minute prickle; *seeds* 1⁄12" long, triangular, black and roughened, with wings about ⅛" long; about 131,000 (71,000–250,000) seeds to the pound. Serotinous (late opening) cones are typical of this species, lodgepole pine, knobcone pine, and a few others. In jack pine, there is considerable variation from one tree to another in the degree of serotiny observed. On some trees, nearly all mature cones remain closed; on others most of them open. When closed cones are subjected to temperatures of 140°F they subsequently open. Cones extracted with alcohol-benzene also open, and it is presumed that resins and perhaps other substances "glue" the scales together. Scales treated in this way, or whose bonds have been fractured mechanically, behave normally, opening when dried, closing when wetted (269).

Bark thin, brown slightly tinged with red, or dark gray; irregularly divided into scaly ridges.

GENERAL DESCRIPTION

Jack pine is essentially a Canadian species which reaches its best development north and west of Lake Superior. It extends southward into the United States through northern New England, also into Michigan,

[1] On young trees (nursery stock), often 3 in. or more in length.

Fig. 27. *Pinus banksiana.* Jack pine. *1.* Staminate flowers shedding pollen × 1. *2.* Closed cones and foliage × ½. *3.* Open cone × ¾. *4.* Seed × 1. *5.* Fascicle of needles × ¾. *6.* Cross section of needle × 35.

Wisconsin, and Minnesota. In these Lake states, jack pine is one of the most important second-growth species. The growing season over this range is somewhat shorter than that of its associate, red pine, but the extremes in temperature are about the same. Under the most favorable conditions, this pine varies from 70 to 80 ft in height and 12 to 15 in. in diameter, but is usually much smaller (max. 100 by 2 ft). In the open an irregular rounded crown is produced, the lower branches of which soon die but persist on the trunk for many years; this gives the tree a scraggly appearance unlike that of other evergreens of the region. When grown in dense stands, the crown is smaller, but the dead lower branches still prune very poorly. The root system, at least after the first few years, is wide-spreading and only moderately deep (67).

Jack pine is very intolerant and occurs in pure stands or open mixtures with quaking aspen and paper birch on dry, sandy, acid soils too poor for such species as red pine or eastern white pine, with which, however, it is often found on the better sites. In fact, much of the land formerly occupied by these two species in the Great Lakes region supports pure stands of jack pine which originated after logging and fire had destroyed the layer of humus, leaving only bare sand. This species serves as a valuable pioneer tree on such areas, but, except on the very poorest, it is eventually replaced by red pine or white pine. On better sandy loam soils, these species may in turn yield to hardwoods such as sugar maple, northern red oak, and basswood.

Like the lodgepole pine of the West, which it resembles in many ways, jack pine is very prolific and begins to produce yearly crops of cones at an early age (5 to 10 years) with larger amounts at three- or four-year intervals. The cones open irregularly, and many remain closed unless heat is applied; in the former instance they are often engulfed by the trunk or branch to which they are attached.[1] This habit of retaining so

PLATE 4. *Pinus banksiana.*

many unopened cones explains the rapidity of natural seeding after a fire has swept through a jack pine forest.

The germination of the seed varies from 60 to 75 percent (even higher in freshly collected seeds); and after the first 3 to 5 years the young trees make rapid growth, usually developing, like pitch pine, two or three false whorls of branches each year. Jack pine matures in about 60 years and subsequently begins to deteriorate, although trees 150 years of age or older have been found (maximum 230 years).

RANGE

Canada; and northern United States east of the Great Plains (see map, Plate 4).

[1] Seeds from completely embedded cones have been found viable.

Pinus rigida Mill.   Pitch pine

BOTANICAL FEATURES

Needles 3″ to 5″ long, in fascicles of 3, yellow-green, stiff, usually somewhat twisted, standing out at nearly right angles to the twig, often produced on short "water sprouts" or in tufts along the trunk; mostly deciduous during the 2d season; *resin canals* 2 to 11, both medial and internal.

Cones 2″ to 3½″ long, nearly sessile, ovoid, usually persistent for many years; *apophysis* light brown, smooth; *umbo* dorsal and armed with a rigid prickle; *seeds* ¼″ long, triangular to oval, dull black, sometimes mottled with gray, with brownish terminal wings; about 62,000 (36,000–83,000) seeds to the pound.

Bark at first dark and very scaly; eventually 1″ to 2″ thick at the base of old trees and smoother with brownish-yellow, flat plates separated by narrow irregular fissures.

Fig. 28. *Pinus rigida.* Pitch pine. *1.* Fascicle of needles × ¾. *2.* Cross section of needle × 35. *3.* Open and closed cones, respectively × ¾. *4.* Seed × 1. *5.* Bark of old tree.

GENERAL DESCRIPTION

Pitch pine is a tree of great diversity in form, habit, and development. In the northern part of its range, through New England, it is commonly a small tree growing on the poorest of acid, sandy, sterile soils in company with gray birch and scrub oak (*Q. ilicifolia* Wangenh.). Farther south, especially in Pennsylvania, it reaches its best development (186) and varies from 50 to 60 ft in height and 1 to 2 ft in diameter (max. 100 by 3 ft).

The form of the tree is exceedingly variable, and on exposed sites it is often very grotesque, while in better situations a tall columnar bole and small open crown are produced; the root system is deep, and the tree is relatively windfirm until overmaturity, when shallower roots predominate.

Although pitch pine is extremely hardy in maintaining itself on the driest, most unproductive sites, best growth is made on sandy loam soils with moderate amounts of moisture. Particularly near the coast (New Jersey), this species may be found on peat soils of Atlantic white-cedar swamps. Very little pitch pine is found on the more favorable areas because of its pronounced intolerance to forest competition, especially that of the hardwoods, which usually preempt the better sites. This pine is found naturally in fairly open, pure stands, or in mixture with such hardwoods as scarlet, black, and chestnut oaks, various hickories, black tupelo, and red maple; best growth is attained in the hardwood mixture.

The production of cones begins very early, and 12-year-old trees often bear quantities of viable seeds.[1] Good crops may occur at 3-year or longer intervals; many of the cones remain unopened until midwinter and then gradually release their seeds upon the snow, in this way providing food for birds and small rodents. However, the time of seed release varies. On some trees it occurs soon after the cones mature, but on others, cones may remain closed for many years.

The stems of seedlings often lie nearly flat on the ground. Subsequent growth to an upright position leaves the tree with a double curvature at the base. Evidence of this juvenile habit disappears as the tree becomes older (224).

PLATE 5. *Pinus rigida.*

On good sites the growth of pitch pine is moderate for about the first 90 years, after which stagnation takes place and the trees deteriorate (maximum age 200 years). An interesting feature of this tree is its periodicity in growth. Instead of one false whorl of lateral branches, two or even three may develop during a single season, with resting stages between successive whorls. Concomitantly, diameter growth is often made

[1] Even 3-year-old trees may yield viable seeds, and flowering cones have been found on 12-month hybrid seedlings (268).

FIG. 29. Bark of young pitch pine.

in installments, with false growth rings resulting. Estimates of age made by counting whorls or rings are, therefore, liable to error unless this habit is understood.

Fire is the most serious enemy of this species, even though it is remarkably resistant. Young trees commonly produce sprouts after burning or other injury, and these persist for many years, a feature rare among the conifers.[1]

Pitch pine seedlings have been produced in large quantities for forest planting, especially in Pennsylvania, and this species may be of considerable importance especially on soils too poor for other trees.

RANGE

The Northeast, and the Appalachian Mountains to Georgia (map, Plate 5). *Altitudinal distribution:* sea level to 3,000 ft, or in some sections to the upper limit of tree growth.

THE SOUTHERN YELLOW PINES

Ten yellow pines are included in the woody flora of southern forests. Five of them, namely, longleaf, shortleaf, loblolly, slash, and Vir-

[1] See also shortleaf and longleaf pines, Chihuahua pine, baldcypress, and redwood.

Species	Needles	Cones	Twigs
P. palustris, longleaf pine	in fascicles of 3, about 12″ long	about 7″ long, dull reddish brown	stout, orange-brown, glabrous; buds with silvery-white scales
P. echinata, shortleaf pine	in fascicles of 2 and 3, about 4″ long	about 2″ long, light reddish brown	slender, green, tinged with a purplish bloom; buds with reddish-brown, appressed scales
P. taeda, loblolly pine	in fascicles of 3, about 7″ long	about 3½″ long, yellowish brown; sessile; apophysis depressed, dull	slender, glabrous; buds with reddish-brown scales, free at the tips
P. elliottii, slash pine	in fascicles of 2 and 3, about 9″ long	about 4″ long, reddish brown; short-stalked; apophysis rounded, shiny	stout; buds with reddish-brown scales, white-ciliate
P. virginiana, Virginia pine	in fascicles of 2, about 2″ long	about 2″ long, dull reddish brown	slender, purplish during the first winter

ginia are of primary importance and will be considered first. (See table above.)

Pinus palustris Mill.   Longleaf pine

BOTANICAL FEATURES

Needles 8″ to 18″ long,[1] in fascicles of 3,[2] bright green, densely tufted, at the ends of stout branch tips, persistent until the end of the second season; *resin canals* 4 to 7, mostly internal, fascicle sheath from 0.6″ to 1.5″ in length.

Cones 6″ to 10″ long, narrowly ovoid-cylindric, when shed usually leaving a few of the basal scales attached to the twig; *apophysis* reddish brown, weathering to an ashy gray, wrinkled; *umbo* armed with a dorsal prickle which curves toward the base of the scale; *seeds* ½″ long, somewhat ridged, pale with dark blotches; wings 1½″ long, striped, oblique at the ends; *cotyledons* 5 to 10; about 4,200 partially dewinged seeds to the pound.

Twigs stout, orange-brown; *buds* large and very conspicuous, covered with silvery-white, fringed scales.

[1] A weeping variety with needles 24 in. long is reported by Coker and Totten for North Carolina (72).

[2] Numerous individuals with needles in 4's and 5's have been found in the Gulf states.

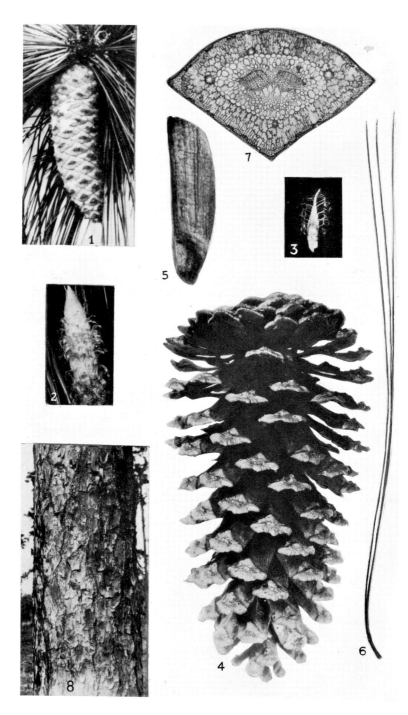

Bark coarsely scaly, with rough plates on older trees; *phellogen layers,* ivory-white (102).

Longleaf pine is one of the most distinctive and important of southern conifers. It is a medium-sized to large tree 80 to 120 ft in height and 2 to 2½ ft in diameter (max. 150 by 4 ft) with a long clear bole and small open crown featured by dense tufts of needles at the ends of the branchlets. The underground system comprises a very deep taproot with many wide-spreading, well-developed laterals.

Although it grows best on deep well-drained acid sandy soils, this species is found on a variety of sites. In the poorest of situations where a hardpan is near the surface, it maintains itself, even though growth is very slow. Flat land of this character is poorly drained and in spring may be covered with shallow pools of standing water, hence possibly the original application of the name *palustris* (swamp) to longleaf pine. During the summer, however, such areas are exceedingly dry, and only trees like blackjack oak or turkey oak are seen scattered through the open nearly pure forests of pine. On these shallow soils underlain by hardpan, the taproot is poorly developed and wind-thrown trees are not uncommon. As previously indicated, best growth is made on better-drained sandy soils, and especially in the southern part of its range, longleaf often occupies low ridges or knolls while slash pine preempts the moister depressions.

Longleaf is very intolerant, and has but few associates; pure open stands are typical with a small accumulation of needles or short grasses on the forest floor. Seed crops are irregular, with exceptionally high yields every five to seven years. The seeds must have mineral soil for best growth. Under natural conditions germination takes place within two to five weeks after the seeds are released, with a viability ranging from 50 to 75 percent or higher.[1] Unless stored airtight at low temperatures or stratified under similar conditions, the germinative capacity is much reduced.

[1] According to Burleigh (56), such birds as the mourning dove, bobwhite, southern meadow lark, and blackbird consistently eat the seeds and also clip off the endosperm raised upon the cotyledons of young seedlings. This often makes reproduction by seeding very unsatisfactory or even a failure. It is notable that there are but few birds present in poor seed years.

FIG. 30. *Pinus palustris.* Longleaf pine. *1.* Closed cone × ¼. *2.* Terminal bud × ¾. *3.* Fringed bud scale × 1½. *4.* Open cone × ¾. *5.* Seed × 1. *6.* Fascicle of needles × ½. *7.* Cross section of needle × 35. *8.* Bark (*Photograph by J. C. Th. Uphof.*)

FIG. 31. "Grass stage" of longleaf pine.

Longleaf pine develops very little aboveground for the first three to six years (exceptionally 12 or more years), but during this time the roots get a firm foothold. Moreover, the young tree does not exhibit annual rings but seems to grow intermittently when conditions permit (280). A dense bunch of green needles is all that appears on the surface, and to the inexperienced eye this is often mistaken for grass; hence the so-called "grass stage" of longleaf pine. By the end of this period the root system is well developed, but the aerial stem shows practically no elongation.[1] Height and diameter growth then increase rapidly, and trees 25 years old average 45 ft in height and 6 in. in diameter. Some 70-year-old stands contain trees average 70 ft in height and 15 in. d.b.h. Maturity is reached in about 150 years, but old trees sometimes show 300 annual rings.

Although the buds may be somewhat resistant to moderate heat, fire is often very destructive to young trees; and many of them are rooted up by hogs searching for food. However, this species is more fire-resistant than are the other southern pines. Although longleaf pine is not considered to propagate by sprouting, one reference indicates that some four-year-old trees cut off just above the root collar produce vigorous sprouts (132).

This pine, in addition to furnishing lumber, is one of the two principal southern species which produce naval stores.[2]

RANGE

South Atlantic and Gulf Coastal plains (map, Plate 6). *Altitudinal distribution:* near sea level up to 1,900 ft in the Appalachian Mountains of Alabama.

---

[1] This unusual growth habit is also found in south Florida slash pine.
[2] For other uses see W. G. Wahlenberg's monograph, which lists 637 references on this species (365).

1. *Pinus palustris.*　　　2. *Pinus echinata.*

PLATE 6

Pinus echinata Mill.　　Shortleaf pine

BOTANICAL FEATURES

Needles 3″ to 5″ long, mostly in fascicles of 2, but also in 3's on the same tree (occasionally with the latter number predominant), dark yellow-green, slender, flexible, persistent until the 2d to 4th seasons, not infrequently occurring from dormant buds along the bole (335); *resin canals* 1 to 4, small, medial, or both medial and internal.

Cones 1½″ to 2½″ long, ovoid-oblong to conical, nearly sessile, usually persistent for several years; *apophysis* reddish brown, rounded; *umbo* dorsal and armed with a small sharp, straight or curved, sometimes deciduous prickle; *seeds* ³⁄₁₆″ long, brown, with black markings; wings ½″ long, broadest near the middle; about 48,000 (36,000–62,000) seeds to the pound.

Twigs at first green and tinged with purple, eventually reddish brown; buds with red-brown scales.

Bark on small trees nearly black, roughly scaly, with small surface pockets or holes; later reddish brown and broken into irregular flat plates, scaly on the surface; *phellogen layers* ivory-white.

GENERAL DESCRIPTION

Shortleaf pine is a medium-sized to large tree 80 to 100 ft in height and 2 to 3 ft in diameter (max. 146° by 4 ft). The clear well-formed bole supports a small narrowly pyramidal crown and terminates underground in a very deep taproot.[1]

Although found on many different sites, this species is most common in pure or mixed stands on dry upland soils which are neither highly acid nor strongly alkaline. Its associates include loblolly and Virginia pines; eastern redcedar; black, blackjack, post, and chestnut oaks; and mockernut hickory. In addition—especially on soils containing more moisture—bitternut hickory and sweetgum are included. Especially west of the Mississippi River, the shortleaf and longleaf pines occur in mixture and often attain maximum development together.

[1] Eight-year-old trees may have taproots 14 ft in length.

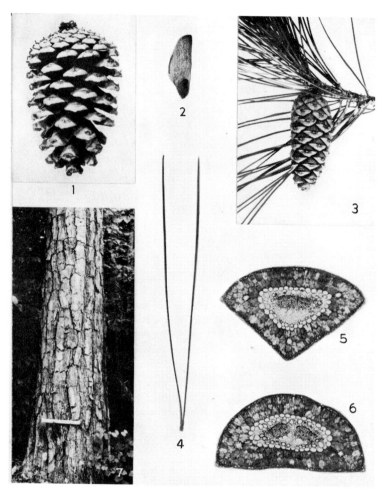

FIG. 32. *Pinus echinata*. Shortleaf pine. *1*. Open cone × ¾. *2*. Seed × 1. *3*. Closed cone and foliage × ½. *4*. Fascicle of needles × ¾. *5* and *6*. Cross section of needles × 35. *7*. Bark of old tree.

In many localities where the ranges of shortleaf and loblolly pines overlap, they are mixed together on dry soils, and since the needles and cones of the latter become somewhat dwarfed under such conditions, separation of the two species may be difficult. Generally, however, these two trees tend to be complementary, with the loblolly pine favoring the heavier, wetter soils, while the shortleaf pine more frequently pre-empts those which are lighter and drier.

Shortleaf pine may produce some seed nearly every year, with good to excellent amounts at 3- to 6-year intervals. The germination averages about 70 percent, and vitality is retained for several years in storage.

Growth of the young trees is moderately rapid, and as in several of the other southern pines, the terminal shoots are multinodal, developing from two to four false whorls of side branches each year; false growth rings are often concomitant and may be mistaken for true seasonal rings. On good sites, trees 35 years old may be 60 ft high and 8 in. in diameter; those 60 years old, 80 ft tall and nearly 12 in. d.b.h.

A remarkable feature of shortleaf pine trees up to eight or ten years old is their ability to sprout after their main stems have been destroyed by either fire or cutting. This ability results from the same peculiar juvenile habit already mentioned for pitch pine. As reported by the Stones (335), the stem of shortleaf seedlings may become prostrate as shoot growth begins. It then turns upward from just above the cotyledons. This produces the second part of a double crook, and leaves the cotyledonary part of the stem near the ground. If the main axis of the young tree is destroyed, dormant buds in the axils of primary leaves above the cotyledons start to grow and develop new sprouts.

This species may be less tolerant than loblolly pine, but will endure suppression for many years, and shows greatly accelerated growth when released; it also surpasses longleaf pine in this respect.

Maturity is reached in about 170 years, while very old trees may reach the four-century mark.

Young trees are damaged by the Nantucket pine-tip moth, and the Southern pine beetle is a serious enemy. The greatest threat is posed by the littleleaf disease.

RANGE

Southeastern United States except for the Appalachian and Mississippi Valley regions and peninsular Florida (see map, Plate 6). *Altitudinal distribution:* sea level up to 3,000 ft in the lower Appalachian Mountains.

Pinus taeda L.   Loblolly pine [1]

BOTANICAL FEATURES

Needles 6″ to 9″ long, in fascicles of 3 (occasionally 2), slender but somewhat stiff, yellow-green, sometimes twisted, persistent until the second autumn; *resin canals* usually 2 (rarely 2 to 4), large, mostly medial.

[1] The name "loblolly," applied by the early colonists to a moist depression, swamp, or mudhole, seems to have a curious origin. On board ship, the doctor's assistant, the "loblolly-boy," dispensed drugs and also a lumpy gruel to the often seasick passengers. It has been suggested that the sound of the gruel bubbling in the pot ("lob-lup") was the origin of the name, and that the colonists somehow connected the appearance of the gruel with the lumpy surface of mudholes in the new land.

Cones 3″ to 6″ long, ovoid-cylindric to narrowly conical, sessile; *apophysis* rather flattened, wrinkled; *umbo* dorsal and armed with a stout sharp spine; *seeds* nearly ¼″ long, dark brown, roughened, with black markings; wings ¾″ long, usually broadest above the center; about 18,400 (16,000–25,000) seeds to the pound.

Twigs yellow-brown or reddish brown; *buds* covered with reddish-brown scales, free at the tips.

Bark variable, on young trees scaly and nearly black, later ¾″ to 2″ thick, with irregular, brownish blocks; or on very old trees, with reddish-brown scaly plates similar to those of shortleaf pine or even red pine; *phellogen layers* slate-gray.

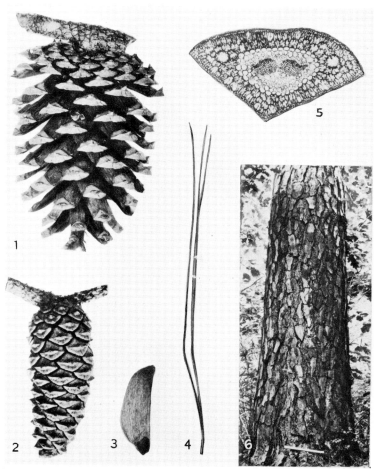

Fig. 33. *Pinus taeda.* Loblolly pine. *1.* Open cone × ¾. *2.* Closed cone × ½. *3.* Seed × 1. *4.* Fascicle of needles × ½. *5.* Cross section of needle × 35. *6.* Bark of old tree.

Loblolly pine, now considered to be the leading commercial timber species in the southern United States [Wahlenberg (364)], is a medium-sized to large tree 90 to 110 ft in height and 2 to 2½ ft in diameter (max. 182 by 5 ft or more). The bole is long and cylindrical, and the crown, although open, is denser than that of the other southern pines. In youth a short taproot is developed, but except on the driest of soils it soon ceases growth in favor of an extensive lateral root system.

This species grows on a very wide variety of soils but does best on those with deep surface layers having plenty of moisture and poor drainage. On such Coastal Plain sites, pure stands are extensive especially on river bottoms; however, even on the drier soils of the Piedmont and inland areas, pure stands also develop. Because this pine occurs on so many different sites from wet to dry, the list of associated species is large, including the other important Southern pines. Loblolly pine–southern hardwood mixtures are also common and include sweetgum, oaks, hickories, and many others. This pine is less tolerant than its hardwood associates but more tolerant than longleaf and slash pines.

Fig. 34. Loblolly pine at margin of Tupelo swamp. (*Photograph by C. A. Brown.*)

When one- to three-year seedlings are cut off, they sprout, but older ones do not retain this ability.

On cutover lands in the South, this species has spread to a remarkable degree and is especially aggressive in forming pure stands on old fields (hence the local name of "old field pine").[1]

Seeds may be produced on 7-year-old trees, and in abundance after about the twenty-fifth year; they show 80 to 90 percent germination. Especially on old fields, the young trees make rapid growth, frequently averaging 3½ ft in height and ½ in. or more in diameter per year for the

[1] See also eastern white pine.

first decade, and annual rings nearly 1 in. wide are sometimes produced. Trees 25 years old may be nearly 70 ft tall and 8 to 10 in. in diameter, those 70 years of age about 90 ft high and 24 in. d.b.h. Loblolly pine matures in about 150 years, while old trees may pass the three-century mark.

The problem in producing more loblolly pine is to extend its original range, and to control the desired proportion of soil-building hardwoods which continually invade the pine stands. Besides its importance for lumber, this species ranks high in paper making. More than half of United States wood pulp comes from the southern pines, with a large percentage from loblolly pine. The sulfate content of the green needles can be used as a measure of contamination in air pollution studies, and correlates well with other criteria (34).

1. *Pinus taeda.*   2. *Pinus elliottii;* ☐
                              Pinus elliottii var. *densa* (Southern
                                 Florida); ▤

PLATE 7

Atlantic and Gulf Coastal plains (map, Plate 7). *Altitudinal distribution:* from near sea level to 800 ft (occasionally up to 1,500 ft).

Pinus elliottii Engelm.   Slash pine

BOTANICAL FEATURES

Needles 7″ to 10″ long, in fascicles of 2 and 3, dark glossy green, tufted at the ends of tapering branches but extending back some distance along the branch (compare with longleaf pine); persistent until the end of the 2d season; *resin canals* 2 to 10, mostly internal, *fascicle sheath* usually 0.5″ or less in length.

Cones 3″ to 6″ long, ovoid-conic, stalked; usually persistent until the following summer; *apophysis* reddish brown, lustrous, commonly full and rounded; *umbo* dorsal and armed with a sharp spine; *seeds* about ¼″ long, ovoid, black, ridged; wings 1″ long, thin and transparent; *cotyledons* 5 to 9; about 14,500 (13,000–16,000) seeds to the pound.

Twigs orange-brown; *buds* covered with reddish-brown white-ciliate scales, free at the tips.

Bark on young trees deeply furrowed, later becoming plated and ¾″ to 1½″ thick, with thin, papery, purplish layers; *phellogen layers* ivory-white.

FIG. 35. *Pinus elliottii.* Slash pine. *1.* Fascicle of needles × ½. *2.* Cross section of needle × 35. *3.* Closed cone × ½. *4.* Open cone × ¾. *5.* Bark. (*Photograph by W. R. Mattoon, U.S. Forest Service.*) *6.* Seed × 1.

GENERAL DESCRIPTION

Slash pine varies from 60 to 100 ft in height and averages about 2 ft in diameter, with large trees sometimes 120 ft tall and 3 ft through. The trunk is straight and erect with a narrow ovoid crown. The root system may reach a depth of 9 to 15 ft or more, unless hampered by the presence of hardpan near the surface.

In virgin forests this tree was found on sandy soils, in depressions, around ponds, or on other low sites with an abundance of moisture in the surface layers. Longleaf pine occupied the drier knolls, and over large areas this alternation of species was frequently seen. Such distribution may have been due in part to the relative susceptibility of slash pine to fire damage. With modern fire protection, this pine invades the drier soils in mixture with the more fire-resistant longleaf pine (329a). On cutover areas, slash pine is very aggressive and, like loblolly pine, quickly preempts abandoned land, especially where the soil is at all moist.

Slash pine, although intolerant, is better able to survive competition than longleaf pine.

The resistance of small trees to damage by hogs is also greater in slash pine whose habit of very fast growth in youth gives it a further advantage. It is not surprising, therefore, that this species is spreading rapidly, even somewhat north of its previous range in the pine belt. It has also been planted experimentally as far north as central North Carolina.

FIG. 36. Bark of old slash pine. (*Photograph by J. C. Th. Uphof.*)

Trees first produce seed abundantly when about 20 years old, with heavy yields at about three-year intervals. By the end of the first year young trees are from 8 to 16 in. tall and in three years may attain heights of from 3 to 5 ft; this is in striking contrast to longleaf pine which in the same time is not yet past the "grass stage" (see page 84). Trees of slash pine 25 years of age average 65 ft in height and about 10 in. d.b.h. Like loblolly pine, young fast-growing trees of this species sometimes show annual rings from $\frac{1}{2}$ to 1 in. in width.

This species, because of its aggressiveness and value for timber and naval stores, will undoubtedly increase in importance in the future. Enemies include red-brown butt rot and bark beetles.

Southeastern United States (map, Plate 7). *Altitudinal distribution:* usually less than 300 ft above sea level.

Pinus elliottii var. **densa** Little and Dorman   South Florida slash pine

Over much of its range this is the only native pine, occurring both in pure stands and scattered through the grasslands. It differs from the typical slash pine in several ways (221). (1) The needles are in 2's (rarely 3's also). (2) The seedlings spend two to six years in a dwarf "grass stage" similar to that of longleaf pine. (3) The trunk divides into large spreading branches forming a flat-topped or rounded crown. (4) The wood is very hard and heavy, with very wide summerwood, and is usually denser than that of the other southern yellow pines. (5) The tree is not worked for naval stores. (6) Typically, this variety is found on dry sites, either sandy flat lands or limestone outcrops.

In the fourth edition of this text, the range [Little and Dorman (221)] for south Florida slash pine was given as south Florida and northward in a narrow strip along both coasts. Further study by Langdon (206) shows that between the two coastal "prongs" there is an area in the central part of the state where the ranges of typical slash pine and south Florida slash pine overlap. The monograph by Squillace (329a) indicates that in the separation features listed above, the variation is essentially continuous or clinal, both within and between varieties. Also, in the northern part of its range, south Florida slash pine may be found on wet sites.

Pinus virginiana Mill.   Virginia pine

Needles 1½ to 3 in. long, in fascicles of 2, yellow-green to gray-green, twisted, often divergent, persistent until the 3rd or 4th year; *resin canals* 2, medial: in the hypoderm, the heavy-walled cells are relatively inconspicuous and usually occur in a single row (or two); in jack and lodgepole pines, both with similar structure, 2 to 3 rows of heavy-walled cells are usually present.
Twigs at first green, becoming purplish glaucous, by the end of the season and through the first winter.
Cones 1½ to 2½ in. long, usually sessile, ovoid-conic, usually not persistent for more more than 3 or 4 years, the scales thin; *apophysis* reddish brown; *umbo* dorsal and armed with a slender prickle; *seeds* about ¼" long, oval, light brown, wings terminal,

FIG. 37. *Pinus virginiana* Mill. Virginia pine. *1.* Open cone and foliage × ¾. *2.* Seed × 1. *3.* Cross section of needle × 35. *4.* Bark.

usually broadest near the middle; about 53,000 (40,000–75,000) seeds to the pound. **Bark** thin and smooth, eventually scaly-plated, reddish brown.

GENERAL DESCRIPTION

Virginia pine is usually a small, often unkempt-appearing tree about 40 ft high and 12 in. d.b.h. (max. 120 by 3 ft), with persisting side branches and a shallow root system. This pine is found on a wide variety of soils,

PLATE 8. *Pinus virginiana.*

but seems to do best on clay, loam, or sandy loam. It is intolerant, and is commonly found in pure stands as a pioneer tree after fires, and on poor eroded sites. Here, it is eventually replaced by hardwoods, but meantime it may produce more pulpwood per acre than other pines of the region. The growing importance of Virginia pine is due to its rapid spread over extensive areas of neglected and abandoned agricultural land. The tree is also being grown in plantations.

RANGE

From Long Island (N.Y.) southwestward to central Alabama, in the Appalachian, Ohio Valley, Piedmont, and part of the Coastal Plain regions (map, Plate 8).

Pinus serotina Michx.   Pond pine

This tree is considered by some writers to be a variety or subspecies of *P. rigida,* and may well be thought of as its southern counterpart. Pond pine's needles are in 3's (rarely 4's), 6 to 9 in. long and flexible; the cones are more nearly globose than those of pitch pine, and the scales are armed with weak, sometimes deciduous prickles. The features of serotinous cones and tufted needles along the trunk are shared by both trees, and the latter distinguishes pond pine from most other southern pines.

Pond pine is a small to medium-sized tree found in pure stands on wet sites including poorly drained boggy areas on low hills between streams. Such areas were called "pocosins" (swamp-on-a-hill) by the Indians, and the name persists. This species is increasing in importance as a pulpwood producer. It ranges over the Coastal Plain from southern New Jersey (sparse) to central and northwestern Florida, and adjacent Alabama.

OTHER SOUTHERN AND EASTERN PINES

P. glabra Walt. (spruce pine). *Needles* in 2's, about 3 in. long, very slender, flexible. *Cones* similar to those of *P. echinata,* but more globose when open, often smaller, the scales nearly unarmed (small weak prickles). *Bark* not plated like other southern pines, finely furrowed, and with cross fissures, similar to that of southern red oak. Spruce pine is a medium-sized tree 80 ft high and 2 ft in diameter (max. 120 by 4°ft). Nowhere abundant, it rarely forms pure stands and is usually seen as a scattered tree among hardwoods and loblolly pine, along stream banks or rich moist hummocks of the Coastal Plain from South Carolina to northern Florida, and west to southeastern Louisiana.

P. clausa (Chapm.) Vasey (sand pine). *Needles* in 2's, about 3 in. long, slender, flexible. *Cones* persisting, closed or open for several years, about 2½ in. long, narrowly oblong-conic, the scales armed with short, stout spines. *Bark* gray, relatively smooth. This pine is mostly a small tree growing on sandy soils of central Florida from the Atlantic to the Gulf of Mexico, and also along the Gulf in the northwestern part of the state and adjacent Alabama. Sand pine is cut for pulpwood.

P. pungens Lamb (table-mountain pine) *Needles* in 2's, about 2½ in. long dark yellow-green, rigid, often twisted. *Cones* persisting for many years, about 3 in. long, ovoid, heavy, the scales armed with large conspicuous sharp spurs. *Bark* reddish brown, plated. This pine is a small to medium-sized tree and occurs sparingly on dry, often rocky slopes of the Appalachian region from central Pennsylvania to northern Georgia and Tennessee. Especially on the southern tablelands, the tree attains sufficient size and quantity (pure stands) to furnish timber.

THE WESTERN YELLOW PINES

There are at least a dozen yellow pines scattered through the timbered areas of western United States, but only three of them, ponderosa, Jeffrey, and lodgepole pine, are of primary importance.

DISTINGUISHING CHARACTERISTICS OF IMPORTANT SPECIES

Species	Needles	Cones	Buds
P. ponderosa, ponderosa pine	in fascicles of 2 and 3, about 7″ long, yellow-green to gray-green	about 4″ long, opening and deciduous at maturity	with exterior resin droplets
P. jeffreyi, Jeffrey pine	same except blue-green and twisted	about 9″ long, opening and deciduous at maturity	without resin droplets
P. contorta, lodgepole pine	in fascicles of 2, about 1½″ long, yellow-green to dark green, twisted	about 1½″ long, mostly remaining unopened and attached for many years	with exterior resin droplets

Pinus ponderosa Laws.   Ponderosa pine

BOTANICAL FEATURES

Needles in 3's, or 2's and 3's on the same tree, 5″ to 11″ long, dark gray-green to yellow-green, flexible, persistent until the 3d season. Crushed needles have a turpentine odor similar to that of most other pines.
Cones 3″ to 6″ long, ovoid to ellipsoidal, sessile, solitary or clustered; usually leaving a few basal scales attached to the twig, when shed; *apophysis* dark reddish brown to dull brownish yellow, transversely ridged and more or less diamond-shaped; *umbo*

dorsal, with a slender, often deciduous prickle; *seeds* ¼" long, ovoid, slightly compressed toward the apex, brownish purple; wings moderately wide, about 1" long; about 12,000 (6,900–23,000) seeds to the pound.

Twigs stout, exhaling a turpentine odor when bruised; *buds* usually covered with droplets of resin.

Bark brown to black and deeply furrowed on vigorous or young trees (bull pines); yellowish brown to a cinnamon-red and broken up into large flat, superficially scaly plates separated by deep irregular fissures on slow-growing and old trunks.

GENERAL DESCRIPTION

This is the most important pine in western North America, and in the United States is found in commercial quantities in every state west of the Great Plains. At present it furnishes more timber than any other American pine and in terms of total annual production of lumber by species is second only to Douglas-fir.

Ponderosa pine is a large tree 150 to 180 ft high and 3 to 4 ft in diameter [1] (max. 262* by 8.6* ft). Even though this species commonly forms open parklike forests, the boles are ordinarily symmetrical and clear for one-half or more of their length; short conical or flat-topped crowns are characteristic of old trees. Four-year-old trees may have taproots four to five ft long. Moderately deep wide-spreading laterals develop as the trees get older. Ponderosa pine is not exacting in its soil requirements, but trees on thin, dry soils are usually dwarfed. Its occurrence on dry sites with the nut pines and certain of the junipers is indicative of its great resistance to drought. This species attains its maximum development, however, on the relatively moist but well-drained western slopes of the Siskiyou and Sierra Nevada Mountains of southern Oregon and California, respectively.

Ponderosa pine occurs in pure and mixed coniferous stands. Excellent pure forests are found in the Black Hills of South Dakota, the Blue Mountains of Oregon, the Columbian Plateau northeast of the Sierra Nevada, and in northern Arizona and New Mexico. It is also commonly the most abundant tree in mixed coniferous stands; east of the summit of the Cascade Range in Washington and Oregon it occurs with western larch, Douglas-fir, and occasionally lodgepole pine; in the central Rocky Mountains with Douglas-fir; and in California with Jeffrey and sugar pines, incense-cedar, Douglas-fir, and white fir. On the Fort Lewis plains in western Washington, near Puget Sound, ponderosa pine is occasionally found in association with Douglas-fir and Oregon white oak.

Small quantities of seed are produced annually, but large crops are released only at intervals of from three to five years. Under forest condi-

[1] On the best sites, 300-year-old dominant trees average about 175 ft high and 48 in. d.b.h.

FIG. 38. *Pinus ponderosa.* Ponderosa pine. *1.* Closed cone × ¾. *2.* Open cone × ¾. *3.* Seed × 1. *4.* Staminate flowers × 1. *5.* Ovulate flowers × 1. *6.* Cross section of needle × 35. *7.* Bark. (*Photograph by U.S. Forest Service.*)

Fig. 39. 1. Ponderosa pine bark flakes × ½. 2. Bark of ponderosa pine. (*Photograph by Paul Graves.*)

tions germination as high as 50 percent may be anticipated, but in the nursery this figure can be increased to 80 percent. Seedlings can exist under the canopy of the parent trees, even though they grow quite slowly, and in such situations often attain a height of only 3 to 4 ft during the first 15 to 20 years. Reproduction is best in clearings made by fire or logging. The seedlings will grow on sterile sites and have been planted extensively in the Nebraska sand hills and elsewhere. Ponderosa pine is classed as intolerant.

The rapidity of growth has a marked effect on the general appearance of the trees of this species. Young, vigorous specimens commonly develop dense crowns of dark green foliage, and bark which is dark brown to nearly black, more or less corky, and deeply furrowed. In contrast, the foliage of old-growth or slow-growing trees is yellow-green, and the bark yellow-brown to cinnamon-red and plated. Those of the first type are commonly called "bull" or "blackjack pines," and to some woodsmen ponderosa pine and bull pine are different trees. Fast-growth bull pines 150 years of age found near Cle Elum, Washington, measured 30 to 40 in. in diameter, while more typical ponderosa pines occurring in the same vicinity were only 10 to 14 in. in diameter at the same age. The growth of this species varies considerably with locality. In California, trees 120 years of age averaged 23 in. d.b.h., while in Arizona trees of the same age were only 16 in., and in the Black Hills 10½ in. Trees over 500 years of age are seldom encountered.[1] Severe damage is caused by bark beetles, and ponderosa pine is also attacked by more than 100 other

[1] Keen (196) considers that this pine may reach an age of 800 years, while Mills (258) reported a tree in southwestern Colorado with 1,047 rings.

kinds of insects. Fires kill seedlings and cause considerable damage even to large trees. Severe fires in the past have completely destroyed hundreds of thousands of acres of ponderosa pine forest. Other destructive agents include mistletoe and fungi.

The common name ponderosa pine is identical with the species name. Previously called western yellow pine, logs of this tree were also sold under such names as Arizona white pine, California white pine, and western soft pine, since the wood resembles that of the white pines rather than that of the hard, moderately heavy wood of the southern yellow pines. Finally the name ponderosa pine was adopted by the U.S. Forest Service, and it is now accepted by the industry.

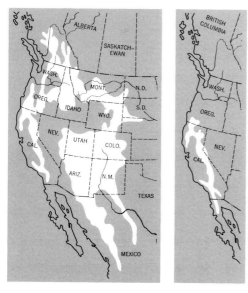

1. *Pinus ponderosa.*   2. *Pinus jeffreyi.*

PLATE 9

RANGE

Western North America (map, Plate 9). *Altitudinal distribution:* 5,000 to 8,000 ft in Arizona, 3,300 to 6,000 ft in Montana and South Dakota, 2,000 to 7,000 ft in northern Idaho, sea level to 6,200 ft in British Columbia and Washington, sea level (Columbia River Valley) to 7,000 ft in Oregon, 300 to 7,000 ft in northern California, 4,000 to 9,000 ft in southern California; for the most part a tree of relatively low elevations.

Pinus ponderosa var. **arizonica** (Engelm.) Shaw   Arizona pine; Arizona ponderosa pine (SPN)

Distinguishing characteristics. *Needles* mostly in 5's (occasionally in clusters of 2 to 5 on the same tree). *Cones* similar to those of *P. ponderosa,* but never more than 2 to 3½ in. long. *Bark* similar to that of *P. ponderosa.*

General description. Arizona pine attains commercial proportions in southern Arizona and New Mexico, but maximum size is reached across the border in the mountains of old Mexico. Under average conditions this pine seldom exceeds a height of 75 to 90 ft and a diameter of 2 to 3 ft (max. 120 by 4 ft). Arizona pine produces a symmetrical, slightly tapered bole which is often clear for one-third to one-half of its total length. The trees occur quite abundantly on rocky flats, slopes, and canyon walls. At low elevations they form pure stands, but at higher levels they are commonly found in mixture with Chihuahua and Apache pines, Arizona cypress, and scrub oaks.

Range. Southern Arizona and New Mexico south across the border into northern Mexico. *Altitudinal distribution:* 6,000 to 8,000 ft.

Pinus jeffreyi Grev. and Balf.   Jeffrey pine

BOTANICAL FEATURES

Needles 5" to 10" long, in fascicles of 3, or 2 and 3 on the same tree, blue-green, somewhat twisted, persistent until the 6th to 9th seasons. Crushed needles have the violet-like or pineapple odor of normal heptane.

Cones 5" to 15" long, ovoid; *apophysis* chestnut-brown, rhomboidal to broadly elliptical, often transversely ridged and occasionally wrinkled; *umbo* dorsal, often chalky white, terminating in a long, stout, incurved, occasionally deciduous prickle; *seeds* about ⅛" long, yellowish brown, mottled with purple; wings 1" to 1¾" long, broadest below the middle; about 4,000 (3,100–5,400) seeds to the pound, dewinged.

Twigs tinged with purple, often glaucous, exhaling a pineapple or violet aroma when crushed; *buds* only slightly resinous, never covered with resin droplets (a common feature of ponderosa pine).

Bark similar to that of ponderosa pine, but darker cinnamon-red and commonly tinged with lavender or purple on old trunks.

GENERAL DESCRIPTION

The status of Jeffrey pine has been a subject of controversy among taxonomists ever since its discovery in 1852 by the Scottish botanist John Jeffrey. Although most of them now agree that it is a separate species, there are still a few who insist that Jeffrey pine is only a variety of *Pinus ponderosa.* Trained observers rarely experience any difficulty in distinguishing between Jeffrey and ponderosa pines in the field.

The oleoresins derived from the wood of these two species exhibit notable chemical differences. Normal heptane (C_7H_{16}), a hydrocarbon of rare occurrence in trees, has been found by Mirov (260) to be the

Fig. 40. *Pinus jeffreyi.* Jeffrey pine. *1.* Fascicle of needles × ¾. *2.* Cone × ¾. *3.* Seed × 1. *4.* Cross section of needle × 35.

principal constituent of Jeffrey pinewood resins.[1] This is lacking in those from ponderosa pine. It may be also of even further interest to note that the scolytid beetle, *Dendroctonus jeffreyi* Hopk., commonly attacks Jeffrey pine but avoids ponderosa pine.

[1] Normal heptane is also found in small to large amounts in digger, Coulter, and Torrey pines, and in a few of the white pine group.

Fig. 41. Bark of Jeffrey pine. (*Photograph by Emanuel Fritz.*)

Throughout its range, Jeffrey pine mingles with ponderosa pine and many of its associates. It can endure greater extremes of climate than ponderosa pine, however, and east of the Sierra, where conditions are more rigorous, this species occurs in some abundance.

The habits of Jeffrey pine are quite similar to those of ponderosa. Seedlings, however, are somewhat frost-hardy and more suitable for reforesting on sites where low temperatures often prevail.

Although a stately tree, Jeffrey pine never reaches the proportions of

Fig. 42. Wind form of Jeffrey pine, growing on Sentinel Dome, Yosemite National Park, California.

ponderosa pine. Under favorable growing conditions mature trees will attain a height of 90 to 100 ft and a diameter of 36 to 60 in. (max. 197° by 7 ft). It is customary to log these two species together, and because of the great similarity of their timbers, no attempt is made to segregate them in the trade.

Southern Oregon to Lower California (map, Plate 9). *Altitudinal distribution:* 3,500 ft in the north to 10,000 ft in the south.

Pinus contorta Dougl.   Lodgepole pine [1]

BOTANICAL FEATURES

Needles 1" to 3" long, in 2's or rarely solitary, dark green to yellow-green, often twisted, persistent until the 4th to 6th seasons; *resin canals* 2, medial; epidermal cells somewhat square in cross section.
Cones ¾" to 2" long, subcylindric to ovoid, asymmetrical at the base, occasionally opening at maturity but often remaining closed for many years; *apophysis* tawny to dark brown, flattened, or those toward the base knoblike; *umbo* dorsal, terminating in a long, recurved, often deciduous prickle; *seeds* about ⅙" long, ovoid, reddish brown, often mottled with black; wings ½" long; about 135,000 (111,000–165,000) seeds to the pound, dewinged.
Twigs moderately stout, dark red-brown to nearly black; *buds* ovoid, slightly resinous.
Bark of coastal trees ¾" to 1" thick, deeply furrowed and transversely fissured, reddish brown to black and superficially scaly; that on mountain trees about ¼" thick, orange-brown to gray, covered by thin, loosely appressed scales.

GENERAL DESCRIPTION

Lodgepole pine is a cosmopolitan tree of wide distribution through western North America. Two distinct forms of the species are recognized. **Shore pine.** This is a small tree ordinarily 25 to 30 ft high and 12 to 18 in. in diameter. It is characterized by a short, often contorted bole and a dense, irregular crown of twisted branches, many of which extend nearly to the ground; the root system is deep, wide-spreading, and includes a persistent taproot, even when growing in bogs or muskegs. The tree is

[1] So called because of its use for poles by the Plains Indians. The lodge or tipi with its movable smoke flaps and symbolic decorations is perhaps the most functional and beautiful dwelling ever designed by nomadic man.

FIG. 43. *Pinus contorta.* Lodgepole pine. *1.* Fascicle of needles × ¾. *2.* Closed cones × ¾. *3.* Open cone × ¾. *4.* Closed cone, shore pine × ¾. *5.* Cluster of staminate flowers × 1. *6.* Ovulate flower × 1. *7.* Seeds × 1. *8.* Bark. (*Photograph by H. E. Troxell.*) *9.* Bark, shore pine.

one of the first to invade the peat bogs of Alaska and British Columbia, as well as those of the Puget Sound basin in western Washington where it may form pure stands. Farther south it is found most abundantly on dry sandy and gravelly sites near the Pacific Ocean to northern California. Here it sometimes mingles with Sitka spruce and occasionally with grand fir. Because of their small size and poorly formed boles, the trees of the coastal form contribute little or nothing to the nation's timber supply. Large stands occasionaly retard the migration of sand dunes, but smaller ones have been completely buried by shifting sands.

Lodgepole pine. This form, by contrast, is a medium-sized tree 70 to 80 ft high and 15 to 30 in. in diameter (max. 150 by 6* ft), with a long, clear, slender, cylindrical bole and short, narrow, open crown. Best development is attained on a moist but well-drained sandy or gravelly loam, although trees reach commercial proportions on a variety of soil types. Unlike the shore pine, which is seldom found far from tide water, the lodgepole pine occurs from 1,500 to 11,500 ft of elevation in either pure dense even-aged stands or in mixture with several other conifers. At the lower limits of its altitudinal range its associates are ponderosa and other western pines, Douglas-fir, and western larch. At higher levels it is found chiefly with Engelmann spruce, subalpine fir, and limber pine in the Rockies; and with limber pine, Jeffrey pine, and California red fir in the Sierra.

This form is one of the most aggressive and hardy of western forest trees and under favorable conditions is capable of fully restocking cutover' lands in a remarkably short time. Following fire it quickly forms dense stands and occasionally usurps areas formerly occupied by Douglas-fir, or at higher levels by Engelmann spruce.

The gregarious habit of this species is traceable to a number of factors. The trees are prolific seeders and often produce fertile seed before they are 10 years of age. Heavy seed crops occur at intervals of 2 or 3 years, but instead of releasing all of the seed at maturity, many of the cones remain closed and attached to the branches for as long as 15 to 20 or more years.[1] When the cones remain closed, large quantities of seed are gradually accumulated. The heat of a forest fire sweeping through the stands starts the opening of the cones. After the fire has passed, the scales open fully and release their seeds upon the freshly exposed mineral soil.[2] The subsequent reproduction is often so dense that it quickly stag-

[1] See Fowells (127) for localities where non-serotinous cones are common.
[2] According to Enos Mills (259), a camping party once built a fire against a solitary lodgepole pine. The tree was killed, as shown by the subsequent loss of its needles. Four years later, a long tattered green pennant, formed by thousands of lodgepole pine seedlings, showed on the mountainside. This pennant, varying in width from 10 to 50 ft., began at the tree and streamed out for more than 700 ft. from its base.

PLATE 10. *Pinus contorta.*

nates. Under normal conditions, growth is rather slow but persistent, and maturity is attained in about 200 years with a maximum of 500 to 600 years. According to Hanzlik (128), trees 100 years of age in the Blue Mountains of southern Oregon average 70 to 80 ft in height and 12 in. in diameter, while trees of the same age in the Sierra are 90 to 100 ft high and 15 to 18 in. in diameter. Lodgepole pine is rated as intolerant.

Bark beetles inflict heavy damage in stagnated stands. Mistletoe causes some damage, and because of the thin bark of the tree, fire is always a serious menace even though heavy new stands result through this agency.

RANGE

Western North America (map, Plate 10). *Altitudinal distribution:* sea level of 2,000 ft in Alaska and British Columbia, sea level to 6,000 ft in Washington and Oregon, sea level to 11,500 ft in California, 6,000 to 11,000 ft in the Rocky Mountains.

OTHER WESTERN YELLOW PINES

Pinus coulteri D. Don   Coulter pine

Distinguishing characteristics. Needles in 3's, about 10 in. long, blue-green, rigid. *Cones* about 10 in. long, heavy, when green often weighing 4 to 6 pounds, subcylindric to oblong-ovoid, short-stalked; *cone scales* with light brownish-yellow, irregularly rhomboidal apophyses, each terminating in a long, sharp, flat claw, those near the base of the cone the longest and exhibiting the greatest curvature; *seeds* ellipsoidal, with

Fig. 44. *Pinus coulteri.* Coulter
pine. *1.* Cone × ⅓. *2.* Seed × ⅔.

Fig. 45. *Pinus sabiniana.* Digger pine. *1.*
Cone × ⅓. *2.* Seed × ⅔.

extremely thick hard coats, the wings longer than the seeds. *Bark* dark brown to nearly black, with broad rounded ridges separated by deep anastomosing fissures.

General description. Coulter pine is a small tree 40 to 50 ft high and 15 to 30 in. in diameter (max. 144° by 5° ft), largely restricted to the mountains of southern coastal California and northern Lower California. At low elevations (3,000 ft) Coulter pine invades chaparral. Here the trees develop a typical open-grown form, the large crowns often extending to within a few feet of the ground. At higher elevations (3,500 to 7,000 ft) it occurs on dry, gravelly, or loamy soils in mixture with live oaks, incense-cedar, ponderosa and sugar pine, and bigcone Douglas-fir.

Range. Mountain slopes of central coastal California to northern Baja California. *Altitudinal distribution:* 3,000 to 7,000 ft.

Pinus sabiniana Dougl.   Digger pine

Since this pine is quite similar to the preceding species, direct comparison will be made between the two.

Comparative botanical features. *Needles* gray-green, flexible. Cones about 8 in. long, heavy, subglobose, their reddish-brown scales with irregularly rhomboidal apophyses, each terminating in a stout dorsal claw. *Seeds* oblong with very short abortive terminal wings and thick hard coats. *Bark* dark brown with flattened anastomosing ridges.

General description. Digger pine is restricted to the low fringe forests of California. As a rule, it is a small to medium-sized tree 40 to 50 ft high and 12 to 24 in. d.b.h. (max. 155° by 5 ft°). The bole is usually short, the crown open and irregular, and the root system moderately deep and spreading. Scattered through the dry foothills and lower mountain slopes it occurs either in pure, open parklike stands or in mixture with one or more of the native oaks. At higher elevations it is occasionally associated with ponderosa pine.

Range. High valleys, foothills, and lower mountain slopes in the coast ranges and west slopes of the Sierra Nevada in California from the Siskiyou Mountains south to the Tehachapi and Sierra de la Liebre Mountains. *Altitudinal distribution:* 500 to 4,000 ft.

Pinus radiata D. Don   Monterey pine

Monterey pine, also designated as *Pinus insignis* Dougl. by some authors, is a medium-sized tree (max. 165° by 5 ft) restricted to three small separated coastal areas of central California; a two-needled variety is found on Guadalupe Island of Baja California. This species is of little or no commercial value within its range, but it is a common decorative tree in many cities along the Pacific slope and appears to be quite hardy as far north as the Puget Sound basin.

This pine has been widely planted in New Zealand, Australia, South Africa, Spain, and Chile, where it grows very rapidly and produces saw timber in a relatively short time. Thirty-year-old plantation trees in New Zealand may be from 100 to 140 ft high

Fig. 46. *Pinus radiata.* Monterey pine. *1.* Cone × ¾. *2.* Seed × 1.

and 30 in. or more in diameter. For a monographic treatment of this pine, see Scott (319). It is estimated that world wide, more than 1½ million acres have been afforested with Monterey pine. The tree may be identified by its rich, dark green, slender and flexible needles of 4" to 6" in length, borne in fascicles of 3, and by its large asymmetrical cones.

Pinus attenuata Lemm. Knobcone pine

This 3-needle pine with narrowly top-shaped, knobby and serotinous cones, is a medium-sized tree largely confined to the mountainous regions of southwestern Oregon south along the coast ranges and Sierra Nevada to central (sporadically southern) California. It frequents dry slopes, rocky spurs, and sun-baked ridges where it may be encountered in pure stands (especially in the north) or in mixture with sugar, ponderosa, and Coulter pines and several chaparral oaks. Its seeding habits are similar to those of lodgepole pine. Following a fire, stores of viable seed are released, and the scorched earth is soon again covered with a green mantle of seedlings.

Pinus torreyana Parry   Torrey pine

Torrey pine has the distinction of having the most restricted range of any American pine. It occurs only in a narrow strip of coastal land in San Diego County, California and adjacent Santa Rosa Island. It is readily distinguished by its stout needles which, unlike other western yellow pines, are borne in fascicles of 5. Its 4- to 5-inch cones with thick scales and ovoid, thick-shelled seeds are also distinctive. Torrey pine has been propagated with some degree of success in New Zealand for sawtimber.

Pinus muricata D. Don   Bishop pine

Bishop pine occurs in seven widely separated coastal areas from northern California to northern Baja California. It often forms pure stands but never occurs in sufficient quantity to be of more than local importance. A preference is shown for swampy sites and peat bogs, although it also grows on much drier soils. This pine bears its needles in 2's; they are thick, rigid, dark yellow-green, and about 5 in. long. The cones are small (2 to 4 in.), commonly borne in clusters of 3 to 5, and are featured by stout, spurlike prickles. They persist for several seasons.

Pinus engelmannii Carr.   Apache pine

Apache pine is principally a Mexican species but is found locally in southeastern Arizona and extreme southwestern New Mexico. It is often called the "longleaf pine" of the Southwest, and may be distinguished from other pines of that region by its dark green needles, borne in fascicles of 2 to 5 (mostly 3), which are often a foot or more in length. From a distance, the mature trees appear quite similar to those of ponderosa pine, a species with which it is often associated; young trees, however, are very distinctive. The seedling sends down a prodigious taproot which descends to a depth of 6 ft or more during the first few years of the tree's development. In the meantime, the aerial portion grows very slowly and is seldom branched.

Pinus leiophylla var. chihuahuana (Engelm.) Shaw   Chihuahua pine

This pine attains its best development in northern Mexico, and is found in the United States only in scattered areas of southwestern New Mexico and southeastern Arizona. The needles, which are in 3's, are 2 to 4 in. long and differ from all other American yellow pines in that the fascicle sheaths are deciduous. The cones are small, armed with minute, often deciduous prickles, and unlike all other American pines, require three seasons to mature. Chihuahua pine produces vigorous stump sprouts after logging, another feature rare among the pines.

INTRODUCED PINES

Scotch (or Scots) pine (*P. sylvestris* L.) should be mentioned since it is an important European conifer and has been widely used in reforestation since the beginning of forestry in this country. In some localities, this tree has achieved a poor reputation on account of the crookedness of the young boles. It is now recognized, however, that the origin of the seed is of great importance, and more recent plantings should be free from this characteristic.

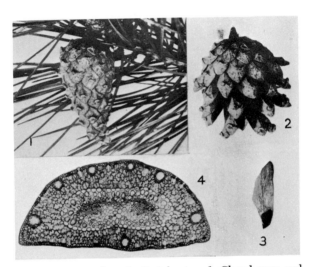

FIG. 47. *Pinus sylvestris*. Scotch pine. *1.* Closed cone and foliage × ¾. *2.* Open cone × ¾. *3.* Seed × 1. *4.* Cross section of needle × 35.

The needles are in fascicles of two (rarely three), mostly blue-green, 1½ to 3 in. long, slightly twisted and sharp-pointed; resin canals are few to many, and external. The cones are oblong-conical and about as long as the needles; the apophysis is flat, or raised and pyramidal, with a small scarcely armed umbo. The bark soon becomes orange in color, and this feature is persistent until the tree reaches nearly full size, at which time it becomes dark and furrowed.

Austrian pine (*P. nigra* Arnold) has been planted extensively in the United States as an ornamental. Superficially, it is similar to the native red pine, but the needles are stouter and stiffer, with medial resin canals; the bark is dark brown to black; the buds silvery; and the cones somewhat larger, with armed umbos. Several varieties are known, as is also the case in the preceding species.

About 15 other exotic pines are cultivated in this country, descriptions of which are included in certain of the various manuals listed under Selected References.

Fig. 48. Some coniferous seedlings. *1.* Red pine. *2.* Balsam fir. *3.* Northern white-cedar. *4.* White spruce. *5.* Eastern hemlock. *6.* European larch.

LARIX Mill.[1]   Larch

Although much larger during previous geological periods, this genus now includes only about 10 species of deciduous trees widely scattered through the forests of eastern and western North America, Europe, and Asia. *L. decidua* Mill., European larch, is an important continental tree used for reforestation in eastern United States where it has now become naturalized in at least one locality (75). The foliage is yellow-green, the twigs yellowish or straw-colored, and the upright cones are about 1¼ in. long. This species, together with its pendulous variety, *L. decidua* var. *pendula* Henk. and Hochst., also finds use as an ornamental in this country; and the Japanese larch, *L. leptolepis* (Sieb. and Zucc.) Gord.,[2] is another exotic similarly employed. An interesting hybrid of these two species, the Dunkeld larch, *Larix* ×*eurolepis* Henry, promises to be of some importance; this form grows very rapidly and appears to be more resistant to insect or fungal attack than either of the parent species.

There are three species of *Larix* native to the United States, one in the Northeast, and two in the West.

Extensive forests of larch are occasionally destroyed by the larch sawfly.

BOTANICAL FEATURES OF THE GENUS

Leaves deciduous, solitary, and spirally arranged on new growth, on older growth recurring in dense false whorls on lateral spurs; *shape*

---

[1] The related golden larch, *Pseudolarix amabilis* Rehd., is distinguished by its cones which at maturity disintegrate like those of either the firs (*Abies*) or the true cedars (*Cedrus*).
[2] *L. kaempferi* Sarg.

FIG. 49. *Larix decidua.* European larch. *1.* Staminate flowers × 1. *2.* Ovulate flower × 1. *3.* Open cones × ¾. *4.* Bark.

linear, more or less flattened, triangular, or less frequently 4-angled in transverse section, keeled below or occasionally above and below, with numerous lines of stomata on all surfaces but most abundant below; *apex* pointed or rounded; *resin canals* 2, medial or occasionally external. **Flowers** solitary, terminal, appearing with the leaves; *staminate* strobili globose, ovoid, or oblong, sessile or pedicelled; yellow to yellowish green, composed of several to many short stamens; *ovulate* cones sub-globose, erect, consisting of few to many, generally scarlet, sharp-pointed

DISTINGUISHING CHARACTERISTICS OF THE IMPORTANT LARCHES

Species	Leaves	Cones	Young twigs
L. laricina, tamarack	about 1″ long, blue-green	about ⅝″ long, oblong-ovoid, bracts shorter than scales	glabrous or glaucous
L. occidentalis, western larch	about 1½″ long, lustrous green	about 1″ long, oblong, the bracts exserted	pale pubescent

bracts, each subtending a short suborbicular to rectangular scale with two inverted ovules; all species monoecious.
Cones short-stalked, erect, subglobose to oblong, maturing in one season; *cone scales* thin, persistent, longer or shorter than the bracts; *bracts* long-acuminate; *seeds* triangular, terminally winged; *cotyledons* 6.
Buds small, subglobose, covered by several imbricated scales, nonresinous.

Larix laricina (Du Roi) K. Koch   Tamarack; eastern larch (SPN)

BOTANICAL FEATURES

Leaves deciduous, linear, ¾″ to 1½″ long, flexible, 3-angled, bright blue-green, turning yellow and falling from the branches in September to November.
Cones ½″ to ¾″ long, erect, oblong-ovoid, short-stalked; *cone scales* slightly longer than broad, sparingly erose on the margin; *bracts* not visible, except near the base of the cone; *seeds* ⅛″ long; wings ¼″ long, light chestnut-brown; about 318,000 (210,000–420,000) seeds to the pound, dewinged.
Twigs brownish, marked by many small leaf scars and fewer buds, on older growth showing conspicuous short spurs; *buds* globose, dark red.
Bark thin and smooth on young stems, later becoming ½″ to ¾″ thick, gray to reddish brown, scaly.

Tamarack is a small to medium-sized tree 40 to 80 ft high and 1 to 2 ft in diameter (max. 100 by 3* ft) with a long clear, cylindrical bole, open pyramidal crown, and shallow wide-spreading root system. In the southern part of its range it is usually restricted to cool swamps or sphagnum bogs; but farther north it makes best growth on moist benches and better-drained uplands. Its chief arborescent associate in bogs is

FIG. 50. *Larix laricina.* Tamarack. *1.* Mature cones × ¾. *2.* Seed × 1. *3.* Foliage showing solitary and clustered leaves × ½. *4.* Bark of old tree. *5.* Spur shoot × ½. *6.* First year's twig × 1½.

black spruce, while on drier sites it is often found in open mixtures with this species and also balsam fir, quaking aspen, paper birch, and jack pine. Tamarack is exceedingly intolerant and is always a dominant tree under forest conditions.

Seeds are produced annually, with larger crops at two- to six-year intervals. Growth of young trees on favorable sites is rapid, but decreases after 40 to 50 years; maturity is reached in 100 to 200 years. On Isle Royale in Lake Superior, very long-lived tamaracks have been found, the oldest with an age of 335 years.

This species is not often damaged by fire because of its wet surroundings, but on dry sites it readily succumbs on account of its thin bark and shallow roots. Two serious insect enemies are the larch sawfly and the introduced (Europe) casebearer. Where defoliation is severe and repeated from year to year, tree death results.

RANGE

Northeastern United States and transcontinental through Canada (map, Plate 11).

Larix occidentalis Nutt.   Western larch [1]

BOTANICAL FEATURES

Leaves deciduous, linear, 1″ to 1¾″ long, pale, green, lustrous 3-angled.
Cones 1″ to 1½″ long, purplish red to reddish brown, oblong, short-stalked; *cone scales* broader than long, occasionally finely toothed at the tip of the reflexed apex; *bracts* exserted, shouldered, terminating in a long spike; *seeds* ¼″ long; wings ½″ long, thin, fragile; about 143,000 (98,000–197,000) seeds to the pound, dewinged.
Twigs stout, at first pale pubescent, but soon becoming orange-brown and glabrous; *buds* chestnut-brown.
Bark reddish brown to cinnamon-red, scaly on young stems; up to 4″ to 6″ thick on old trunks and then with flat-plated ridges separated by deep irregular fissures.

GENERAL DESCRIPTION

This tree was discovered in 1806 by the Lewis and Clark Expedition on the upper watershed of the Clearwater River in western Montana. David Douglas found this larch in northeastern Washington in 1827. He erroneously concluded, however, that he had encountered a natural extension of the European larch into the New World. Thus it was not until 1849, when Thomas Nuttall recognized that the larches in the Blue Mountains

[1] The name larch has been applied by lumbermen to certain western species of the genus *Abies,* notably *A. procera* and *A. amabilis.*

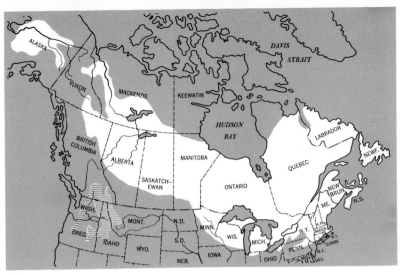

1. *Larix occidentalis;*   2. *Larix laricina;*

PLATE 11

of northeastern Oregon did indeed comprise a new species, that the identity of this tree was correctly established.

Western larch is the largest of the American larches and one of the most important trees of the Inland Empire. The boles of mature trees are clear for a considerable length, characteristically tapered, often "churn-butted," and vary from 140 to 180 ft in height and 3 to 4 ft in diameter (max. 210 by 8 ft). The crowns are usually short, open, and essentially pyramidal; in the summer they are distinguishable at a considerable distance by their light, lustrous green foliage and in winter by their bareness. Excellent anchorage is afforded by a deep wide-spreading root system, and the trees are seldom wind-thrown. Western larch attains maximum size on deep, moist, porous soils in high valleys and on mountain slopes of northern and western exposure, although thrifty trees often occur on drier gravelly soils. Nearly pure open forests of western larch are found in northwestern Montana, northern Idaho, and northeastern Washington. It is often the most abundant species in the western larch–Douglas-fir forests of the northern Rockies, where it is also associated with western white pine, and at higher elevations with lodgepole pine, Engelmann spruce, and subalpine fir. Its other forest associates include western hemlock, grand fir, ponderosa pine, and occasionally western redcedar.

Small amounts of seed are released annually, and heavy crops are produced at intervals of from five to seven years. Germination is fairly good on mineral soil but poor in duff and thick forest litter. Seedling

Fig. 51. *Larix occidentalis.* Western larch. *1.* Foliage × ½. *2.* Ovulate flowers × 1. *3.* Staminate flowers × 1. *4.* Closed cone × ¾. *5.* Open cone × ¾. *6.* Seeds × 1. *7.* Bark. (*Photograph by British Columbia Forest Service.*)

growth is extremely vigorous, and plants only four years of age are often 4 ft or more in height. Considering the relatively short growing season, this seems all the more remarkable since Douglas-fir and ponderosa pine on the same site rarely exceed a height of 20 in., and Engelmann spruce seedlings of the same age are usually less than 1 ft high. Western larch is very intolerant throughout life and is dominant in old-growth mixed stands. Maturity is ordinarily reached in 300 to 400 years, but trees from 700 to 900 years of age have been reported. Commercially, this species attains its best development in the Priest River country of northern Idaho.

The bark of old trees is thick and moderately fire-resistant, but young trees are severely damaged by only a light ground fire. Wood-destroying fungi commonly attack overmature timber, and mistletoe reaches epidemic proportions in some localities.

RANGE

Inland Empire (map, Plate 11). *Altitudinal distribution:* 2,000 to 7,000 ft.

Larix lyallii Parl.   Subalpine larch

Subalpine larch is a small timberline tree with long, willowy, often pendulous branches, found on several high watersheds in the Cascade, Bitterroot, and northern Rocky Mountains. It occurs in pure open groves or intermingled with whitebark pine, mountain hemlock, subalpine fir, and Engelmann spruce. Because of its small size, poor form, and inaccessibility, subalpine larch is of no commercial importance. It can be recognized by its four-angled needles, dense woolly twigs, and erect 2″ cones with exserted bracts.

PICEA A. Dietr.   Spruce

The genus *Picea* includes nearly 40 species of trees which are largely restricted to the cooler regions of the Northern Hemisphere; about half of them are in China.[1]

The wood of the spruces is strong for its weight, moderately long-fibered, odorless, but slightly resinous, and is of primary importance in the manufacture of pulp and paper. The most important European species is *Picea abies* (L.) Karst. (syn. *P. excelsa* Link), the Norway spruce. This is a tall tree which may be readily identified by its dark yellow-green, usually drooping foliage, somewhat laterally compressed leaves, and large cones (4 to 7 in. long). This species, together with many of its varieties, both natural and horticultural, are common ornamentals in many sections of the United States. Norway spruce has been also widely

[1] Investigations on leaf anatomy [Marco (233)] and the findings of Chen [through (233)] indicate that the number 18 for Chinese species is probably too large.

Fig. 52. Cone and seeds of Norway spruce × ¾.

used in forest plantations, especially in the East where it grows more rapidly than the native spruces.[1] The resinous bark exudations of this tree furnish the so-called Burgundy pitch which is the basic material for a number of varnishes and medicinal compounds; while the new leafy shoots are often used in brewing spruce beer. In Asia the Himalayan spruce, *Picea smithiana* (Walt.) Boiss., is one of the most important of indigenous softwood species. *Picea jezoensis* (Sieb. & Zucc.) Carr., the yezo or jeddo spruce, and *Picea polita* Carr., the tigertail spruce, are two oriental species suitable for decorative purposes in the United States.

The natural enemies of the spruces are rather numerous, and some of them cause considerable damage to immature timber. Because of the flammable nature of the bark and foliage, fire is always a serious menace. The trees are also subject to periodic attacks of the eastern spruce gall aphid, which lays its eggs at the base of partially developed leaves near the tips of twigs. A large conelike gall soon develops, beyond which all growth ceases. The spruce budworm often destroys whole stands of young timber, while the white pine weevil may damage certain species. Trees growing in large industrial cities are frequently affected by smoke and flue gases.

[1] It is not as hardy to low temperatures as red spruce or white spruce, and also tends to die at the top when 60 to 70 years old.

Seven spruces are native to North America (exclusive of Mexico). The Brewer spruce, *Picea breweriana* S. Wats., a small tree in the Siskiyou Mountains of southern Oregon and northern California, is the only one which is of little or no commercial value.

BOTANICAL FEATURES OF THE GENUS

Leaves spirally arranged, extending from all sides of the twigs or massed toward the upper surface; *shape* linear or nearly acicular; flattened, laterally compressed, or more commonly 4- (rarely 3-) angled, with numerous stomatiferous lines on the lower surfaces, or in many forms on all surfaces; *apex* usually sharp-pointed; persistent for 7 to 10 years, sessile upon conspicuous peglike projections of the twig; when bruised not infrequently emitting an aromatic, or fetid, odor; resin *canals* 1 or 2, commonly segmented longitudinally; external for the most part.

Flowers unisexual; *staminate* strobili erect or pendent, stalked, consisting of numerous spirally arranged stamens, appearing from axillary buds on the shoots of the previous season or terminal; *ovulate* strobili terminal, erect or nearly so, composed of numerous purple or green scales each of which bears 2 inverted ovules and is subtended by a bract; all species monoecious.

Cones pendent (rarely nearly erect), woody, comprising a number of persistent, unarmed scales, often erose along the margins, and much longer than the bracts; *seeds* 2 to each cone scale, ovoid to cylindrical, often compressed, terminally winged; *cotyledons* 4 to 15.

Buds conic to ovoid, with numerous imbricated scales, resinous or nonresinous.

THE EASTERN AND TRANSCONTINENTAL SPRUCES

DISTINGUISHING CHARACTERISTICS

Species	Leaves	Cones	Twigs
P. rubens, red spruce	shiny, dark yellow-green	about 1¾" long, ovoid-oblong; scales rounded on margin, sparingly erose or entire	more or less pubescent
P. mariana, black spruce	dull blue-green, more or less glaucous	about 1" long, ovoid; scales rounded on margin, erose	pubescent
P. glauca, white spruce	blue-green, glaucous, more or less fetid when crushed	about 2" long, oblong-cylindric; scales truncate on margin, entire	glaucous

Picea rubens Sarg. [*Picea rubra* (Du Roi) Link.]   Red spruce

BOTANICAL FEATURES

Leaves ½″ to ⅝″ long, linear, 4-sided, shiny yellow-green, apex blunt or acute.
Cones 1¼″ to 2″ long, ovoid-oblong, chestnut-brown at maturity, falling during the first winter or following spring; *scales* rigid, rounded, entire on the margin or very slightly erose; *seeds* ⅛″ long, dark brown; wings ¼″ long; about 140,000 (100,000–289,000) seeds to the pound, dewinged.
Twigs orange-brown, more or less pubescent; *buds* ovoid, reddish brown.
Bark ¼″ to ½″ thick, separating into close, irregular, grayish- to reddish-brown scales; inner layers reddish brown.

GENERAL DESCRIPTION

Red spruce is one of the most important of northeastern conifers and is especially characteristic of the mountainous regions in northern New York and New England. In old-growth stands, trees 60 to 70 ft high and 12 to 24 in. in diameter are not uncommon.

Maximum development of the species occurs in the southern Appalachians where humidity and rainfall are especially high during the grow-

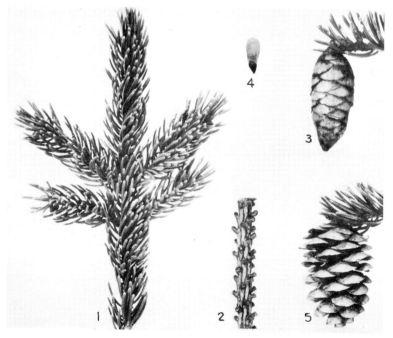

Fig. 53. *Picea rubens.* Red spruce. *1.* Foliage × ½. *2.* Dead twig showing sterigmata × 2. *3.* Closed cone × ¾. *4.* Seed × 1. *5.* Open cone × ¾.

ing season. Here the largest recorded tree was 162 ft high and 57 in. in diameter.

Open-grown trees develop a broadly conical crown which extends nearly to the ground; under forest conditions the crown is restricted to the upper portion of the tree and is somewhat pagoda-shaped. The boles of forest-grown trees are long and cylindrical; the root system is shallow and wide-spreading.

Red spruce occurs in pure stands or groups, and also in mixture with other northern species. It is found in swamps or bogs with black spruce, tamarack, balsam fir, and red maple but does not make satisfactory growth on such sites. Faster growth is made on adjacent better-drained flats in company with such species as balsam fir, eastern hemlock, eastern white pine, and yellow birch; while scattered trees occur throughout the neighboring hardwood mixture (sugar maple, yellow birch, and beech, on higher ground), and here development is probably best. This species is also found in pure groups on upper slopes where the soil is very thin and rocky. In general, acid sandy loam soils with considerable moisture support the best spruce.

Abundant moisture is also essential for good reproduction, and the

Fig. 54. Bark of red spruce.

most favorable conditions are found under mixed stands of hardwoods and conifers. Open-grown spruce may begin to yield good seed crops when 30 to 40 years old, but in old-growth stands it is usually much later. Good seed years occur at three- to eight-year intervals; the germination of the seeds may average 60 percent. The young trees are very tolerant, more so than those of the associated species, with the possible exception of eastern hemlock, sugar maple, and American beech; but they grow slowly under forest cover (1 ft in height may represent 15 years' growth); and even in the open they do not make rapid growth.

This spruce is long-lived and scarcely reaches maturity in less than 200 years, while trees with 350 to 400 annual rings have been reported. Because of the shallow root system, red spruce is susceptible to wind throw; it is also severely damaged by fire, and defoliated by the spruce budworm.

RANGE

The Northeast and Appalachian Mountains to Georgia (map, Plate 12). *Altitudinal distribution:* from near sea level in the North to 6,000 ft in the South; most of the red spruce in the United States is above the 1,000-ft level.

PLATE 12. *Picea rubens.*

Picea mariana (Mill.) B.S.P.   Black spruce [1]

BOTANICAL FEATURES

Leaves ¼″ to ½″ long, linear, 4-sided, dull blue-green, blunt-pointed; more or less glaucous.

[1] Where the ranges of the Appalachian and Northeastern red spruce, and the transcontinental black spruce overlap, numerous hybrids with intermediate characters are often found. These intermediate forms have puzzled botanists and foresters for a century or more. An excellent account of these introgressive spruce hybrids is given by Morgenstern and Farrar (262).

Cones ¾″ to 1½″ long, ovoid, purplish, turning brown at maturity; *scales* brittle, rigid, rounded, erose on the margin; *seeds* ⅛″ long, dark brown; wings ¼″ to ⅜″ long; about 404,000 (335,000–510,000) seeds to the pound, dewinged. The cones persist for many years (20 to 30) and often form large clusters easily seen at a distance. Although most of the good seed is released during the first 4 years, viable seed may come from 15-year-old cones. Fire may start the opening of these semiserotinous cones, and large amounts of seed are then released.

Twigs pubescent, brownish; *buds* ovoid, somewhat puberulous.

Bark ¼″ to ½″ thick, broken into thin, flaky, grayish-brown to reddish-brown scales; freshly exposed inner layers somewhat olive-green.

GENERAL DESCRIPTION

Black spruce is a small to medium-sized tree 30 to 40 ft high and 6 to 12 in. in diameter (max. 100 by 3 ft), with a long, straight, tapering bole, irregularly cylindrical crown and a shallow, spreading root system. In the southern part of its range, this species is commonly restricted to cool sphagnum bogs; in the far north it is also found on dry slopes but makes its best growth on moist, well-drained alluvial bottoms. Among the conifers, this species is of interest since with white spruce and tamarack it marks "the northern limit of tree growth" and assumes there a prostrate or shrubby habit. Black spruce is especially characteristic as a pioneer tree on the floating mats extending outward from the shores of small ponds which are slowly becoming bogs ("muskegs") through the deposition of plant material. In such situations growth is exceedingly

Fig. 55. *Picea mariana.* Black spruce. *1.* Closed cone × ¾. *2.* Open cone × ¾. *3.* Bark. (*Photograph by Canadian Forest Service.*)

slow, and "trees" 2 in. in diameter may show from 80 to 90 or more growth rings in cross section.[1]

Black spruce occurs in dense pure stands or in mixture with such species as tamarack, balsam fir, northern white-cedar, black ash, quaking aspen, and paper birch. Like most of the other spruces, it is tolerant, but less so than balsam fir and northern white-cedar. Natural pruning is poor, and unless the tree is grown in very dense stands, the side branches persist for many years.

Some seed is produced each year, with larger crops at irregular intervals; germination is about 60 percent. Propagation on wet sites also takes place by "layering"; the lower branches become embedded in the moist sphagnum and sprout roots which eventually support the erect branch without aid from the parent tree. Black spruce may attain an age of 250 years.

[1] In the interior of Alaska near northern timberline, Robert Marshall (personal correspondence) found on poorly drained soil a dwarfed black spruce 1 in. in diameter at the root collar, which showed 128 rings, while many others were growing almost as slowly.

PLATE 13. *Picea mariana.*

Northeastern United States and transcontinental through Canada (map, Plate 13). *Altitudinal distribution:* sea level up to 5,000 ft.

Picea glauca (Moench) Voss   White spruce

BOTANICAL FEATURES

Leaves ⅓" to ¾" long, linear, 4-sided, blue-green, and glaucous; apex acute but not sharp to the touch; tending to be crowded on the upper side of the branch by a twist at the base of those below; crushed foliage often with a pungent odor; hence the common name "cat spruce."
Cones 1½" to 2½" long, narrowly oblong, light brown; *scales* thin and flexible, usually truncate, rounded, or slightly emarginate at the apex; *seeds* ⅛" long, pale brown; wings ¼" to ⅜" long; about 240,000 (142,000–398,000) seeds to the pound, dewinged.
Twigs glabrous, or somewhat glaucous, orange-brown to gray; *buds* ovoid, with sometimes reflexed scales, ragged, or occasionally ciliate on the margin.
Bark thin, flaky or scaly, ashy brown; freshly exposed layers somewhat silvery.

GENERAL DESCRIPTION

White spruce is one of the most important and widely distributed conifers of Canada, and extends southward into several of the northern United States. When grown in the open, it develops a handsome conical crown which extends nearly to the ground. Forest trees are from 60 to 70 ft in height and 18 to 24 in. in diameter (max. 184 by 4 ft). The maximum age is more than 200 years.

This species forms extensive pure stands but also occurs in mixture with quaking aspen, paper birch, jack and lodgepole pines, balsam fir, and black and red spruces. Best growth is made on moist loam or alluvial

Fig. 56. *Picea glauca.* White spruce. *1.* Closed cone and foliage × ¾. *2.* Open cone × ¾. *3.* Bark. (*Photograph by Canadian Forest Service.*)

soils; and although found on many different sites, white spruce is especially typical of stream banks, lake shores, and adjacent slopes.

The silvical and other features are similar to those of the preceding species, but white spruce is probably shorter-lived and in its early years makes faster growth. It is used for reforestation both in the United States and Canada, and is also a widely planted ornamental. The pliable roots of white spruce are used by the Indians for lacing birchbark canoes, and making woven baskets (320).

Along the Canadian Rockies where the ranges of white spruce and Engelmann spruce overlap, certain varieties of white spruce have been recognized, including western white spruce *P. glauca* var. *albertiana* (S. Brown) Sarg. In this region, so much natural hybridizing is taking place between white and Engelmann spruces that perhaps varieties should not be recognized (389). There is considerable variation in cone size and scale structure on these spruces.

RANGE

Northern United States and transcontinental through Canada (map, Plate 14). *Altitudinal distribution:* sea level up to 5,000 ft elevation.

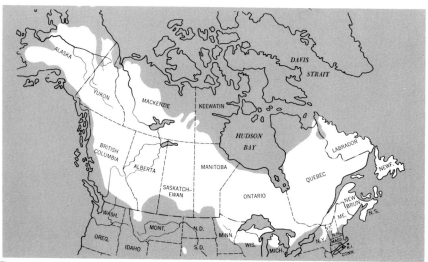

PLATE 14. *Picea glauca.*

DISTINGUISHING CHARACTERISTICS OF IMPORTANT SPECIES

Species	Leaves	Cones	Twigs
P. sitchensis, Sitka spruce	flattened, bright yellow-green above, blue-green below, sharp-pointed	about 3″ long, with erose, wedge-shaped, papery scales	glabrous
P. engelmannii, Engelmann spruce	4-angled, blue-green, often fetid, acute but not sharp-pointed	about 2″ long, otherwise similar to above	more or less pubescent

Picea sitchensis (Bong.) Carr.   Sitka spruce

BOTANICAL FEATURES

Leaves ½″ to 1⅛″ long, linear, flattened, bright yellow-green above, bluish white, glaucous below, very sharp-pointed, tending to extend outward at right angles from all sides of a twig.
Cones 2″ to 4″ long, ovoid-oblong, falling in the late autumn and early winter; *scales* thin, papery but stiff, wedge-shaped, erose at the apex; *seeds* ⅛″ long, reddish brown, their wings ⅛″ to ½″ long; about 210,000 (155,000–400,000) to the pound dewinged.
Twigs glabrous, orange-brown; *buds* ovoid, their scales obtuse.
Bark thin, rarely as much as 1″ thick even on the largest trunks, divided at the surface into thin, loosely appressed, concave, and elliptical silvery-gray to purplish-gray scales.

GENERAL DESCRIPTION

Sitka spruce, which is also known in the lumber trade as tidewater spruce, is one of the major timber-producing species of the Pacific Northwest. Mature trees on the Olympic peninsula of western Washington vary from 180 to 200 ft in height and from 3½ to 4½ ft in diameter (max. 300 by 17* ft). Many individuals yield from 6,000 to 8,000 board feet of lumber, and an occasional tree contains as much as 40,000 ft B.M.

Forest-grown trees feature long, clear, cylindrical boles which terminate in short, open crowns with horizontal and ascending branches terminating in pendulous branchlets. The typically shallow wide-spreading root system provides only moderate resistance to wind throw.

Sitka spruce forms extensive pure forests in many parts of its range, and also occurs in mixture with several other softwoods and hardwoods. In Alaska and elsewhere its chief associate is western hemlock. In British Columbia, Washington, and north-central Oregon it mingles with Douglas-fir, western redcedar, Pacific silver and grand firs, red alder, bigleaf maple, and black cottonwood. Occasional associates in southern Oregon include redwood and Port-Orford-cedar. The largest trees throughout its

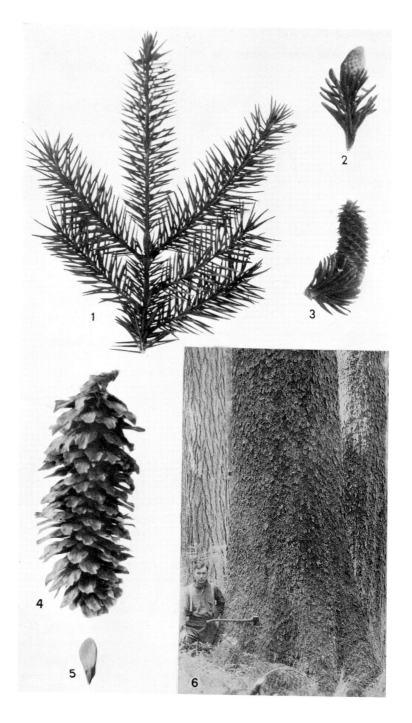

range occur on deep loams of high moisture retention. This species also invades peat bogs of the Puget Sound region. Trees on such sites, however, are of poor form and rarely attain commercial size. Sitka spruce is a coastal species usually found no more than 30 miles from tidewater and often much closer, as the coastal plain is narrow and the mountains sometimes rise almost directly from the sea. An interesting growth form of this species is found on the dry sandy soils and dunes along the coasts of Oregon and northern California. Here, with no protection from the winds that blow in almost continuously from the Pacific Ocean, individuals are greatly dwarfed, sprawling, or even prostrate. In some cases their boles are actually bent away from the direction of the prevailing winds, and their branches are twisted and contorted in such a manner that they appear to arise from the leeward sides of the stems.

Sitka spruce ordinarily produces some seed each fall, and usually releases copious crops every third or fourth year. Germination is good (60 to 70 percent), and seedlings become readily established on a variety of soil types. Growth is vigorous in youth, and the trees soon overtop their forest associates. This spruce is rated as tolerant, but not as much so as western hemlock. Maturity is reached in about 500 years, but occasional forest monarchs 700 to 800 years old have been reported.

RANGE

West coast of North America (map, Plate 15). *Altitudinal distribution:* sea level up to 3,000 ft; commercial range, sea level to 1,200 ft.

Picea engelmannii Parry   Engelmann spruce

BOTANICAL FEATURES

Leaves 1" to 1⅛" long, linear, 4-sided, blue-green, flexible, apex often blunt; exhaling a rank odor when crushed; often somewhat appressed and tending to point toward the tip of the twig.

Cones 1" to 2½" long, ovoid-oblong; *scales* thin and somewhat papery, wedge-shaped, and commonly erose at the apex; *seeds* ⅛" long, nearly black; wings about ½" long, oblique; about 135,000 (69,000–200,000) seeds to the pound, dewinged.

Twigs more or less pubescent, light brown to gray; *bud scales* more often appressed than in blue spruce.

Bark very thin, broken into large purplish brown to russet-red, thin, loosely attached scales.

Fig. 57. *Picea sitchensis.* Sitka spruce. *1.* Foliage × ½. *2.* Staminate flowers × 1. *3.* Ovulate flower × 1. *4.* Open cone × ¾. *5.* Seed × 1. *6.* Bark. (*Photograph by J. D. Cress, Seattle, Wash.*)

1. *Picea sitchensis.*   2. *Picea engelmannii.*

PLATE 15

The name of this spruce commemorates Dr. George Engelmann, noted German-American physician and botanist of the middle nineteenth century.

Englemann spruce is typically a mountain species and under favorable conditions for growth attains a height of from 100 to 120 ft and a d.b.h. of 18 to 30 in., although somewhat larger trees (max. 165 by 6 ft) occur on the best sites. Its general habit is quite similar to that of Sitka spruce, and like that species, it reaches its maximum size on deep, rich, loamy soils of high moisture content.

Besides occurring in extensive pure stands, Engelmann spruce is found with other species comprising some 14 recognized forest types. The most common associate is subalpine fir. Through the central Rocky Mountains, lodgepole, limber, and whitebark pines, Douglas-fir, and quaking aspen may also be included.[1] Where the ranges of Engelmann and white spruce overlap, a confusing array of natural hybrids is to be found. Both Colorado blue and Sitka spruce also produce hybrids with this species.

Engelmann spruce produces large crops of seed every 3 to 6 years. Germination is particularly high (up to 97 percent) in beds of moist mineral soil, although seedling development is also good in moist duff soils covering the floor of virgin forests. A few trees are also traceable to layering, but individuals produced in this way never attain commercial proportions.

[1] For a listing of other species see Fowells (127).

Fig. 58. *Picea engelmannii.* Engelmann spruce. *1.* Foliage × ½. *2.* Closed cone × ¾. *3.* Open cone × ¾. *4.* Seed × 1. *5.* Bud × 1. *6.* Bark. (*Courtesy of Western Pine Association.*)

This spruce is tolerant, and among its common associates is exceeded only by subalpine fir and the hemlocks. Trees of all ages are often found under the canopy of old trees, and individuals often suppressed for 50 to 100 years quickly recover upon being released. Growth is restricted by a short summer season; and trees 16 to 22 in. in diameter are often 350 to 450 years of age. The average maximum age for Engelmann spruce appears to be in the neighborhood of 400 years. Occasional trees over 500 years of age have been reported, and Bates [1] observed one stem with 660 growth rings.

Periodic outbreaks of the Engelmann spruce bark beetle have been extremely damaging to mature stands in the central Rocky Mountain region. The bark is thin even on old trunks, and fires cause extensive damage.

Fig. 59. Engelmann spruce near timberline.

RANGE

Rocky Mountains, Cascade Mountains, and northeastern California (map, Plate 15). *Altitudinal distribution:* 1,500 to 12,000 ft in British Columbia, the Cascades, and northern Rockies; 9,000 to 11,000 ft through the central Rockies; and 10,000 to 12,000 ft in the southern Rockies.

Picea pungens Engelm.   Blue spruce; Colorado spruce (SPN)

Those who are familiar only with the shapely and beautiful silvery-blue ornamental varieties of this species would scarcely recognize the blue spruce in its central Rocky

[1] See *Colorado Forester,* 1926.

Mountain domain. Found on the middle and upper slopes, and sculptured by gale-force winds and heavy snows, the trees often bear little resemblance to the carefully nurtured specimens of park and dooryards. Even the foliage, except for a brief time in early spring when the needles are coated with a powdery waxy bloom, is dull dark green to blue-green with only an occasional tree silvery. The blue spruce often resembles the Engelmann spruce, with which it is sometimes associated at the lower elevations. Since both species may be seen as ornamentals outside their natural range, the following comparisons may be useful.

TABLE OF COMPARISON

Feature	Blue spruce	Engelmann spruce
Needles	sharp, extending at right angles to the twig; when chewed, have a sharp, acid, pungent taste	more or less blunt, usually pointing forward; lacking a sharp acid taste
Twigs	essentially glabrous	more or less pubescent
Bud scales	reflexed	usually appressed
Cones	about 3″ long, scales often narrow	1″ to 2½″ long, scales relatively broad
Form	branch arrangement gives crown a layered appearance	crown not layered

This species and several of its varieties,[1] because of their habit, beautiful foliage, and ability to withstand drought and extremes of temperatures, are highly prized ornamentals in many parts of the United States.

Range. Yellowstone National Park near the Montana state line and northwestern Wyoming, south along the mountains to south-central New Mexico; in the West, south through extreme eastern Idaho, central Utah, and central Arizona to southeastern Arizona. *Altitudinal distribution:* 6,000 to 9,000 ft in the North, 8,000 to 11,000 ft in the South.

Picea breweriana S. Wats.   Brewer spruce

This rare and little-known tree is restricted to the upper limits of tree growth in the Siskiyou Mountains and neighboring coast ranges in southern Oregon and northern California. It is readily distinguished from other American spruces by its weeping habit, dark green, flattened or remotely three-angled needles, and entire-margined cone scales.

[1] The commonest is var. *argentea,* often erroneously called Koster's blue spruce; the true var. *kosteri* is a weeping form seldom seen.

PSEUDOTSUGA Carr.   Douglas-fir

This genus includes about six species [1] of trees widely scattered through the forests of western North America, southwestern China, Japan, and Taiwan. While these were originally included under *Abies*, they are readily distinguished by their pointed buds, petiolate leaves, persistent cone scales, and three-lobed bracts. Douglas-fir itself, *P. menziesii* (Mirb.) Franco, is the only important species in the group and is one of the two found in western United States.

BOTANICAL FEATURES OF THE GENUS

Leaves spirally arranged; *shape* linear, grooved on the upper surface and with a broad band of stomata on each side of the midrib below; *apex* blunt to rather sharply pointed; *base* constricted; petioled, persistent for 5 to 8 years and leaving a suborbicular, slightly raised leaf cushion upon removal, or when shed; exhaling a characteristic odor when crushed; *resin canals* 2, external.

Flowers solitary; *staminate* strobili axillary, consisting of a number of spirally arranged, short-stalked, subglobose anthers; *ovulate* strobili conical, terminal or in the axils of the upper leaves, composed of several spirally arranged, imbricated, 3-lobed bracts each subtending a small ovate scale with 2 basal ovules; all species monoecious.

Fruit an ovoid-cylindrical, pendant cone maturing at the end of the first season; the conspicuous 3-lobed bracts longer than the rounded cone scales; *seeds* more or less triangular, with a large, rounded terminal wing which partially envelops the seed; *cotyledons* 6 to 12.

Buds fusiform, sharp-pointed, covered by several imbricated, shining brown scales.

Pseudotsuga menziesii (Mirb.) Franco [2]   Douglas-fir; Douglas fir (Tr)

BOTANICAL FEATURES

Leaves ¾″ to 1¼″ long, yellow-green or blue-green, more or less flattened, standing out from all sides of the twig or with a tendency to be somewhat 2-ranked; *apex* rounded-obtuse or rarely acute, stomatiferous below, persistent for 8 or more years.

[1] Eight species, if the native Douglas-fir is split into three species, as has been done by certain European authors (171).

[2] *P. taxifolia* (Poir.) Britt. used for many years was based on an earlier name found to lack priority [Check List (212)].

FIG. 60. *Pseudotsuga menziesii*. Douglas-fir. *1*. Foliage × ¾. *2*. Buds × 1. *3*. Closed con, coast form × ¾. *4*. Ovulate and staminate flowers, respectively, × 1. *5*. Open cone, Rocky Mountain form × ¾. *6*. Seed × 1. *7*. Bark.

1

2

3

♀

4

♂

5

6

7

Cones 3″ to 4″ long, pendent, ovoid-cylindric, with exserted, 3-lobed, forklike, appressed or strongly reflexed bracts; *seeds* triangular, terminally winged; about 42,000 seeds to the pound, dewinged.

Buds fusiform, sharp-pointed, lustrous brown.

Bark on young stems smooth except for resin blisters; at length becoming 6″ to 24″ thick on old trees, and then divided into thick reddish-brown ridges separated by deep irregular fissures. In a few instances the bark is "tight" (fine-textured) on old trees and corky on others, particularly those of the mountain form.

GENERAL DESCRIPTION

Douglas-fir, monarch of Pacific Northwest forests, was first observed by Menzies on Vancouver Island when he accompanied the British naval captain Vancouver on an expedition to the Pacific Coast in the early 1790s. For more than a quarter of a century this tree was variously classified as a spruce, hemlock, true fir, and even as a pine; in fact logs exported by the Hudson's Bay outpost near the mouth of the Columbia River were listed in European ports as "Oregon pine," a name which has persisted in the trade to this day, especially in Australia. It remained for David Douglas, a Scottish botanist sent out by the Royal Horticultural Society in 1825, to study this tree, to show that it was sufficiently different to be considered as separate from other previously described conifers; later Carrière coined the new generic name *Pseudotsuga*. This name was

PLATE 16. *Pseudotsuga menziesii.*

a rather unfortunate choice, since it literally means "false hemlock." The common name, Douglas-fir,[1] commemorates Douglas, and in addition serves to distinguish this species from the true fir (*Abies*).

Douglas-fir is a dimorphic species with two more or less distinct forms.[2] One of these is restricted to the forests of the Pacific slope, and the other to those of the Rocky Mountain region.

The Rocky Mountain form of Douglas-fir is considered distinct from the coast form by some taxonomists, who accordingly classify it as *Pseudotsuga glauca* Mayr. or *Pseudotsuga menziesii* var. *glauca* (Beissn.) Franco. However, in certain sections, the two types intergrade. Usually the foliage of the Rocky Mountain tree is blue-green, but sometimes trees with blue-green foliage and others with yellow-green leaves are found standing together. Similarly, although yellow-green crowns are typical of the coast form, some trees show a blue-green coloration. The principal botanical difference between these two forms lies in the structure of their cones. Rocky Mountain trees have small cones rarely 3 in. in length, with much-exserted and strongly reflexed bracts. By contrast, the cones of the coastal form are often 4 in. long and have straight, more or less appressed bracts.

Douglas-fir comprises about 50 percent of the standing timber of our western forests. It produces more timber than any other American species and at the present time furnishes about one-fifth of the total annual cut.

COAST FORM

Douglas-fir is the largest tree in the Northwest, and in the United States it is second only to the giant sequoias of California. Trees in virgin forests average 180 to 250 ft in height and 4 to 6 ft in diameter, although heights of 325 ft and diameters of 8 to 10 ft are not uncommon. The tallest known specimen in the United States stood near Mineral, Washington, and was approximately 385 ft in height and 15 ft in diameter. In the Olympic National Park, Washington state, a tree was reported to have a height of 221 ft and a circumference breast high of 53 ft 4 in.

Old trees are characterized by an exceptionally clear, long, cylindrical bole and either a rounded or an irregularly flat-topped crown. However, in closed stands of young trees, early natural pruning is poor, and a clear butt log may not begin to develop before the 80th year (127). Anchorage is provided by a strong, well-developed, wide-spreading lateral root sys-

[1] The names red fir and yellow fir have been used by loggers and lumbermen to differentiate locally certain specimens on the basis of ring width, color, and softness.
[2] Several European workers (171) have claimed that there are three species of Douglas-fir; this is based largely upon needle structure. Studies by W. E. Kilgore at the New York State College of Forestry have failed to substantiate this viewpoint.

tem. Trees are found on a variety of soils but make their best growth on deep, rich, well-drained, porous loams in regions where there is an abundance of both soil and atmospheric moisture. In youth, Douglas-fir forms extensive, pure, even-aged stands, but these are later commonly invaded by other species. In the Pacific Northwest coniferous associates include western redcedar, western hemlock, Sitka spruce, and grand, Pacific silver, and noble firs. Although rated as intermediate in tolerance, Douglas-fir is less so than these associates, with the exception of noble fir. Red alder and Oregon white oak are also found in Douglas-fir forests. In the principal timber belt of the Sierra it occurs chiefly with white fir and ponderosa pine, in the northern coast ranges of California with ponderosa pine, tanoak, and Oregon white oak, and in the redwood belt with redwood.

Seed is produced after about the twenty-fifth year, with heavy crops at intervals of 5 to 7 years. Germination is good in both mineral and humus soils, and dense thickets spring up rapidly after logging, provided fires are excluded. Under favorable conditions trees 10 years of age may be 12 to 15 ft in height and 1 to 2 in. in diameter. Pole size is often attained in 30 to 40 years, and saw logs may be harvested in less than 80 years. The trees attain great age and are commonly found with over 700 (maximum 1,375) growth rings. Second-growth stands may produce more than 30,000 ft B.M. to the acre in less than 50 years.

Principal enemies are fire, the Douglas-fir bark beetle, and certain heart rots.

ROCKY MOUNTAIN FORM

The Rocky Mountain form of Douglas-fir rarely exceeds a height of more than 130 ft or a diameter of 3 ft. It occurs in both pure and mixed stands with ponderosa pine, western larch, and grand fir. Other associates include western hemlock, western white and lodgepole pines, Engelmann spruce, white fir, and aspen. Douglas-fir is more tolerant than these except the hemlock and spruce.

Although most abundant on moist sites, Rocky Mountain Douglas-fir is quite drought-resistant and is often found on arid areas with ponderosa pine. It is frost-resistant and hardy in the East and is a common ornamental of that region. The trees are grown for timber in Europe and have been planted successfully in many parts of the world.

RANGE

Western United States and British Columbia (see map, Plate 16). *Altitudinal distribution:* sea level to 5,000 ft along the coast; 4,000 to 6,000 ft inland; 10,000 ft in the southern Rocky Mountains.

FIG. 61. Old-growth Douglas-fir. (*Photograph by J. D. Cress.*)

Pseudotsuga macrocarpa (Vasey) Mayr.   Bigcone Douglas-fir

This tree, restricted to the mountains of southern California and Baja California, never attains the grandeur or stature of the Douglas-fir, which it resembles. Large 5-in. cones with rigid, woody scales subtended by trident bracts of about equal length provide its most distinctive feature. Its rapidly tapering bole (max 120° by 2° ft), usually clothed for the greater part—if not all—of its length in a massive pyramidal crown, is seldom used for the production of lumber in commercial quantities. This tree contributes little or nothing to the nation's timber supply, but it is a valuable cover tree and aids materially in erosion control.

Range. Southern California from eastern Santa Barbara County south along the mountains to Lower California. *Altitudinal distribution:* 1,500 to 7,000 ft.

TSUGA (Endl.) Carr.   Hemlock

The genus *Tsuga* is comprised of about 14 species of evergreen, usually pyramidal-shaped trees confined to the forests of eastern and western North America, Japan, Taiwan, China, and the Himalaya. Hemlock pollen has been identified in several French and Polish peat bogs, and fossil wood has been unearthed in other sections of Europe; but hemlocks are not found in the modern forests of that continent.

The Japanese hemlocks, *T. sieboldii* Carr. and *T. diversifolia* (Maxim.) Mast., respectively, and the Chinese species, *T. chinensis* (Franch.) Pritz., are oriental timber-producing species; they are frequently used for ornamental purposes in other parts of the world, including the United States.

Four species of *Tsuga* are indigenous to North America; two in the East and two in the West, respectively. Of these, the western hemlock is at present the most important timber-producing species in this genus. Hemlock bark contains from 7 to 12 percent tannin, and in the United States that of the eastern hemlock was one of the principal commercial sources of this material for many years.

BOTANICAL FEATURES OF THE GENUS

Leaves spirally arranged, but commonly 2-ranked by a twist in the petiole, variable in length, those on the upper side of the branchlet usually the shortest; *shape* linear, flattened or less frequently angular or semicircular in transverse section, generally grooved above, with 2 broad bands of stomata below; *margin* frequently serrulate above the middle; *apex* blunt; conspicuously petioled; persistent for 3 to 6 years; borne on short peglike projections from the twig; *resin canals* 1, embedded in the lower central portion of the leaf.

Flowers solitary; *staminate* strobili axillary, globose, consisting of a number of short stamens; *ovulate* cones erect, terminal on the lateral branchlets, consisting of a number of membranous bracts each subtending a nearly orbicular scale with two basal ovules; *bracts* and *scales* of nearly the same length; all species monoecious.

Cones pendent, globose to ovoid or oblong, subsessile, maturing in one season; scales orbicular to ovate-polygonal, mostly with entire margins, several times longer than the bracts; *bracts* inconspicuous (rarely exserted); *seeds* small, ovoid-oblong, dotted with minute resin vesicles, with obovate, terminal wings; *cotyledons* 3 to 6.

Buds small, ovoid to globose, nonresinous.

DISTINGUISHING CHARACTERISTICS OF THE IMPORTANT HEMLOCKS

Species	Leaves	Cones
T. canadensis, eastern hemlock	tapering from base to apex, bands of stomata well defined below	about ¾″ long, oblong-ovoid; scale margins not undulate
T. heterophylla, western hemlock	uniform in width from base to apex, bands of stomata poorly defined below, upper surface grooved	about ⅞″ long, ovoid; scale margins undulate

Tsuga canadensis (L.) Carr.   Eastern hemlock; Canada hemlock (SPN)

BOTANICAL FEATURES

Leaves ⅓″ to ⅔″ long, linear, tapering from base to apex, dark yellow-green, rounded or slightly emarginate, marked below with 2 white lines of stomata; persistent until the 3d season.

Cones ½″ to ¾″ long, oblong-ovoid, with suborbicular, smooth-margined scales; shedding their seeds during the winter and often persistent during the next season; *seeds* ¹⁄₁₆″ long, with several resin vesicles; wings terminal, broad; about 187,000 (132,000–360,000) seeds to the pound, dewinged.

Bark on young trees flaky or scaly; soon with wide, flat ridges; on old trees heavily and deeply furrowed; freshly cut surfaces showing purplish streaks.

GENERAL DESCRIPTION

Eastern hemlock is usually a medium-sized tree 60 to 70 ft high and 2 to 3 ft in diameter, although in the mountains of West Virginia, North Carolina, and Tennessee it sometimes attains a maximum height of 160 ft and a diameter of 6 to 7 ft. This species is exceedingly graceful in youth, and open-grown trees develop a dense, pyramidal crown, with the lower branches often touching the ground. The slender terminal leader in hemlocks (*Tsuga*) is rare among conifers in that the new growth droops or curves away from the vertical as much as 90 deg or more. During this first

Fig. 62. *Tsuga canadensis.* Eastern hemlock. *1.* Ovulate flower × 2. *2.* Staminate flowers × 2. *3.* Closed cone × ¾. *4.* Open cone × ¾. *5.* Seed × 1. *6.* Foliage × ½. *7.* Leaf showing white bands below × 2. *8.* Bark of old tree.

season, compression wood develops on the under surface of the curve, and straightening begins (250, 372). Several years may pass before this is completed, and the curved tip is at any season an excellent mark of identification. The crowns of old trees are inclined to be ragged in outline; even in dense stands the lower branches remain alive for many years and when dead prune poorly. This causes knots, which in this species are often remarkably hard and flintlike. The bole, except in old trees, shows considerable taper and is supported below by a superficial, wide-spreading root system.

This tree is found on many types of soil, and it reaches its best development in cool, moist situations. Eastern hemlock is remarkably tolerant, perhaps more so than any of its associates. Growth rings of trees under heavy shade may be so narrow that a hand lens is needed to see them.

When such a suppressed tree is liberated by the removal of others around it, the sudden increase in growth is often amazing. Rings 10 times the width of the previous ones may be produced.

In the North, common associates of eastern hemlock are eastern white pine, red spruce, sugar maple, American beech, and yellow birch; while farther south additional ones include white ash, yellow-poplar, basswood, and several white and red oaks. Eastern hemlock occurs in several forest types with these and other species, and over long periods of time tends to replace them; pure stands, however, are of limited extent.

Abundant seed is produced at two- to three-year intervals, and seedling reproduction is plentiful on moist, shaded humus; in fact, the seeds even germinate on old, partially rotted stumps or logs, and occasionally on mossy boulders. In this respect, yellow birch is the chief competitor, and it is common to find a good-sized hemlock and a birch with their roots intertwined endeavoring to exist on the top of a stump a foot or more above the forest floor. Although some reproduction may occur on bare, exposed soil, this hemlock usually starts under the shade of other species and, growing very slowly, forces its way, during a period of a century or more, into the crown cover overhead. A maximum age of 600 years or more may be attained.

Hemlocks are valued as ornamentals, and young trees may show great variation in form and foliage. About 70 cultivars of the eastern hemlock have been described (101).

RANGE

Southern Canada, the Northeast, Lake states, and Appalachian Mountains to Georgia (map, Plate 17). *Altitudinal distribution:* in the North, sea level to 2,500 ft; in the Southern Appalachians mostly from 2,000 to 5,000 ft.

Tsuga caroliniana Engelm.   Carolina hemlock

This is a relatively rare tree of the upper slopes of the Appalachian Mountains from Virginia to Georgia. The cones and leaves are slightly longer than those of eastern

Fig. 63. Cone of Carolina hemlock × ¾.

1. *Tsuga canadensis.*   2. *Tsuga heterophylla.*

PLATE 17

hemlock, and the leaves are not two-ranked. Carolina hemlock is well adapted as an ornamental and is gaining favor for this purpose.

Tsuga heterophylla (Raf.) Sarg.   Western hemlock; Pacific hemlock (SPN)

BOTANICAL FEATURES

Leaves ¼" to ¾" long, flattened, of uniform width from base to apex, dark shiny green, grooved above, with 2 poorly defined bands of stomata below; mostly rounded or blunt at the apex, persistent for 4 to 7 years.
Cones ¾" to 1" long, ovoid, light brown; *cone scales* suborbicular, often more or less wavy along the margin; *seeds* ¹⁄₁₆" long, ovoid, nearly surrounded by a large straw-colored wing; about 297,000 (220,000–508,000) seeds to the pound, dewinged.
Bark thin even on the largest trees, separated by deep, narrow fissures into broad, flat, russet-brown ridges; inner bark dark red streaked with purple.

GENERAL DESCRIPTION

Western hemlock is one of the four major timber-contributing species in the Pacific Northwest.[1] Largest of the four American hemlocks, this tree varies from 125 to 175 ft in height and 2 to 4 ft in diameter (max. 259 by 9 ft). Forest trees produce a long, clear, symmetrical bole and a shallow, wide-spreading root system. The crown is short, open, and pyramidal, and, like the eastern hemlock, features a drooping terminal leader. An abundance of both soil and atmospheric moisture is requisite for rapid growth, and the largest trees are invariably found on moist porous soils in

[1] The others are Douglas-fir, Sitka spruce, and western redcedar.

Fig. 64. *Tsuga heterophylla*. Western hemlock. *1*. Foliage and cones × ¾. *2*. Seed × 1. *3*. Bark.

regions where the annual precipitation is at least 70 in. per year. In drier situations the trees are somewhat smaller and slower-growing, but do eventually reach commercial proportions. Western hemlock occurs in pure, dense, even-age forests and as an occasional tree in mixed hardwood and coniferous stands, then commonly as an understory species. Nearly pure, extensive forests of western hemlock occur in southeastern Alaska, coastal British Columbia, and western Washington. Those restricted to the middle-upper western slopes of the Cascade and Olympic Mountains usually occur above the Douglas-fir belt. At low elevations hemlock commonly invades forests chiefly composed of Douglas-fir, Pacific silver and grand firs, western redcedar, black cottonwood, bigleaf maple, and red alder. At higher levels its associates include noble fir, Alaska-cedar, mountain hemlock, and western white pine. Western hemlock is a major component of 5 forest types, and a minor species in 11 others (127).

Western hemlock begins to produce seed after the twenty-fifth to thirtieth year, and large crops are borne every three or four years thereafter. Nearly any sort of soil provides a satisfactory seedbed, and when supplied with an abundance of moisture, the percentage of germination is usually high. Partially rotted stumps and logs are often literally covered with hemlock seedlings, and fresh mineral soil, moist duff, or even sphagnum peat are suitable for seedling development. This species often usurps cutover and burned-over areas formerly occupied by other species when moisture is not a limiting factor. The trees are very tolerant throughout life. Rate of growth compares favorably with that of Douglas-fir, and trees 90 to 100 years of age are commonly 110 to 130 ft high and 15 to 18 in. in diameter. The largest trees rarely attain an age of more than 500 years. Western hemlock is susceptible to fire injury, butt rot is prevalent in overmature trees, and dwarf mistletoe is a common parasite.

Western hemlock timber was virtually unknown until the close of World War I, except locally. However, since then it has found a ready market in many of the world's leading lumber centers. The bark of this tree contains tannin (9 to 16 percent), but it is rarely used commercially.

RANGE

West coast of North America and the Inland Empire (map, Plate 17). *Altitudinal distribution:* sea level to 7,000 ft.

Tsuga mertensiana (Bong.) Carr.   Mountain hemlock

Distinguishing characteristics. Leaves about ¾ in. long, blue-green, semicircular in transverse section, the upper surface often keeled or grooved; extending from all sides of the twig or crowded toward the upper side, stomatiferous on all surfaces. *Cones* ¾ to 3½ in. long (the largest cones are found on trees toward the southern limits of the range), oblong-cylindric, yellow-green to purple, the scales often strongly reflexed after shedding their seeds; *seeds* ⅛ in. long, with one or two resin vesicles; the wings terminal, about ½ in. long. *Bark* dull purplish brown to reddish brown, divided into narrow flattened ridges by deep, narrow fissures.

General description. Mountain hemlock, although one of the largest of alpine trees, is often a low, sprawling, or even prostrate shrub on windswept ridges at timberline. Forest trees, however, average 75 to 100 ft in height and 2½ to 3½ ft in diameter and are characterized by a shallow root system which supports a long, clear or limby bole with a narrow pyramidal crown of drooping or even pendulous branches. Trees on the sides of canyons and on very steep slopes are commonly pistol-butted. In open situations, particularly in high alpine meadows, the boles are excessively tapered. Here mountain hemlock forms pure, parklike stands or mingles with subalpine fir, subalpine larch, Engelmann spruce, and whitebark pine. The best stands of this species, however, are found on moist slopes, flats, and heads of ravines of northerly exposure. While pure stands are seldom extensive, mountain hemlock commonly constitutes 85 percent or more of certain mixed coniferous forests. This species reaches its maximum development in southern Oregon, and fully stocked stands are found in the vicinity of Crater Lake National Park.

Seed is borne at an early age, and regular crops are produced annually after the twenty-fifth to thirtieth year. The seeds exhibit transient vitality, but under favorable

Fig. 65. Foliage and cones of mountain hemlock × ½.

conditions germination is good either in moist duff or on bare mineral soil. Seedlings are very tolerant, comparing favorably in this respect with those of western hemlock. Dense shade causes suppression, but the trees recover rapidly upon being released. Growth is at no time rapid, and trees 200 to 300 years of age are seldom ever more than 18 to 24 in. in diameter on the best sites. Trees 500 years of age or more are rarely found.

This species is used as an ornamental in a number of European countries, and several horticultural varieties are now known. The bark of mature trees contains large quantities of tannin, but owing to the relative inaccessibility of the trees, it is not used at the present time. Like the subalpine fir, it promises to be a more important timber tree in the future.

Range. Southern Alaska south along the coast ranges of British Columbia, Washington, and Oregon; and inland on the upper slopes of the Sierra Nevada to central California; also in southeastern British Columbia, northern Idaho, and western Montana. *Altitudinal distribution:* sea level (near Sitka, Alaska) to 10,000 ft.

ABIES Mill.   Fir

The genus *Abies* includes about 40 species of trees, widely scattered through the forests of North and Central America, Europe, Asia, and northern Africa. Trees growing in southern latitudes are usually restricted to the upper slopes of mountains and are not infrequently found on sites at or near timberline; those in boreal forests, however, are largely confined to regions of relatively low elevations, with only a few forms ascending to the upper limits of tree growth.

This group comprises a number of important species, although the timber produced is somewhat inferior to that of the spruces. Several species, including balsam fir, furnish pulpwood. Other forest products traceable to certain of the firs include the oleoresins known to the trade as Canada balsam or Strasburg turpentine, and leaf oils. The former are obtained from superficial pitch blisters on the bark and are used chiefly in the manufacture of medicinal compounds and varnishes, as a mounting medium in the preparation of slides for the microscope, and for cementing lenses in this and other optical instruments. Leaf oils are largely used in the manufacture of pharmaceutical compounds.

A. *pindrow* Royle, the Himalayan silver fir, is a valuable species indigenous to India. A. *alba* Mill., silver fir or "Swiss pine," is an important timber tree of southern and central Europe. The Japanese momi and nikko firs, A. *firma* Sieb. and Zucc. and A. *homolepis* Sieb. and Zucc., respectively, are two noteworthy trees of Japan, the former being one of its principal pulpwood species. In Central America the wood of the sacred fir, A. *religiosa* Lindl., is used, particularly in Mexico and Guatemala, for structural purposes. The Siberian fir, A. *sibirica* Ledeb., forms extensive forests through northern and eastern Russia, Siberia, and Turkestan. Some of the timber produced by this species has been offered to the world's trade, and it may become a serious competitor of the American pulpwood species.

A number of the introduced firs are highly prized for decorative purposes in this country. The Spanish fir, A. *pinsapo* Boiss., a tree with sprucelike needles, is a common ornamental in the Pacific Northwest. The stately Greek fir, A. *cephalonica* Lud., the Nordmann fir, A. *nordmanniana* (Steven) Spach, and the nikko fir previously mentioned are other trees favored for decorative use.

Nine species of *Abies* are included in the coniferous flora of the United States. Seven of these are scattered through the forests of the West, while two of them are found in the East.

BOTANICAL FEATURES OF THE GENUS

Leaves spirally arranged, often more or less pectinate, sessile;[1] *shape* linear, flattened in cross section, or rarely 4-angled and then grooved above, with numerous lines of stomata on the lower or occasionally all surfaces; *apex* acute, rounded, or shallowly to deeply notched or bifid; persistent for 7 to 10 years and leaving a circular leaf scar upon falling or when removed; usually exhaling a balsamic, or turpentinelike, odor when bruised; *resin canals* 2 or rarely 4, external or occasionally medial. **Flowers** solitary; *staminate* strobili appearing from buds of the previous

[1] But often narrowed near the base.

season, and borne on the underside of the lower crown branches in the axils of leaves; *ovulate* cones erect, composed of many bracts each subtending a large scale with two inverted basal ovules; strobili axillary on the upper crown branches of the previous season's growth; all species monoecious.

Cones erect, maturing at the end of the first season; *scales* thin, broadly fan-shaped, particularly near the center of the cone, longer or shorter than the bracts; *bracts* apiculate, often shouldered, their margins erose; both scales and bracts together deciduous at maturity, leaving a mostly bare spikelike axis which frequently persists through the winter.

Seeds ovoid to oblong, with conspicuous resin vesicles; the broad terminal wings often delicately tinted with shades of pink, rose, lavender, or brown; *cotyledons* 5 to 7.

Buds ovoid to oblong, blunt, less commonly pointed, resinous or rarely nonresinous.

EASTERN BALSAM FIRS

Abies balsamea (L.) Mill.   Balsam fir

BOTANICAL FEATURES

Leaves linear, flattened, dark shiny green above, silvery banded below, on sterile side branches ¾″ to 1½″ long, blunt, or slightly notched at the apex, 2-ranked; on upper branches much shorter, often sharp-pointed, and tending to crowd toward the upper surface of the twig; [1] *resin canals* 2, medial.

Cones 2″ to 3½″ long, oblong-cylindric, green tinged with purple; *bracts* usually shorter than the scales, with rounded erose shoulders and short, pointed tips; *seeds* about ⅛″ long, with broad purplish-brown wings; about 60,000 (30,000–94,000) seeds to the pound, dewinged.

Buds ⅛″ to ¼″ long, subglobose, resinous, with orange-green scales.

Bark ½″ thick, dull green, later with grayish patches, smooth except for numerous raised resin blisters; eventually breaking up into small reddish-brown, irregular scaly plates.

GENERAL DESCRIPTION

Balsam fir is a small to medium-sized tree 40 to 60 ft high and 12 to 18 in. in diameter (max. 125 by 3* ft). It is perhaps the most symmetrical of northeastern trees with its dense, dark green, narrowly pyramidal crown, terminating in a stiff, spirelike tip. The moderately tapering bole usually retains small dead, persistent branches, and is supported by a shallow, wide-spreading root system.

[1] This variation between the leaves on sterile side branches and upper (often cone-bearing) branchlets, respectively, is typical of many species of fir.

Fig. 66. *Abies balsamea*. Balsam fir. *1*. Foliage × ½. *2*. Mature cone × ½. *3*. Dead twig showing smooth leaf scars × 1½. *4*. Cone with scales partly fallen × ¾. *5*. Cone scales nearly all fallen × ¾. *6*. Back of cone scale showing bract × 1¼. *7*. Face of cone scale showing seeds × 1¼. *8*. Bark of old tree.

Balsam fir is a cold-climate tree, requiring abundant moisture for best development. In swamps it often forms pure stands but does best in association with spruce on the adjacent flats which are better drained; even here pure stands or groups are commonly found. On higher ground, balsam fir occurs as a scattered tree in mixture with other northern species. It appears again in dwarfed, matted, pure stands, or entangled with black spruce near the windswept summits of mountains where great extremes in temperature are experienced.

Good seed years occur at two- to four-year intervals, and large quantities of seeds are then produced. Although germination is low (about 22 percent), this species is aggressive in restocking cutover lands, and makes rapid growth. Propagation of new fir trees by layering is common, and on some areas important. Balsam fir is more shade-tolerant than most of its associates, including tamarack, the pines, white spruce, aspens, and white birch. [For complete list of associates and tolerances see Bakuzis and Hansen (22).]

This fir is short-lived, and although it may reach an age of nearly 200 years, trees over 90 years old show a high percentage of heart rot caused by wood-destroying fungi. The chief insect enemies of balsam fir are the spruce budworm and the balsam woolly aphid; fire also causes severe loss.

"Canada balsam," the liquid resin collected from the bark blisters, is the traditional cement used to cover thin specimens for permanent mounting under cover glass upon glass slides; it is also valued for cementing the elements in compound lenses.

For many years the leading Christmas tree, the use of balsam fir for this purpose is declining in favor of plantation-grown pines (104).

RANGE

Canada and the northeastern United States (map, Plate 18). *Altitudinal distribution:* sea level to about 5,000 ft.

Abies fraseri (Pursh) Poir.   Fraser fir; Fraser balsam fir (SPN)

This is a tree of the high mountains in southern Virginia, North Carolina, and Tennessee. It is very similar to *A. balsamea*, except for the ovuliferous bracts, which are longer than the scales and strongly reflexed.

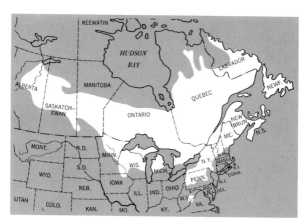

PLATE 18. *Abies balsamea*

WESTERN FIRS

DISTINGUISHING CHARACTERISTICS OF IMPORTANT SPECIES

Species	Lower crown leaves	Cones	Bark
A. amabilis, Pacific silver fir	about 1″ long, flattened, stomatiferous below	about 4½″ long, the bracts shorter than the scales	silvery white to ashy gray
A. magnifica, California red fir	about 1″ long, 4-angled, stomatiferous on all surfaces	about 7½″ long, the bracts shorter than the scales	red-brown
A. procera, noble fir	about 1¼″ long, 4-angled, grooved above, stomatiferous on all surfaces	about 5″ long, the bracts exserted	dark gray, tinged with purple
A. grandis, grand fir	about 1¼″ long, flattened, stomatiferous below, 2-ranked	about 3″ long, the bracts shorter than the scales	gray-brown to reddish brown
A. concolor, white fir	about 2½″ long, flattened, stomatiferous on both sides, obscurely 2-ranked	about 4″ long, the bracts shorter than the scales	dark ashy gray to nearly black, horny

Abies amabilis (Dougl.) Forbes   Pacific silver fir; Cascades fir (SPN)

BOTANICAL FEATURES

Leaves ¾" to 1¼" long, lustrous dark green above, silvery white (stomatiferous) below; flattened in transverse section, deeply grooved above; crowded toward the upper side of the twig, those above often twisted at the base in such a way that they appear to be appressed along the twig; notched or pointed at the apex; needles from cone-bearing branches occasionally somewhat thicker and often also stomatiferous on the upper surface at the apex.
Cones 3½" to 6" long, cylindrical to barrel-shaped, deep purple; *bracts* shorter than the scales, with rounded, poorly defined shoulders, and a broad, wedgelike spinose tip; *seeds* ½" long, yellowish brown, the wings very broad, straw-colored; about 11,300 (8,200–14,900) seeds to the pound, dewinged.
Twigs stout, yellowish brown, puberulous; *buds* ¼" long, subglobose, dark purple, resinous.
Bark, ashy gray, with large, irregular chalky-colored blotches and resin blisters on stems up to 3 ft in diameter; superficially scaly on the largest trunks.

GENERAL DESCRIPTION

Pacific silver fir and noble fir have long been known as "larch," since that name was once commonly applied to lumber manufactured from these two species and shipped to the Orient.

Pacific silver fir is the most abundant fir in the Pacific Northwest and forms extensive pure stands in many localities. It attains its largest proportions in the Olympic Mountains in western Washington, where mature trees vary from 140 to 160 ft in height and 2 to 4 ft in diameter (max. 245° by 8° ft). The bole and root systems are similar to those of other firs of low altitudes, but the crown, particularly of old trees, is usually pyramidal or even spirelike; hence it is readily distinguished from that of either the noble, or grand fir, which is usually domelike. The trees are most abundant on deep moist soil covering slopes of southern and western exposure and grow on a variety of soil types. In mixed stands at low levels this species is commonly associated with Sitka spruce, Douglas-fir, grand fir, western hemlock, and western redcedar; while at higher altitudes it occurs with Engelmann spruce, subalpine and noble firs, Alaska-cedar, western larch, western white pine, and mountain hemlock.

Large seed crops are borne every two or three years, but the percentage of germination is relatively low and vitality is very transient. Seedlings become readily established in either a duff or mineral soil and are very tolerant. In fact, this species is considered as tolerant as western hemlock and western redcedar, and it may be that the true climax forest west of the Cascades and in the Olympics is one of Pacific silver fir. Although excessive shade results in extremely slow growth, excellent recovery is made upon release. Even so, growth is not rapid, and forest trees

Fig. 67. *Abies amabilis.* Pacific silver fir. *1.* Foliage × ½. *2.* Seed × 1. *3.* Cone × ¾. *4.* Cone scale and subtending bract × 1. *5.* Bark.

150 to 250 years of age are often only 15 to 24 in. in diameter. Maturity is attained in about 250 years; trees of a much greater age are seldom found (max. 540 years).

Because of its beautifully shaped crown and dense lustrous foliage, the silver fir is commonly used ornamentally, particularly in Europe. Outbreaks of balsam woolly aphid have reached epidemic proportions in recent years, and have taken a heavy toll. Wood-destroying fungi are common in overmature timber.

RANGE

West Coast, Alaska to Oregon (map, Plate 19). *Altitudinal distribution:* sea level in Alaska and British Columbia; 1,000 to 5,000 (rarely 6,000) ft in Washington and Oregon.

| 1. *Abies* | 2. *Abies* |
| amabilis | magnifica |

PLATE 19

Abies magnifica A. Murr.   California red fir; red fir (SPN)

BOTANICAL FEATURES

Leaves ¾″ to 1¼″ long, silvery-blue to dark blue-green, on new shoots often silvery white; 4-angled, stomatiferous on all sides, usually pointed at the apex, crowded toward the upper side of the branchlets.

Cones 6″ to 9″ long, 2″ to 3″ in diameter, cylindrical to barrel-shaped, purplish brown; *bracts* shorter than the scales, with more or less parallel edges and terminating rather abruptly in a spikelike tip; *seeds* ½″ to ¾″ long, dark brown, with large, broad, reddish-purple terminal wings; about 6,600 (4,000–11,000) seeds to the pound, dewinged.

Twigs light brown; *buds* ¼″ long, ovoid, dark brown, nonresinous, or slightly resinous.

Bark smooth and chalky on young stems; 4″ to 6″ thick on old trunks and divided by deep furrows into rounded or plated reddish-colored ridges.

Fig. 68. *Abies magnifica.* California red fir. *1.* Foliage × ½. *2.* Cone × ¾. *3.* Seed × 1. *4.* Cone scale and subtending bract × 1. *5.* Bark.

This is one of the two largest North American firs and at maturity varies from 150 to 180 ft in height and 4 or 5 ft in diameter (max. 230 by 10 ft). Under forest conditions it is similar in form to noble fir, but is at once distinguished from that species by its reddish-colored bark. The largest trees are found on cool, moist, gravelly, or sandy soils in sheltered ravines and gulches, or on protected mountain slopes, although this species also reaches commercial proportions on much poorer sites. California red fir occurs in pure forests above the white fir belt and in some sections is a common tree at timberline. In mixed stands it is found with many species; in southern Oregon and northern California these include Douglas-fir, sugar pine, and ponderosa pine at lower altitudes, and mountain hemlock and lodgepole pine at higher levels. In the Sierra it is found with white and Shasta firs, lodgepole, western white, ponderosa, Jeffrey, and sugar pines, incense-cedar, giant sequoia, and mountain hemlock. Trees at high elevations standing on exposed ridges frequently lose their upper crowns from the action of gale-force winds. Such destroyed crowns may be replaced by upsweeping lateral branches from just below the broken top. This replacement growth is often distinctive when silhouetted against the sky.

Red fir produces large seed crops every two or three years. Although germination is low (average, 25 percent) seedlings are hardy and survive well. They are moderately tolerant, but older trees cannot meet intensive forest competition and are intermediate in this respect. Growth is never rapid, and trees 250 to 350 years of age are commonly only 20 to 35 in. in diameter. The longevity of this species is not too well known, but trees in excess of 500 years of age have been reported.

RANGE

Southern Oregon and California (map, Plate 19). *Altitudinal distribution:* 5,000 to 10,000 ft.

Abies magnifica var. **shastensis** Lemm.   Shasta red fir

Distinguishing characteristics. *Leaves* and *bark* similar to those of the species. *Cones* about 8 in. long, cylindrical, purple; *bracts* exserted, strongly reflexed, fan-shaped, with large erose shoulders, and terminating in a short mucro or spine.
General description. Aside from variations in cone structure, there are no reliable botanical features by which this variety can be distinguished from California red fir. In typical cones of Shasta red fir, the bracts are much longer than the scales, strongly reflexed, and commonly fan-shaped. Those in cones of red fir are never exserted and are occasionally tapered, rather than flared at the apex. There are intermediate forms between these two types, however, for in some cones the bracts barely protrude, in

others they are more or less exserted but weakly reflexed, and in still others they are more or less acute rather than fanlike at the apex.

The silvical features of Shasta red fir are similar to those of red fir, with which it is often associated.

Range. Southern Cascade, Siskiyou, and Sierra Nevada Mountains, and possibly elsewhere (range imperfectly known). *Altitudinal distribution:* 5,000 to 10,000 ft.

FIG. 69. Cone scale and bract of Shasta red fir × 1.

Abies procera Rehd. [*Abies nobilis* (Dougl.) Lind.]   Noble fir

BOTANICAL FEATURES

Leaves 1″ to 1½″ long, blue-green, 4-angled in transverse section, stomatiferous on all surfaces, grooved above, pointed at the apex, and crowded toward the upper side of the twig; those on sterile branches flexible, somewhat flattened; those on cone-bearing shoots stout, stiff, and nearly equally 4-sided.

Cones 4″ to 6″ long, 1¾″ to 2¼″ in diameter, cylindrical, olive-brown to purple; *bracts* exserted, strongly reflexed, and imbricate, thus completely ensheathing the cone; *seeds* ½″ long, dull brown, often tinged with red; wings lustrous light brown to straw-colored; about 14,600 (11,200–19,300) seeds to the pound, dewinged.

Twigs slender, reddish brown, finely pubescent; *buds* ⅛″ long, blunt, oblong-conic, resinous.

Bark 1″ to 2″ thick, gray and smooth for many years, with prominent resin blisters; eventually dark gray, often tinged with purple and broken up into thin, nearly rectangular plates separated by deep fissures on old trunks.

GENERAL DESCRIPTION

Noble fir, the largest (max. 278° by 9° ft) of the Cascade firs, and the one producing the best timber, has, unfortunately, the smallest range. It was first discovered in 1825 by David Douglas in the Oregon Cascades near the Columbia River. The finest stands have long since been logged, and those which remain are for the most part relatively inaccessible at the present time. Mature trees produce a long, clear, columnar bole, with an essentially domelike crown, and are anchored by a moderately deep and spreading root system. A deep, moist, cool soil is preferred, although good growth is also made on thin, rocky soils if provided with an abundance of moisture. Noble fir usually occurs singly or in small

FIG. 70. *Abies procera*. Noble fir. *1*. Foliage × ½. *2*. Cone × ¾. *3*. Seed × 1. *4*. Cone scale and subtending bract × 1. *5*. Bark. (*Photograph by C. F. Brockman.*)

groups in association with other conifers. Douglas-fir, western hemlock, Pacific silver and subalpine firs, western white pine, and western redcedar are its principal forest associates in northerly portions of its range, while toward the southern limit it also mingles with white fir and sugar pine.

Noble fir is not a prolific seeder. Small quantities of seed are borne annually, but heavy crops are released only at wide and irregular intervals. Average germination is about 24 percent. Unlike other firs of the Pacific Northwest, noble fir is somewhat intolerant, although it may not be as much so as previously reported (127). Growth in both height and diameter is moderately rapid during the first century, as is shown by the fact that trees 100 to 120 years of age are commonly 90 to 120 ft in height and 20 to 24 in. in diameter. Maturity is reached in about 350 years, although trees with 500 to 600 annual rings have been reported.

The bark of noble fir is very thin, and trees of all age classes are easily killed by fire. Overmature trees are frequently damaged by one or more species of decay-producing fungi, including the Indian paint fungus. Damage by insects is rarely severe.

RANGE

Pacific Northwest (map, Plate 20). *Altitudinal distribution:* 2,000 to 5,000 ft.

Abies grandis (Dougl.) Lindl.   Grand fir

BOTANICAL FEATURES

Leaves ½" to 2" long, flattened, lustrous, dark yellow-green above, silvery (stomatiferous) below, those on sterile side branches 2-ranked, the ones from the upper side shorter than the laterals or those from underneath; often crowded on the upper side of cone-bearing branches, blunt or emarginate at the apex.

Cones 2½" to 4¼" long, cylindrical, yellowish green to greenish purple; *bracts* shorter than the scales, the shoulders erose, rounded-truncate or cordate, terminating in a short spikelike tip; *seeds* ⅜" long, pale yellow-brown; wings about ¾" long, straw-colored; about 23,200 (12,600–44,300) seeds to the pound, dewinged.

Twigs slender, brown, puberulous; *buds* ¼" long, subglobose, resinous.

Bark smooth, gray-brown with resin blisters and chalky-white blotches on young stems; reddish brown, plated, or more commonly deeply furrowed or divided into flat ridges on old trunks.

GENERAL DESCRIPTION

Grand fir is one of the two firs found in the northern Rocky Mountain region, and one of four common to the forests of the Pacific Northwest. Except in the southern part of its range where it is often confused with

Fɪɢ. 71. *Abies grandis*. Grand fir. *1*. Foliage × ½. *2*. Cone × ¾. *3*. Cone scales and subtending bracts × 1. *4*. Seeds × 1. *5*. Bark.

white fir, this species is readily distinguished from other firs by its needles, which are distinctly two-ranked. Trees in coastal forests reach 140 to 160 ft in height and 2 to 4 ft in diameter (max. 250 by 7° ft), but in the Rocky Mountains they are rarely more than 120 ft high or 3 ft in diameter. Mature trees are featured by long, clear, columnar boles and domelike crowns; the roots are deep and spreading. Grand fir occurs most frequently on deep, moist alluvial soils in gulches, along streams, and on gentle mountain slopes. While it not infrequently forms limited pure stands, it is much more abundant in mixed hardwood and coniferous forests. Douglas-fir, western larch, and ponderosa and lodgepole pines are its common associates in the Rocky Mountains; in the Bitterroot Mountains to the west it occurs with western larch, western white pine, Engelmann spruce, and subalpine fir. At sea level and low elevations in the Cascade Mountains of western Washington and Oregon, grand fir mingles with Sitka spruce, Pacific silver fir, western redcedar, western hemlock, Douglas-fir, Oregon ash, red alder, bigleaf maple, and black cottonwood. Redwood is an associated species at the southern limit of its range, and at higher elevations to the south, grand fir occurs with Shasta red, white, noble, and subalpine firs, and western white pine.

The seeding habits of grand fir are similar to those of white fir (see page 165). Grand fir is a tolerant tree, but it is less so than western hemlock or western redcedar. Early height growth in Idaho often compares favorably with that of western white pine and on the Pacific coast with that of Douglas-fir. Maturity is reached in about 200 years.

Overmature trees are frequent hosts of the brown stringy rot fungus, and young trees are commonly attacked by the eastern spruce budworm.

1. *Abies procera.*   2. *Abies grandis.*

PLATE 20

RANGE

Pacific Northwest and Inland Empire (map, Plate 20).

Abies concolor (Gord. and Glend.) Lindl.   White fir

Leaves 2″ to 3″ long, silvery-blue to silvery-green, extending at nearly right angles from all sides of the twig or more or less obscurely 2-ranked; flattened, stomatiferous above and below, rounded or acute at the apex.

Cones 3″ to 5″ long, oblong, olive-green to purple; *bracts* shorter than the scales, with short, broad erose shoulders, and a spikelike tip; *seeds* ½″ long, yellow-brown, the wings rose-tinted; about 15,000 (8,200–27,200) seeds to the pound, dewinged.

Twigs moderately stout, yellowish green to brownish green; *buds* ¼″ long, sub-globose, yellowish brown, resinous.

Bark 4″ to 7″ thick on old trunks, ashy gray and divided by deep irregular furrows into thick, horny flattened ridges; young stems with conspicuous resin blisters.

GENERAL DESCRIPTION

White fir has the largest range of any of the commercial western firs. It attains its maximum development in the Sierra, where it becomes 130 to 150 ft in height and 3 to 4 ft in diameter (max. 200 by 8* ft). The Rocky Mountain trees are usually much smaller and rarely attain a height of 100 ft or a diameter of 15 to 30 in. In youth the crown is often elongated and clothes a slightly tapered bole from one-half to two-thirds of its length. Older trees usually have a domelike crown unless malformed by the fir dwarf mistletoe. The root system is shallow and wide-spreading. White fir occurs most abundantly on deep, rich, moist but well-drained, gravelly, or sandy loam-covered slopes and benches with a northerly exposure. However, this species requires less moisture than other western firs and possesses a remarkable ability to exist on dry, thin layers of partially decomposed granite or nearly barren rocks. Trees on such sites however, are small and often malformed.

Pure stands of white fir are seldom encountered, except as second-growth, but forests comprising up to 80 percent of this species are fairly numerous in some parts of the Sierra Nevada. Sugar, ponderosa, and Jeffrey pines, incense-cedar, California red fir, and Douglas-fir are common associates. Forests composed of sugar pine and white fir are not uncommon, and in the Canadian zone, a red fir–white fir combination occurs quite frequently. White fir–ponderosa pine stands may be found east of the Sierra. White fir is also found with grand fir in the Cascade Mountains of southern Oregon, where intermediate forms exist between the two species, and where specific identification of either is sometimes difficult.

Good seed crops occur at about 5-year intervals. The seeds show transient viability, and germination averages about 30 percent. Nearly any soil except heavy clay makes a satisfactory seedbed.

Seedlings develop readily under the canopy of old trees and are even

FIG. 72. *Abies concolor*. White fir. *1*. Foliage × ½. *2*. Cone × ¾. *3*. Seeds adhering to cone scale × 1. *4*. Cone scale and subtending bract × 1. *5*. Bark. (*Photograph by Emanuel Fritz.*)

166

tolerant in later life provided they receive ample supplies of moisture. Late spring freezes often decimate seedlings, and reproduction is usually sparse on burns and logged-off lands until a cover of shrubs and numerous herbaceous species has become well established. Growth in both height and diameter is usually slow for the first 25 to 30 years, but after this period it is comparable to or even faster than that of its associated species. Growth rate gradually diminishes after the first century, and maturity is attained in about 300 years. Trees more than 350 years old are seldom encountered.

White fir is severely damaged by mistletoe, while the fir engraver beetle causes extremely heavy damage in some areas; heart rots are quite prevalent in others.

This fir is commonly used as an ornamental in many parts of the United States, particularly in the East. Some of the very glaucous forms produce a beautiful effect when planted formally with certain of the more somber evergreens.

RANGE

Western United States (map, Plate 21). *Altitudinal distribution:* 6,000 to 11,000 ft in the Rockies; elsewhere lower limit sometimes below 3,000 ft.

PLATE 21. *Abies concolor.*

Abies lasiocarpa (Hook.) Nutt.   Subalpine fir

Distinguishing characteristics. *Leaves* 1″ to 1¾″ long, pale blue-green, stomatiferous on both surfaces. *Cones* 2¼″ to 4″ long, cylindrical, purplish gray to nearly black; *bracts* shorter than the scales, with erose rounded shoulders and long spine-like tips. *Bark* smooth and chalky on young stems; furrowed and scaly on old trunks.

General description. Subalpine fir was first observed by Lewis and Clark when they crossed the Bitterroot Mountains in Montana and Idaho in September, 1805. It is largely restricted to high western forests, and on exposed sites at timberline it is often reduced to a grotesque shrub of sprawling or prostrate habit. On protected sites of good quality, however, trees attain a height of 60 to 100 ft with a diameter of 18 to 24 in. (max. 160 by 6° ft), and under average conditions develop dense,

PINACEAE   167

Fig. 73. *Abies lasiocarpa*. Subalpine fir. *1.* Foliage × ½. *2.* Cone × ¾. *3.* Cone scale and subtending bract × 1. *4.* Seeds × 1. *5.* Bark. (*Photograph by British Columbia Forest Service.*)

narrowly pyramidal crowns and symmetrical, moderately tapering boles which are often clear for 30 to 40 ft. Open-grown trees, particularly in subalpine meadows, feature excessively tapered trunks and dense spirelike crowns of great beauty that commonly extend to the ground.

Subalpine fir forms limited pure stands but also occurs in mixed forests. It is an almost constant companion of Engelmann spruce in the Rocky Mountains, although to the north it is also found with mountain hemlock, lodgepole, whitebark, and limber pines, and subalpine larch; farther south bristlecone pine, corkbark fir, and quaking aspen are also associated species. In the Bitterroot Mountains of northern Idaho, where it attains large size if not its maximum development, it mingles with grand fir, western white pine, Engelmann spruce, and western larch. Mountain hemlock, whitebark pine, and Alaska-cedar are its principal companions in high alpine forests along the Pacific Coast.

Because of inaccessibility, subalpine fir is currently of little commercial importance except locally, but serves principally as a cover tree on high watersheds.

Fig. 74. Subalpine fir.

Range. Western North America. *Altitudinal distribution:* sea level to 3,000 ft in Alaska; 2,000 to 7,000 ft in British Columbia; 2,000 to 7,900 ft in Washington and Oregon; 3,500 to 9,500 ft in the Rocky Mountains.

Abies lasiocarpa var. arizonica (Merriam) Lemm. [*Abies arizonica* Merriam]   Corkbark fir

Corkbar fir is a small tree of the southern Rocky Mountains and occurs on thin gravelly or rocky soils at elevations of from 8,000 to 10,000 ft. It is accorded specific rank by several taxonomists and as such is given the technical name *Abies arizonica* Merriam. Typical corkbark fir is readily separated from other balsam firs by its thick, corky bark, which is free of resin blisters. The foliage of corkbark fir is similar to that of subalpine fir, but the cones of these two species sometimes show minor differences. In subalpine fir the cone scales are mostly wedge-shaped, while in corkbark fir they are often halberdlike at the base. There appear to be a number of integrading forms wherein these differences are not consistent and hence cannot always be relied upon for specific separation.

In southern Colorado, corkbark fir replaces subalpine fir as an associate of Engelmann spruce and as such is logged and distributed as white fir. However, the relative inaccessibility of this species, together with its smaller size and limited distribution, prevents it from ever becoming commercially important except locally.

Abies bracteata D. Don   Bristlecone fir

Bristlecone fir is a small to medium-sized tree of rare occurrence scattered through the forests of central western California between elevations of 2,000 and 5,000 ft (Santa Lucia Mountains of Monterey County). The needles are flat, 1 to 2 in. long, sharp-pointed, and are arranged in several ranks. The most distinctive feature of this species, however, is the cone, which has spiny, exserted bracts often 1 to 2 in. or more in length.

Taxodiaceae: The Redwood family

During the mild, humid climate of the Miocene epoch, the Taxodiaceae were very abundant and formed extensive forests throughout the world, particularly in the Northern Hemisphere. Many forms have long since become extinct, however; and at present the family comprises but 9 genera (5 monotypes) and 13 to 15 species. *Athrotaxis* with 3 species is found in the mountainous forests of Tasmania, while *Cunninghamia* includes 2 species, one endemic to China, the other to Taiwan. *Cryptomeria, Taiwania, Sciadopitys,* and *Glyptostrobus,* all monotypic, are scattered through the forests of eastern and southern Asia, including Japan and Taiwan. *Metasequoia,* the most recently discovered genus (monotypic), is found in central China (179, 180). The two American genera, *Taxodium* and *Sequoia,* include trees noted for great size and length of life.

Leaves persistent or deciduous, spirally arranged (opposite in *Metasequoia*), linear, or ovate to awl-shaped.
Flowers with bracts and ovuliferous scales partially fused; ovules erect, 2 to 12 on each scale; all species monoecious.
Cones woody, composed of several peltate scales; maturing in 1 or 2 years; *seeds* with 2 or 3 lateral wings.

CONSPECTUS OF NATIVE GENERA

Genus	Leaves	Cones	Seeds
Sequoia	persistent	ovoid, with 2 to 9 seeds on each scale, subglobose, with 2 seeds on each scale	ovoid, laterally 2-winged
Taxodium	lateral branchlets with their attached leaves deciduous (except in 1 species)	subglobose, with 2 seeds on each scale	unequally 3-angled, laterally 3-winged

SEQUOIA Endl.   Sequoia

This group is of ancient lineage and flourished during the Cretaceous and Tertiary periods; about 40 fossil forms have been described. While many forms, now extinct, were widely scattered through the forests of the Northern Hemisphere, the modern genus consists of but two species, both of which are found in relatively small areas in California.[1] The name Sequoia commemorates Sequoiah, a talented half-breed Cherokee Indian who developed the first alphabet used by his tribe.

BOTANICAL FEATURES OF THE GENUS

Leaves persistent, spirally arranged, of two sorts, respectively: (1) linear and 2-ranked, or (2) ovate-lanceolate, in several ranks, and more or less appressed.
Flowers solitary; *staminate* strobili ovoid to oblong, composed of numerous spirally arranged filaments, each subtended by 2 to 5 pendent anthers; *ovulate* cones consisting of several peltate scales, each bearing 3 to 12 erect ovules. Both species monoecious.
Fruit a pendent, ovoid, woody cone reaching full size the first season but

---

[1] One of these species also extends into southwestern Oregon.

Fig. 75. Scene in Jedediah Smith Redwoods State Park, Del Norte Co., California. (*Photograph by Richard St. Barbe Baker.*)

in one species requiring an additional year for seed maturation; composed of several woody, peltate, or wedge-shaped scales which are transversely depressed or wrinkled at the apex, or armed with a small mucro; *seeds* 2 to 9 on each scale, ovoid-oblong, laterally compressed and laterally 2-winged; *cotyledons* usually 2 or 4.

Species	Leaves	Cones
S. *sempervirens*, redwood	linear, 2-ranked, dark yellow-green	about 1″ long, maturing at the end of one season
S. *gigantea*, giant sequoia	ovate-lanceolate, in several ranks, blue-green	about 2½″ long, reaching full size the 1st season, but the seeds maturing the following year.

Sequoia sempervirens (D. Don) Endl. Redwood

BOTANICAL FEATURES

Leaves spirally arranged, of two sorts: (1) those on lateral branches ½″ to 1″ long, linear or lanceolate, 2-ranked; *apex* acute; *base* truncate and twisted; (2) on tips of leaders and fertile branches about ¼″ long, oblong to acicular, in several ranks; *apex*

FIG. 76. *Sequoia sempervirens.* Redwood. *1.* Foliage × ¾. *2.* Staminate flowers × 1¼. *3.* Ovulate flower × 1¼. *4.* Open cone × ¾. *5.* Seeds × 1¼. Bark, see Fig. 75.

incurved, sharp-pointed; *surfaces* dark yellow-green above, with a broad band or stomata on either side of the midrib below; *resin canals* 3, external.
Flowers as for the genus, the ovulate with 15 to 20 pointed scales.
Cones ¾″ to 1″ in diameter, ovoid to subglobose, reddish brown, with 15 to 20 peltate, wrinkled scales, maturing at the end of one season; *seeds* ¹⁄₁₆″ long, light brown, with narrow lateral wings; about 122,000 (59,000–300,000) seeds to the pound.
Buds globose, covered by several acute, imbricate scales.
Bark reddish brown to cinnamon red, deeply furrowed, fibrous, 3″ to 12″ thick.

GENERAL DESCRIPTION

Redwood is a massive tree commonly 200 to 275 ft in height and 8 to 12 ft in diameter (max. about 370 [1] by 20 ft). From a relatively shallow wide-spreading root system rises a clear, impressively tall, buttressed, and somewhat tapering trunk which supports a short, narrow, irregularly conical crown.

Redwood is restricted to a number of separated areas through the California "fog belt," a narrow strip of coast about 450 miles in length and from 20 to 40 miles in width, extending from extreme southwestern Oregon near the California border to Monterey south of San Francisco Bay. Its eastern limits appear to be governed by atmospheric moisture; inland, beyond points where the ocean fogs are cut off by the high coastal mountain ridges, redwood disappears.

Redwood is the dominating species throughout this belt; forests containing 80 percent or more of redwood are extensive, and on moist benches and alluvial bottoms 90 percent or even more of the standing timber is redwood. Douglas-fir, Sitka spruce, grand fir, western hemlock, tanoak, Pacific madrone, red alder, and California-laurel are common associates.

The redwood is a prolific annual seeder, but a large percentage of the seeds are empty or tannin-filled, and average germination may not be more than 10 percent. Although seeds will germinate on moist duff, the young trees can scarcely penetrate it and usually die from drying out. Fresh mineral soil is best. This may result when a large tree falls and the upturned roots strip away the overlying litter and humus. On alluvial flats where the best stands of redwood are found, periodic floods may deposit from several inches to 2 ft of fresh silt, which is soon covered with a thick growth of seedlings. Logging and fire also uncover extensive areas for new reproduction. Unlike nearly all other conifers, redwood stumps produce vigorous sprouts which reach tree size in a remarkably short time.

[1] Because of difficulties in determining the exact ground level, the roughness of terrain, and other problems inherent in measuring trees of such great height, it is probable that an error of ±5 feet must be accepted even when the best instruments are used. According to Frederick A. Meyer, California State Park Forester, Dr. Paul Zinke, School of Forestry, measured a redwood 369.2 ft tall, growing near the "Founders Tree" in Humboldt Redwoods State Park. There may be taller trees not yet measured.

On the best sites, 20-year-old sprouts attain an average height of 50 ft and a d.b.h. of 8 in., and in 50 years they commonly reach merchantable proportions. Where coppice growth is removed, a second generation of equally vigorous sprouts soon makes its appearance about the collar of the new stumps, and ultimately, they too reach commercial size.

The original redwood forests covered about 1,950,000 acres. Most of those which remain are privately owned; however, the state of California has acquired some 50,000 acres of virgin redwood forests which are administered as state parks. The only important federally owned tract has been Muir Woods National Monument north of San Francisco, but the new Redwood National Park greatly expands federal holdings.

The largest stands of timber in the world are found in the redwood belt. On alluvial bottomlands bordering the Smith and Eel Rivers through Humboldt and Del Norte Counties in north coastal California, where redwood attains its maximum development, mature stands average 125,000 to 150,000 ft B.M. to the acre, and some river flats have yielded as high as 1,000,000 ft of scaled logs per acre. Jepson (189) reported a single tree which upon being sawn into lumber yielded 480,000 ft B.M., excluding waste.

The rate of growth of redwood both in height and in diameter measurably exceeds that of most American timber-producing species, and research in the second-growth forests indicates that no other species, with the possible exception of eastern cottonwood, is capable of producing as large a tree or as great a volume of wood in the same period of time. Jepson (loc. cit.) states that the leaders of open-grown trees 4 to 10 years of age commonly elongate 2 to 6 ft a year and that the annual terminal shoots for these same trees are rarely less than 2 ft in length during the next 20 to 30 years. Redwood is remarkably tolerant, and trees which have been suppressed for protracted lengths of time quickly recover once they are released. This even applies to old trees. When a 1,000-year-old tree was partially freed from competition, the ring count changed from 30 to 6 per inch (127). It is difficult to ascertain at what age redwood matures since old trees exhibit from 400 to 1,800 growth rings.[1]

Most of the damage in redwood forests is traceable either directly or indirectly to fire. The bark on old trees is very thick and hence offers considerable resistance, but young reproduction is readily killed even by a moderately light ground fire. Most, if not all, of the dry rot found in the

[1] According to Professor Emanuel Fritz of the School of Forestry, University of California, the great ages sometimes reported for redwood trees are grossly exaggerated. On a 30-acre plot containing 567 trees he found only 17 trees over 1,000 years of age, the oldest 1,380 years. He also reports having seen several trees in other locations which were about 2,200 years old. Also, a tree of this age was cut many years ago in Humboldt Redwoods State Park.

basal portions of old trees had its inception near fire scars or seams. Recurring fires are responsible for hollow butts or "goose pens" so common in old growth, and while neither heart rot nor the formation of goose pens actually kills trees, both serve to weaken them materially, and much high-grade saw timber is also destroyed.

Burls, those small to very large excrescences which appear along the bole of many trees, are also a feature of this species. The large ones, if solid, are removed from logs and cut into beautifully figured veneers. Smaller ones are frequently turned on the lathe into trays, nut bowls, and similar objects, or, because of their ability to sprout when placed in water, are offered for sale along with other redwood novelties. A perfume extracted from the leaves is another product of this species offered to the tourist trade.

RANGE

West Coast (southwestern Oregon and California) (map, Plate 22). *Altitudinal distribution:* sea level to about 2,500 ft.

PLATE 22. 1. *Sequoia gigantea;* □
2. *Sequoia sempervirens;* ⊟

Sequoia gigantea (Lindl.) Decne.[1] [*Sequoia washingtoniana* (Winsl.) Sudw.] Giant sequoia; bigtree

BOTANICAL FEATURES

Leaves on leaders, ½″ long, lanceolate; on lateral and lower branches, ¼″ long, ovate, blue-green; spreading or appressed; turning brown at the end of the 2d or 3d season, but persistent for several years.

Cones 2″ to 3½″ in length, ovoid-oblong, reaching full size the first season after emerging from the bud, but requiring an additional year for the seed to mature; and persistent, mostly unopened, for a number of years; *cone scales* 25 to 40, peltate or

[1] Buchholz (54), with considerable justification, has made a new monotypic genus of this taxon with the species name *Sequoiadendron giganteum* (Lindl.) Buchholz.

wedge-shaped; *apophyses* rugose, depressed; *seeds* ¼″ long, straw-colored, laterally broadly winged; usually not shed until the next October after maturity, and then irregularly for several years; about 91,000 (54,000–132,000) seeds to the pound.
Buds naked.
Bark 12″ to 24″ thick on old trunks, cinnamon-red, fibrous, divided into broad rounded ridges by deep fissures; very fire resistant.

GENERAL DESCRIPTION

The giant sequoias, or bigtrees, often referred to as "the sentinels of the Sierra," are numbered among the largest and oldest of living organisms, and some of them may have been 2,000 to 2,500 years old at the birth of Christ.[1] In their presence, all sense of proportion is lost, and trees which may be 4 to 10 ft in diameter appear small by comparison. It is small wonder, therefore, that a feeling of reverence comes over one upon entering a grove of these patriarchs whose gigantic red trunks are like the supports of some vast outdoor cathedral. The emotions aroused by the silent ageless majesty of these great trees are akin to those of primitive man for whom they would have been objects of worship, and it is unlikely that centuries of scientific training will ever completely efface this elemental feeling.

Giant sequoia does not attain the height of either the redwood or the Douglas-fir, but greatly surpasses either of them in diameter. The General Sherman tree in Sequoia National Park, for example, averages 30.7 ft in diameter at its base, 27.4 ft at a point 8 ft from the ground, and 17.5 ft at a height of 60 ft. The total height, however, is only 272 ft (76). In general the larger giant sequoias commonly attain a diameter of 10 to 15 ft and a height of 250 to 280 ft (max. probably about 347 by 37.3 ft).[2] A better appreciation of their size perhaps may be gained when it is discovered that a man of normal height could lie crosswise on the largest branch (7 ft in diameter) of the General Sherman tree and not be seen from the ground 130 ft. below. Furthermore, it has been estimated that the weight of this forest monarch's trunk is between 1,300 and 1,400 tons.

It has already been mentioned that various species of *Sequoia* were once widely distributed, and it is of more than passing interest that the giant sequoia, and even the redwood, are now so restricted in range. In terms of geological time, the former may be thought of as making its last

[1] John Muir studied a deep burn cavity in one big tree, and estimated its age at about 4,000 years. Fry and White (130) indicate that an even greater age may be attained. See also bristlecone pine, p. 71.
[2] According to C. A. Harwell (*Yosemite Nature Notes*, **10**, no. 6, 1931) the Clothespin tree in the Mariposa Grove is 293 ft high and is the tallest standing giant sequoia upon which accurate measurements have been made. Other tall specimens of this species are the Hart, Massachusetts, and Columbia trees which are 278, 280, and 290 ft in height, respectively.

Fig. 77. *Sequoia gigantea*. Giant sequoia. *1.* Cones and foliage × ¾. *2.* Foliage × 1½. *3.* Seeds × 1¼. *4.* Bark. (*Photograph by U.S. Forest Service.*)

stand in scattered groves along the western middle slopes of the Sierra. How many more tens of centuries the giant sequoia might maintain itself is problematical, as is also the effect of man in clearing the lesser vegetation around certain individual trees. It is known that any general disturbance of the forest litter under the bigtrees not infrequently results in the death of many small fibrous roots; and their death, if in large numbers, is sooner or later reflected in the effectiveness of the whole anchorage system. Even in the primeval forest it is not certain but that the final overthrow of the largest trees is caused by the gradual shifting of the center of gravity until the balance of the massive trunk is upset, since trees have fallen on days when there was little or no wind.

Insects and fungi cause but minor damage, and no large bigtree killed by them has ever been found. Fires have in the past eroded the bark at ground level, and sometimes as much as three-fourths of the circumference has been destroyed, but the tree still lives on. Lightning causes spectacular damage to certain individuals.

FIG. 78. Longitudinal section through cone of giant sequoia × ¾. (Note spiral arrangement of the peltate scales and the large woody core.)

The principal associates of giant sequoia include sugar, ponderosa, and Jeffrey pines, California red and white firs, and incense-cedar.

Buchholz (52) worked out the life history of the giant sequoia seed cone. He noted that pollination, fertilization, and growth to full size all take place the first season after emergence of the ovulate flower from the bud (the former is present in embryonic form the previous season). While full size is thus attained in one season, a second year elapses before the embryos are developed and the seed matures. Perhaps the most remarkable feature, however, is that the cone remains green and usually closed for as many as 20 years after maturity. During this time the peduncle develops growth rings (with occasional lapses). Few seeds are shed until the cone dies or is detached from the tree.

For so large a tree, the sequoia possesses what might seem to be very small seeds, furnishing a good illustration of the fact that there is no correlation between the sizes of trees and their seeds. Another interesting feature is the presence in the cones of a powdery dark red pigment which is released together with the seeds when the cones are dried artificially. When dissolved in water, this substance furnishes a nonfading writing fluid or ink. The natural function of the pigment, which has a high tannin content, is not well known, but seeds shed normally are always more or less coated with a thin water-deposited layer of this substance. Experiments seem to indicate a slightly higher percentage of germination for seeds treated naturally or artificially with solutions of the pigment, while the vigor of seedlings developed from such seeds is somewhat greater than from untreated samples (130).

Although the giant sequoia produces large quantities of seeds almost every year, the percentage of germination averages only about 25 percent, and bare earth is necessary for seedling development. At one time, the trail- and road-building activities of the Civilian Conservation Corps in the giant sequoia belt did much to stimulate natural reproduction, and where mineral soil was laid bare, many young trees appeared.

The securing of seeds in quantity would be a problem were it not for the activities of squirrels, which cut from the trees the otherwise persistent cones. The extracted seeds, especially when treated with the pigment solution and dried, can be stored under proper conditions for 20 years or more without losing their viability.

The seedlings develop a short taproot, but after a few years this ceases to develop; thereafter the tree is characterized by a relatively shallow wide-spreading system of laterals. The crown of young trees is dense and conical, with the branches reaching to the ground. Later the much-tapered bole clears itself of lower limbs, while the crown still maintains its juvenile shape; eventually very old trees become rounded or irregular in outline.

This species is commonly used ornamentally along the Pacific Coast, and also in some of the eastern states and abroad.

The wood is exceedingly brittle, but like that of the redwood, durable almost beyond belief, and trees which fell more than a thousand years ago are still perfectly sound, with the exception of the sapwood which soon decays. From trees of this sort have been obtained the oldest records of forest fires; and the story of early climatic conditions as told by a study of the growth rings has been of interest to climatologists the world over.

Although the giant sequoia no longer contributes much lumber, the length of description seems deserved, since this species is without doubt the most famous tree of North America, if not of the entire world.[1]

[1] For an account of other giant trees of the world see article by Tiemann (354).

In separated groves along the Sierra Nevada Mountains (map, Plate 22). *Altitudinal distribution:* mostly from 4,500 to 7,500 ft.

TAXODIUM Rich.   Baldcypress

This genus was once widely distributed in the prehistoric forests of Europe and North America. Now, however, there are but two species, *T. distichum* (L.) Rich., native to the southeastern United States, and *T. mucronatum* Ten., Montezuma baldycypress, found from Guatemala through Mexico to southwestern Texas. A tree of the last-named species standing near Oaxaca, Mexico, has a circumference of approximately 115 ft [1] and has been estimated to be between 4,000 and 5,000 years old. The height, however, is not proportionate, being only between 130 and 140 ft (82).

BOTANICAL FEATURES OF THE GENUS

Leaves deciduous or persistent; either (1) linear-lanceolate and 2-ranked, sometimes conspicuously stomatiferous below, or (2) nearly scalelike and appressed (mostly on fertile branches).

Flowers unisexual; *staminate* flowers in drooping panicles, each composed of 6 to 8 stamens opposite in 2 ranks; *ovulate* cones subglobose, comprising several spirally arranged peltate scales, each bearing 2 erect, basal ovules; all species monoecious.

Fruit an obovoid or globose woody cone maturing in 1 season, comprising several peltate scales; *scales* 4-angled in cross section, resinous-glandular on the inner surface, and terminating in a short, transverse mucro; *seeds* irregularly 3-angled and 3-winged.

Buds subglobose, covered with several sharp-pointed, imbricate scales.

Taxodium distichum (L.) Rich.   Baldcypress; common baldcypress (SPN); southern cypress (Tr)

[1] During the summer of 1948, Dr. Paul H. Fluck measured the circumference, at 4½ ft above the ground, of the giant Montezuma baldcypress near Oaxaca. The measurement was repeated several times with the tape stretched tightly, and the figure obtained was between 114 and 115 ft. Previous measurements of this great tree have presumably been made at ground level, or by tacking the tape in the deeply embedded bays of the tree. Furthermore, it is not easy to translate circumference into diameter, since the trunk of the tree is somewhat oval in cross section, and the shorter diameter is considerably less than the longer one. Professor Emanuel Fritz is of the opinion that

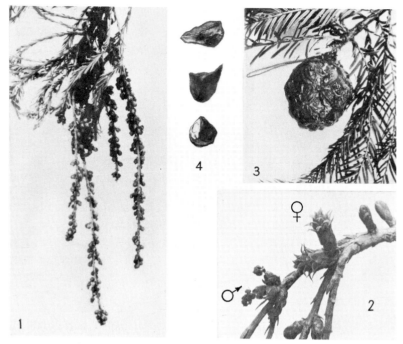

Fig. 79. *Taxodium distichum.* Baldcypress. *1.* Staminate flowers × ¾. *2.* Ovulate flowers × 1. *3.* Mature cone and foliage × ¾. *4.* Seeds × 1.

BOTANICAL FEATURES

Leaves ½″ to ¾″ long,[1] linear, 2-ranked, yellow-green. Lateral branchlets with their attached leaves deciduous, the terminal shoots bearing axillary buds, persistent.
Cones ¾″ to 1″ in diameter, subglobose, rugose, usually disintegrating at maturity; seeds irregular in shape, about 4,800 (1,300–9,100) to the pound.
Bark variable; fibrous and up to 1½″ in thickness, or scaly and thin, reddish brown, but often weathering to an ashy-gray color on the surface.

---

this tree may have resulted from the natural grafting together of several trees originally planted close together. He states that, according to Professor C. Conzatti, the tree's age is probably about 2,000 years.
[1] Shorter and more scalelike on fertile branchlets (see generic description), in pondcypress, *T. distichum* var. *nutans* (Ait.) Sweet, previously called *T. ascendens* Brongn., the leaves are appressed in several ranks and are mostly short and more scalelike than in typical baldcypress. However, these features are variable, and intergrading forms are not uncommon.

This species is most distinctive of southern conifers. In the dim light of an old-growth baldcypress forest, the massive, often ashy-gray columnar trunks with their peculiarly swollen, fluted bases, and branches bearded with Spanish moss, produce an unforgettable impression.

Baldcypress is a large tree, 100 to 120 ft high and 3 to 5 ft in diameter (max. 150 by 12 ft).[1] The trunk of young trees shows considerable taper and supports an open, narrowly pyramidal crown; with age the bole becomes more cylindrical and the crown irregularly flattened. The root system is the most distinctive feature of the tree. It consists of several descending roots providing anchorage, and many shallow, wide-spreading roots from which rise, especially on wetter sites, the peculiar conical structures called "knees." What function these outgrowths may have is not known. Although they have been called aerating organs, their removal seems to have no measurable effect on subsequent tree growth. Baldcypress is exceptionally windfirm, and even on the most unstable silts it is successful in rearing its massive bulk, which even winds of hurricane strength rarely overturn (242).

[1] These maximum dimensions are given by Sargent (312). According to the A.F.A., the largest standing baldcypress is near Sharon, Tenn. This trees is 122 ft high, with a circumference of 39 ft 8 in. at 4½ ft about the ground. Another large baldcypress with a comparable circumference of 35 ft 7 in. stands near Orlando, Fla.

FIG. 80. Old-growth baldcypress. (*Photograph by U.S. Forest Service.*)

Best growth of this species is made on deep, fine, sandy loams with plenty of moisture in the surface layers and moderately good drainage. Baldcypress is rarely found, however, on such areas, presumably because of hardwood competition, and in contrast is typical of permanent swamps, where it forms extensive pure stands. In such situations it has few associates, but probably the most common is water tupelo; on slightly higher ground the bottomland hardwood species such as sweetgum, green ash, the soft maples, American elm, and certain of the oaks, are more aggressive, and the baldcypress eventually disappears. This species, although preeminently adapted to freshwater swamps, extends into the coastal region of brackish tidewater, where it makes poor growth.

Reproduction by seeds is persistent but not widespread because their weight precludes distribution by wind. Germination averages about 40 percent, but an abundant supply of moisture is necessary during one to three months after dispersal.

Trees up to 40 to 60 years old sprout vigorously from the stump, and even much older trees often produce a few sprouts. Baldcypress is apparently more tolerant than such species as water tupelo, swamp cottonwood, and sweetgum, but less so than the oaks, soft maples, slash pine, and Atlantic white-cedar.

Baldcypress has been considered a slow-growing tree, but studies of old stands do not indicate what may be expected of young trees, which often reach a foot in height the first season, nearly 2 ft the second, and in 10 years as much as 18 ft. Second-growth trees 100 years old are about 100 ft tall and 15 to 20 in. in diameter. Trees in virgin stands were 400 to 600 years old, and certain ones in South Carolina and Georgia were reported to attain ages of up to 1,200 years. Because of its great durability (resistance to decay), the wood of baldcypress is often known in the trade as the "wood everlasting."

RANGE

Atlantic and Gulf Coastal Plains (map, Plate 23). *Altitudinal distribution: 90 percent of this species is within an elevation of 100 ft above sea level;*

PLATE 23. *Taxodium distichum.*

in the Mississippi Valley 500 ft is the limit, and in western Texas 1,000 to 1,750 ft.

Baldcypress has been planted far north of its natural range, in several of the northern states, and southern Canada. A few 75-year-old trees are growing in a moist sheltered valley in Syracuse, N.Y. The largest is about 70 ft tall and 18 in. D.B.H. This tree is near a spring hole, and from the shallow roots that extend toward it some 30 knees are growing, one of them 30 ft away from the base of the trunk. These trees have withstood minimum winter temperatures of −20 to −30 deg F.

Cupressaceae: The Cypress or Cedar [1] family

The Cypress family includes 15 genera, 6 of which are monotypic, and about 140 species, widely scattered throughout the world, and occurring abundantly in forests of both the Northern and Southern Hemispheres. *Juniperus*, the largest genus, includes about 60 species.[2] The Cupressaceae are represented in the United States by 26 species included in 5 genera, namely, *Libocedrus, Thuja, Chamaecyparis, Cupressus,* and *Juniperus.*

BOTANICAL FEATURES OF THE FAMILY

Leaves persistent, scalelike or awl-shaped, the former mostly decussate, the later often ternate; both types present on the same individual in certain species.

Flowers with bract and ovuliferous scale completely united; ovules erect, 2 to many on each cone scale; the species monoecious, or in some genera dioecious.

Cones woody, leathery, or semifleshy; few-scaled, the scales opposite, peltate, or thin and flattened, the basal pairs often sterile; *seeds* laterally winged or wingless.

LIBOCEDRUS Endl.   Incense-cedar

Libocedrus is a small genus of evergreen trees consisting of about 10 species encircling the Pacific Ocean in the forests of western North America, South America, New Zealand, New Caledonia, New Guinea, southern China, and Taiwan. *L. chilensis* Endl. and *L. tetragona* Endl. are endemic to the Chilean Andes Mountains. Both species are commercially important in South America and furnish timber to the local trade; the

[1] Although the true cedars are included in the genus *Cedrus* of the Pinaceae, many species in the Cupressaceae are known at least locally by the name "cedar."
[2] According to some writers, 40 species, with the others rated as varieties.

Genus	Leaves	Fruit	Branchlets
Libocedrus	scalelike, oblong-obovate, in whorls of 4	oblong with 6 thin, leathery scales; matures in 1 season	flattened
Thuja	scalelike, decussate, lateral pairs keeled, facial pairs flattened, often glandular	ovoid-oblong, with 8 to 12 thin leathery to woody scales; matures in 1 season	flattened
Cupressus	scalelike, decussate, often glandular	globose, with 6 to 12 woody, bossed, peltate scales; matures in 2 seasons	4-angled
Chamaecyparis	same as above	globose, with 4 to 8 leathery to semifleshy peltate scales; matures in 1 or 2 seasons	flattened
Juniperus	dimorphic; the scalelike leaves decussate; the subulate leaves ternate or occasionally decussate	globose, berrylike, composed of 3 to 8 semifleshy scales; matures in 1 to 3 seasons	4-angled

former is used ornamentally in several countries of the Northern Hemisphere. *L. bidwillii* is an important timber tree of New Zealand. *L. macrolepis* B. and H. is a large tree of southern China and Formosa. Logs of this species buried in past geologic ages have been perfectly preserved, and these are not infrequently "mined" and sawed into boards to be used for coffin stock. A single native species, *L. decurrens* Torr., the incense-cedar, is found in western United States, and to avoid repetition, the generic description as such is omitted.

Libocedrus decurrens Torr.   Incense-cedar

BOTANICAL FEATURES

Leaves ⅛″ to ½″ long, lustrous, dark yellow-green, oblong-ovate, in whorls of 4, decurrent and adnate to the twigs except at the tips; glandular, exhaling an aromatic odor when crushed; laterals keeled, almost wholly ensheathing the facial pairs.
Flowers terminal; *staminate* with 12 to 16 decussate, filamentous, 4-celled anthers; *ovulate cones* composed of 6 scales, 2 bearing 2 erect basal ovules; all species monoecious.

Cones ¾″ to 1½″ long, pendent, leathery, 2 of the 6 scales becoming greatly enlarged and giving to the partially open cone the appearance of a duck's bill; *seeds* ⅓″ to ½″ long, unequally laterally winged, straw-colored; about 15,000 (6,400–29,000) to the pound; *cotyledons* 2, rarely 3.

Bark thin, smooth, and gray-green or scaly and tinged with red on young stems; on old trunks thick (3″ to 8″) yellowish brown to cinnamon-red, fibrous, deeply and irregularly furrowed.

Fig. 81. *Libocedrus decurrens.* Incense-cedar. *1.* Foliage × 2. *2.* Closed cone × ¾. *3.* Seeds × 1. *4.* Open cone and foliage × ¾. *5.* Preformed staminate cones × ¾. *6.* Bark. (*Photograph by Paul Graves.*)

Frémont first discovered incense-cedar on the south fork of the American River in California in 1844. Specimens which he collected two years later at the headwaters of the Sacramento River were used by Torrey in compiling the original botanical description of this species.

At maturity this tree attains a height of from 75 to 110 ft and a diameter of 3 to 4 ft (max. 200 by 11° ft). Old trees are usually broadly buttressed at the base and have rapidly tapering trunks which are often fluted and clothed for nearly one-half of their length in crowns of lustrous foliage. In youth the crown is typically conical, but that of old trees is more irregular and often deformed by mistletoe and witches'-brooms. Seedlings develop profusely branched root systems, and old trees possess well-developed, moderately deep lateral roots.

Incense-cedar grows best on cool, moist sites in the transition zone. Pure stands are virtually unknown, although it may form up to 50 percent of forests chiefly composed of sugar pine, ponderosa pine, and white fir. It is also a nearly constant companion of the giant sequoia. Ponderosa and Jeffrey pines, together with small amounts of bigcone Douglas-fir and white fir, are its principal associates in southern California; it also occurs in the coast ranges east of the redwood belt with both hardwoods and softwoods. In the Cascades of southern Oregon, incense-cedar invades the mixed coniferous forests composed largely of sugar, ponderosa, and western white pines, white fir, and Douglas-fir.

Good seed years occur every three to six years. Reproduction is abundant in moist, organic litter, although good survival may also be found on moist mineral soils. In regions where prolonged drought occurs, this species is usually sparse or wholly wanting. Incense-cedar exhibits greater tolerance than most of the conifers with which it is associated and grows quite persistently under moderate cover when assured of plenty of soil moisture. Sudworth (344) observed that reproduction was usually good under old trees and in open situations, but that it was especially abundant in dense thickets under thinned stands where the more intolerant species could not compete. Growth is at no time rapid; trees 200 years of age vary from 90 to 95 ft in height and 25 to 30 in. in diameter, while trees twice as old are rarely more than 110 ft high and 40 in. in diameter. Maturity appears to be attained in about 300 years, and trees more than 500 years old [1] are rarely encountered.

Pocket dry rot is responsible for considerable damage in old trees. A rust fungus and witches'-brooms are also prevalent in some sections, but

[1] Dr. Duncan Dunning, one-time silviculturist for the California Forest and Range Experimental Station, reported six trees over 500 years of age, but no records of a tree with more than 600 rings.

PLATE 24. *Libocedrus decurrens.*

they are relatively unimportant. Trees of all age classes are quite susceptible to fire.

RANGE

Central Oregon to lower California (map, Plate 24). *Altitudinal distribution:* 1,000 to 5,000 ft in Oregon; 1,000 to 9,000 ft in California; 3,500 to 7,000 ft in Nevada.

THUJA L.[1]   Thuja; arborvitae

This is a small genus consisting of 5 or 6 species of trees or large shrubs scattered through the forests of China, Taiwan, Korea, Japan, and North America. The oriental arborvitae and the Japanese "hiba," *Biota orientalis* (L) Endl.[2] and *Thujopsis dolabrata* Sieb. and Zucc., respectively were formerly included in this genus; however, it is now agreed by many taxonomists that these two species are monotypes.

Two species, one a small to medium-sized northeastern tree, the other a large northwestern form, are the only representatives of *Thuja* in North America.

BOTANICAL FEATURES OF THE GENUS

Leaves persistent, small, scalelike, decussate; the facial leaves flattened, grooved, and often glandular, the lateral leaves rounded or keeled; on leading shoots ovate to lanceolate and somewhat larger than those on the lateral branchlets.

---

[1] Also spelled *Thuya.*
[2] The oriental arborvitae, *Biota orientalis,* (L.) Endl. has been much used as an ornamental in this country and may be distinguished by its somewhat "lacy" foliage and peculiar semifleshy, hooked cone, scales with wingless seeds. It is not hardy in the Northeast during extremely cold winters.

Flowers terminal; *staminate* strobili arising from branchlets near the base of the shoot, individual strobili ovoid to globose, consisting of 3 to 6 pairs of decussate stamens, each with a scalelike filament and 2 to 4 subglobose anthers; *ovulate* cones appearing at the tips of short terminal branchlets, and comprising 8 to 12 scales, each scale bearing 2 or 3 erect ovules; all species monoecious.

Fruit an erect, ovoid-cylindrical, leathery to semiwoody cone composed of several thin scales only a few of which are fertile; cones solitary for the most part and maturing in one season; *seeds* small, laterally 2-winged; *cotyledons* 2.

DISTINGUISHING CHARACTERISTICS OF THE ARBORVITAES

Species	Leaves	Cones
T. occidentalis, northern white-cedar	dull green, glandular-pitted	with 4 fertile scales, spine tips very minute or lacking
T. plicata, western redcedar	dark glossy green, eglandular for the most part	with 6 fertile scales, usually spine-tipped

Thuja occidentalis L.   Northern white-cedar; eastern arborvitae (SPN)

BOTANICAL FEATURES

Leaves yellow-green, not lustrous; on leading shoots nearly $\frac{1}{4}''$ long, glandular, and long-pointed; on lateral branchlets scalelike and flattened, $\frac{1}{8}''$ long, obscurely glandular-pitted, the foliage sprays often fanlike.

Cones $\frac{1}{3}''$ to $\frac{1}{2}''$ long, erect, oblong; releasing their seeds in the fall, but persisting during the winter, tips of the scales rounded or with a very minute spine; usually 4 scales fertile; *seeds* $\frac{1}{8}''$ long, wings as wide as the body; about 346,000 (184,000–568,000) seeds to the pound; *cotyledons* 2.

Bark $\frac{1}{4}''$ to $\frac{1}{3}''$ thick, reddish to grayish brown, fibrous, forming a more or less close network of connecting ridges and shallow furrows, grayish on the surface.

GENERAL DESCRIPTION

Trees of northern white-cedar are commonly 40 to 50 ft tall and 2 to 3 ft in diameter (max. 125* by 6 ft). The crown, narrowly pyramidal in youth, later becomes irregularly oblong, and the tapering bole is supported by a shallow, wide-spreading root system.

This species occurs on a wide variety of soils but reaches its best development and outlying stations both in the North and in the South, on limestone outcrops. Even though it is in this respect a calcicole, white-cedar is also characteristic of shallow sphagnum-covered basins such as

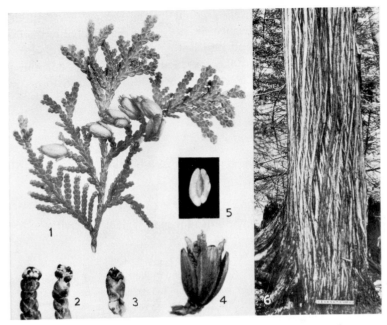

Fig. 82. *Thuja occidentalis*. Northern white-cedar. *1*. Foliage and cones × ¾. *2*. Staminate flowers before and after shedding pollen × 2. *3*. Ovulate flower × 2. *4*. Open cone × 2. *5*. Seed × 2. *6*. Bark of old tree.

those in the Adirondack Mountains, where, however, the growth is very slow, about 1 ft in diameter in 200 years (154). Growth may be from two to three times faster on the best sites.

Some seeds are produced annually, with large crops at three to five year intervals. In suitable locations, especially on swampy ground or limestone areas, extensive pure stands develop. In mixed stands, balsam fir, eastern hemlock, eastern white pine, spruces, tamarack, black ash, yellow birch, and the northern maples are common associates. Northern white-cedar is moderately tolerant. An age of 400 years or more is probably attained; ring counts are not satisfactory, since about 80 percent of old trees are rotten at the heart.

"Arborvitae" is the Latin form of "l'arbre de vie," or tree of life, the name said to have been given this species by the king of France in the early sixteenth century. Members of Jacques Cartier's expedition which discovered the St. Lawrence River (249) were given by the Indians a decoction called Annedda [1] to cure scurvy; and it is thought that the

[1] This early report credits the "Annedda" to eastern arborvitae, but A. C. Parker, of the Rochester, New York, Museum, traced Annedda through Ahnehdah to Oh-neh-ta, the Iroquois name for hemlock. The foliage of either arborvitae or hemlock could be used as an antiscorbutic, and New York Indians did make a tea from the steeped leaves of hemlock.

French, believing themselves cured by the extract, in gratitude carried the arborvitae back to France. It was in this way probably the first American tree to be introduced into Europe, where it soon found favor as an ornamental. More than 100 cultivars are known (101), and these may be easily propagated by cuttings. On wet sites, this tree forms new individuals by layering.

RANGE

Southern Canada, Lake states, Northeast, and Appalachian Mountains (see map, Plate 25).

Thuja plicata Donn   Western redcedar; [1] giant arborvitae (SPN)

BOTANICAL FEATURES

Leaves lustrous dark yellow-green, usually without glandular pits, similar to those of *T. occidentalis* but somewhat coarser; the foliage sprays long, drooping, and often fernlike, or stringy.
Cones also similar to those of the preceding species, but more often with weakly spine-tipped scales, 6 of which are fertile; *seeds* ⅛″ long, the lateral wings about as wide as the seed; about 414,000 (203,000–504,000) seeds to the pound.
Bark ½″ to 1″ thick, fibrous, cinnamon-red on young stems, gray on old trunks, and forming a closely interlacing network.

GENERAL DESCRIPTION

Western redcedar, the larger of our two American species of arborvitae, was first observed by the Malaspina Expedition on the west side of Vancouver Island, British Columbia, near Nootka Sound in 1791. Today it is one of the four most important species of the Pacific Northwest and is the principal timber tree used in shingle manufacture both in the United States and in Canada.

Under favorable conditions for growth, forest trees attain gigantic proportions and vary from 150 to 200 ft in height and 4 to 8 ft in diameter (max. 250 by 21° ft). A shallow, wide-spreading root system supports a

[2] Although this is the preferred common name among lumbermen, it unfortunately links the species with *Juniperus virginiana*, or eastern redcedar, which is in a different genus. The name "giant arborvitae" is not used by the lumber trade, although it would seem a more logical one for *Thuja plicata* than that now applied.

Fig. 83. *Thuja plicata*. Western redcedar. *1*. Foliage and closed cones × ¾. *2*. Seed × 2. *3*. Open cones × ¾. *4*. Ovulate flowers × 2. *5*. Staminate flowers × 2. *6*. Bark.

broadly buttressed, often fluted base and rapidly tapering bole. The crown is typically irregular and is usually composed of numerous more or less horizontal or drooping branches which bend upward near their tips to form a distinct hook.

This species generally inhabits moist flats and slopes, the banks of rivers and swamps, and is found even in bogs (297). It avoids dry soils, although stunted growth is occasionally found on such sites. Western red-cedar seldom occurs in pure stands but often constitutes up to 50 percent of mixed forests. Of its important associates along the Pacific slope, mention should be made of Sitka spruce, western hemlock, Douglas-fir, grand and Pacific silver firs, Pacific yew, red alder, black cottonwood, and big-leaf maple. In Rocky Mountain forests western larch, western white pine, western hemlock, grand fir, Douglas-fir, and Engelmann spruce are its principal companions.

1. *Thuja occidentalis.* 2. *Thuja plicata.*

PLATE 25

Western redcedar releases prodigious amounts of seed at about 3-year intervals, with smaller amounts almost every year. Germination is high (70 percent) on both mineral soils and duff, provided they remain moist. Seedling mortality from drought, fungi, birds, and insects is often excessive, and only a few trees may result from the tremendous number of seeds released. Tree growth is relatively slow although individuals 80 years old may average 20 in. in diameter and 100 ft in height. Maturity is reached in about 350 years, but trees with more than 1,000 growth rings have been reported. This species is very tolerant.

Because of its shallow root system and thin bark, western redcedar is readily killed by fire. Pecky heart rot is commonly found in overmature trees, and almost all very old trees are hollow-butted.

Western redcedar wood is extremely durable. One old wind-thrown tree on the Olympic peninsula was found supporting 14 hemlocks which were over 100 years of age, and while the sapwood of the redcedar had rotted away, the heartwood was sound in every respect.

Several ornamental forms of this species are now under cultivation.

RANGE

Pacific Northwest and Inland Empire (map, Plate 25). *Altitudinal distribution:* sea level to 4,000 ft near the coast; 2,000 to 7,000 ft in the Rocky Mountains.

CUPRESSUS L.   Cypress [1]

Cupressus consists of about 15 species of trees and shrubs found in western North America, Mexico, the Mediterranean basin, the Himalaya Mountains, and western China. The Italian cypress, *C. sempervirens* L., is a large and important tree of columnar habit widely scattered through forests of the Mediterranean basin. In this region it is planted extensively as an ornamental, especially along avenues for formal effects. Several species of *Cupressus,* including the Italian cypress, are widely used ornamentals in the warmer portions of other countries.

Five species are native to the Pacific slope and one to the southwestern states; some of these trees produce timber used locally.

BOTANICAL FEATURES OF THE GENUS

Leaves persistent, scalelike (often awl-shaped on juvenile or vigorous growth), decussate in 4 uniform ranks, or the lateral pairs boat-shaped and the facial pairs flattened; finely serrate on the margin and commonly glandular on the back; with irregularly disposed 4-angled branchlets, or rarely with flattened sprays and branchlets.

Flowers terminal; *staminate* strobili cylindrical, composed of numerous filaments, each bearing 2 to 6 subglobose anthers; *ovulate* cones consisting of 6 to 12 peltate scales, each with a terminal mucro and 6 to many basal ovules arranged in 2 or more rows; all species monoecious.

Fruit a globose, woody, or leathery cone maturing at the end of the second season; scales peltate, each with a central boss or mucro; *seeds* 6 to many on each scale; compressed, with narrow lateral wings; *cotyledons* 2 to 5.

[1] See also the genus *Taxodium.* A taxonomic treatment of the native cypresses is that of C. B. Wolf and W. W. Wagener (384).

Cupressus arizonica Greene Arizona cypress

Distinguishing characteristics. *Leaves* scalelike, gray-green, exhaling a fetid odor when bruised. *Cones* ¾ to 1 in. in diameter, subglobose, dark reddish brown, with 6 to 8 bossed scales. *Bark* breaking into thin irregular scales on young stems, furrowed and fibrous on old trunks.

General description. Arizona cypress is the only cypress native to the Southwest. Under favorable growing conditions, this tree is 50 to 60 ft high and 15 to 30 in. in diameter (max. 102° by 5° ft). The bole of mature trees exhibits considerable taper and is clothed for half of its length in a dense conical crown composed of short, stout, horizontal branches. The largest trees are found on moist, gravelly slopes and benches and in coves of northerly exposure. Trees on dry, sterile, rocky mountain slopes and canyon walls are small or even dwarfed, but may persist on such sites for many years. This species occurs most abundantly in open pure forests, but it is occasionally observed in mixture with Arizona pine and live oaks.

Seed is borne in abundance every year, but owing to the fact that much of it never finds conditions suitable for germination, reproduction is usually scanty. The trees are tolerant throughout life. Growth is seldom rapid, and trees 6 to 12 in. in diameter frequently show 70 to 100 growth rings; the largest trees are rarely more than 400 years old.

Range. Mountains of central, southern, and eastern Arizona, western New Mexico, and northern Mexico. *Altitudinal distribution:* 4,500 to 8,000 ft.

Fig. 84. *Cupressus arizonica.* Arizona cypress. *1.* Fruiting branchlet × ¾. *2.* Seeds × 2.

CHAMAECYPARIS Spach Whitecedar; falsecypress (SPN)

This group includes six species and is considered by some authors to be a section of the genus *Cupressus*. There are several botanical features, however, which serve to distinguish between the two groups (see page

186). Three species of *Chamaecyparis* are indigenous to North America; one of these, *C. thyoides* (L.) B.S.P., is a small coastal species of the East, and *C. nootkatensis* (D. Don) Spach and *C. lawsoniana* (A. Murr.) Parl. are important trees of the Pacific Coast. The Japanese Sawara-tree and Hinoki-cypress, *C. pisifera* (Sieb. and Zucc.) Endl. and *C. obtusa* (Sieb. and Zucc.) Endl., respectively, together with many of their varieties, are favored ornamental trees in many sections of the United States. The remaining species, *C. formosensis* Matsum., is a massive tree native to Taiwan. This tree is said to attain a maximum height of 195 ft, a diameter of 23 ft, and an estimated age of 1,500 years (85).

BOTANICAL FEATURES OF THE GENUS

Leaves persistent, scalelike, decussate, ovate, acuminate, entire on the margin, the lateral pairs boat-shaped, the facial pairs flattened; on terminal shoots linear-lanceolate or needlelike, spreading; usually turning brown after the 2d or 3d season, but persistent for many years.

Flowers both sexes terminal but on separate branches; *staminate* strobili cylindrical, composed of numerous decussate stamens, each with 2 to 6 subglobose anthers; *ovulate* strobili subglobose, usually consisting of 6

DISTINGUISHING CHARACTERISTICS OF THE NATIVE SPECIES OF CHAMAECYPARIS

Species	Leaves	Cones
C. thyoides, Atlantic white-cedar	about 1⁄16″ long, glandular	about 1⁄4″ in diameter, somewhat fleshy, maturing in one season; scales terminating in a reflexed boss; seeds 1 or 2 per scale
C. lawsoniana, Port-Orford-cedar	same	about 1⁄3″ in diameter, woody, maturing in 1 season; scales same as above; seeds 2 to 4 per scale
C. nootkatensis, Alaska-cedar	about 1⁄8″, sharp, essentially eglandular	about 1⁄2″ in diameter, maturing in 2 seasons, woody; scales terminating in an erect boss; seeds same as *C. lawsoniana*.

to 12 decussate, peltate, ovuliferous scales, each bearing 2 to 5 erect ovules; all species monoecious.

Fruit an erect, globose, leathery or semifleshy cone maturing in one or two years; *cone scales* peltate, each with a central boss; *seeds* 2 rarely up to 5 on each scale, slightly compressed, laterally winged; *cotyledons* 2.

Chamaecyparis thyoides (L.) B.S.P.   Atlantic white-cedar; [1]
whitecedar falsecypress (SPN)

BOTANICAL FEATURES

Leaves ⅟₁₆″ to ⅛″ long, keeled, and glandular on the back, dark blue-green, turning brown the second year, but persistent for several years.
Cones ¼″ in diameter, somewhat fleshy; at maturity bluish purple, glaucous, later turning brown: *seeds* 1 or 2 for each fertile scale, ⅛″ long or smaller; about 460,000 (420,000–500,000) seeds to the pound.
Bark thin, but on old trunks ¾″ to 1″ thick, ashy gray to reddish brown, somewhat similar in appearance to that of northern white-cedar.

GENERAL DESCRIPTION

Atlantic white-cedar on good sites averages 80 to 85 ft in height and 10 to 14 in. in diameter (max. 120 by 5 ft). The bole of mature trees grown in moderately dense stands is long, cylindrical, and clear of branches for

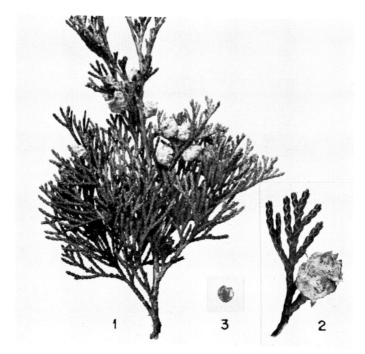

Fɪɢ. 85. *Chamaecyparis thyoides.* Atlantic white-cedar. *1.* Foliage and cones × ¾. *2.* Closed cone × 2. *3.* Seed × 2.

[1] Previously called southern white cedar, the U.S. Forest Service's Committee on Tree Names suggests "Atlantic" as more appropriate (see range).

about three-quarters of its length, making it an ideal pole or post timber. The crown of forest trees is small, narrowly conical, and composed of slender limbs with somewhat drooping branchlets; the root system is superficial and wide-spreading.

This species is characteristic of fresh-water swamps and bogs, wet depressions, or stream banks, and is rarely found except on such sites; extensive pure stands are the rule, occurring on shallow peat-covered soils underlain by sand. Because of the extensive north-south distribution of Atlantic white-cedar, the list of trees which may be found growing with it is large. Some of the more common are hemlock, eastern white pine, gray birch, black tupelo, and red maple in the North; and in the South, slash and pond pines, baldcypress, and sweetbay. Young trees are nearly as tolerant as balsam fir or hemlock, and much more so than the pines or baldcypress; however, they do not survive under the dense cover of older growth, especially hardwoods.

The production of seed in dense stands begins between the ages of 10 and 20 years (earlier in open-grown trees), and good crops are borne nearly every year. The small winged seeds are widely disseminated by wind and on favorable sites show from 70 to 90 percent germination. Following fires, pure, even-aged stands occur from which merchantable timber can be harvested in 75 to 100 years or less. However, much of the crop is used for poles and posts.

RANGE

Atlantic and Gulf Coastal Plains (map, Plate 26).

PLATE 26. *Chamaecyparis thyoides.*

Chamaecyparis lawsoniana (A. Murr.) Parl.   Port-Orford-cedar;
Lawson falsecypress (SPN)

BOTANICAL FEATURES

Leaves $\frac{1}{16}''$ long, yellow-green to blue-green, blunt, glandular, stomatiferous on the lower facial leaves; forming fine, flattened, feathery or lacy sprays; persistent until the 3d or 4th seasons.

Cones $\frac{1}{3}''$ in diameter, reddish brown, often glaucous, globose, composed of 3 pairs of peltate scales each bearing 2 to 4 seeds, maturing in one season; *seeds* $\frac{1}{8}''$ long, reddish brown, with 2 broad lateral wings; about 210,000 (80,000–600,000) seeds to the pound.

Bark 6″ to 10″ thick on old trees, silvery-brown, fibrous, divided into thick, rounded ridges separated by deep irregular furrows.

GENERAL DESCRIPTION

Port-Orford-cedar, also known as Oregon white-cedar and Lawson cypress, is a large tree, 140 to 180 ft in height and 4 to 6 ft in diameter (max. 225 by 16 ft), restricted to the coastal forests of southwestern Oregon and northern California. The boles of large trees are sometimes buttressed and commonly clear for 150 ft or more of their length. The crown is characteristically short, conical, and composed of numerous more or less horizontal or somewhat pendulous branches; the roots are shallow to moderately deep and spreading.

This species does best in regions where there is an abundance of both soil and atmospheric moisture. It is less exacting in this respect, however, than redwood, and it frequently occurs on rather high, dry, sandy ridges which are often 30 to 40 miles inland. Except in the vicinity of Coos Bay, Oregon, Port-Orford-cedar is rarely found in pure stands. Although found in a relatively small area, this species spans the floristic transition zone between the trees of California and those of the Pacific Northwest. Common associates in coastal Oregon include Douglas-fir, Sitka spruce, western hemlock, and western redcedar. Farther inland and southward, it is found with such species as western white and sugar pines, incense-cedar, red fir, and red alder.

Port-Orford-cedar reproduces readily on burned or unburned sites with about equal aggressiveness. Large seed crops occur every four to five years with smaller amounts annually. Although showing transient vitality, the seeds germinate well (up to 65 percent) if they encounter suitable conditions shortly after their release. Seedling trees grow persistently in either shade or full sunlight, although under very dense cover they are usually suppressed and eventually die. Growth continues at a

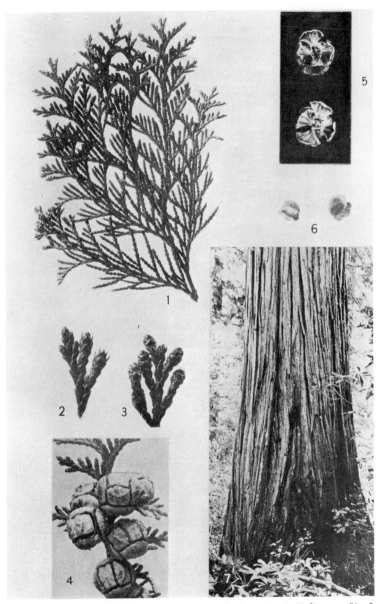

Fig. 86. *Chamaecyparis lawsoniana*. Port-Orford-cedar. *1.* Foliage × ¾. *2.* Ovulate flowers × 2. *3.* Staminate flowers × 2. *4.* Mature cones × 2. *5.* Open cones × 2. *6.* Seeds × 2. *7.* Bark. (*Photograph by U.S. Forest Service.*)

moderate rate, and the trees reach maturity in about 300 to 350 years. The oldest trees are often 500 or more years of age.

Port-Orford-cedar is one of the most commonly used trees for ornamental planting, both in North America and Europe. Great variation in color and form have been found, and some 198 cultivars are listed by Den Ouden and Boom (101).

This species is relatively free from insect and fungal diseases, but fire causes considerable damage to the thin-barked young trees. Wind throw is also a hazard.

RANGE

West Coast (Oregon and California) (see map, Plate 27). *Altitudinal distribution:* sea level to nearly 5,000 ft.

Chamaecyparis nootkatensis (D. Don) Spach   Alaska-cedar; Nootka falsecypress (SPN)

BOTANICAL FEATURES

Leaves about ⅛″ long, acute, blue-green to gray-green, occasionally glandular on the back, appressed, but with the apices of the lateral pairs often free, turning brown during the 2d season but persistent until the 3d.
Cones ¼″ to ½″ in diameter, purplish brown to reddish brown, with 4 to 6 peltate, bossed scales each bearing 2 to 4 seeds; maturing at the end of the 2d season; *seeds* about ¼″ long, the lateral wings about twice as wide as the seed; about 108,000 (66,000–180,000) seeds to the pound.
Bark thin, grayish brown, scaly on young stems; forming thin, narrow, flattened, interlacing ridges on old trunks.

GENERAL DESCRIPTION

This species, known in the trade as Alaska-cypress, yellow-cypress, or yellow-cedar, is typical of the Pacific Northwest region. It is a medium-sized tree, 60 to 90 ft high and 2 to 3 ft in diameter (max. 175° by 8° ft). In the forest it usually develops a broadly buttressed, often fluted base and rapidly tapering bole which is often clear for about one-half of its length. The conical crown is composed of numerous drooping branches with long, pendulous, flattened sprays of foliage. The root system varies with the site; in moist soils it is shallow, but in drier situations it penetrates to much greater depths.

Alaska-cedar reaches its maximum development on the islands of southeastern Alaska and British Columbia near tide water, where both soil and atmospheric moisture are abundant. Much of the timber in this

Fig. 87. *Chamaecyparis nootkatensis.* Alaska-cedar. *1.* Foliage and cones ×
¾. *2.* Seed × 2. *3.* Bark. (*Photograph by Kenneth Walin.*)

region has been logged, however, and the best stands are now located
in the humid forests of the Olympic and Cascade Mountains in northern
Washington. Here it forms limited pure forests but usually occurs in
mixture with other conifers. At low elevations, these include western
hemlock, Sitka spruce, Pacific yew, Pacific silver and grand firs, and
western redcedar; at high altitudes are found subalpine fir, mountain
hemlock, western white, and whitebark pines, Engelmann spruce, and
western larch. Timberline trees are often reduced to a sprawling shrublike habit, or they may become even prostrate on wholly unprotected
sites. This species is considered tolerant, more so than western white
pine or western larch, but less than Engelmann spruce, subalpine fir, or
the hemlocks.

Alaska-cedar generally produces a small amount of seed yearly, and
large crops are released only at irregular intervals. The seeds exhibit
transient viability, and the percentage of seedling survival is never very
great. The seeds are able to germinate in rocky, gravelly, or clay soil,
leaf litter, or even moss, provided there is an abundance of soil moisture.
The seedling, once it has become established, continues to grow very
slowly but persistently both in height and in diameter. Pole-sized trees

PLATE 27. *Chamaecyparis nootkatensis;*
Chamaecyparis lawsoniana;

may be 100 to 200 years old. This species is one of the longest-lived of western conifers. An age of 1,000 years is not uncommon, and one old tree was reported to show 3,500 growth rings.

RANGE

Coastal Alaska to Washington; the Cascades to Oregon (map, Plate 27). *Altitudinal distribution:* sea level to 3,000 ft in Alaska and British Columbia; 2,500 to 7,500 ft in Washington and Oregon.

JUNIPERUS L.   Juniper

The junipers constitute a group of from 50 to 70 species of trees and shrubs widely scattered through North and Central America, Japan, Taiwan, China, the Himalaya, the Mediterranean basin, northern Africa, Abyssinia, the Canary Islands, the Azores, and the West Indies.

J. communis L. (common juniper) is a small tree, which together with its shrubby varieties, is circumpolar in the Northern Hemisphere. The geographic variety *depressa* Pursh, oldfield common juniper, is a sprawling shrub common to many sections of northeastern and northwestern United States and Canada. It is readily recognized by its peculiar bushy habit of growth, its long-subulate, ternate leaves, and its glaucous blue berrylike fruits. Several varieties of *J. communis* are used as ornamentals.

Oil obtained from both the wood and leaves of certain species is used in the manufacture of perfumes and medicines. The leaf oils possess diuretic properties, and cattlemen exercise particular care in making sure that their grazing livestock do not forage on juniperous vegetation. Gin derives its characteristic taste from juniper "berries."

About thirteen species of *Juniperus* are native to the United States; the most important is *J. virginiana* L.

Leaves persistent, opposite or ternate; always needlelike or subulate on juvenile growth; on older plants (1) wholly acicular to subulate, and ternate, (2) wholly scalelike and decussate, (3) both 1 and 2 on the same plant; leaves with or without glands; the acicular ones frequently conspicuously stomatiferous and with a single medial resin canal.

Flowers terminal or axillary; *staminate* strobili composed of several decussate and peltate filaments, each with 2 to 6 globose anthers; *ovulate* cones with basal scalelike bracts, composed of 3 to 8 decussate or ternate pointed scales, some or all bearing 1 or 2 basal ovules; the species dioecious or rarely monoecious.

Fruit a red-brown, blue, or blue-black, often glaucous, berrylike cone, maturing in 1, 2, or 3 seasons and bearing 1 to 12 ovoid, terete or angular, unwinged seeds which usually require 2 or more seasons to germinate; cotyledons 2, or 4 to 6.

EASTERN JUNIPERS

Juniperus virginiana L.   Eastern redcedar

BOTANICAL FEATURES

Leaves about $\frac{1}{16}$" long, opposite, (rarely ternate) dark green, scalelike, and arranged to form a 4-sided branchlet; the long sharp-pointed juvenile leaves predominate for a number of years and are usually present in small numbers even on old trees.

Cones $\frac{1}{4}$" to $\frac{1}{3}$" in diameter, subglobose, ripening the first season, pale green turning to dark blue at maturity, glaucous; *seeds* 1 or 2, rarely 3 or 4, requiring 2 or 3 years to germinate; *cotyledons* 2; about 43,200 (17,600–59,000) seeds to the pound.

Bark $\frac{1}{8}$" to $\frac{1}{4}$" thick, light reddish brown, fibrous, separating into long, narrow, fringed scales; often ashy gray on exposed surfaces.

GENERAL DESCRIPTION

Eastern redcedar is a small to medium-sized tree 40 to 50 ft high and 12 to 24 in. in diameter (max. 120 by 4 ft). The crown is dense and narrowly pyramidal, or in some forms columnar, and the tapering bole terminates below in a deep root system.

This species has a very wide distribution and is found on many types of soil ranging from acid sands to those derived from limestone. Although best growth is made on deep alluvial soils, hardwood competition elimi-

FIG. 88. *Juniperus virginiana.* Eastern redcedar. *1.* Juvenile foliage × ¾.
2. Mature type of foliage and cones × ¾. *3.* Bark. (*Photograph by U.S.
Forest Service.*)

nates most redcedars from such sites. The tree is most common on the
poorest of dry soils in pure stands or open mixtures with shortleaf and
Virginia pines, or the dry soil oaks, hickories and other hardwoods. The
so-called cedar barrens of Tennessee and northern Alabama have supplied much of the commercial timber produced.

Dissemination of the seeds is facilitated by birds, which eat the berrylike fruits in large numbers. Delayed germination is the rule, and the

FIG. 89. Open-grown eastern redcedar.

seedlings do not appear until the second season after the seeds are sown. Eastern redcedar is a slow-growing, intolerant tree reaching a maximum age of about 300 years.

Seedling variation is pronounced, and many ornamental forms have been discovered and propagated vegetatively; in fact, redcedar and its cultivars are among the best of native ornamental evergreens. "Cedar apples," galls caused by a fungus, are often conspicuous features.

RANGE

Eastern United States and southern Ontario (map, Plate 28).

PLATE 28. *Juniperus virginiana.*

WESTERN JUNIPERS

There are 10 junipers indigenous to western North America. As a group they are mostly large bushy or sprawling shrubs, or small stunted trees on poor, dry soils in arid regions. Those that do attain arborescent stature, however, usually feature a stout, rapidly tapering bole partially clothed in a dense pyramidal to subglobose crown of more or less irregular outline. These trees are of little or no value for sawtimber, but they are sometimes used in the round for poles, posts, crossties, and mine props. For purposes of convenience the western junipers may be divided into two groups which are known as the "blue-berried junipers" and the "red-berried junipers," respectively.

Included in the blue-fruited group is *Juniperus communis* L., a circumpolar species (see page 204), and the Rocky Mountain, western, and Ashe junipers. One-seed juniper, *Juniperus monosperma* (Engelm.) Sarg., a shrub or small tree of semiarid slopes and benches in the central and southern Rocky Mountains, while often classed with the blue-fruited forms, does indeed commonly produce glaucous-brown globular cones. Cones of both colors, however, ordinarily encase a single (rarely 2) seed with four sharp ridges.

The Rocky Mountain juniper, *Juniperus scopulorum* Sarg., ranges over the Rockies from western Texas northward to Alberta, Canada, thence east to the Black Hills in South Dakota and westward to tidewater in British Columbia and Washington. While the cones of other blue-fruited species mature in a single season, two years are required for the maturation of Rocky Mountain juniper cones.

Closely related and similar in appearance to the one-seed juniper is the Ashe juniper, *Juniperus ashei* Buchholz, a tree extending from southwestern Missouri to the Trans-Pecos region of Texas and then south over the Mexican highlands. Occasionally attaining a height of as much as 100 ft, this species may be recognized by its essentially eglandular, dark blue-green foliage and smooth or only remotely ridged seeds.

The remaining species in the blue-fruited group is the western juniper, *Juniperus occidentalis* Hook. This is a tree of the Pacific Slope ranging from southwestern Idaho south over the east slopes of the Cascades and crests of the Sierra to southern California. It features opposite as well as ternate foliage and cones containing 2 or 3 seeds.

Fig. 90. *Juniperus scopulorum*. Rocky Mountain juniper. *1*. Foliage and 1-year-old cones × ¾. *2*. Foliage and 2-year-old mature cones × ¾. *3*. Bark.

Numbered among the red-berried junipers is the alligator juniper, *Juniperus deppeana* Steud. This distinctive tree, like the Rocky Mountain juniper, and unlike others with reddish, berrylike fruits, also matures its cones at the end of two growing seasons. Its thick, reddish-brown bark is divided into small squares or blocks which give to the bole an alligator hide–like appearance.

Another distinctive tree is the drooping juniper, *Juniperus flaccida* Schlecht. Featuring long, slender, pendulous branchlets, this tree may be observed in Trans-Pecos Texas and in the mountains of Mexico.

The Utah juniper, *Juniperus osteosperma* (Torr.) Little, is probably the most widely distributed red-fruited species, and is found at elevations from 5,000 to 8,000 feet in the Great Basin region from western Wyoming to Idaho and Nevada and south to western New Mexico and eastern California. A common growth form features several stems rising from the same root system.

The California juniper, *Juniperus californica* Carr., as its name suggests, is largely restricted to California. Unlike other red-fruited species, its needles are mostly ternate.

Taxaceae: The Yew family

The Yew family comprises 3 genera and about 13 species. *Torreya* (or *Tumion*) and *Taxus* are represented in the American flora. The third genus, *Austrotaxus*, is a monotype of New Caledonia in the South Seas.

BOTANICAL FEATURES OF THE FAMILY

Leaves persistent, mostly alternate, linear, or less commonly, scalelike.
Flowers with ovules erect, or occasionally partially inverted; the species dioecious, or rarely monoecious.
Fruit a single seed surrounded by a fleshy aril; or drupelike.

CONSPECTUS OF NATIVE GENERA

Genus	Leaves	Flowers	Fruit
Torreya	linear, with 2 glaucous white stomatiferous bands below	staminate flowers solitary	a single seed, drupelike, the outer seed coat fleshy; maturing in 2 seasons
Taxus	linear, pale yellow-green below	staminate flowers in globose heads	a single seed surrounded by a resinous or fleshy, scarlet cuplike aril; maturing in 1 season

TORREYA Arn. *Tumion* Raf.   Torreya; nutmeg

This is a small genus consisting of five species of trees and shrubs found in North America, China, and Japan. Wooden novelties such as chessmen, rings, and articles of turnery are manufactured from the Japanese kaya, *Torreya nucifera* (L.) Sieb. and Zucc.

Two species are found in the United States: *Torreya taxifolia* Arn., Florida torreya (stinking-cedar), is rare and local; it is found along the Appalachicola River in western Florida and in southwestern Georgia. *Torreya californica* Torr., California torreya, is restricted to the west slopes of the Sierra Nevada and central coast region of California.

Leaves persistent, often aromatic, linear, acuminate, often bristle-tipped; spirally arranged and commonly 2-ranked; convex above, with a wide band of stomata on each side of the midrib below.

Flowers unisexual; *staminate* solitary, axillary on the new shoots, consisting of several stamens in whorls of 4, each composed of a filament supporting 4 anthers; *ovulate* in pairs near the base of new shoots; species mostly dioecious.

Fruit a seed with an outer fleshy layer; drupelike; *cotyledons* 2.

Buds ovoid, acute, covered by a few shining scales which are opposite in pairs.

TAXUS L.   Yew

This genus includes 7 species [1] of trees and shrubs of wide distribution through eastern Asia, Asia Minor, northern Africa, Europe, and North America. *Taxus baccata* L., the English yew, and about 40 of its natural and horticultural varieties are commonly used as ornamentals throughout the Northern Hemisphere. Japanese yew, *T. cuspidata* Sieb. and Zucc., and its varieties are similarly employed.

Three species of *Taxus* are native to the United States: *T. canadensis* Marsh., commonly designated as ground-hemlock or Canadian yew, is a low sprawling shrub found in moist, shady situations through the northeastern states and Canada; *T. floridana* Nutt.,[2] the Florida yew, is a small tree frequenting river banks and ravines in western Florida; *T. brevifolia* Nutt., the Pacific yew, is a small to medium-sized tree of the Pacific Coast and is the only native species of any commercial importance.

Leaves persistent linear-lanceolate, often rigid, acuminate; spirally arranged (rarely opposite) and generally 2-ranked; persistent from 2 to many years.

Flowers unisexual; *staminate* in stalked globose heads composed of 6 to 14 filamentous stamens, each with 5 to 9 anthers; *ovulate* flowers composed of several scales, the apical scale bearing a solitary ovule with a basal disk; species dioecious (rarely monoecious).

Fruit a single erect, ovoid, bony-covered seed partially enveloped by a scarlet fleshy aril; maturing in one season; *cotyledons*, 2.

Buds obtuse, with a number of closely imbricated scales.

[1] According to Engler and Prantl (117) one species and several varieties.
[2] According to Engler and Prantl (117) a form of *T. canadensis*.

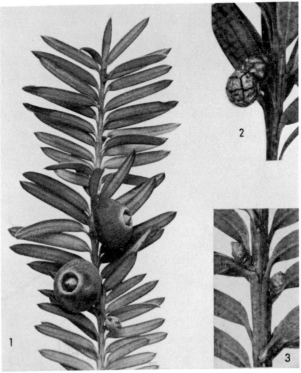

Fɪɢ. 91. *1*. Fruits and foliage of Pacific yew × 1. *2*. Staminate flower structures × 3. *3*. Ovulate flower structures × 3.

Taxus brevifolia Nutt.   Pacific yew

Distinguishing characteristics.   *Leaves* about 1 in. long, linear, dark yellow-green to blue-green above, paler below, petiolate. *Flowers* dioecious. *Fruit* an ovoid-oblong seed ⅛ in. in length, partially surrounded by a scarlet aril. *Bark* dark reddish purple, thin, and scaly.

General description.   The Pacific yew is not confined to the Pacific Coast as its name implies but extends eastward over the Cascade Mountains in Washington to the Rocky Mountains in Idaho and Montana. It is usually a small tree or large shrub 20 to 40 ft high and 12 to 15 in. in diameter, although larger trees are occasionally found on the best sites. The crown is large and conical; and even forest trees produce "limby," often fluted, and occasionally contorted boles; the root system is deep and wide-spreading. This tree is usually found on deep, rich, moist soils near lakes and streams, as well as on protected flats, benches, and gentle slopes up to 8,000 ft. On such sites it ordinarily occurs as an occasional understory tree in mixed coniferous forests composed of Douglas-fir, western hemlock, western redcedar, grand and Pacific silver firs, lodge-pole and western white pines, western larch, and Engelmann spruce. It is occasionally found as a much dwarfed and often sprawling shrub at or near timberline with white-bark pine and Alaska-cedar.

Pacific yew produces some seed every year, and large crops occur at irregular intervals. The seeds are largely bird-disseminated, and those falling on wet moss, decaying wood, or leaf litter ordinarily germinate. This species is probably the most tolerant of northwestern forest trees. Growth proceeds very slowly, and maturity is attained in about 250 to 350 years. The largest trunks are usually hollow-butted and often exhibit spiral grain.

Range. Southeastern Alaska along the coast to Monterey Bay, California (about half-way down the coast from the Oregon line); also in the Sierra Nevada Mountains; eastward through British Columbia and Washington to the west slopes of the Rockies in Montana and Idaho. *Altitudinal distribution:* sea level to 8,000 ft.

ANGIOSPERMS

Angiospermae

The angiosperms are the commonest, most complex, and most widely distributed plants now inhabiting the earth's surface. They supply food, clothing, and shelter for both man and beast, and also innumerable drugs, oils, dyes, and other products. Numbering some 250,000 species, they are found from the luxuriant, rain-drenched forests of the tropics to the wastes of the tundra in polar regions. Many of them form the only cover on hot, dry soils in arid regions, others ascend mountains to the highest levels of plant growth, and still others of hydrophytic habit invade fresh or even brackish waters. Showing great variation in size and structure, some of the angiosperms are small floating disklike bodies, while certain terrestrial forms are not infrequently 300 ft or more in height or length. Some complete their life history within a few short weeks, while others require one or two years (described as *annuals* and *biennials,* respectively); the life cycle of still others may span several years or even centuries (*perennials*).

The origin of the angiosperms was nearly concomitant with that of the mammals, and although fossils of the former have not been found below the Jurassic, the exceedingly complex structure of many of them would imply that they had developed from even older forms, the remains of which have not yet been discovered. Consequently most paleobotanists agree that the angiosperms had their probable origin during the close of the Paleozoic era. It is also now quite generally conceded that the gymnosperms probably gave rise to the angiosperms, although the manner in which this took place is still a disputed matter. Engler and Prantl hold that the "primitive amentiferae," i.e., the willows, birches, walnuts, and related species, trace their lineage back to the Gnetales, and that the

213

unisexual ament or catkin of these plants is homologous with the unisexual strobile of the Gnetales. Opposed to this is the theory supported by Bessey, Bentham and Hooker, and others, namely, that the bisexual strobile of certain primitive cycadlike plants, or perhaps that of the Bennettitales, a race now extinct, is equivalent to the bisexual actinomorphic flowers of the Ranales and related groups; and that the angiosperms were evolved from either one or possibly both of these groups. Botanists in favor of this theory further contend that the sepals and petals are simply sterile sporophylls, and that unisexual or apetalous flowers represent advanced types which have become simple through reduction.

The angiosperms are further divided into two classes, namely, the *Monocotyledoneae* and the *Dicotyledoneae*. Engler and Diels (115) divide the monocots into 11 orders, the dicots into 44 orders.[1] It is generally agreed among taxonomists that the monocots are of more recent origin than the dicots, although for many years the monocots were held to be the more primitive. There are no important monocotyledonous timber trees in the United States;[2] hence further mention of this group will be omitted. The distinguishing features of the two groups, however, are tabulated below:

Class	Cotyledons	Leaf venation	Flower parts	Fibrovascular bundles
Monocotyledons	1	parallel	usually in 3's or 6's, never in 5's	distributed throughout the stem
Dicotyledons	2 (rarely 1 to 8)	netted	various, often in 4's or 5's	separate or fused, forming a ring around a central pith

THE PLANT FAMILIES

The distinguishing features of the dicotyledonous families included in this text are outlined in the following tables. For convenience they are divided into two major groups, namely, the *Amentiferae*, or catkin-bearing plants, and the *Floriferae*, or non-catkin-bearing plants.

[1] A much larger number according to some writers.
[2] With the possible exception of *Sabal palmetto* (Walt.) Lodd., cabbage palmetto, sometimes used for marine piling.

I. AMENTIFERAE

Families	Leaves	Flowers	Fruit
1. Salicaceae	Deciduous, alternate, simple, stipulate	Imperfect; both sexes in aments; species dioecious	A capsule
2. Myricaceae	Deciduous (rarely persistent), alternate, simple, stipulate [a]	Imperfect; both sexes in aments; species monoecious or dioecious	A drupe
3. Leitneriaceae	Deciduous, alternate, simple, stipulate	Imperfect; both sexes in aments; species dioecious	A drupe
4. Juglandaceae	Deciduous, alternate, pinnately compound, estipulate	Imperfect; staminate in aments, pistillate in spikes or solitary; species monoecious	A nut encased in a leathery or semi-woody husk; or drupaceous
5. Betulaceae	Deciduous, alternate, simple, stipulate	Imperfect; both sexes in aments or the pistillate in clusters or spikes; species monoecious	(1) A nut subtended by an involucre or bract, or (2) a winged nutlet borne in a strobile
6. Fagaceae	Deciduous or persistent, alternate, simple, stipulate	Imperfect; staminate in aments or heads; pistillate in spikes or in bisexual aments; species monoecious	A nut, more or less encased in a scaly or spiny involucre

II. FLORIFERAE

A. *Apetalae*—flowers without petals

1. Ulmaceae	Deciduous (rarely persistent), alternate, simple, stipulate	Perfect or imperfect	A samara, drupe, or nut
2. Moraceae	Deciduous or persistent, alternate, simple, stipulate	Imperfect; in spikes or heads or within a hollow receptacle; species monoecious or dioecious	An achene or drupe, often borne in multiples

B. *Polypetalae*—corolla with separate petals

1. Magnoliaceae	Deciduous or persistent, alternate, simple, stipulate	Perfect; solitary	An aggregate of samaras or follicles
2. Lauraceae	Deciduous or persistent, alternate (rarely opposite), simple, estipulate	Perfect or imperfect	A 1-seeded berry or drupe

[a] One species with stipules.

Families	Leaves	Flowers	Fruit
3. Saxifragaceae	Deciduous (rarely persistent), opposite or alternate, simple, mostly estipulate	Perfect or imperfect	A capsule or berry
4. Hamamelidaceae	Deciduous or persistent, alternate, simple, stipulate	Perfect or imperfect; if the latter, species monoecious	A 2-celled woody capsule
5. Platanaceae	Deciduous, alternate, simple, stipulate	Imperfect; both sexes in globose heads; species monoecious	A globose multiple of achenes
6. Rosaceae	Deciduous or persistent, alternate (rarely opposite), simple or compound, mostly stipulate	Perfect; 5- (rarely 4-) merous	A pome, drupe, capsule, follicle or achene
7. Leguminosae	Deciduous or persistent, alternate (rarely opposite) 1- to 3-pinnately compound or simple, stipulate	Perfect or imperfect; actinomorphic or zygomorphic	A legume
8. Zygophyllaceae	Deciduous or persistent, mostly opposite, and pinnately compound, stipulate	Mostly perfect	A capsule
9. Rutaceae	Deciduous or persistent, compound or simple, alternate or opposite; estipulate or with spinescent stipules	Perfect; regular, 4- or 5-merous	A capsule, berry or drupaceous
10. Simaroubaceae	Deciduous or persistent, alternate or rarely opposite, pinnately compound (rarely simple), estipulate	Perfect or imperfect; regular	A samara, or drupe
11. Meliaceae	Deciduous or persistent, alternate, pinnately compound, estipulate	Perfect	A capsule, drupe, or berry
12. Anacardiaceae	Deciduous or persistent, alternate or rarely opposite, pinnately compound or simple, rarely stipulate	Perfect or imperfect	A drupe, or nutlike

Families	Leaves	Flowers	Fruit
13. Aquifoli- aceae	Deciduous or persist- ent, alternate, simple, stipulate	Imperfect; cymose or solitary; species dioecious	A berrylike drupe
14. Aceraceae	Deciduous, opposite, simple or compound, estipulate	Perfect or imperfect; species polygamous or dioecious	A double (rarely triple) samara
15. Hippocas- tanaceae	Deciduous, opposite, palmately com- pound, estipulate	Perfect or imperfect	A capsule
16. Rhamnaceae	Deciduous or persist- ent, alternate or sub- opposite, simple, stipulate	Perfect or imperfect	Drupaceous, sama- roid, or capsular
17. Tiliaceae	Deciduous, alter- nate, simple, stipu- late	Perfect; cymose or corymbose	A capsule, drupe, berry, or nut
18. Cactaceae	Alternate, simple, re- duced to spines, or sometimes scalelike	Perfect; regular	A berry
19. Nyssaceae	Deciduous, alter- nate, simple, estipu- late	Perfect or imperfect	A drupe, or sa- maralike
20. Cornaceae	Deciduous, opposite (rarely alternate), simple, estipulate	Perfect or rarely im- perfect	A drupe or berry

C. *Sympetalae*—petals more or less united to form a lobed, funnel-shaped, or tubular corolla

1. Ericaceae	Deciduous or persist- ent, alternate (rarely opposite or whorled), simple	Perfect; 4- or 5-mer- ous	A capsule, berry, or drupe
2. Ebenaceae	Deciduous (rarely persistent), alter- nate, simple	Perfect or imperfect; regular	A berry
3. Oleaceae	Deciduous or persist- ent, opposite, simple or compound, estip- ulate	Perfect or imperfect	A samara, capsule, berry, or drupe
4. Bignoniaceae	Deciduous (rarely persistent), mostly opposite or whorled, simple or compound	Perfect	A 2-valved cap- sule, or a berry

I. AMENTIFERAE

Salicaceae: The Willow or Poplar family

The Salicaceae include 2 genera [1] and about 335 species of trees and shrubs widely distributed throughout the world, but most abundant in the cooler regions of the Northern Hemisphere. The tropical species are restricted to mountainous regions where they usually occur at or near timberline. The willow family is not a timber-contributing group of major importance, although many of its species play an active part in the natural regeneration of our forests and in the conservation of both soil and water.

The willows and poplars, perhaps because of their minute seeds with only transient vitality, are usually restricted to locations which are moist at least during late spring when seed dispersal takes place. In many species, propagation by cuttings or root sprouts is exceptionally good, and this feature is sometimes of value in obtaining a network of fast-growing roots for erosion control.

Certain species in this family are often difficult to separate from each other, and numerous natural hybrids have also been described. In contrast, some forms are very distinctive in appearance and are widely used as ornamentals. *Salix* and *Populus* are represented in North America by more than 120 species.

BOTANICAL FEATURES OF THE FAMILY

Leaves deciduous, alternate, simple, stipulate; the petioles often glandular.

Flowers imperfect (species dioecious) in some cases also androgynous (201), both sexes in aments, usually appearing before the leaves; individual flowers solitary, each subtended by a bract; staminate flowers with 1 to many stamens; pistillate flowers consisting of a 1-celled pistil with 2 to 4 parietal placentae bearing many ovules, the styles with 2 to 4, often 2-lobed stigmas.

Fruit a 1-celled, 2- to 4-valved capsule containing numerous small tufted seeds which are shed in late spring or early summer. These are extremely light in weight and are often carried considerable distances by wind. They rapidly lose their vitality, however, and unless a moist location is found within a few hours after their release, they soon dry out and die. Given proper conditions, germination takes place rapidly, often within 24 to 48 hours.

---

[1] Three other genera are recognized by some taxonomists.

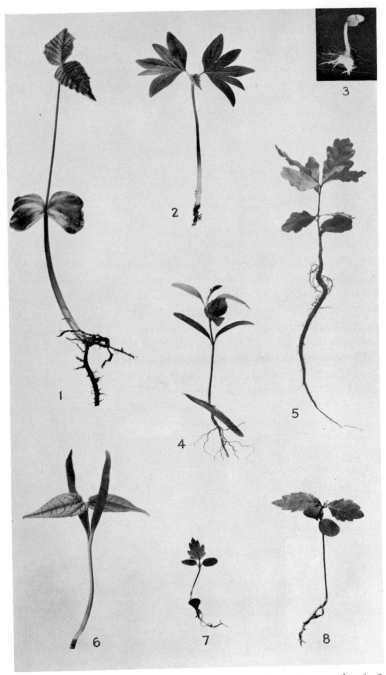

FIG. 92. Some broad-leaved seedlings. *1.* Beech × ¾. *2.* Basswood × 1. *3.* Aspen × 3. *4.* White ash × ½. *5.* White oak × ⅓. *6.* Sugar maple × ½. *7.* Yellow birch × 1. *8.* American elm × 1.

Genus	Leaves	Flowers	Fruit	Buds
Salix	usually several times longer than broad; short-petioled	with nectar glands; bract margins entire	not inserted upon a disk	covered by a single caplike scale
Populus	usually about as long as broad; long-petioled	without nectar glands; bract margins laciniate	inserted upon a disk	covered by several imbricated scales

SALIX L.   Willow

The genus *Salix* numbers about 300 species which are largely scattered through the cooler regions of the Northern Hemisphere. A few forms are tropical (Indonesia), and some are found in South Africa and southern South America. Others extend beyond the Arctic Circle to the northern limits of tree growth, where they become greatly dwarfed and in some instances are actually reduced to a creeping or matlike habit. The willows as a group require considerable moisture, and many of them frequent the banks of streams, where their interlacing roots help to protect the soil from washing away; coarsely woven mats of willow branches are used to effect the same purpose in artificial stream control. A number

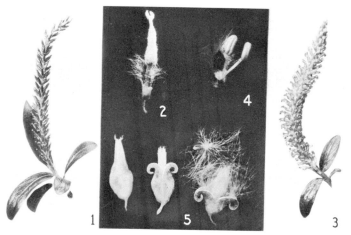

FIG. 93. *Salix*. Willow. *1*. Pistillate ament × ¾. *2*. Pistillate flower showing basal nectar gland × 6. *3*. Staminate ament × ¾. *4*. Staminate flower × 6. *5*. Successive stages in the opening of the capsular fruit with the liberation of a seed × 5.

of shrubby forms serve as browse in the western cattle country, and the honeybee obtains much of its pollen and nectar for rearing spring broods from the early-flowering species. In the chemical history of aspirin, extract of willow bark is one of the precursors (73). Among the exotics commonly used for ornamental purposes are the graceful and stately Babylon weeping willow (*S. babylonica* L.) of eastern Asia; laurel willow (*S. pentandra* L.), yellowstem white willow [*S. alba* var. *vitellina* (L.) Stokes], and crack willow (*S. fragilis* L.), all of European origin. The last two are common escapes and are found naturalized over a large portion of the eastern United States.

About 70 species of *Salix* are native to North America (for some authors more than 100), but only about 38 of them attain tree size. Most of the commercial willow timber is produced by *S. nigra* Marsh.

BOTANICAL FEATURES OF THE GENUS

Leaves alternate or rarely subopposite, mostly lanceolate to elliptical, the margins entire or finely to coarsely toothed, usually short-petioled, or sessile; the stipules often persisting for several weeks or longer.

Flowers entomophilous and also anemophilous; aments ascending, the individual flowers (both sexes) with a basal nectar gland and a densely pubescent, entire-margined bract; *staminate* flowers with 1 to 12 (mostly 2) stamens; *pistillate* flowers with a single pistil composed of 2 carpels.

Fruit a 2-valved, 1-celled capsule containing a number of cottony or silky-haired seeds.

Twigs slender to stout, often brittle, glabrous, pubescent or hoary-tomentose; ranging through shades of red, orange, yellow, green, purple, or brown; lenticellate; *terminal buds* absent; *lateral buds* usually appressed, covered by a single caplike scale; *leaf scars* V-shaped, usually with 3 bundle scars; *stipule scars* often inconspicuous; *pith* homogeneous, terete.

Salix nigra Marsh.   Black willow

BOTANICAL FEATURES

Leaves 3" to 6" long, ⅜" to ¾" wide; *shape* lanceolate; *margin* finely serrate; *apex* acuminate, often falcate; *base* obtuse or rounded; *surfaces* light green and somewhat lustrous above, glabrous below (except on the veins); *petiole* short, terete.

Flowers, aments terminal, appearing on short leafy twigs; *staminate flowers* with 3 to 5 long, yellow, filamentous stamens; *pistillate* with a solitary pistil and 2 nearly sessile stigmas.

Fruit a capsule about ¼" long, slender, ovoid-conic, short-stalked, glabrous; seeds 2 to 3 million to the pound.

FIG. 94. *Salix nigra.* Black willow. *1.* Bark. *2.* Leaf showing semi-persistent stipules × ½. *3.* Fruiting ament × ¾. *4.* Buds × 1¼.

Twigs slender, purplish green to pale orange-brown, usually rather brittle; *terminal buds* absent, the twig scar inconspicuous; *lateral buds* reddish brown, ⅟₁₆″ long. **Bark** brown to nearly black, divided into deep fissures separating thick, interlacing, sometimes scaly ridges.

GENERAL DESCRIPTION

Black willow is a small to medium-sized tree 30 to 60 ft high and about 14 in. in diameter (max. 140 by 8* ft) with a broad, irregular crown and a superficial root system. This species is usually found on moist or wet soils along the banks of streams and lakes or in swamps. Reproduction by seeds may be somewhat restricted since they must find moist mineral soil soon after being shed; however, propagation by natural or man-made cuttings, sprouts, and root suckers is excellent.

Growth is rapid, and maturity is reached in 50 to 70 years. Like most willows, this species is very intolerant and is usually found as a dominant tree in hardwood mixtures or in pure stands. In the South, especially along the Mississippi River, pioneer well-stocked stands of black willow develop. On the best of alluvial silts, trees 40 years old may be 100 ft tall and nearly 20 in. d.b.h., with straight boles clear of limbs for as much as 40 ft.

PLATE 29. *Salix nigra.*

Eastern United States (see map, Plate 29).

POPULUS L.　　Cottonwood; poplar

The genus *Populus*, which includes the aspens, cottonwoods, and balsam poplars, consists of about 35 species widely distributed throughout the Northern Hemisphere, ranging from the forests of northern Africa, the Himalaya, China, and Japan northward beyond the Arctic Circle. In the New World, poplars are found from Alaska and Canada to northern Mexico.

In many sections of our semiarid West, the cottonwoods are the only species attaining tree size, and here they are very characteristic of stream banks, which in summer show their presence at some distance by the green band of cottonwoods along their margins.

Several exotic species are used as street and shade trees in American cities. These include the Simon poplar (*P. simonii* Carr.), a tree readily identified by its reddish-brown, sharp-pointed buds and its bright green, nearly rhombic leaves; the clone Lombardy poplar (*P. nigra* var. *italica* Muenchh.), a large tree with a narrow columnar crown of ascending branches; and the European white poplar (*P. alba* L.) with several of its varieties, characterized by white tomentose buds and palmately lobed leaves which are not infrequently white tomentose below. The latter species is very aggressive and often produces thickets of root sprouts around the base of the parent tree. The common and widely cultivated Carolina poplar, *Populus* × *eugenei* Simon-Louis, also originated in Europe and is believed to be a hybrid clone (*P. deltoides* × *P. nigra* L.); [1] only the staminate form of Carolina poplar is known. Widely used as a street tree on account of its rapid growth, it has been removed by many cities on account of the litter of catkins in the spring and the tendency of the roots to obstruct sewers. The leaves may be separated from those of eastern cottonwood by their obtuse, usually eglandular bases and the finer serrations of the margin.

About 10 species of *Populus* are native to North America, but only 5 or 6 of them occur in commercial size and quantity.

BOTANICAL FEATURES OF THE GENUS

Leaves ovate to deltoid (lanecolate or nearly so in *P. angustifolia* James and *P.* × *acuminata* Rydb. of the Rocky Mountains); entire-margined, crenate-serrate, dentate, or lobed; usually with long, terete, or laterally compressed petioles.

Flowers anemophilous, in drooping aments appearing in advance of the leaves, individual flowers (both sexes) solitary, inserted on a disk and subtended by a pubescent, laciniate bract; *staminate* flowers with either 6 to 12, or 12 to many stamens; *pistillate* flowers with a single pistil composed of 2 or 3 (rarely 4) carpels.

Fruit a 2- to 4-valved capsule containing a number of tufted seeds; the seeds are shed in large numbers and at the height of their dispersal, wind-blown masses of white "cotton" may accumulate to a depth of 6 in. or more in neighboring depressions.

Twigs stout to slender, mostly olive-brown to lustrous reddish brown, glabrous, pubescent, or hoary-pubescent; *terminal bud* present, resinous or nonresinous, covered by several imbricated scales; *lateral buds* of nearly the same size as the terminal buds, divergent or appressed, the

DISTINGUISHING CHARACTERISTICS OF ASPENS AND COTTONWOODS

Group	Flowers	Capsules	Buds
Aspens	with 6 to 12 stamens	thin-walled	essentially nonresinous
Cottonwoods (and balsam poplars)	with 12 to 60 stamens	thick-walled	resinous and aromatic

[1] According to L. H. Bailey, the original tree was found in the nursery of Simon-Louis, near Metz, France, in 1832. This tree was measured by Henry in 1913 (81 years later) and found to be 150 ft in height and nearly 8 ft in diameter. The Check List (212) states that *P.* ×*eugenei* also includes hybrid clones from other places.

first or lowest scale directly above the leaf scar; flower buds conspicuously larger; *leaf scars* nearly deltoid to elliptical, with 3 bundle scars, either single or divided; *pith* homogeneous, stellate in transverse section.

THE ASPENS

Populus tremuloides Michx.   Quaking aspen; trembling aspen; popple

BOTANICAL FEATURES

Leaves 1½″ to 3″ in diameter; *shape* suborbicular to broadly ovate; *margin* finely crenate-serrate; *apex* acute to acuminate; *base* rounded; *surfaces* somewhat lustrous, green and glabrous above, duller and glabrous below; *petioles* laterally flattened,[1] ½″ to 3″ long; especially in the var. *aurea*, the leaves turn a bright yellow in the autumn.
Fruit about ¼″ long, narrowly conical, curved; *seeds* about 3,600,000 to the pound.
Twigs slender, lustrous, reddish brown; *terminal buds* conical, sharp-pointed, sometimes very slightly resinous, covered by 6 to 7 visible, reddish-brown, imbricated scales; *lateral buds* incurved, similar to the terminal buds but smaller.
Bark smooth, greenish white to cream-colored, at length furrowed, dark brown or gray, often roughened by numerous wartlike excrescences.

GENERAL DESCRIPTION

Quaking aspen is the most widely distributed tree of North America. It is fast growing, relatively shortlived, and commonly attains heights of 50 to 60 ft and diameters of 1 to 2 ft (max. 120 by 4½ ft[2]). This tree is very intolerant and under competition develops a long, clear bole and small rounded crown. The root system is widespreading, and sometimes surface roots may extend as far as 80 ft from the base of the tree (141). Depending upon soil depth, other roots may go down 3 to 5 ft or more (127). Over its vast range, quaking aspen is found on many types of soil from moist loamy sands to shallow rocky soils and clay.

In old-growth forests, this species occurred as a scattered dominant tree, or along the edges of openings or water courses where there was sufficient light. Logging and subsequent fires usually destroyed the organic litter over wide areas and exposed mineral soil. Such sites are favorable to aspen, a prolific seeder, and extensive pure stands of this species spring up and serve as a cover for the more tolerant northern conifers and hardwoods which develop slowly beneath this semi-open canopy. After 30 years or more, competition becomes excessive, much of the aspen dies, and the relatively few trees which are left maintain a posi-

---

[1] On young sprouts the petioles are often nearly terete, and the leaf shape is like that in balsam poplar.
[2] P. E. Packer reported a tree of this size growing in the Manti National Forest, 28 miles west of Castle Dale, Utah.

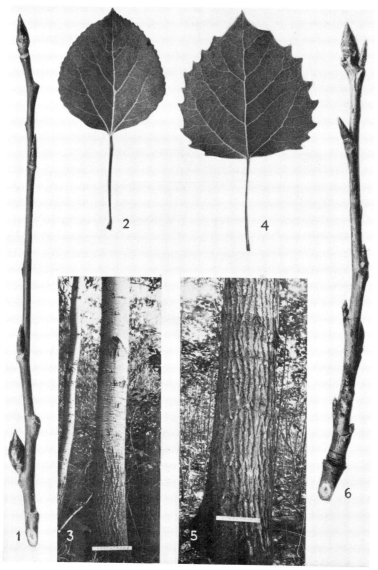

FIG. 95. *Populus tremuloides,* Quaking aspen; and *P. grandidentata,* Bigtooth aspen. *1. P. tremuloides* twig × 1¼. *2.* Leaf × ½. *3.* Bark of young tree showing transition, near base, of smooth surface to furrows typical of old trees. *4. P. grandidentata* leaf × ½. *5.* Bark of old tree. *6.* Twig × 1¼.

tion of dominance over the dense growth of other species below. In the Lake States, these include the northern pines, spruces, and balsam fir, which in turn are finally replaced by hemlock and maples. Other aspen associates are many, including bigtooth aspen, paper birch, and balsam poplar, and in the west Douglas-fir, lodgepole pine, and white fir.

PLATE 30. *Populus tremuloides.*

Unless managed, the pioneer stand of aspen is transient, and although some individual trees may reach an age of 150 years (200 in the west), most Lake States aspen over 60 years old is not worth harvesting because of its rapid deterioration. At least 500 organisms from deer and beaver to insects, fungi, and viruses feed upon aspen (141).

When aspen stands are cut, innumerable root suckers grow quickly from the shallow roots and form a dense new forest (122). In Michigan, Minnesota, and Wisconsin, there are extensive areas of aspen forests which are especially valuable for pulpwood production.

Transcontinental through Canada, northern United States, and western mountains (map, Plate 30).

Populus grandidentata Michx.   Bigtooth aspen

Distinguishing characteristics. *Leaves* suborbicular to ovate, usually larger than those of the preceding species, coarsely toothed, with a long, slender, flattened petiole (young leaves whitish tomentose). *Fruit* similar to that of quaking aspen. *Twigs* often stouter than those of quaking aspen, dull, brownish gray; lateral buds gray, puberulous, divergent. *Bark* olive-green but often not readily separated from that of the preceding species, later brown and furrowed.

General description. Bigtooth aspen is a medium-sized tree, 60 to 70 ft high and 2 ft in diameter (max. 95° by 5° ft). It is similar in its silvical features to the preceding species. However, in the Lake States, bigtooth aspen is less adaptable to site variation than quaking aspen and predominates on well-drained uplands of medium to good quality. With the cessation or control of forest fires, conditions are increasingly unfavorable for the development of new extensive stands of the aspens. Since these two species, especially bigtooth aspen, will produce under management in Michigan more wood per acre per year than any other tree native to the state (141), it is important to develop the best silvicultural methods for growing them.

Range. Nova Scotia and New Brunswick westward through southern Canada to northeastern North Dakota; southeast through central Illinois to the Ohio River and along the mountains to Tennessee; in the East, along the coast to New Jersey, and in the mountains to North Carolina.

THE COTTONWOODS AND BALSAM POPLARS

This group includes about 8 native species and a number of varieties. Although 6 of these are starred in the Check List (212), it is doubtful whether more than 3 are of first importance, except perhaps locally.

DISTINGUISHING CHARACTERISTICS OF IMPORTANT SPECIES

Species	Leaves	Fruit
P. balsamifera, balsam poplar	ovate-lanceolate; petiole terete	2-valved, glabrous
P. deltoides, eastern cottonwood	deltoid; petiole compressed, glandular at the apex	3- or 4-valved, glabrous
P. trichocarpa, black cottonwood	ovate-lanceolate; petiole terete	3-valved, pubescent

Populus balsamifera L. [*Populus tacamahaca* Mill.]   Balsam poplar;
Tacamahac poplar (SPN)

BOTANICAL FEATURES

Leaves 3″ to 6″ long, 2″ to 4″ wide; *shape* broadly ovate to ovate-lanceolate; *margin* finely crenate-serrate; *apex* abruptly acute to acuminate; *base* rounded or cordate; *surfaces* lustrous dark green, glabrous above, pale green or commonly with rusty-brown blotches below; *petiole* terete, 2″ to 3½″ long.
Fruit ¼″ to ⅓″ long, ovoid, 2-valved, glabrous.
Twigs moderately stout, reddish brown to dark brown, lustrous, lenticellate; *terminal buds* ovate to narrowly conical, covered by 5 imbricated scales sealed by a fragrant amber-colored resin; *lateral buds* smaller, appressed, or divergent near the apex.
Bark on young stems and limbs greenish brown to reddish brown, on older trunks eventually becoming gray to grayish black and dividing into flat, scaly, or shaggy ridges separated by narrow fissures.

Fig. 96. *Populus balsamifera.* Balsam poplar. *1.* Bark. *2.* Leaf × ½. *3.* Fruit × 2. *4.* Twig × 1¼.

GENERAL DESCRIPTION

Balsam poplar is a fast-growing, medium-sized tree 60 to 80 ft high and 12 to 24 in. in diameter (max. 100 by 5 to 6 ft) with a long cylindrical bole, narrow, open, pyramidal crown, and shallow root system. It is characteristic of alluvial bottomlands and stream banks and reaches its greatest size in the far Northwest (Mackenzie River Valley of north-western Canada). In this region, considered too cold for most trees, it is the largest, most characteristic species and occurs in open pure stands or mixed with other northern trees. Throughout its wide range, the associates of balsam poplar include balsam fir, white spruce, the aspens, and paper birch. Like other poplars, this species is intolerant. Besides the timber and pulpwood which it furnishes, balsam poplar serves as a cover crop for white spruce in certain sections of Canada.

RANGE

Transcontinental through Canada and northern United States (map, Plate 31).

PLATE 31. *Populus balsamifera.*

Balm-of-Gilead poplar is similar to balsam poplar except that the leaves are more cordate, and pubescent below. According to Stout (337), Balm-of-Gilead, a well-known planted tree in northeastern United States and adjacent Canada, is a sterile clone from (1) a single pistillate tree of *P. balsamifera* var. *subcordata* Hylander, heartleaf balsam poplar, or (2) a hybrid of this variety.

Populus deltoides Bartr.   Eastern cottonwood; eastern poplar (SPN)

BOTANICAL FEATURES

Leaves 3" to 6" long, 4" to 5" wide; *shape* deltoid to ovate-deltoid; *margin* crenate-serrate, the teeth glandular; *apex* acuminate to acute; *base* truncate to cordate; *surfaces* lustrous green, glabrous above, somewhat paler and glabrous below; *petiole* flattened, 1½" to 3" long, glandular.
Fruit ¼" to ⅓" long, ovoid, 3- or 4-valved; *seeds* about 350,000 (200,000–590,000) to the pound.
Twigs stout, angular, yellowish brown, glabrous; *terminal buds* about ¾" long, narrowly ellipsoidal to conical, lustrous brown, resinous, covered by 6 or 7 imbricated scales; *lateral buds* somewhat smaller, divergent.
Bark light greenish yellow on young stems, eventually becoming ash-gray and dividing into thick, flattened or rounded ridges separated by deep fissures.

GENERAL DESCRIPTION

This species, the most important of the eastern poplars, is a medium-sized to large tree 80 to 100 ft high and 3 to 4 ft in diameter (max. 175 by 12 ft). Open-grown trees have a spreading crown supported by a massive trunk which is often divided near the ground and terminates below in an extensive superficial root system; in the forest, the bole is long, clear, and cylindrical, and the crown much smaller.

Not common in the Northeast and Appalachian regions, eastern cottonwood, together with its varieties or closely related species, covers a wide range from the Rocky Mountains to the southern Atlantic Coast. It is especially common on moist alluvial soils through the plains and prairie states, where a winding belt of green cottonwood crowns usually indicates the presence of a stream or water course. Although not found naturally on dry soils, this species was planted extensively around homesteads by the early settlers and when once established has proved to be relatively drought-resistant.

On the best alluvial soils in the Mississippi Valley growth is exceedingly fast, and young trees commonly grow 5 ft or more in height and 1 in. in diameter yearly. Cottonwood is very intolerant and occurs in pure stands or open mixtures with such species as black willow, sycamore, American elm, and some of the bottomland oaks. In the South, cottonwood may seed in heavily on old fields in mixture with sweetgum, by which it is eventually replaced.

Like other poplars, eastern cottonwood liberates large quantities of silky-haired seeds which may travel by air or on the surface of water for many miles. Although germination is high (60 to 90 percent), vitality is transient, and this probably accounts for the distribution of this species along water courses where in late spring moist silt is available for the

1

2

3

5

4

6

7

sprouting seeds. Propagation by cuttings is good, and young trees produced in this way make rapid growth; two-year-old trees sometimes
attain heights of 30 ft and diameters of nearly 5 in. (127). Cottonwood
is a short-lived species; trees over 70 years old rapidly deteriorate, and
the maximum life span is probably not greater than two centuries.

RANGE

(Including that of the plains cottonwood, var. *occidentalis* Rydb. known
also as *P. sargentii* Dode) Eastern United States and the Great Plains
(map, Plate 32).

PLATE 32. *Populus deltoides.*

Populus trichocarpa Torr. and Gray   Black cottonwood; California
poplar (SPN)

BOTANICAL FEATURES

Leaves 5″ to 6″ long; *shape* ovate to ovate-lanceolate; *margin* finely crenate to
crenate-serrate; *apex* acute to long-acuminate; *base* rounded or slightly cordate;
surfaces dark green, glabrous above, rusty brown to silvery white, or occasionally
pale green below; *petioles* 1½″ to 3″ long, terete in transverse section.
Fruit ⅛″ to ½″ long, 3-valved, pubescent.
Twigs slender to moderately stout, orange-brown to light yellow-brown or greenish
brown, slightly angular, lenticellate; *terminal buds* ¾″ long, ovoid-conical, with 6 or
7 visible imbricated scales, resinous and exhaling a fragrant odor when crushed;
lateral buds smaller, often divergent and falcate.
Bark tawny yellow to gray, and smooth on young stems; later, dark gray to grayish
brown and separated by deep furrows into narrow, flat-topped ridges.

FIG. 97. *Populus deltoides.* Eastern cottonwood. *1.* Twig × 1¼. *2.* Leaf × ½. *3.* Staminate aments × ½. *4.* Staminate flowers, front and rear views, respectively, × 3. *5.*
Pistillate flower and laciniate bract × 3. *6.* Fruit clusters × ⅔. *7.* Bark. Base of tree
has been covered with river silt, therefore butt swell is not visible.

FIG. 98. *Populus trichocarpa.* Black cottonwood. *1.* Twig × 1¼. *2.* Pistillate ament × ½. *3.* Staminate ament × ½. *4.* Staminate flower (bract removed) × 3. *5.* Pistillate flower (bract removed) × 3. *6.* Mature capsule × 2. *7.* Open capsule releasing seed × 2. *8.* Leaf × ½. *9.* Bark. (*Photograph by G. B. Sudworth, U.S. Forest Service.*)

Black cottonwood, the largest of the American cottonwoods, is also the tallest broadleaved tree of the Pacific Northwest. In the Puget Sound basin and vicinity, trees sometimes attain heights of from 125 to 150 ft and diameters of from 48 to 60 in. (max. 225 by 10* ft). Forest trees develop long, clear boles with narrow, cylindrical, round-topped crowns. This species occurs most frequently on moist, sandy, gravelly, or deep alluvial soils. Dwarfed trees may be seen occasionally on poor, dry sterile sites.

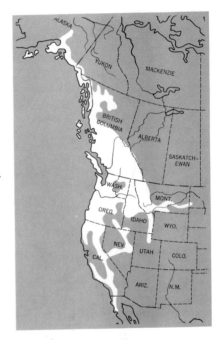

PLATE 33. *Populus trichocarpa.*

Black cottonwood forms limited pure stands and groves, especially on newly formed river bars. It also occurs with such species as Douglas-fir, western white pine, white spruce, western redcedar, western hemlock, paper birch, red alder, vine (*Acer circinatum* Pursh) and bigleaf maples, and numerous willows.

Large seed crops are released annually. The seed exhibits a high degree of viability, but its capacity to germinate is of very short duration. A moist sandy soil provides a suitable seedbed, and vigorous seedling development usually occurs on such sites. This species is very intolerant, and trees lacking vigor are soon suppressed by their more rapidly growing associates. Growth is quite rapid, particularly through the seedling

SALICACEAE 235

and sapling stages. According to a Forest Service report (127), a number of nine-year-old stems growing on Lady Island in the Columbia River near Camas, Washington averaged 48.5 ft in height and 6.7 in. in diameter. Trees on good sites grow fairly rapidly throughout their life span, with maturity being attained in about 150 to 200 years.

RANGE

West Coast and Inland Empire (map, Plate 33). *Altitudinal Distribution:* sea level to 2,000 ft in the North, as high as 7,000 to 9,000 ft at its southern limits in California.

Populus heterophylla L.   Swamp cottonwood; swamp poplar (SPN)

Distinguishing characteristics. *Leaves* ovate, crenate-serrate, cordate or rounded at the base, with a terete petiole. *Fruit* ovoid, 2- or 3-valved, long pedicelled. *Twigs* moderately slender, brownish gray, with an orange pith and slightly resinous, stout buds. *Bark* furrowed, somewhat scaly.

General description. Swamp cottonwood is a medium-sized tree scattered through the bottomland forests of the southern Coastal Plain. It is similar in its habits to the other cottonwoods and although utilized locally is of secondary importance among the southern hardwoods.

Range. Along the coastal plain from southern Connecticut to northern Florida, west in the Gulf States to western Louisiana, and north in the Mississippi Valley to southern Illinois, Indiana, and Ohio (also said to occur in Michigan).

Myricaceae: The Waxmyrtle family

This family comprises two genera and about 40 species of shrubs and small trees found usually in swamps or on dry sandy soils in the temperate and warmer parts of the world. The leaves are aromatic and bear minute resin dots, visible with a hand lens. *Comptonia peregrina* (L.) Coult. with pinnatifid, fernlike, linear-lanceolate leaves is the common "sweet-fern" of the Northeast. The Myricas, or bayberries, have leaves with entire or toothed margins. The waxy covering of the fruit of *Myrica pensylvanica* Loisel furnishes most of the bayberry wax used for candles, while the bark of *Myrica cerifera* L. contains volatile oils. For a description of candle making see Dengler (100a).

Myrica californica Cham., a West Coast species, occurs quite abundantly on low hills, sand dunes, and riverbanks near Puget Sound and the Pacific Ocean.

Leitneriaceae: The Corkwood family

Although of no commercial importance, this family is of interest botanically, and also because it produces the lightest wood grown in the United States. It is the only family in the order Leitneriales and comprises only 1 genus and 1 species.

The single species, corkwood (*Leitneria floridana* Chapm.), is a shrub or small tree native to swamps in scattered areas of the southern Coastal Plain and lower Mississippi Valley. The leaves are alternate, 4 to 6 in. long, oblong to elliptic-lanceolate, and pubescent. The flowers are unisexual on separate trees, and the fruit is a dry drupe. The wood has a specific gravity of about 0.21 (cork 0.24, balsa wood 0.12).

Juglandaceae: The Walnut family

The Juglandaceae comprise 6 or 7 genera and about 60 species of trees and large shrubs which are widely distributed through the forests of the North Temperate Zone, and to a lesser extent in the tropical forests of both the Northern and Southern Hemispheres. The importance of this family lies chiefly in the many valuable timber trees which it includes. The genera *Juglans*, *Engelhardtia*, and *Pterocarya* produce cabinet woods, while those of *Carya* are extremely tough and are suitable for many purposes where strength is required. The fruits of several species of *Carya* and *Juglans* are used as food in many localities; and the bark and fruit husks of a few species are sources of yellow dyes and tannic compounds. Two genera and about 25 species of the Juglandaceae are found in the United States.

BOTANICAL FEATURES OF THE FAMILY

Leaves deciduous, mostly alternate,[1] pinnately compound, estipulate, more or less aromatic.

Flowers imperfect (species monoecious), appearing with or after the leaves; *staminate* in drooping axillary aments, the individual flowers consisting of 3 to 105 often nearly sessile stamens surrounded by a 3- to 6-lobed calyx and subtended by a bract; *pistillate* solitary or in few-flowered spikes terminating the new growth, the individual flowers comprising a 1- to 4-celled pistil, short style, and 2 plumose stigmas, the ovary clothed by a 3- to 5-lobed or parted calyx and subtended by an adnate involucre consisting of a bract and 2 bracteoles.

Fruit (1) drupaceous; or (2) a bony nut (or nutlike)[2] encased in a semifleshy or woody, dehiscent "husk"; seed exalbuminous, with large cotyledons.

[1] Two Mexican and Central American genera have certain species with opposite leaves.
[2] In the Juglandaceae, the "husk" consists of the semifleshy outer ovary wall, together with the fused bract and bracteoles. By definition, a drupe should not include the involucre; hence the indehiscent fruit of *Juglans* may at most be called "drupaceous" or drupelike. The fruit of *Carya* by contrast presents a dehiscent "husk," which, however, comprises not only the bracts but also the outer ovary wall as in *Juglans*.

Genus	Flowers	Fruit	Pith
Juglans	staminate aments unbranched; stamens, 7 to 105	shell of nut corrugated or rugose; husk indehiscent	chambered after the first season
Carya (*Hicoria*)	staminate aments 3-branched; stamens, 3 to 7	shell of nut smooth although generally ribbed; husk usually dehiscent along 4 sutures	homogeneous

JUGLANS L.   Walnut

The walnuts, although numerous and widely distributed during past geological periods (Tertiary), now comprise only about 20 species. These are found in the forests of North, Central, and South America (231), the West Indies, southern Europe, and southern and eastern Asia. The French, Turkish, Italian, and Circassian walnut timbers, respectively, are produced by the cosmopolite *Juglans regia* L., which is also an important timber-contributing species of India. The so-called English walnuts are the fruits of this tree, and in recent years large plantations have been developed in both Oregon and California.

Six species of *Juglans* are native to the United States, but only two of them (*J. nigra* and *J. cinerea*) are important as producers of lumber. *J. hindsii* Jeps. and *J. californica* S. Wats. are two California species. The former is used as a stock for English walnut cultivation along the Pacific slope, and occasionally as a shade tree. Little walnut, *J. microcarpa* Berlandier, the fifth species, is a small tree native to Texas, Arizona, and northern Mexico, and the remaining southwestern species is Arizona walnut, *J. major* (Torr.) Heller.

BOTANICAL FEATURES OF THE GENUS

Leaves odd-pinnately compound, consisting of 9 to 23 sessile or nearly sessile leaflets; *leaflets* more or less oblong-lanceolate, each with an acute to acuminate apex, inequilateral base, and finely serrate margin; *rachis* stout, usually pubescent.

Flowers imperfect (species monoecious); *staminate aments* preformed, appearing as small, scaly, conelike buds, unbranched; *stamens* 7 to 105;

FIG. 99. *Juglans.* Walnut. *1.* Pistillate (upper) and staminate (lower) flowers × ½. *2.* Staminate flower (face view) × 3. *3.* Pistillate flower × 3. *4.* Staminate flower (back view) × 3.

pistillate in 2- to 8-flowered spikes, the individual flowers consisting of a 2- to 4-celled pistil surmounted by a short style and two divergent, plumose stigmas.

Fruit drupaceous; outer ovary wall ("husk") semifleshy, indehiscent; *pit* nutlike, thick-walled, rugose or deeply corrugated; *seed* sweet, often oily.

Twigs stout, with an acrid taste, pubescent or glabrous; *pith* chambered after the first season except between the seasons' growth, stellate in transverse section; *terminal buds* few-scaled, often appearing naked; *lateral buds* commonly superposed; *leaf scars* obcordate to obdeltoid, with three sets of equidistant U-shaped bundle scars.

Species	Leaves	Fruit	Pith	Bark
J. nigra black walnut	with 15 to 23 ovate-lanceolate leaflets	globose; nut corrugations rounded	buff-colored	dark brown to black, with thin anastomosing ridges
J. cinerea, butternut	with 11 to 17 oblong-lanceolate leaflets	oblong-ovoid; nut corrugations sharp	chocolate-colored	ashy gray, with broad, anastomosing ridges

Juglans nigra L.   Black walnut; eastern black walnut (SPN)

BOTANICAL FEATURES

Leaves 12″ to 24″ long, with 15 to 23 nearly sessile leaflets attached to a stout puberulous rachis, the terminal leaflet often suppressed; *leaflets* 3″ to 3½″ long, 1″ to 1¼″ wide, ovate-lanceolate; *margin* finely serrate; *apex* acute to acuminate; *base* inequilateral; *surfaces* lustrous, dark yellow-green and glabrous above, pale green and pubescent below; *petiole* very short, puberulous.

Flowers appearing in late May and early June; *staminate* with 17 to 50 nearly sessile stamens.

Fruit 1½″ to 2″ in diameter, globose or nearly so, solitary or in clusters of 2 or 3; with a thick, semifleshy, yellowish-green, pubescent husk; *pit* corrugated, with rounded ridges; *seed* sweet, oily; about 40 (20–100) of the pits (without husks) to the pound.

Twigs stout, light brown to orange-brown, lenticellate; *pith* chambered, with thin diaphragms, buff-colored; *terminal buds* short, blunt, covered by a few pubescent scales; *lateral buds* much smaller, often superposed; *leaf scars* elevated, obcordate, without a hairy fringe on the upper margin; *bundle scars* in 3 U-shaped clusters.

Bark dark brown to grayish black, divided by deep, narrow furrows into thin ridges, the whole forming a roughly diamond-shaped pattern.

GENERAL DESCRIPTION

Black walnut is not only first in importance among the native species of *Juglans,* but it is also one of the most highly valued of North American hardwoods. Although usually a medium-sized tree 70 to 90 ft high and 2 to 3 ft in diameter, it may reach a maximum height of 150 ft and a diameter of 8 ft.

This species is very intolerant, and under forest competition develops a tall, well-formed clear bole, with a small, open crown which is always dominant in the stand; the root system is deep and wide-spreading, with a definite taproot, at least in early life.

Small amounts of seed may be produced nearly every year, with large

Fig. 100. *Juglans nigra*. Black walnut. *1*. Leaf × ⅕. *2*. Bark. *3*. Fruit × ¾. *4*. Nut × ¾. *5*. Transverse section of fruit × ¾. *6*. Twig × 1¼.

crops at irregular intervals; rodents are the chief means of dispersal, although they also use many of the nuts for food. If stratified in the fall, the seeds show a high percentage of germination the following spring, but when allowed to dry out, vitality is decreased, and many will not germinate until the second year.

On deep, rich, moist soils, of alluvial origin, young seedlings may grow 3 ft in height the first season and double this figure the second year; logs 10 in. in diameter may be produced in 35 years. This species, however, is very sensitive to soil conditions and grows much more slowly on poorer sites; large pure stands are rare, but walnut groves are frequently found, apparently from seeds buried by squirrels. The chief associates of black walnut include yellow-poplar, white ash, black cherry, basswood, American beech, numerous oaks, and hickories. Black walnut matures in about 150 years, but its life span may embrace 2½ centuries.

The supply of black walnut timber has been greatly depleted, but efforts have been made to popularize the planting of this valuable species.[1] Besides the timber which it produces, the fruit is sold locally, and new varieties are being developed with thinner shells.

RANGE

Eastern United States except on southern Coastal Plain (map, Plate 34).

1. *Juglans nigra.*

2. *Juglans cinerea.*

PLATE 34

[1] If used ornamentally, it should be known that the fruit husks contain a brown dye substance capable of permanently staining cloth (so used by the pioneers); and substances liberated by the roots poison certain nearby crops such as tomatoes and potatoes (87). However, black walnut is a good pasture tree. The more valuable grasses grow better within its root area than outside of it (49).

Juglans cinerea L.   Butternut

Leaves 15" to 30" long, with 11 to 17 nearly sessile leaflets attached to a stout, pubescent rachis; *leaflets* 3" to 4" long, 1¼" to 2" wide, oblong-lanceolate; *margin* serrate; *apex* acute to acuminate; *base* inequilateral and rounded; *surfaces* yellowish green, rugose above, paler and soft pubescent below; *petioles* extremely short, pubescent.

Flowers appearing in late May or early June; *staminate* with 7 to 15 nearly sessile stamens.

Fruit 1½" to 2½" long, oblong-ovoid, in clusters of 2 to 5, or solitary; with a semi-fleshy, greenish-bronze, indehiscent husk clothed with glandular pubescence, sticky to the touch; *pit* deeply corrugated, with sharp ridges; *seed* sweet and very oily; about 30 (15–40) of the pits (without husks) to the pound.

Twigs stout, greenish gray to reddish brown, lenticellate; *pith* chambered, with thick diaphragms, dark chocolate-brown to nearly black; *terminal buds* somewhat elongated, blunt, covered by a few pubescent scales, the outer ones lobed; *lateral buds* much smaller, often superposed, covered by rusty-brown tomentum; *leaf scars* elevated, obcordate with a dense hairy cushion on the upper margin; *bundle scars* in 3 U-shaped clusters.

Bark light gray, divided by shallow to moderately deep fissures into broad, flat ridges, later more closely furrowed with a roughly diamond-shaped pattern.

Butternut, or white walnut as this species is known in some localities, is a small to medium-sized tree, 40 to 60 ft high and 12 to 24 in. in diameter (max. 110 by 3 ft). The bole is often short and divides into a few stout, ascending limbs which form a broad, open, somewhat irregular, flat or round-topped crown. The root system comprises a taproot and a number of deep-seated but wide-spreading laterals; however, the roots of trees growing on shallow soils are superficial and devoid of anything resembling a taproot. This species commonly frequents the moist, rich loams of ravines and coves, although it also grows quite well on drier, rocky soils, especially of limestone origin.

Butternut never occurs in pure stands, although it is occasionally abundant locally in mixed hardwood forests, where its associates include black cherry, basswood, hickories, American beech, oaks, yellow-poplar, chestnut, and elms. At the northern limits of its range it is not infrequently mixed with sugar maple and yellow birch, and rarely with eastern white pine.

The silvical features of butternut are similar to those of the preceding species, but it is shorter-lived, usually not reaching a greater age than 75 years.

In addition to the timber produced (a minor species), the nuts are used

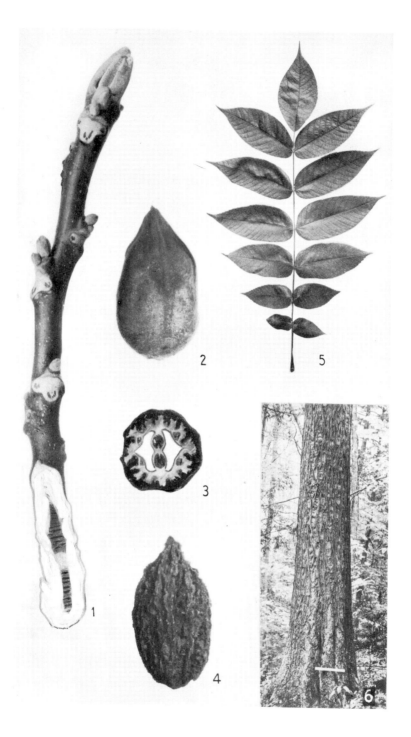

1　　2　　3

5

4

6

for food, a sweet sugary sirup may be obtained by boiling down the sap, the green husks liberate a dye which colors cloth orange or yellow, and the dried inner bark of the roots contains natural substances used in medicine.

Eastern United States except for the south Atlantic and Gulf Coastal Plains (up to 4,800 ft in the Virginias) (map, Plate 34).

CARYA Nutt. [*Hicoria Raf.*[1]]   Hickory

It is known that numerous species of the genus *Carya* were included in the ancient floras of Europe, northern Africa, Asia, and North America prior to the Glacial Epoch. Many of them since have been exterminated, until today there remain about 17 species. There are two each in mainland China and Mexico. The remaining ones range through eastern and southern United States; several of these are also found in adjacent Canada and Mexico.

About eight of the native hickories come under the heading of "true hickories," while the remaining five species are classified as "pecan hickories." Both groups contain a number of varieties and hybrids which are often difficult to identify; *Carya* is not a stable genus.

Hickories produce strong, especially shock-resistant wood; pecan hickory, besides furnishing timber, is valuable for its edible fruit.

BOTANICAL FEATURES OF THE GENUS

Leaves odd-pinnately compound, consisting of 3 to 17 sessile or nearly sessile leaflets; *leaflets* ovate to obovate, with acute to acuminate apices, inequilateral bases, and finely serrate margins; *rachis* usually stout, glabrous or pubescent.

Flowers imperfect (species monoecious); *staminate* in 3-branched aments, in clusters on the new growth or near the summit of the previous season's; individual flowers with 3 to 7 stamens, and a 2- or 3-lobed calyx; *pistillate* flowers in 2- to 10-flowered terminal spikes; the individual flowers with a

[1] The Indians made a fermented aqueous drink, called "powcohiccora," from the crushed nuts of the shagbark hickory, hence the name *Hicoria*.

FIG. 101. *Juglans cinerea*. Butternut. *1.* Twig × 1¼. *2.* Fruit × ¾. *3.* Transverse section of fruit. *4.* Nut showing sharp corrugations × ¾. *5.* Leaf × ⅕. *6.* Bark.

Fig. 102. *Carya*. Hickory. *1*. Flowers showing 3-branched habit of aments × ½. *2*. Pistillate flowers × 3. *3*. Staminate flower × 3.

bract and three bracteoles and a 1-celled ovary surmounted by 2 sessile stigmas.

Fruit an ovoid, pyriform or globose nut (or nutlike), encased in a semi-woody "husk" which splits along 4 sutures; *nut* ribbed, smooth, or slightly rugose, with a thick or thin shell; *seed* bitter or sweet.

Twigs stout to moderately slender, dark brown to orange-brown for the most part; *terminal buds* much larger than the laterals, covered by numerous imbricated or few valvate scales; *leaf scars* lobed or obdeltoid, the bundle scars in 3 U-shaped groups or scattered; *pith* homogeneous, somewhat stellate.

CONSPECTUS OF SUBGENERA

Subgenus	Leaves	Fruit Husks	Bud Scales
True hickories (*Eucarya*)	with 3 to 9 (mostly 5 to 7) leaflets	unwinged, occasionally ribbed at the sutures	imbricate with more than 6 scales
Pecan hickories (*Apocarya*)	with 5 to 17 (mostly more than 7) commonly falcate leaflets	usually broadly winged at the sutures	valvate with 4 to 6 scales

DISTINGUISHING CHARACTERISTICS OF IMPORTANT SPECIES

Species	Leaves	Fruit	Bark
C. ovata, shagbark hickory	10″ to 14″ long, usually with 5 leaflets; essentially glabrous	about 1½″ in diameter; husk ¼″ to ½″ thick; nut 4-ribbed, thick-shelled	broken into long shaggy plates
C. laciniosa, shellbark hickory	usually with 7 leaflets; velvety beneath	about 1¾″ in diameter; husk same; nut 4- to 6-ribbed	same
C. tomentosa, mockernut hickory	aromatic, usually with 7 or 9 leaflets; pubescent beneath, and on the rachis	about 1¼″ in diameter; husk ⅛″ to ¼″ thick; nut 4-ribbed	with anastomosing ridges; shallowly furrowed
C. ovalis, red hickory *ᵃ*	commonly with 7 leaflets; essentially glabrous	about 1″ long, oval in vertical section; husk less than ⅛″ thick; nut 4-ribbed above the middle	same but deeply furrowed, often flaky at the surface
C. glabra, pignut hickory	commonly with 5 leaflets; essentially glabrous	about 1″ in diameter, pyriform; husk thin, only partially dehiscent, nut not ribbed	with rounded anastomosing ridges, but often similar to the above

ᵃ Included under *C. glabra* in the Check List.

Carya ovata (Mill.) K. Koch   Shagbark hickory

BOTANICAL FEATURES

Leaves 10″ to 14″ long, with 5 (rarely 7) ovate-lanceolate to obovate, sessile or nearly sessile leaflets; *terminal leaflets* 5″ to 8″ long, 2″ to 3″ wide, usually larger than the lateral leaflets; *margin* finely serrate, ciliate; *apex* acute to acuminate; *base* cuneate; *surfaces* dark yellow-green, glabrous above; pale yellow-green, glabrous or puberulous below; *rachis* stout, grooved, glabrous or puberulous.
Fruit 1″ to 2½″ in diameter, solitary or paired, subglobose, depressed at the apex; *nut* subglobose, brownish white to pinkish white, 4-ribbed, with a reddish-brown to nearly black, readily dehiscent husk, ¼″ to ½″ thick; *seed* sweet; about 100 (80–150) nuts to the pound.[1]
Twigs stout, gray-brown to reddish brown, usually somewhat pubescent, lenticellate; *terminal buds* ½″ to ¾″ long, broadly ovoid to ellipsoidal, obtuse, covered with 3 or

[1] In this and other hickories, the numbers per pound do not include the husks.

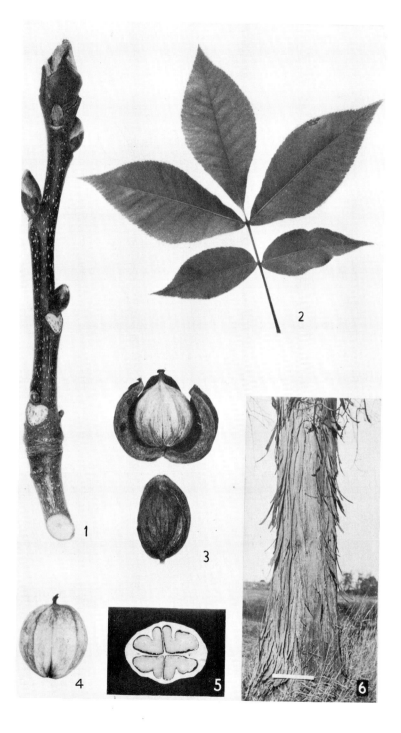

4 visible dark brown, loosely fitting pubescent scales; *lateral buds* somewhat smaller, ovoid, divergent; *leaf scars* slightly elevated, somewhat obdeltoid to semicircular; *bundle scars* scattered.

Bark smooth and gray on young stems, soon breaking up into thin plates which curve away from the trunk, thus giving it a shaggy appearance.

GENERAL DESCRIPTION

Shagbark hickory is a medium-sized tree 70 to 80 ft high and 12 to 24 in. in diameter (max. 130 by 4 ft) and in the forest develops a clear, straight, cylindrical bole with a small, open crown; if given sufficient space, however, the crown is typically oblong, and this shape characterizes many of the hickories when grown in the open. Seedlings of shagbark hickory develop a large and remarkably deep taproot which may penetrate downward 2 to 3 ft the first season with a corresponding top growth of only a few inches; this feature is typical of most of the hickories except those found on wet soils.

This species varies greatly over its range in the kind of site occupied; in the North it is often found on upland slopes in company with other hickories and oaks, while farther south it is commonest in deep, moist soils of alluvial origin, with the hardwoods of that region. Shagbark hickory, at least in youth, will stand considerable forest competition and may be rated as moderately tolerant.

Large crops of seed are produced nearly every other year, especially by trees in the open, and it is not unusual to obtain two to three bushels of nuts from a single large tree.[1] These are distributed by squirrels and other rodents. Where plentiful, the fruit reaches the local markets. Squirrels fail to claim some of their buried stores, and the following year young hickory seedlings spring up, often in the most unlooked-for places. The percentage of germination is high if seed is properly stratified the preceeding fall. Young trees produce sprouts when cut, and root suckers are also common, especially from older trees.

Shagbark hickory is a slow-growing tree and attains an age of 250 to 300 years. The shaggy bark makes it picturesque as a specimen tree when used ornamentally, but the litter of husks and fruit does not recommend it for city planting. Like most hickories, this tree is highly susceptible to damage by fire.

[1] Reports indicate that occasionally a large tree may yield from 15 to 18 bushels of nuts.

Fig. 103. *Carya ovata.* Shagbark hickory. *1.* Twig × 1¼. *2.* Leaf × ¼. *3.* Fruit × ¾. *4.* Nut × ¾. *5.* Transverse section of nut × ¾. *6.* Bark.

Eastern United States except for the south Atlantic and Gulf Coastal Plains (map, Plate 35).

1. *Carya ovata.*   2. *Carya laciniosa.*

PLATE 35

Carya carolinae-septentrionalis (Ashe) Engl. & Graebn.   Carolina hickory; southern shagbark hickory

This species resembles *C. ovata* except for its smaller leaves and fruit, slender twigs, and smaller, nearly glabrous, black or brownish-black cylindrical buds. It reaches commercial proportions and is very abundant in the Piedmont and ranges from central North Carolina to northern Georgia and northeastern Mississippi, and west through eastern Tennessee.

Carya laciniosa (Michx. f.) Loud.   Shellbark hickory; bigleaf shagbark hickory

BOTANICAL FEATURES

Leaves 15″ to 22″ long, with 5 to 9 (usually 7) ovate, oblong-lanceolate, or obovate, sessile or nearly sessile leaflets; *terminal leaflets* 5″ to 9″ long, 3″ to 4″ wide, usually larger than the laterals; *margin* finely serrate; *apex* acute to acuminate; *base* cuneate or inequilaterally rounded; *surfaces* dark green, lustrous above, pale yellow-green to yellowish brown, velvety pubescent below; *rachis* stout, grooved, glabrous or pubescent.

Fruit 1¾″ to 2½″ long, solitary or paired, ellipsoidal to subglobose, depressed at the apex, with an orange to chestnut-brown husk, ¼″ to ½″ thick; *nut* subglobose to obovoid, yellowish brown to reddish brown; 4- to 6-ribbed; *seed* sweet; about 30 (25–35) nuts to the pound.

Twigs stout, orange-brown, prominently orange lenticellate; *terminal buds* ¾″ to 1″

Fig. 104. *Carya laciniosa*. Shellbark hickory. *1.* Twig × 1¼. *2.* Side view of husk × ¾. *3.* Nut × ¾.

long, ovoid, obtuse, covered with 6 to 8 visible dark-brown, loosely fitting scales; *lateral buds* smaller, ovoid-oblong, divergent; *leaf scars* obcordate; *bundle scars* scattered.

Bark similar to that of the preceding species, but usually with straighter plates.

GENERAL DESCRIPTION

This hickory, as its common name indicates, is very similar to shagbark hickory. It is, however, much more frequently found on wet alluvial bottoms, and often occurs in nearly pure groves, or mixed with other bottomland hardwoods, on areas which are inundated for several weeks during high water. Some of the common associates include bur, swamp chestnut, cherrybark and pin oaks, red maple, American elm, and sweetgum.

RANGE

Ohio and Mississippi River Valleys (map, Plate 35).

Carya tomentosa Nutt.　　Mockernut hickory

BOTANICAL FEATURES

Leaves 9″ to 14″ long,[1] with 7 or 9 (rarely 5) sessile or nearly sessile, lanceolate to obovate-oblanceolate, glandular-resinous, fragrant leaflets; *terminal leaflets* 4″ to 6″

[1] Especially in the South, leaves on lower branches in the shade are often much larger (up to 20 in. in length).

Fig. 105. *Carya tomentosa*. Mockernut hickory. *1*. Leaf × ¼. *2*. Portion of tomentose petiole × 2. *3*. Twig × 1¼. *4*. Nut × ¾. *5*. Transverse section of nut × ¾. *6*. Fruit × ¾. *7*. Bark.

long, 2″ to 3″ wide, usually larger than the lateral leaflets; *margin* finely to coarsely serrate; *apex* acute to acuminate; *base* inequilaterally rounded or cuneate; *surfaces* dark yellow-green, lustrous above, pale yellow-green to orange-brown, pubescent below; *rachis* stout, grooved, glandular pubescent.

Fruit 1½″ to 2″ long, solitary or paired, obovoid to ellipsoidal, deeply 4-channeled from the base to the depressed apex, with a dark red-brown husk ⅛″ to ¼″ thick; *nut* reddish brown, 4-ribbed, somewhat laterally compressed; *seed* sweet; about 90 (34–113) nuts to the pound.

Twigs stout, reddish brown to brownish gray, pubescent; *terminal buds* ½″ to ¾″ long, subglobose, reddish brown, tomentose, the outer scales soon deciduous, showing the paler, silky ones beneath; *lateral buds* similar but smaller, somewhat divergent; *leaf scars* 3-lobed to obcordate, with a cluster of bundle scars in each lobe, or scattered.

Bark firm, close, with low, rounded interlaced ridges and shallow furrows.

GENERAL DESCRIPTION

Mockernut hickory is a small to medium-sized tree, 40 to 60 ft high and 10 to 20 in. in diameter, but it may attain a maximum size of 112* ft by 3 ft. It is found on many soil types with varying amounts of moisture. This tree is the only hickory on the dry sandy soils in the pine forests of the southern coastal plain; it is common on terraces in the second bottoms along the Mississippi (288) and reaches its best development in Arkansas, Missouri, and the lower Ohio river valley. Most of the commercial mockernut is found on fertile uplands. Hardwood associates include other oaks and hickories, sweetgum, maples, American beech and many others depending upon the site (dry, medium, wet).

RANGE

Eastern United States (map, Plate 36).

1. *Carya tomentosa.*   2. *Carya ovalis.*

PLATE 36

Carya ovalis (Wangenh.) Sarg.[1]   Red hickory; oval pignut hickory

Leaves 8″ to 12″ long, 5 or 7 (mostly 7) sessile or nearly sessile, lanceolate to ob-lanceolate or obovate leaflets; *terminal leaflets* 4″ to 6″ long, 1½″ to 2″ wide, some-what larger than the lateral leaflets; *margin* finely serrate; *apex* acute to acuminate; *base* cuneate or inequilaterally rounded; *surfaces* dark yellow-green, glabrous above; more or less pubescent to glabrous below; *rachis* slender, glabrous.

Flowers at least in the South, appearing much later than those of the associated species.

Fruit 1″ to 1¼″ long, oval in vertical section, with a husk ¹⁄₁₂″ to ¹⁄₁₀″ thick, splitting freely to the base; *nut* brownish white, thin-shelled, 4-ribbed above the center; *seed* sweet, or only slightly astringent.

Twigs slender to stout, lustrous reddish brown, glabrous; *terminal buds* ¼″ to ½″ long, ovoid to subglobose, obtuse to acuminate, covered by a few reddish-brown, glabrous scales, the outer usually deciduous; *lateral buds* smaller, somewhat divergent; *leaf scars* obdeltoid to cordate, commonly with 3 equidistant groups of bundle scars.

Bark at first smooth, on older trunks often somewhat platy so that it may be mistaken for that of shagbark hickory; eventually closely and deeply furrowed with interlacing ridges, scaly or ragged on the surface.

Red hickory is usually a medium-sized tree 50 to 60 ft high and 12 to 24 in. in diameter (max. 145° by 4° ft). It is an important upland species occurring in mixture with black, red, and white oaks and pignut hickory. At least in the northern part of its range, it is found on dry, upland clay soils of glacial origin, as well as in more favorable locations.

It is probable that red hickory with its several varieties is much more widely distributed than formerly supposed. This is because of its great similarity to *C. glabra* (pignut), with which it is associated. Although the range sometimes given extends southeast from western New York, red hickory in one or more of its forms is a common hickory in the central part of the state (Syracuse) and makes up a considerable portion of the trees previously considered as "pignut."

Since these two upland hickories are also similar in their silvical habits, it is likely that they will not be separated, except by those primarily interested in taxonomy, even though typical specimens are quite different from each other.

[1] The current Check List (212) reduces this species to synonymy with *C. glabra* (p. 256). Fruit and other differences compel us to agree with Sargent (262), Deam (95), Manning (230), Fernald (124), and Braun (43) that these two species should not be combined.

Fɪɢ. 106. *Carya ovalis*. Red hickory. *1*. Twig × 1¼. *2*. Leaf × ⅓. *3*. Fruit × ¾. *4*. Transverse section of nut × ¾. *5*. Nut × ¾. *6*. Bark.

1 2 3 4 5 6

Eastern United States except for the south Atlantic and Gulf Coastal Plains (map, Plate 36).

Carya glabra (Mill.) Sweet   Pignut hickory

Since this hickory is similar to the preceding species, direct comparison will be made between the two.

Fig. 107. Fruit of pignut × ¾. Note incomplete dehiscence.

Comparative botanical features. *Leaves* with 5 leaflets, less often also 7 on the same tree. *Fruit* obovoid or pyriform, the husk tardily dehiscent about halfway to the base, often not releasing the nut after it falls to the ground; *nut* smooth, not ribbed. *Bark* on young trees smooth, not shaggy, eventually developing rounded ridges. *Habitat* commonly found along streams or on moist hillsides, but also on drier sites.

Range. Eastern United States except Coastal Plains (map, Plate 37). A large-fruited form, var. *megacarpa* (Sarg.) Sarg., extends over the Coastal Plains from Virginia and Louisiana.

Plate 37. *Carya glabra.*

Carya leiodermis Sarg.   Swamp hickory

This is a southern species, also known as "pignut hickory," and is found from northwestern Mississippi through Louisiana and southern Arkansas. The leaflets, usually seven in number, are narrow, and pubescent below, especially along the midrib; the fruit husk is ¼ in. or less in thickness and splits to the base at maturity. This tree is common in low wet woods and is included among the "terrace hickories" of the lower Mississippi Valley (288).

Carya pallida (Ashe) Engl. and Graebn.   Sand hickory

Sand hickory (pale hickory), also called "pignut," is found on dry soils from southern New Jersey through the Piedmont and Coastal Plains to western Florida and Louisiana. The young leaves are conspicuously silvery below, and the crown is denser than that of the other associated hickories.

APOCARYA

DISTINGUISHING CHARACTERISTICS OF IMPORTANT SPECIES

Species	Leaves	Fruits
C. illinoensis, pecan	about 15″ long, with 9 to 17 lanceolate (often falcate) leaflets	ellipsoidal; husk 4-winged from base to apex; seed sweet
C. cordiformis, bitternut hickory	about 9″ long, with 7 to 11 oblong-lanceolate leaflets	subglobose; husk 4-winged above the middle; seed bitter

Carya illinoensis (Wangenh.) K. Koch [Carya pecan (Marsh.) Engl. and Graebn.]   Pecan

BOTANICAL FEATURES

Leaves 12″ to 20″ long, with 9 to 17 sessile or nearly sessile, lanceolate to oblanceolate, usually falcate leaflets; *leaflets* 4″ to 8″ long, 1″ to 3″ wide; *margin* serrate or doubly serrate; *apex* acute to acuminate; *base* cuneate or unequally rounded; *surfaces* dark yellow-green, glabrous or nearly so above, pale yellow-green, glabrous or pubescent below; *rachis* slender, glabrous or pubescent.
Fruit usually in clusters of 3 to 12, ellipsoidal, 1″ to 2½″ long; with a dark-brown husk, 4-winged from apex to base; *nut* ellipsoidal, bright reddish brown, smooth or slightly 4-ridged; *seed* sweet; about 100 (55–160) nuts to the pound.
Twigs moderately stout, reddish brown, dotted with orange-brown lenticels, usually more or less pubescent; *terminal buds* ¼″ to ½″ long, acute, somewhat 4-angled, valvate, yellowish brown, scurfy; *lateral buds* smaller, often divergent; *leaf scars* obovate; bundle scars scattered or variously clustered.
Bark on mature trees light brown to brownish gray, divided into interlacing, somewhat scaly ridges separated by narrow fissures.

GENERAL DESCRIPTION

Pecan is said to be the largest of the native hickories and varies from 110 to 140 ft in height and 2 to 4 ft in diameter (max. 180 by 6 ft [1]). This

[1] Trees with even larger diameters have been reported.

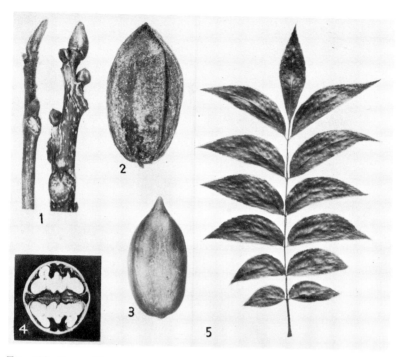

Fig. 108. *Carya illinoensis.* Pecan. *1.* Twigs, fast-growing and slow-growing, respectively, × 1¼. *2.* Fruit × ¾. *3.* Nut × ¾. *4.* Transverse section of nut × ¾. *5.* Leaf × ¼.

species is found as a scattered tree on moist but well-drained ridges in river bottoms in company with sycamore, sweetgum, American elm, willow and water oaks, persimmon, poplars, hackberries, black willow, and other bottomland hardwoods.

The timber produced from the pecan hickories is not as strong or heavy as that of the "true hickories," but it is suitable for flooring and furniture. *Carya illinoensis* is valuable chiefly for its fruit, which is produced in large amounts and used widely in the United States. Efforts to

Fig. 109. Nut of cultivated pecan × ¾; "papershell" variety.

Fig. 110. Pecan bark.

improve the size and quality of the nuts have been successful (hence "papershell pecans"), and fruit from large planted groves of these trees is harvested on a commercial scale; pecan is now found planted through all the southern states as far north as Virginia.

RANGE

Mississippi River Valley (map, Plate 38).

1. *Carya illinoensis.*   2. *Carya cordiformis.*

PLATE 38

Carya cordiformis (Wangenh.) K. Koch   Bitternut hickory

BOTANICAL FEATURES

Leaves 7" to 10" long, with 7 to 11 sessile or nearly sessile, lanceolate or ovate-lanceolate to oblong-lanceolate leaflets; *terminal leaflets* 3" to 6" long, 1" to 1¼" wide; slightly larger than the lateral leaflets; *margin* finely to coarsely serrate; *apex* acuminate; *base* cuneate to unequally rounded; *surfaces* bright green, lustrous, glabrous above; pale green, pubescent or glabrous below; *rachis* slender, slightly grooved, pubescent.

Fruit about 1" long, solitary or paired, subglobose, with a yellowish-green, often minutely scurfy husk, 4-winged above the middle; *nut* subglobose, light reddish brown or gray-brown, thin-shelled; *seed* bitter; about 156 (125–185) nuts to the pound.

Twigs moderately stout, greenish brown to gray-brown, more or less pubescent, lenticellate; *terminal buds* ⅓" to ¾" long, cylindrical or somewhat 4-angled, valvate, sulfur-yellow, and scurfy pubescent; *lateral buds* smaller, often short-stalked, divergent; *leaf scars* 3-lobed, obcordate, with a number of scattered or grouped bundle scars; *pith* brownish white.

Bark close and firm, remaining smooth for many years, eventually with shallow furrows and low, narrow, interlacing ridges, sometimes slightly scaly on the surface.

GENERAL DESCRIPTION

Bitternut hickory, the only member of the pecan group in the North, is a medium-sized tree and commonly attains a height of 50 to 60 ft and a diameter of 12 to 24 in. (max. 171° by 4° ft). Like mockernut hickory it is found on many soil types, from those of dry gravelly uplands to rich, moist bottomlands. Bitternut hickory is associated chiefly with other hickories and oaks, but many other hardwoods may also be in the mixture.

Probably the most abundant and uniformly distributed of the hickories, it reaches its largest size in the bottomlands of the lower Ohio basin; it is also the common hickory of Kansas, Nebraska, and Iowa, where it occurs on gravelly ridges bordering streams.

RANGE

Eastern United States except for portions of the south Atlantic and Gulf Coastal Plains (map, Plate 38).

Carya aquatica (Michx. f.) Nutt.   Water hickory; bitter pecan

This species is common in swamps and on other low wet sites through the Coastal Plains from Virginia to Florida, west to eastern Texas, and north in the Mississippi Valley to southern Illinois. It is most similar to *C. illinoensis* but differs in its fruit, which is shorter and contains a flattened, obovoid, four-ribbed nut with a bitter seed. In the absence of the nut, it is often difficult to separate the two species. Water

Fig. 111. *Carya cordiformis.* Bitternut hickory. *1.* Twig × 1¼. *2.* Leaf × ⅓. *3.* Fruit × ¾. *4.* Nut × ¾. *5.* Transverse section of nut showing thin shell × ¾. *6.* Bark.

hickory, although of minor importance, will grow on sites too poor for the better-grade hardwoods, and hence merits some consideration. Its most common associates include overcup and Nuttall oaks, green ash, American and cedar elms, waterlocust, and hackberries.

Carya myristicaeformis (Michx. f.) Nutt.   Nutmeg hickory

Nutmeg hickory tends to have fewer leaflets (7 or 9, sometimes 5), than others in the pecan group. The thin husk is ridged along the sutures from apex to base, and the shape of the broadly ellipsoidal to obovoid nut suggests that of a nutmeg; the seed is sweet. The bark is thin and finely scaly. This hickory is found along stream banks or elsewhere on rich moist soils. Although reaching 80 to 100 ft by 2 ft in diameter, it is of minor importance because of its scattered occurrence. Small widely separated patches are found in South Carolina, Alabama, Mississippi, Arkansas, Louisiana, and Texas; reappearing (rare) on the mountains of northeastern Mexico; found along the Red River Valley in Louisiana, Arkansas, Oklahoma, and Texas.

Betulaceae: The Birch family

Although somewhat larger during previous geological periods, the Betu-laceae now number but 6 genera and about 100 species of deciduous trees and shrubs which, with few exceptions,[1] are restricted to the cooler regions of the Northern Hemisphere.

The introduced European hornbeam, *Carpinus betulus* L., is some-times used ornamentally in the United States, especially on the Pacific Coast. Another European species, *Corylus avellana* L., produces the filbert nuts of commerce, but in recent years most of the local supply has come from American-grown trees of this species.

Five genera with about 25 species are represented in this country. The remaining genus *Ostryopsis* (monotypic) is restricted to eastern Asia.

BOTANICAL FEATURES OF THE FAMILY

Leaves deciduous, alternate, simple, stipulate.

Flowers imperfect (species monoecious), mostly anemophilous, appear-ing before or with the leaves, or rarely autumnal; *staminate* aments pre-formed (except in *Carpinus*), the individual flowers borne in clusters of 1 to 6 in the axils of bracts; consisting of 2 to 20 stamens inserted on a receptacle with or without a calyx; *pistillate* flowers in short, spikelike or capitate aments, the individual flowers borne at the base of bracts, solitary or in clusters of 2 or 3, comprising a 2-celled ovary surmounted by a short style and a 2-lobed stigma, calyx present or absent.

[1] A few species of *Alnus* extend southward through the mountains of Mexico and Central America to the Peruvian Andes.

Fruit a very minute to medium-sized 1-celled, 1-seeded nut, winged or unwinged, subtended by a papery or semiwoody involucre, or scale; in *Betula* and *Alnus* the small fruits are compounded to form a cone or strobilus.

CONSPECTUS OF NATIVE GENERA

Genus	Fruit
Betula	nutlets very small, laterally winged; borne in a strobile whose scales (bracts) are usually deciduous at maturity (Fig. 115, 6)
Alnus	nutlets similar to those of *Betula,* but strobile scales persistent at maturity (Fig. 118, 3)
Carpinus	nuts small, not winged; each subtended by a characteristic usually 3-lobed bract (Fig. 119), borne in leafy spikelike clusters
Ostrya	nuts small, not winged; each enclosed in a bladderlike sac (Fig. 120), borne in conelike clusters
Corylus	nuts large and not winged; in a leathery foliaceous involucre or husk

BETULA L.   Birch

The genus *Betula* numbers about 40 species of trees and shrubs widely scattered through the Northern Hemisphere from the Arctic Circle to southern Europe, the Himalaya, China, and Japan in the Old World, and in North America from the Arctic regions to the southern United States. Several species form vast forests in countries of the far north, while others, which are extremely dwarfed in habit, are found on the slopes of mountains at or near timberline. The resin birch, *B. glandulosa* Michx., a small shrub common to the peat bogs and high mountains of the West,[1] is a suitable browse plant for both sheep and cattle. In Alaska the ground birch, *B. rotundifolia* Sarg., is one of the important summer grazing plants for reindeer.

Because of their handsome foliage and showy bark, many of the birches are used for decorative purposes. The exotic most commonly favored is the European white birch, *B. pendula* Roth. (Syn. *B. alba* L. in part), and its varieties.

About 15 species of *Betula* are endemic to the cooler regions of North America. Of the 7 arborescent species, 3 attain commercial size and abundance.

[1] Circumpolar; also in mountainous regions of some of the northeastern states.

Leaves mostly ovate to triangular; serrate, dentate, or lobulate.

Flowers *staminate* aments preformed, borne in clusters of 2 or 3, or solitary, the individual flowers consisting of 4 stamens adnate to a 4-parted calyx, each bract bearing 3 flowers; *pistillate* aments solitary, the individual flowers naked, borne in clusters of 3 and subtended by a 3-lobed bract.

Fruit a small nutlet borne in an erect or pendent strobile, the scales usually deciduous from the persistent cone axis at maturity, releasing the nutlets; *nutlets* [1] compressed, laterally winged. A key to the nutlets of Northeastern birches has been published by Cunningham (83).

Twigs slender, in certain species aromatic; usually greenish to reddish brown, glabrous or pubescent; spur shoots commonly present on old growth; *terminal buds* absent; *lateral buds* with several imbricated scales, only 3 of which usually show; *leaf scars* lunate to semioval, with 3 nearly equidistant bundle scars; *pith* small, homogeneous, terete, or remotely triangular.

DISTINGUISHING CHARACTERISTICS OF IMPORTANT SPECIES

Species	Leaves	Fruiting strobiles	Twigs	Young bark
B. alleghaniensis, yellow birch	doubly serrate, base rounded to remotely cordate	ovoid, erect; scales pubescent	aromatic	bronze
B. lenta, sweet birch	essentially singly serrate, base cordate	oblong, erect; scales essentially glabrous	aromatic	black
B. papyrifera, paper birch	doubly serrate, obtuse or round at the base, glandular below	cylindrical, pendent	nonaromatic	chalky white

Betula alleghaniensis Britton [Betula lutea Michx. f.]   Yellow birch

BOTANICAL FEATURES

Leaves 3″ to 4½″ long, 1½″ to 2″ wide; *shape* ovate to oblong-ovate; *margin* sharply doubly serrate; *apex* acute to acuminate; *base* rounded or remotely cordate

---

[1] Birch seeds, when first collected and dried in the fall, require very high temperatures (90°F) for germination, but if stratified at 32 to 40°F, the germinating temperature steadily drops until at the end of several months the seeds begin to germinate even at the low temperature chosen for stratification. This habit is unusual if not unique among seed plants as a group (81).

Fig. 112. *Betula alleghaniensis.* Yellow birch. *1.* Twig × 1¼. *2.* Spur shoot × 1¼. *3.* Fruiting strobile (cone) × ¾. *4.* Fruit × 3. *5.* Bract, or cone scale, × 3. *6.* Leaf × ½. *7.* Bark of young tree. *8.* Bark of old tree.

and inequilateral; *surfaces* dull, dark green, glabrous above; pale yellow-green and with tufts of pubescence in the axils of the principal veins below; *petiole* slender, pubescent, ½″ to ¾″ long.

Flowers *staminate* aments (preformed) ¾″ to 1″ long; the *pistillate* ½″ to ⅔″ long.
Fruit in an ovoid, sessile or short-stalked, erect strobile, at maturity 1″ to 1½″ long; *scales* pubescent on the back, longer than broad, often tardily deciduous; *nutlet*

pubescent toward the apex, oval to ovate, about as wide as its lateral wings; about 447,000 (278,000–907,000) nutlets to the pound.

Twigs slender, yellowish brown to dark brown, aromatic, with a wintergreen taste; *terminal buds* absent; *lateral buds* ovate, acute, with chestnut-brown scales, ciliate on the margin; *spurs* numerous on old growth.

Bark on young stems and branches golden gray to bronze-colored, separating at the surface and peeling horizontally into thin, curly, papery strips; eventually breaking up into reddish-brown plates on mature trunks.

GENERAL DESCRIPTION

This species, the most important of the native birches, is a medium-sized tree 60 to 70 ft high and 2 to 2½ ft in diameter (max. 100 by 4½ ft). In the forest, the crown is irregularly rounded, and the long, usually well-formed bole terminates below in a shallow, wide-spreading root system.

Yellow birch is probably the most typical of northeastern hardwoods, and in the mountainous sections is found on sandy loam soils in mixture with sugar maple and American beech (beech-birch-maple mixture); the associated conifers include eastern hemlock, red spruce, balsam fir, and eastern white pine. Farther south, yellow birch occurs on a variety of soils but always in moist, cool locations such as steep northerly slopes and the edges of sphagnum bogs. Temperature seems to be an important factor influencing distribution, and it may be more than coincidental that the southern limit for the species follows roughly the 70°F summer isotherm.

Yellow birch is a prolific seeder, usually producing some seed each year and very large crops at irregular intervals. The winged nutlets are light and are carried a considerable distance by the wind; this probably accounts for the excellent reproduction which often takes place after fires. In virgin woods, seeds germinate on almost any moist place, including moss-covered boulders and old partially rotted stumps. The young seedlings not only thrive in such situations but commonly persist for many years, and eventually may even send their roots downward over the surface of the boulder or stump until they reach the ground. Eventually, the stump may rot away completely and the tree be left on "stilts." Among the conifers, hemlock is the chief competitor of yellow birch in this respect, and it is common to find several small trees of each species striving for the supremacy of a single stump. Elsewhere, after a good seed year, there are countless thousands of small birch seedlings scattered over the forest floor. The roots have difficulty in growing through the layer of leaves and other litter. Disturbance of this layer by logging or fire greatly improves subsequent seedling reproduction.

Yellow birch is moderately tolerant—less so than hemlock, sugar maple, and American beech, but more so than the aspens and pin cherry under whose shade it develops after fire. Growth is not rapid, and trees 50 years old may be 50 ft tall and 6 in. in diameter. Maturity is reached in about 150 years, and old trees may reach the three-century mark.

The papery bark curls are highly flammable and burn even when wet, a useful feature to know when starting a campfire in rain-soaked northern woods. Oil of wintergreen may be obtained by distilling the young twigs or inner bark, but the amount is much less than in sweet birch.

RANGE

Southern Canada, Lake States, Northeast, and Appalachian Mountains (map, Plate 39).

1. *Betula alleghaniensis.* 2. *Betula lenta.*

PLATE 39

Betula lenta L.   Sweet birch; black birch

BOTANICAL FEATURES

Leaves 2½″ to 5″ long, 1½″ to 3″ wide; *shape* ovate to oblong-ovate; *margin* sharply singly or inconspicuously doubly serrate; *apex* acute; *base* cordate, or unequally rounded; *surfaces* dull, dark green, glabrous above, pale yellow-green, with tufts of white pubescence in the axils of the principal veins below; *petiole* stout, pubescent, ½″ to ¾″ long.

Flowers *staminate* aments (preformed) ¾″ to 1″ long; *pistillate* ½″ to ¾″ long.

Fruit in an oblong-ovoid, short-stalked or sessile, erect strobile 1″ to 1½″ long, *scales* glabrous, or sparingly ciliate and slightly pubescent near the base, usually somewhat longer than broad, tardily deciduous; *nutlet* glabrous, obovoid, slightly broader than its lateral wings; about 646,000 (493,000–933,000) nutlets to the pound.

Twigs slender, light reddish brown, lenticellate, with a strong wintergreen odor and taste; *terminal buds* absent; *lateral buds* lustrous, sharply pointed, chestnut-brown, divergent; *spurs* numerous on old growth.

Bark on young trees reddish brown to nearly black, with prominent horizontal lenticels; on mature trees brownish black and breaking up into large thin irregular scaly plates.

Fig. 113. *Betula lenta.* Sweet birch. *1.* Bark (Photograph by H. P. Brown).
2. Bud × 1¼. *3.* Spur shoot × 1¼. *4.* Leaf × ½. *5.* Fruiting strobile (cone)
× ¾. *6.* Fruit × 3. *7.* Bract, or cone scale × 3.

GENERAL DESCRIPTION

Sweet birch is a medium-sized tree 50 to 60 ft high and 12 to 24 in. in diameter (max. 80 by 5 ft), and in the forest develops a long, clear bole which terminates below in a rather deep, wide-spreading root system. This species reaches its best development in Tennessee and Kentucky, but is often more abundant in the North. Deep, rich, and moist but well-drained soils are preferred, yet this tree is also found on rocky sites where the roots often grow over and around boulders and rocky ledges, a habit much more typical, however, of the yellow birch. Never occurring in pure stands, sweet birch is found as a scattered tree in company with such species as white pine, hemlock, yellow birch, sugar maple, beech, black cherry, white ash, basswood, and yellow-poplar.

Sweet birch resembles yellow birch in its botanical features, and these two species differ from the other native birches by the presence of wintergreen oil in the inner bark of stems and roots.

The seeding habits and other silvical features of the sweet and yellow birches, respectively, are similar, except that the former species is not so aggressive and is more exacting in its seedbed requirements. Oil of wintergreen may be extracted from the twigs and bark of sweet birch.

FIG. 114. Young sweet birch, with yellow birch in the background.

Appalachian Mountains and adjacent regions; also southern Michigan (map, Plate 39).

Betula papyrifera Marsh.   Paper birch; white birch

BOTANICAL FEATURES

Leaves 2″ to 3″ long, 1½″ to 2″ wide; *shape* ovate to oval; *margin* coarsely doubly serrate; *apex* acute to acuminate; *base* rounded or obtuse (cordate in var. *cordifolia*); *surfaces* dull, dark green, glabrous above; pale yellowish green, glabrous or pubescent, minutely glandular below; *petiole* black-glandular, slender, ¾″ to 1″ long.
Flowers *staminate* aments (preformed) ¾″ to 1¼″ long, usually borne in 2's or 3's; *pistillate* 1″ to 1¼″ long.
Fruit in a pendent, cylindrical, stalked strobile, 1″ to 1½″ long; *scales* puberulous on the back, about as long as broad, more or less deciduous at maturity; *nutlet* glabrous, elliptical to oval, narrower than its lateral wings; about 1,380,000 (610,000–4,120,000) nutlets to the pound.
Twigs slender, dull reddish brown to orange-brown, lenticellate; *terminal buds* absent; *lateral buds* ovoid, acute, gummy, covered with chestnut-brown scales; *spurs* numerous on old growth.
Bark at first dark brown, soon turning chalky to creamy white, separating into thin, papery strips; at the base of old trees, nearly black and deeply fissured.

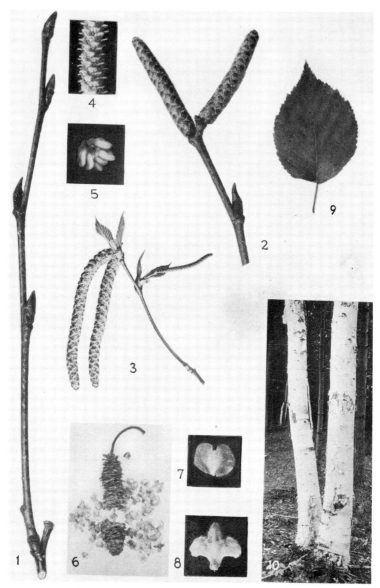

Fɪɢ. 115. *Betula papyrifera.* Paper birch. *1.* Twig × 1¼. *2.* Preformed staminate aments × 1¼. *3.* Flowers; staminate aments pendent, the pistillate one, lateral × ½. *4.* Portion of pistillate ament × 5. *5.* Staminate flower × 5. *6.* Fruiting strobile (cone) shedding its scales and winged nutlets × ¾. *7.* Fruit × 3. *8.* Bract, or cone scale × 3. *9.* Leaf × ½. *10.* Bark of young tree.

Paper birch, the most widely distributed of the native birches, is primarily a Canadian species and only extends southward through the northern United States, where it is found in mountainous regions or in other localities where a cool, moist site is available.

This species is a medium-sized tree 50 to 70 ft high and 12 to 24 in. in diameter (max. 120 by 5° ft). The crown is pyramidal or later irregularly rounded, relatively open, and the long, cylindrical, often curved bole terminates below in a shallow root system.

Paper birch occurs as a scattered tree in the mixed coniferous-hardwood forests of the North; here its associates include white, red, and jack pines, red, black, and white spruces, balsam fir, maples, American beech, yellow birch, and black ash. In some localities this birch, together with white spruce and balsam fir, comprises a large portion of the permanent forest. After fire, paper birch often seeds in over large areas where mineral soil has been exposed, and especially on moist sites it may form nearly pure stands; in this respect, paper birch is similar to the aspens and is commonly found in mixture with them on old burns. These species are all intolerant and often serve as a cover under which the slower-growing, more tolerant trees (especially spruce) become established.

PLATE 40. *Betula papyrifera.*

Paper birch is a fast-growing, short-lived tree and rarely attains an age of more than 80 years (max. 140).

The bark was used by the Indians for utensils, canoes, and wigwam covers, and is utilized for novelties of various sorts; it is also flammable and useful in starting a fire. Such uses by increasing numbers of campers have resulted in extremely unsightly peeled birches at northern campsites.

Although valued along with the European white birch as an ornamental, both trees may be damaged or killed by the bronze birch borer.

RANGE

Including that of the several varieties in the Check List (212), transcontinental through Canada and the northern United States (map, Plate 40).

Betula populifolia Marsh.   Gray birch

Distinguishing characteristics. *Leaves* triangular, with a narrow, pointed apex, doubly serrate. *Staminate aments* usually solitary. *Fruit* in a spreading or ascending, cylindrical, glabrous or puberulous strobile with deciduous scales; *scales* about the same in length as in width; *nutlet* somewhat narrower than its lateral wings. *Twigs* slender, lenticels warty-glandular, terminal bud wanting, laterals ovoid, gummy. *Bark* at first brownish, soon grayish white, exfoliating very little in comparison with that of paper birch; with black triangular patches usually present on the trunk below the branch insertions.

General description. Gray birch is the smallest of the northeastern tree birches and commonly attains a height of only 20 to 30 ft and a diameter of 15 in. or less (max. 60° ft by 2° ft). The root system is shallow, and the bole usually poorly shaped and limby, with an irregular, open, pyramidal crown. This birch is now very plentiful, especially through New England, and covers large areas on abandoned farms and burned-over land; it will grow on the poorest of sterile soils, and by prolific seeding has gained a foothold in advance of other species. In this respect, it is similar to both

Fig. 116. *Betula populifolia.* Gray birch. *1.* Leaf × ½. *2.* Bract, or cone scale × 3. *3.* Fruit × 3. *4.* Fruiting strobile (cone) × ¾. *5.* Lateral bud × 1¼.

paper birch and the aspens. On sterile sites, gray birch is often associated with pitch pine and scrub oak (*Q. ilicifolia* Wangenh.), these three species forming a very monotonous type covering wide areas. Farther south, or on better soils, other oaks occur with this species, and among the conifers white pine is most frequently seen. Gray birch serves at first as a cover crop for white pine but soon causes it considerable damage by excessive crowding. In its silvical features, gray birch is similar to paper birch.

Range. Newfoundland south to northern Delaware; northwest to the southern shore of Lake Ontario and along the north bank of the St. Lawrence River to its mouth (also in Indiana at the foot of Lake Michigan, and in Madison County, Virginia).

Betula nigra L.   River birch; red birch

Distinguishing characteristics. *Leaves* rhombic-ovate, conspicuously and often deeply doubly serrate, with a broadly wedge-shaped base. *Fruit* in a cylindrical, erect, pubescent strobile with deciduous scales, maturing in late spring; *scales* longer than broad; *nutlet* somewhat broader than its lateral wings. *Twigs* reddish brown, slender, usually pubescent, terminal bud lacking, laterals acute. *Bark* salmon-pink, papery, later becoming coarsely scaly (this change is similar to that taking place in yellow birch).

General description. River birch, the only species of *Betula* at low elevations in the South, is a medium-sized tree 70 to 80 ft high and 2 to 3 ft in diameter, usually much smaller (max. 100 by 5 ft), with a trunk which often divides 15 to 20 ft from the ground into several arching branches. It is commonest along stream banks throughout its range, and occurs as a scattered tree with such species as sycamore, elm, silver and red maples, willows, and cottonwoods.

Fig. 117. *Betula nigra.* River birch. *1.* Fruiting strobile (cone) × ¾. *2.* Bract, or cone scale, × 3. *3.* Fruit × 3. *4.* Leaf × ½. *5.* Bark.

Besides the distinction of being the only typically southern birch, it is also the only one which matures its fruit in late spring. At this time high water is receding and silty shore lines are exposed which offer the best possible place for the wind-blown or water-borne seeds to germinate.

The silvical features are similar to those of the other birches. Although one of the commonest of southern trees, locally this species is seldom cut, partly because of its poor form. Its use as an ornamental seems to be increasing, and even north of the natural range, river birch makes a desirable specimen tree for parks or estates, where it often makes good growth even on dry soils. It is occasionally used as a street tree in the Pacific Northwest.

Range. Southern New Hampshire through north central Pennsylvania, southern Ohio and Indiana, central Illinois and southern Wisconsin to southeastern Minnesota; south through extreme eastern Kansas and Oklahoma, to eastern Texas; in the East, south to northern Florida (not common in the higher Appalachians, and throughout its range restricted to stream banks and other moist places at low to medium elevations).

ALNUS B. Ehrh. Alder

The genus *Alnus* numbers about 30 species of trees and large shrubs mostly distributed through the cooler regions of the Northern Hemisphere. The Eurasian species extend southward to northern Africa, Iran, the Himalaya, and Taiwan. In the New World, alders are found from Alaska and Canada to Guatemala, and on mountains to Argentina.

The European alder, *A. glutinosa* (L.) Gaertn., originally introduced for charcoal manufacture, is now used ornamentally in the eastern United States and has become naturalized. About ten species of *Alnus*, seven of which attain tree size, are native to the United States. Only one western species, however, reaches commercial proportions and abundance. The common stream-bank alder of the eastern states and Canada from Saskatchewan and Nebraska, eastward, is *A. rugosa* (Du Roi) Spreng. [*A. incana* (L.) Moench.], speckled alder.

BOTANICAL FEATURES OF THE GENUS

Leaves mostly ovate, oval, or obovate; usually irregularly serrate or dentate.

Flowers *staminate* aments preformed, in racemose clusters of 3 to 5, the individual flowers consisting of 1 to 4 stamens attached to a 4-parted calyx and subtended by 3 to 5 bractlets, with 3 to 6 flowers for each scale; *pistillate* aments often preformed, in clusters of 2 or 3, the individual flowers composed of a naked ovary surmounted by 2 stigmas and subtended by 2 to 4 bractlets, in clusters of 2 to 4 at the base of bracts.

Fruit a small nutlet borne in a persistent semiwoody strobile or cone; *nutlets* compressed, laterally winged, chestnut-brown.

Twigs slender to moderately stout, reddish or tinged with red; *buds* stalked (American species), covered by 2 or 3 valvate or imbricate scales; *leaf scars* raised, more or less triangular to semicircular, generally with 3 bundle scars; *pith* homogeneous, triangular in cross section.

Alnus rubra Bong.   Red alder

BOTANICAL FEATURES

Leaves 3″ to 6″ long, 1½″ to 3″ wide; *shape* ovate to elliptical; *margin* doubly serrate-dentate, the teeth glandular, slightly revolute; *apex* acute; *base* obtuse or rounded; *surfaces* dark green, glabrous or glabrate above, paler and rusty pubescent on the midrib and principal veins below; *petiole* grooved, ¼″ to ½″ long.
Flowers preformed, the staminate aments 1¼″ to 1½″ long.
Fruit in an oblong to ovoid, long-stalked or rarely sessile strobile, ½″ to 1¼″ long; *scales* truncate, with greatly thickened, often rugose apices; *nutlets* orbicular to obovoid, with membranous lateral wings or a single encircling wing; about 666,000 (363,000–1,087,000) nutlets to the pound.
Twigs slender to moderately stout, bright red to reddish brown, terete or somewhat 3-angled on vigorous shoots; *terminal buds* ⅛″ to ⅔″ long, stalked, covered by 2 or 3 red, scurfy-pubescent scales; *lateral* buds slightly smaller, somewhat divergent; *leaf scars* raised, triangular to semicircular, with 3 bundle scars; *pith* remotely triangular in cross section, greenish white.
Bark grayish white, pale gray, or blue-gray at the surface, smooth or covered with small warty excrescences; on large trees breaking up into large flat plates of irregular contour; inner bark bright reddish brown.

GENERAL DESCRIPTION

Red alder is the most important hardwood in the Pacific Northwest, a region supporting few commercial broadleaved trees. Its wood is used for furniture, veneers, and wooden novelties. The mature tree commonly varies from 80 to 130 ft in height and 10 to 36 in. in diameter (max. diameter 5° ft). In dense stands it develops a clear, symmetrical, slightly tapered bole, rising from a shallow, spreading root system, and supporting a narrow, domelike crown. The crown of open-grown trees, however, is broadly conical and often extends nearly to the ground. Red alder is essentially a coastal species, and except in northern Washington and Idaho, where it occurs sporadically, it is rarely found more than 50 miles from salt water or above 2,500 ft in elevation. It makes its best growth on moist rich loamy bottomlands, slopes, and benches, although it also attains tree size on dry gravelly or rocky soils. This species occurs in pure stands or in mixture with Douglas-fir, Sitka spruce, western redcedar, western hemlock, Pacific yew, Oregon ash, black cottonwood, bigleaf and vine maples, and Pacific dogwood.

1

2

3

4

5

6

Red alder is one of the first trees to appear on burned and logged areas. Like aspen, it never forms a permanent forest but prepares the soil for other species; first by building up an organic litter on the forest floor, and second, by increasing the nitrogen content of the soil through the agency of nitrogen-fixing nodules on its roots. The nitrogen content of the leaves is also high. This tree is an annual seeder, with exceptional crops at about 4-year intervals. The seeds germinate well on either organic or mineral soils. Partial shade may be tolerated for the first 2 or 3 years, but after that, full light is needed. Growth is rapid, and 10-year-old trees may be 35 to 40 ft tall. Sawlogs are produced in 40 to 60 years. Red alder is rated as intolerant in comparison with its associates, except the poplars. Maturity is reached in 60 to 90 years. Sprouts from the stump are often vigorous, but seldom reach large size. Whole stands may be defoliated by the tent caterpillar, but the attacks are cyclic, and little permanent damage results.

It is estimated that the supply of red alder timber runs well over 1 billion board ft, three-quarters of which is confined to the coastal forests of Oregon.

RANGE

West Coast (map, Plate 41).

PLATE 41. *Alnus rubra.*

FIG. 118. *Alnus rubra.* Red alder. *1.* Twig × 1¼. *2.* Staminate (left) and pistillate (right) catkins × ¾. *3.* Strobiles × 1¼. *4.* Nutlets × 2. *5.* Leaf × ½. *6.* Bark.

Alnus rhombifolia Nutt.   White alder; Sierra alder (SPN)

Distinguishing characteristics. *Leaves* ovate, or oval to nearly orbicular, singly (rarely doubly) serrate or serrate-dentate, the teeth glandular; midrib often glandular above. *Flowers* preformed, the staminate with one to three stamens. *Fruiting strobile* oblong, about ¾" long; *nutlet* ovoid, remotely winged. *Twigs* slender, orange-red, both terminal and lateral buds stalked; *pith* triangular in cross section. *Bark* gray, divided into irregular plates covered by thin, appressed scales.

General description. Under favorable conditions this tree attains a height of 50 to 80 ft and a d.b.h. of 18 to 36 in. (max. 115 by 3½ ft). Pure stands or belts occur along the banks of streams and in canyon bottoms when moisture is plentiful, but white alder is seldom observed along water courses where the stream flow is intermittent. California sycamore, bigleaf maple, Pacific dogwood, and Oregon ash are the principal associates in mixed forests. Few species compare in altitudinal distribution with white alder. Along the north central California coast it often occurs only a few feet above sea level, while in the southern Sierra it ascends to elevations of 8,000 ft.

Like most alders, this species is a prolific seeder. Young trees endure considerable competition and often form dense thickets when provided with plenty of moisture. Growth is fairly rapid, and maturity is reached in about 50 to 70 years.

White alder produces low-grade lumber, and it is doubtful if the wood will ever be of value except for fuel.

Range. Northern Idaho to the east slopes of the Cascades in Washington, south along the mountains to southern Oregon; thence south through the coastal ranges of California and on the west slopes of the Sierra Nevada Mountains.

CARPINUS L.   Hornbeam

About 26 species are included in this genus, which is restricted to the Northern Hemisphere. Unlike the other genera of the birch family, *Carpinus* does not exhibit preformed staminate aments. One species, *C. caroliniana* Walt., American hornbeam (bluebeech, water beech), is found in the United States east of the Great Plains. It is a small, usually poorly formed tree with elliptical, doubly serrate leaves, and a twisted, fluted trunk, dark bluish gray in color. The fruit is easily identified by the three-lobed, leafy involucre which subtends the small nut. The species is very tolerant and commonly occurs as an understory in hardwood mixtures. American hornbeam is usually regarded as a "weed tree" because of its small size and poor form.

Fig. 119. Fruit and bract of American hornbeam × 1.

Fɪɢ. 120. Fruit of hophornbeam. The one on the right has part of the sac removed, showing the seed × 1.

OSTRYA Scop.   Hophornbeam

Of the seven or eight known species of *Ostrya,* three are native to North America. Eastern hophornbeam, *O. virginiana* (Mill.) K. Koch, has about the same range as American hornbeam, but extends farther west in the plains region. The habits of the two species are somewhat similar, but the American hornbeam is perhaps commonest on moist sites. Eastern hophornbeam is easily distinguished from other trees by its bark, which has a "shreddy" appearance and is broken into small, shaggy plates which curve away from the trunk; the leaves are similar to those of yellow birch; the fruit, however, is very different and consists of a small nut enclosed in an oval, flattened papery sac (borne in conelike clusters). The wood is extremely hard and tough, hence the common name "ironwood" often applied to this species.

Ostrya knowltonii Cov. is restricted to small isolated areas in Arizona and Utah, and *O. baileyi* Rose is found in western Texas and New Mexico.

CORYLUS L.   Hazel; filbert

There are about 15 species of *Corylus* scattered throughout the Northern Hemisphere, and 2 are native to the United States. A western variety, *C. cornuta* var. *californica* (A. DC.) Sharp, California hazel, is a shrub or small tree, and the two eastern species, *C. americana* Walt. and *C. cornuta* Marsh. [*C. rostrata* Ait.], are both small shrubs with oval to elliptical, doubly serrate leaves, more or less pubescent on both surfaces. *C. cornuta* is known as beaked hazel and may be distinguished from the American hazel by the involucre, which forms a tubelike beak at the apex of the nut.

Fagaceae: The Beech family

The Beech family comprises 6 genera and about 600 species of trees and shrubs scattered throughout both hemispheres, but is most characteristic of the forests in the North Temperate Zone. The importance of this group to American foresters can hardly be overemphasized, since in this country it takes first place among the hardwoods in the production of lumber and other forest products. The most important genus is *Quercus* (oak) to be discussed later.

Five genera with about 90 species are found in North America. Two, *Lithocarpus* and *Castanopsis,* are confined to the Pacific Coast region; *Castanea* and *Fagus* are restricted to the East, and *Quercus* is widely distributed over a large portion of the United States and southern Canada, with the exception of the Great Plains.

Leaves deciduous or persistent,[1] alternate, simple, stipulate, usually penniveined and short-petioled.

Flowers imperfect (species monoecious) and borne in one of several ways. The staminate are usually in aments, but in *Fagus* form a globose head. The aments may be pendent or erect, and the flowers are variously grouped on the axis; the *staminate* flowers comprise a 4- to 7-lobed calyx and from 4 to 8 (rarely more) stamens; the *pistillate* flowers are borne in short few-flowered spikes on the new growth (*Fagus* and *Quercus*), or in clusters near the base of the smaller staminate aments (*Castanea, Castanopsis, Lithocarpus*). When such bisexual aments occur, there are also others of the purely staminate type present. The pistillate flower

CONSPECTUS OF NATIVE ARBORESCENT GENERA [a]

Genus	Leaves	Flowers	Fruit
Fagus	deciduous	staminate in heads, pistillate in short 2- to 4-flowered spikes	a nut, triangular in section, occurring usually in 2's within a bur covered with weak, unbranched spines; fruit maturing in one season
Castanea	deciduous	in erect, unisexual and bisexual aments	a rounded nut, occurring singly or in 2's or 3's within a bur covered with sharp, rigid, branched spines; maturing in one season
Castanopsis	persistent	similar to those of *Castanea*	similar to that of *Castanea* but requiring 2 seasons to mature
Lithocarpus	persistent	similar to those of *Castanea*	an acorn, maturing at the end of the second season
Quercus	deciduous or persistent	staminate in aments, pistillate in several-flowered spikes	an acorn, maturing in one or two seasons, respectively

[a] The genus *Nothofagus* was created to include the beeches [about 34 species (84)] of the Southern Hemisphere; these have small, persistent or deciduous leaves, and fruit which is similar to that of the native beech.

[1] Many of the subtropical species have evergreen leaves, and this trait is *approached* in varying degrees by certain of the more northern species, including beech and some of the oaks which tend to hold their dead leaves until the following spring.

consists of a 4- to 8-lobed calyx adnate to a 3- (rarely 6-) celled ovary with a style for each cell, containing 1 to 2 ovules, only one of which matures.

Fruit a nut with an outer cartilaginous coat, and partially or wholly encased in an involucre; *nut* one-seeded by abortion, *seed* exalbuminous; *cotyledons* large and fleshy, and as in *Juglans, Carya,* and certain other genera with large seeds, always remaining (with the exception of *Fagus*) within the seed coats upon germination.

FAGUS L.   Beech

There are about ten beeches, all of them in the Northern Hemisphere. Besides the single North American species (eastern United States, Canada, and Mexico), one is European, another is in the Caucasus, and the others range through temperate eastern Asia.

European beech, *Fagus sylvatica* L., is one of the important timber trees of Europe, where it is grown in pure or mixed stands under forest management. It is used in this country as an ornamental and is represented by several varieties; var. *atropunicea* West, purple beech, has dark bronze-purple leaves; var. *pendula* Loud. is characterized by drooping branches; and var. *laciniata* Vignet. is a cutleaf form. The leaves, buds, and bark of *F. sylvatica* are darker than those of the American species. The fruit, known as "beech mast," is used in Europe for fattening hogs and as a source of vegetable oil.

The name beech has a very ancient origin and may perhaps signify book.[1] It is said that the early writings of the Germanic peoples were inscribed upon tablets of this wood. The bluish-gray bark of the beech is a most distinctive feature; unfortunately, in parks or other much frequented places the bark is often made very unsightly by initials carved upon its smooth surface. Unless education can change this unfortunate practice, the continued use of beech as an "ornamental" must be at least questioned.

Since only one species of beech is native to the United States, the generic description is omitted.

Fagus grandifolia Ehrh.   American beech

BOTANICAL FEATURES

Leaves deciduous; 2½" to 6" long, 1" to 2½" wide; *shape* elliptical to oblong-ovate; *margin* remotely serrate with sharp, incurved teeth; *apex* acuminate; *base* broadly cuneate; *surfaces* glabrous above, and below except for axillary tufts, secondary

[1] Both "beech" and "book" may be traced from similar Anglo-Saxon words.

Fig. 121. *Fagus grandifolia.* American beech. *1.* Twig × 1¼. *2.* Flowers × ½. *3.* Leaf × ½. *4.* Fruit × ¼. *5.* Fruit after opening, showing trigonous nuts × ¾. *6.* Bark.

veins parallel to each other; texture of the leaf somewhat papery to the touch; *petiole* short; *stipules* 1″ to 1½″ long, straplike, membranous.

Flowers appearing after the unfolding of the leaves in the spring; *staminate* in globose heads, each flower with a 4- to 8-lobed calyx and 8 to 16 stamens; *pistillate* in 2- to 4-flowered spikes, surrounded by an involucre, each flower comprising a 4- to 5-lobed calyx attached to a 3-celled ovary.

Fruit an edible nut, ½" to ¾" long, triangular in cross section; paired or in 3's within a woody, 4-parted involucre or bur covered with weak, unbranched spines; about 1,600 (1,300–2,300) nuts to the pound.

Twigs slender, at times slightly zigzag; *pith* homogeneous, terete; *terminal buds* ¾" to 1" long, slender, lance-shaped, sharp-pointed; *scales* numerous and imbricated in 4 ranks; *lateral buds* similar to the terminals; *leaf scars* small, inconspicuous; *stipule scars* narrow, nearly encircling the twig.

Bark thin, smooth, light blue-gray in color, often mottled; does not change appreciably as the tree grows older.

GENERAL DESCRIPTION

American beech is one of the most distinctive and common trees of the eastern hardwood forest, and its smooth blue-gray trunk is easily recognized, even at some distance. The tree averages 70 to 80 ft in height and 2 to 3 ft in diameter (max. 120 by 5* ft). In the open it is featured by a short, stocky bole with a wide-spreading crown, while under forest conditions a clear, straight, massive trunk and smaller crown are developed. The root system is shallow and extensive and has a tendency to produce sprouts. Such root suckering is very characteristic of beech, and old trees are often surrounded by thickets of young growth, mostly of this origin rather than from seed. It is doubtful whether these root sprouts ever attain much size, at least during the life of the parent tree.

American beech is found on a wide variety of soils from the sandy loams of the Northeast to the alluvial bottoms of the Ohio and Mississippi Valleys. Moisture seems to be the controlling factor, and trees are not usually found on soils where the surface layers dry out quickly. This species may be the most tolerant of northern hardwoods,[1] and with sugar maple and yellow birch it forms the typical maple-beech-birch forest of that region. Other associates include red spruce, white pine, hemlock, black cherry, northern red oak, and white ash. Several of these are also southern associates, and to them may be added such species as southern magnolia, basswood, sweetgum, oaks, and hickories.

American beech reaches its largest size on the better-drained sites of alluvial bottoms in the Ohio and Mississippi Valleys, and on western slopes of the southern Appalachians.

Large crops of seed may be produced at 2- to 3-year or longer intervals; the germination is usually high (max. 95 percent). This species may attain an age of 300 to 400 years, but old trees are usually affected by butt rot.

American beech is a variable species and shows at least three different races (59). The northern form is "gray beech" found from Nova Scotia to the Great Lakes, and on the higher mountains of North Carolina and

[1] Depending upon the site, either beech or sugar maple may be the most tolerant.

Tennessee mainly on neutral to alkaline soils. "White beech" is found on the southern coastal plain and northward on poorly drained acid sites. Between these two forms, mainly on well-drained acid sites and mixing with them, is "red beech." The beech of much of the glaciated area is a hybrid complex derived in various combinations from the three basic forms. Careful studies are needed to clarify this situation on a local basis, since each stand is not only variable but has a "norm" often differing from that of adjacent sites.

The thin bark and shallow root system make beech very susceptible to damage by fire.

RANGE

Eastern United States and also Mexico (map, Plate 42). A Mexican beech, *F. mexicana* Martínez, described in 1940, has been reduced to *F. grandifolia* var. *mexicana* (Martínez) Little (214).

1. *Fagus grandifolia.*   2. *Castanea dentata.*

PLATE 42

CASTANEA Mill.   Chestnut; chinkapin

This is a small genus with about 10 species found in southern Europe, northern Africa, southwestern and eastern Asia, and the eastern United States. The fruits of the Chinese chestnut (*C. mollissima* Bl.) and those of the Japanese chestnut (*C. crenata* Sieb. and Zucc.) are not only important sources of food locally, but large quantities of them are annually exported to the United States. These two species, together with *C. sativa* Mill., the Spanish chestnut, are used ornamentally.

Leaves deciduous, serrate, stipulate.

Flowers borne in ascending, staminate, and also bisexual aments, after the leaves are nearly full grown; *staminate* in clusters of 3 to 7 along the ament axis, each comprising a 6-lobed calyx and 10 to 20 long-filamented stamens; *pistillate* solitary, or in clusters of 2 to 3, in an involucre at the base of special, short, staminate aments (bisexual aments); calyx 6-lobed, adnate to a 6-celled ovary bearing occasionally a few abortive stamens.

Fruit a lustrous-brown, rounded, edible nut borne singly or in clusters of 2 or 3 in a 2- to 4-valved bur covered with needle-sharp branched spines.

Twigs slender to moderately stout, usually brown, glabrous or tomentose, *pith* stellate; *terminal buds* lacking; *lateral buds* with 2 or 3 visible scales; *leaf scars* half round; *bundle scars* 3 or more; *stipule scars* present.

Castanea dentata (Marsh.) Borkh.   American chestnut

BOTANICAL FEATURES

Leaves 5½" to 8" long, about 2" wide; *shape* oblong-lanceolate; *margin* coarsely and sharply serrate, with bristle-tipped or hair-tipped teeth; *apex* acuminate; *base* acute; *surfaces* dull yellow-green and glabrous; *phyllotaxy* variable, usually ½ or ⅖.

Fruit 2" to 2½" in diameter, covered with sharp, branched spines; *nut* ½" to 1" wide, nearly flat on one side, borne 2 or 3 in each bur; about 130 nuts to the pound.

Twigs somewhat lustrous, chestnut-brown; *lateral buds* about ¼" long, ovoid, brown, with 2 or 3 visible scales.

Bark dark brown, shallowly fissured into broad, flat ridges.

GENERAL DESCRIPTION

The American chestnut was a highly valued tree; its growth was rapid, the wood durable, and the flavorful roasted nuts contributed to the food supply. At the turn of the century, the possible extinction of such a vigorous and widespread species would have seemed most improbable. However, just such a calamity has happened. In 1904, chestnut blight disease, caused by a fungus presumably brought in from eastern Asia, was found on a few trees in the New York Zoological Garden. Within 50 years the blight had spread over the entire range of the chestnut, causing wholesale destruction (105).

Chestnut, a fast-growing tree, attained a height of 70 to 90 ft with a diameter of 3 to 4 ft (max. 120 by 10 ft); one specimen 17 ft in diameter was reported by Illick (184). Chestnut developed a taproot and was

Fɪɢ. 122. *Castanea dentata.* American chestnut. *1.* Twig × 1¼. *2.* Leaf × ½. *3.* Flowers × ⅓. *4.* Portion of staminate ament showing clusters of flowers × 1. *5.* Basal portion of bisexual ament showing a pistillate flower × 1. *6.* Nut × 1. *7.* Fruit × ¾. *8.* Chestnut sprouts (old trunks blight-killed).

commonly found on sandy loams in company with other hardwoods. Its ability to sprout vigorously from the stump has helped it to exist in spite of continued attacks of the fungus which persists in the living stumps and eventually kills the larger sprouts.

When it appeared that all attempts to stop the spread of the disease would be futile, the U.S. Department of Agriculture secured 250 bushels of seed from the resistant Chinese and Japanese chestnuts and raised some 320,000 seedlings, which were widely planted throughout the eastern United States (105). A vigorous program of hybridization was begun, crossing the somewhat poorly formed but resistant Asiatic species with the tall-growing American chestnut. Of the many thousands of hybrids produced during a 30-year period, only about 3 percent were found to be blight-resistant and of good form and growth. However, at least two of them show great promise. The Clapper chestnut, a new cultivar, resulted from a hybrid produced by R. B. Clapper near Carter-ville, Ill. in 1946 (220). The parents are a Chinese chestnut and an American chestnut, the hybrid backcrossed upon the same American tree [(*C. mollissima* ♀ × *dentata* ♂) ♀ × *dentata* ♂]. In 1963 the tree was 45 ft tall and 7.3 in. d.b.h.

The Connecticut Agricultural Experimental Station, continuing the many years' work of A. H. Graves (143), has produced promising hybrids of Chinese × Japanese-American chestnut. And so it appears that "chestnut" may once more be a valuable tree in the forests of North America.

RANGE

Northeast, Appalachian region, and Ohio Valley (map, Plate 42).

THE CHINKAPINS

The remaining native species of *Castanea* are designated as the chinkapins (Indian for chestnut). According to the Check List (172), there are three species, all small trees or shrubs found in the southern states. Collectively, they differ from chestnut in their smaller, tomentose leaves, single-seeded burs, and usually tomentose twigs.

One species, *Castanea pumila* Mill., is starred in the Check List. It is a small tree of the Coastal Plain from southern Pennsylvania and New Jersey to northern Florida, west to eastern Texas, and northward as far as southwestern Missouri.

CASTANOPSIS (D. Don) Spach   Chinkapin; Evergreen chinkapin (SPN)

This genus embraces about 30 species of evergreen trees and shrubs, the majority of which are scattered through the forests of China, India, and the Malayan Archipelago. The American flora includes but two species, both native to the Pacific Coast. *C. sempervirens* Dudl. [*C. chrysophylla* var. *sempervirens* (Dudl.) Henry] is a small,

FIG. 123. Fruits of *Castanea pumila* × ¾.

timberline shrub common in the coast ranges and the high Sierra Nevada of California.

BOTANICAL FEATURES OF THE GENUS

Leaves persistent, coriaceous, entire or dentate, stipulate.

Flowers in erect, unisexual or bisexual aments; *staminate* in cymose clusters of 3 along the amentiferous stalk, the individual flowers similar to those of the chestnut; *pistillate* solitary or in clusters of 2 or 3, the ovary 3-celled.

Fruit a large, lustrous, brown to yellowish-brown nut borne solitary or in clusters of 2 or 3 and encased in a 4-valved involucre with branched spines, maturing at the end of the second season (American species).

Castanopsis chrysophylla (Dougl.) A.DC. Golden chinkapin; giant evergreen chinkapin (SPN)

Distinguishing characteristics. *Leaves* lanceolate to oblong-ovate, entire, often slightly revolute, dark green above, covered with minute golden-yellow persistent scales below. *Flowers* like those of chestnut, appearing between June and February. *Fruit* densely covered with branched spines, the husk containing one or two edible nuts which mature at the end of the second season. *Twigs* at first covered with golden-yellow scales, at length reddish brown and somewhat scurfy.

General description. The golden chinkapin, which is never more than a large shrub in Washington, attains tree size in Oregon and California. Under average conditions for growth it will reach a height of 60 to 80 ft and a diameter of about half as many inches, although trees up to 150 ft high and 8 ft in diameter have been observed in the moist valleys of northern coastal California. Under forest conditions this species develops a clear bole for one-half to two-thirds of its length, and a dense, ovoid to conical crown; the crown of open-grown trees is generally large and wide-spreading. A taproot is developed by juvenile trees, but this gives way in later life to a well-developed lateral system of anchorage.

Considerable seed is produced at frequent intervals, and natural regeneration by this means is generally satisfactory. Some renewal is also traceable to stump sprouts. Growth is moderately rapid, and maturity is reached in about 200 to 500 years.

This species is quite gregarious on poor, dry soils and often forms pure stands over wide areas. The tree also appears as an understory species in stands of redwood and Douglas-fir, or mixed with western juniper, Jeffrey pine, canyon live oak, and as a component of chaparral.

Range. A disjunct on Hoods Canal near Hoodsport, Washington; thence south from the Columbia River along the west slopes of the Cascades through Oregon; in California along the coastal ranges to the San Jacinto Mountains; rarely ever found above 4,000-ft elevation.

FIG. 124. *Castanopsis chrysophylla.* Golden chinkapin. *1.* Leaf showing revolute margin × ¾. *2.* Fruit × 1. *3.* Nut × 1. *4.* Bark. (*Photograph by Emanuel Fritz.*)

LITHOCARPUS Blume   Tanoak

Lithocarpus numbers about 100 species of evergreen trees and shrubs. The genus is widespread through southeastern Asia and Indonesia but is not found elsewhere except for a single species indigenous to western North America. The Asiatic forms will not endure cold winters, and hence their use as ornamentals is not possible in the cooler regions of the Temperate Zone. A few species have been successfully introduced into southern United States, but they are rarely ever used for decorative purposes. The fruits of *L. edulis* Rehd. and *L. cornea* Rehd. of Japan and south China, respectively, are rather sweet and fit for human consumption. Botanically, this genus is very interesting, owing to the fact that its flowers are nearly identical with those of either *Castanea* or *Castanopsis*, while its fruit resembles that of the *Erythrobalanus* oaks.

BOTANICAL FEATURES OF THE GENUS

Leaves persistent, stipulate.
Flowers similar to those of *Castanea* or *Castanopsis*.
Fruit a nut (acorn), partially or rarely wholly enveloped by a cuplike involucre; maturing at the end of the second season.

Lithocarpus densiflorus (Hook. and Arn.) Rehd.   Tanoak

Distinguishing characteristics. *Leaves* oblong to oblong-lanceolate, repand-dentate to entire-revolute, rounded-truncate at the base, light green above, brownish woolly pubescent in early summer below, ultimately becoming bluish white and sparsely pubescent toward the end of the season; *petiole* tomentose. *Flowers* similar to those of *Castanopsis*. *Fruit* a bitter acorn, about ¾" long, the cup shallow, tomentose, lined with lustrous red pubescence. *Twigs* at first densely pubescent but at length dark reddish brown and often covered with a glaucous bloom. *Bark* broken into heavy rounded ridges separated by deep narrow fissures.

General description. Tanoak or tanbark-oak, a name by which this species is equally well known, is a moderately large tree 70 to 90 ft in height and 24 to 36 in. d.b.h., but under the most favorable conditions reaching somewhat larger proportions (max. 150 by 7° ft). The boles of forest trees are clear, but often asymmetrical, and support narrow pyramidal crowns of ascending branches; open-grown trunks are short and often disappear in a mass of widespread limbs which form broad, nearly globose crowns. The anchorage consists of a deep, well-developed taproot and a number of short laterals. Best development is reached on deep, rich, moist, but well-drained, gravelly and sandy soils in admixture with redwood, Douglas-fir, Oregon white oak, golden chinkapin, and California black oak. At altitudes of 3,500 to 4,500 ft along the middle-west slopes of the Sierra, tanoak occurs in mixture with black oak, Pacific madrone, bigleaf maple, white fir, sugar pine, ponderosa pine, and Douglas-fir. It also appears, although usually shrubby in habit, in forests above the chaparral. Fairly extensive, nearly pure stands of coppice growth appear on cutover areas.

Viable seed is borne in abundance after the thirtieth to fortieth season. Some natural regeneration, as indicated above, is also traceable to coppice. The growth of seedlings proceeds at a moderate rate, and the trees reach maturity between 200 and 300 years. Tanoak can exist under forest cover throughout its life, and the rapidity

Fig. 125. *Lithocarpus densiflorus.* Tanoak. *1.* Leaf × ¾. *2.* Acorn × 1.

with which suppressed trees often develop upon being released from dense shade is remarkable.

The bark of tanoak contains appreciable amounts of tannin and at one time was an important commercial source of this material.

Range. Southern Oregon south along the coast ranges to the Santa Ynez Mountains in California; south in the Sierra to Mariposa County. *Altitudinal distribution:* sea level to nearly 5,000 ft.

QUERCUS L.   Oak

The oak group with its many species is the most important aggregation of hardwoods found on the North American continent, if not in the entire Northern Hemisphere; in fact, the central and southern hardwood forests of the United States may be thought of as oak forests, with the other broad-leaved species playing a secondary role. The oaks furnish more native timber annually than any other related group of broad-leaved trees, and the amount is surpassed only by the conifers, which occupy first place in this respect. Other products of lesser importance but widespread use include cork from two southern European forms,[1] tannin from the bark of certain others, and ink derived from the insect leaf galls of a few Old World species; the sweet acorns of several western North American oaks were used extensively for food by the Indians.

The sturdy qualities and appearance of many of the oaks, together with their longevity in comparison with other hardwoods, have made them from very ancient times the objects of admiration and worship among the early people of the Old World. This feeling still persists in a modified form, and many of the historic as well as ornamental trees of the United States and other countries are oaks of one species or another.

From the botanical standpoint, the species included in the genus *Quercus* furnish in many instances one of the foremost taxonomic puzzles awaiting solution, on account of the extreme variability exhibited. The

Fig. 126. Stripping an introduced cork oak tree near Monrovia, California. (*Photograph courtesy of the Crown Cork and Seal Co.*)

[1] The world's cork supply is obtained chiefly from *Q. suber* L. and *Q. suber* var. *occidentalis* Areang. See Cooke (77), Ryan (308), and Fowells (126) for reports on growing these trees in the United States.

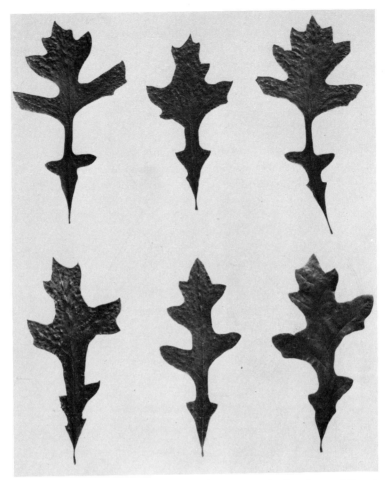

Fig. 127. Leaves from the same tree of overcup oak, showing variation in shape.

total number of species is variously estimated at 200 to 300 or more, but the inclusion of all the known hybrid forms would increase these figures considerably.

The oaks are widely distributed throughout the temperate regions of the Northern Hemisphere and extend southward at higher altitudes to the tropics (Columbia in the Western, northern Africa and Indonesia in the Eastern Hemisphere). There are possibly 60 to 70 species native to the United States, and according to the Check List (212) 58 of these reach tree size. There are also listed 69 hybrids.[1]

Because of the size and complexity of this group, it is obviously not

[1] For an account of North American hybrid oaks, see Palmer (274).

expedient in an elementary text to cover all the native forms, or even species. Only the more important or characteristic are fully described; if one becomes thoroughly familiar with the distinguishing features of these, the identification of other local species, with one of the specialized floras listed under Selected References, can be accomplished.

BOTANICAL FEATURES OF THE GENUS

Leaves deciduous or persistent, alternate; *margin* lobed, crenate, serrate, or entire; *shape* and *size* often very variable even on the same tree; *stipules* usually deciduous, at times persistent at the upper nodes; *phyllotaxy* ⅖.

FIG. 128. *Quercus*. Oak. *1*. Flowering branchlet × ½. *2*. Pistillate flowers × 4. *3*. Staminate flower × 4.

Flowers imperfect (species monoecious), appearing on the old or new growth, with or after the unfolding of the new leaves; *staminate* aments pendent, clustered; individual flowers comprising a 4- to 7-lobed calyx which encloses 6 stamens (rarely 4 to 12); *pistillate* flowers solitary or in few- to many-flowered spikes from the axils of the new leaves; individual flowers consisting of a 6-lobed calyx surrounding a 3- (rarely 4- to 5-) celled ovary, the whole partly enclosed in an involucre.

Fruit an acorn maturing in 1 or 2 seasons, respectively; *nut* partially enclosed by a scaly cup (the modified involucre); usually 1-seeded by abortion.

Twigs stout to slender, straight, commonly angled; *pith* homogeneous, stellate; *buds* clustered at the ends of the twig, *terminal bud* present,

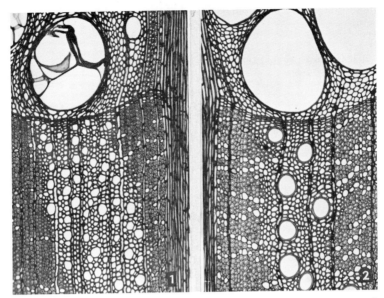

Fɪɢ. 129. Transverse sections × 60. *1.* White oak wood. *2.* Red oak wood.
(*Photomicrographs by Simon Williams, courtesy of Bull. Torr. Bot. Club.*)

with many scales imbricated in 5 ranks; *lateral buds* similar; *leaf scars* semicircular; *bundle scars* scattered, numerous; *stipule scars* minute.

SUBGENERA

On the basis of similarities in botanical features, the oaks can be separated into three subgenera. Two of these include the native oaks as indicated below. *Leucobalanus* comprises the so-called "white oaks," while *Erythrobalanus* is the group name applied to the "red or black oaks."[1]

Although the concept of subgenera as applied to the oaks has been generally accepted, the actual assignment of certain species to one group or the other has not been an easy task. No matter what feature was chosen, there were always a few species which could be put in either group because of overlapping characteristics. Williams (377) reclassified the native oaks, and in so doing found that wood anatomy is the most trustworthy feature to employ since no exceptions occur. The chief difference between the old and the new classification is that the "live oaks" are all placed in the red oak group instead of being partly in one group and partly in the other. It is believed that this is a more logical arrangement, and it has therefore been adopted, even though it means

[1] *Cyclobalanus* is the third subgenus and includes certain foreign species; in this group, the acorn-cup scales are fused together in concentric rings.

including a tree previously called Arizona "white" oak in the red oak group.

CONSPECTUS OF SUBGENERA

Subgenus	Leaves	Wood	Fruit [a]
Leucobalanus (white oaks)	without spinose teeth or bristle-tipped lobes	summerwood pores angled, small and thin-walled (Fig. 129)	maturing in one season; inner surface of shell glabrous; seed sweet
Erythrobalanus (red oaks)	mostly with bristle-tipped lobes; if unlobed, margins, apices, or both often with spines or bristles	summerwood pores rounded, large and thick-walled	usually maturing in two seasons; inner surface of shell generally tomentose; seed usually bitter [b]

[a] The fruit features have been retained from the older classification since they still apply, with one exception, to the eastern species covered by this text.
[b] For exceptions, see individual specific descriptions.

The following key indicates to some extent the variation found in the oaks and arranges the species described in smaller, more readily usable groups.

Condensed key to subgenera and smaller groups

A. White oaks (see above for distinguishing features).
    B. Leaves more or less deeply lobed—*Q. alba, macrocarpa, lyrata, stellata, garryana, lobata.*
    BB. Leaves coarsely or sinuately toothed, or shallowly lobed (chestnut oaks)—*Q. prinus, michauxii, bicolor, muehlenbergii.*
AA. Red oaks (see above for distinguishing features).
    B. Leaves persistent 1 to 4 years (live oaks)—*Q. chrysolepis, agrifolia, wislizenii, virginiana, emoryi, arizonica, oblongifolia.*
    BB. Leaves deciduous the first autumn or following spring.
        C. Leaves pinnately lobed, or broadly obovate and lobed at the apex—*Q. rubra, velutina, shumardii, coccinea, palustris, ellipsoidalis, falcata, laevis, marilandica, nigra, nuttallii, kelloggii, douglasii.*
        CC. Leaves entire, usually oblong to lanceolate (willow oaks)— *Q. phellos, imbricaria, laurifolia* (some forms of *Q. nigra* also included here).

General regional distribution of the oaks

South Atlantic and Gulf Coastal Plains in addition to varying distances north in the Mississippi, Missouri, and Ohio River Valleys, and adjacent regions:

overcup oak, *Q. lyrata*
swamp chestnut oak, *Q. michauxii*
live oak, *Q. virginiana*
Shumard oak, *Q. shumardii*
southern red oak, *Q. falcata* (and its varieties)
Nuttall oak, *Q. nuttallii*
turkey oak, *Q. laevis*
water oak, *Q. nigra*
laurel oak, *Q. laurifolia*
willow oak, *Q. phellos*

The general region east of the Great Plains—including the above:

white oak, *Q. alba*
post oak, *Q. stellata*
black oak, *Q. velutina*
blackjack oak, *Q. marilandica*

Not on the Coastal Plain; in general, north, east, or central:

chinkapin oak, *Q. muehlenbergii*
bur oak, *Q. macrocarpa*
chestnut oak, *Q. prinus*
swamp white oak, *Q. bicolor*
northern red oak, *Q. rubra*
scarlet oak, *Q. coccinea*
pin oak, *Q. palustris*
northern pin oak, *Q. ellipsoidalis*
shingle oak, *Q. imbricaria*

WESTERN OAKS

Rocky Mountains or the Southwest:

bur oak, *Q. macrocarpa* (stunted)
Emory oak, *Q. emoryi*
Arizona oak, *Q. arizonica*
Mexican blue oak, *Q. oblongifolia*

Pacific Coast states:

Oregon white oak, *Q. garryana*
California white oak, *Q. lobata*
blue oak, *Q. douglasii*
California black oak, *Q. kelloggii*

canyon live oak, *Q. chrysolepis*
California live oak, *Q. agrifolia*
interior live oak, *Q. wislizenii*

THE WHITE OAKS

DISTINGUISHING CHARACTERISTICS OF IMPORTANT SPECIES [a]

Species	Leaves	Fruit
Q. alba, white oak	deeply to shallowly lobed, sinuses narrow; green and glabrous below	about ¾″ long; nut ovoid-oblong; cup bowl-like with warty scales
Q. macrocarpa, bur oak	irregularly lobed, the center pair of sinuses the deepest; pale below	about 1½″ long; nut broadly ovoid; cup deep, conspicuously fringed on the margin
Q. lyrata, overcup oak	deeply lobed, with broad irregular sinuses; green or pale below	about 1″ long; nut subglobose, almost wholly enclosed in a deep, thin, unfringed cup
Q. stellata, post oak	cruciform; tawny tomentose below	about ½″ long; nut ovoid-oblong; cup bowl-like with thin scales
Q. garryana, Oregon white oak	evenly and deeply lobed; orange-pubescent below	about 1″ long; ovoid to obovoid; cup shallow with pubescent scales

[a] For chestnut oak subgroup, see page 306.

Quercus alba L.   White oak

BOTANICAL FEATURES

Leaves deciduous, 5″ to 9″ long, 2″ to 4″ wide; *shape* oblong-obovate; *margin* 7- to 9-lobed, with deep to shallow sinuses extending evenly toward the midrib; *apex* rounded; *base* cuneate; *surfaces* glabrous, bright green above, slightly paler below.
Fruit solitary or paired, sessile or short-stalked; *nut* ½″ to ¾″ long, ovoid-oblong, enclosed for one-quarter of its length in a light chestnut-brown, bowl-like cup with thickened, warty scales; about 150 (70–210) nuts to the pound.
Twigs moderately stout, purplish gray to greenish red; *terminal buds* ⅛″ to ³⁄₁₆″ long, globose to broadly ovoid, reddish brown, glabrous; *lateral buds* similar but smaller.
Bark light ashy gray, very variable in appearance; on young to medium-sized trees often broken up into small, vertically aligned blocks, scaly on the surface; later irregularly plated, with the plates attached on one side, or deeply fissured, with narrow rounded ridges. (Fig. 130, 5, 6 shows the amount of variation to be expected, with 5 the more common except on very old trees.)

Fig. 130. *Quercus alba*. White oak. *1*. Twig × 1¼. *2*. Deeply lobed leaf × ½. *3*. Shallowly lobed leaf × ½. *4*. Acorn × 1. *5*. Bark. *6*. Bark of very old tree.

This tree is the most important species of the white oak group and is said to furnish nearly three-fourths of the timber harvested as white oak. Any estimate, however, is subject to error since only "white oak" and "red oak," respectively, are recognized in the trade; each division includes the wood of a number of species which lose their identity when the logs are manufactured into lumber or other forest products.

White oak at its best is a large tree 80 to 100 ft high and 3 to 4 ft in diameter (max. 150 by 8 ft). In the open it is characterized by a short stocky bole and a wide-spreading crown of rugged appearance; this outline with some variation is a feature of most oaks. Under forest conditions, white oak develops a tall straight trunk with a small crown.

The oaks as a group are noted for their deep root systems; and at the end of the first season, white oak seedlings with but 3 to 4 in. of slender top growth terminate below in a prodigious taproot $\frac{1}{4}$ to $\frac{1}{2}$ in. in diameter at the surface and extending 1 ft or more into the ground (see page 219).

Although white oak is found on many types of soil, it reaches its best development in coves or on the higher bottomlands where the soil is deep and moist, with good drainage. Common associates include hickories, other oaks, basswood, white ash, black cherry, yellow-poplar, and sweetgum; a complete list would include a much larger number of species (127). Some of the finest old-growth white oak was in central New York in mixture with eastern white pine, eastern hemlock, sugar maple, and hickories. Although usually found in uneven-aged mixed hardwood forests, this oak, after clearcutting, may form even-aged pure stands. Propagation by stump sprouts is good, especially from young trees damaged by fire or cut down. Such growth from low stumps or seedlings results in trees of excellent quality. Sprout growth from high stumps is often affected by heart rot.

White oak is often a prolific seeder, but good seed years do not occur regularly, and locally several years (4 to 10) may pass without any crop whatever. Like many of the white oak group, the acorns of this species germinate in the fall soon after they are released. This is a disadvantage because the roots often do not have time to penetrate the soil and are killed by freezing; germination varies from 75 to 95 percent. Seton (320) emphasized the importance of the gray squirrel in distributing the fruit of white oak, and indicated that a diminishing squirrel population affects adversely the spread of this tree in our forests. Werthner (370) stated that the acorns of the white oak were used for food by the Indians and early settlers, who made them more palatable by boiling in water to remove tannins.

The growth of white oak is not fast, and like many slow-growing trees it may attain a considerable age, in some instances a maximum of 500 to 600 years. This species, like a number of other oaks, is intermediate in tolerance, with a tendency to become more intolerant with age.

RANGE

Eastern United States (map, Plate 43).

1. *Quercus alba.*   2. *Quercus macrocarpa.*

PLATE 43

Quercus macrocarpa Michx.   Bur oak; mossycup oak

BOTANICAL FEATURES

Leaves deciduous, 6″ to 12″ long, 3″ to 6″ wide; *shape* obovate to oblong; *margin* 5- to 9-lobed, the two center sinuses usually reaching nearly to the midrib; *apex* rounded; *base* cuneate; *surfaces* dark green and lustrous above, pale and pubescent below.
Fruit solitary, usually stalked, variable in size; *nut* usually ¾″ to 1½″ long (max. nearly 2″ in the South), broadly ovoid, downy at the apex, enclosed one-half or more in a deep cup which is conspicuously fringed on the margin; about 75 (40–135) nuts to the pound.
Twigs stout, yellowish brown, usually pubescent; after the second year often with conspicuous corky ridges; *terminal buds* mostly obtuse, usually tawny pubescent; *lateral buds* similar but smaller.
Bark similar to that of *Q. alba* but darker and more definitely ridged vertically.

GENERAL DESCRIPTION

Bur oak is a medium-sized to large tree 70 to 80 ft high, and 2 to 3 ft in diameter (max. 170 by 7 ft) with a massive trunk and broad crown of

Fig. 131. *Quercus macrocarpa.* Bur oak. *1.* Twig × 1¼. *2.* Leaf × ½. *3.* Acorn × ¾. *4.* Bark.

stout branches. On dry upland soils, the root system is remarkably deep; the taproots of 8-year-old saplings may be more than 14 ft in length (127). Over its very extensive range, this oak is found in mixture with numerous hardwoods on many types of soil from sandy plains to moist alluvial bottoms; on uplands, limestone soils are favored. Bur oak is noted for its resistance to drought; invading the grasslands of the Prairies and Great Plains, it may form extensive open, park-like stands. As a small tree or shrub it extends even to the arid foothills of the Rocky Mountains.

Besides its value as a timber producer, the distinctive leaves, fringed acorns, and corky twigs recommend bur oak as an ornamental; it is also more resistant to city smoke and gas injury than most other oaks.

RANGE

Eastern United States except for the south Atlantic and Gulf Coastal Plains (map, Plate 43).

Quercus lyrata Walt.   Overcup oak

BOTANICAL FEATURES

Leaves deciduous, 6″ to 10″ long, 1″ to 4″ wide; *shape* oblong-obovate; *margin* very variable, mostly with 5 to 9 lobes separated by broad irregular sinuses; *apex* acute; *base* cuneate; *surfaces* dark green and glabrous above, green and nearly glabrous, or silvery white and downy below.
Fruit solitary or paired, sessile or stalked; *nut* ½″ to 1″ long, the diameter usually greater than the length, subglobose to ovoid, two-thirds to almost entirely enclosed in a deep, unfringed cup; about 130 nuts to the pound.
Twigs slender, gray; *terminal buds* about ⅛″ long; ovoid to globose, and covered with light chestnut-brown, somewhat tomentose scales; *lateral buds* similar but smaller; *stipules* often persistent near the tip of the twig.

Fig. 132. *Quercus lyrata.* Overcup oak. *1.* Bark. *2.* Twig × 1¼. *3.* Acorn × 1. *4.* Leaf × ½.

Bark somewhat similar to that of *Q. alba*, but brownish gray and rough, with large irregular plates or ridges; trunk frequently with a twisted appearance.

GENERAL DESCRIPTION

Overcup oak perhaps more nearly resembles bur oak than any other associated species, because of its deeply cupped acorns and somewhat similar leaves. It is usually of poor form with a short, often crooked or twisted bole and a large, open crown featured by crooked branches with relatively few smaller branchlets. Overcup oak may attain a height of 114* ft and a diameter of nearly 5* ft, but it is commonly much smaller.

This species is not abundant or important except in the main bottomlands of the lower Mississippi and the lower valleys of its tributaries. Here overcup oak is one of the most common swampland trees growing on wet, poorly drained clay soils, and is better adapted to withstand prolonged inundation than most of the accompanying species. Common associates are water hickory, willow and Nuttall oaks, American and cedar elms, green ash, water locust, persimmon, sugarberry, water tupelo, and baldcypress.

Although overcup oak usually produces timber of poor quality, it merits consideration because of its abundance over large areas and its ability to grow upon the poorest of the bottomland sites.

RANGE

Atlantic and Gulf Coastal Plains and Mississippi River Valley (map, Plate 44).

1. *Quercus lyrata.* 2. *Quercus stellata.*

PLATE 44

Quercus stellata Wangenh.   Post oak

BOTANICAL FEATURES

Leaves deciduous, thick, somewhat leathery, 4″ to 6″ long, 3″ to 4″ wide; *shape* oblong-obovate; *margin* usually deeply 5-lobed, the two middle lobes squarish and nearly opposite, giving the leaf a cruciform appearance; *apex* rounded; *base* cuneate; *surfaces* dark green with scattered stellate-pubescence above, tawny tomentose below. **Fruit** solitary or paired, sessile or short-stalked; *nut* ½″ to ⅔″ long, ovoid-oblong, sometimes slightly striped, smooth or pubescent at the apex; enclosed for about one-third of its length in a bowl-shaped cup with thin scales (less often warty like those of white oak); about 400 (240–635) nuts to the pound.

Twigs somewhat tawny-tomentose; *terminal buds* about ⅛″ long, subglobose to broadly ovoid, covered with chestnut-brown pubescent scales; *lateral buds* similar but smaller.

Bark similar to that of *Q. alba* but often reddish brown and with more definite longitudinal ridges.

FIG. 133. *Quercus stellata.* Post oak. *1.* Twig × 1¼. *2.* Acorn × 1. *3.* Leaf × ½. *4.* Bark.

GENERAL DESCRIPTION

Unlike the two preceding species, post oak is typically found on dry, gravelly or sandy soils and on rocky ridges. It is a small to medium-sized tree 40 to 50 ft high and 12 to 24 in. in diameter (max. 100 by 4* ft), but may attain only shrubby proportions under adverse conditions. The crown usually consists of fewer large branches than in white oak, and they are characteristically gnarled or somewhat twisted in appearance.

The associates of post oak on the so-called "barrens" or in sand-plain country include black, blackjack, and scarlet oaks, pitch pine, and eastern redcedar.

In the lower Mississippi Valley on the silty loam soils of the second or higher bottoms, post oak attains its largest size and best quality; in fact, it seems so different from the dry-soil form of the same region that the specific name *mississippiensis* was given to it by W. W. Ashe (14). It is now recognized as Delta post oak, *Q. stellata* var. *mississippiensis* (Ashe) Little. The usual associates of this bottomland form include swamp chestnut, white, willow, water, and cherrybark oaks; sweetgum, elms, ashes, hickories, and occasionally loblolly pine.

Several other forms of post oak have been distinguished, and one of the commonest is var. *margaretta* (Ashe) Sarg. (sand post oak). This is the common variety of the Coastal Plains from Virginia to Texas; the lobes of the leaves are more rounded and less cruciform than those of the species, the acorn-cup scales are sometimes thinner, and the winter buds may be larger and more acute.

RANGE

Eastern United States (map, Plate 44).

THE CHESTNUT OAKS

The leaves of the species included in this smaller division of the white oak group are coarsely serrate to dentate-crenate, or shallowly lobed.

DISTINGUISHING CHARACTERISTICS OF IMPORTANT SPECIES

Species	Leaves	Fruit
Q. michauxii, swamp chestnut oak	obovate, crenate-dentate	sessile or nearly so, cup thick, the scales wedge-shaped
Q. prinus, chestnut oak	elliptical or nearly so, crenate	long-stalked, cup thin, the scales more or less fused

Quercus michauxii Nutt. [*Quercus prinus* L.]   Swamp chestnut oak; cow oak

BOTANICAL FEATURES

Leaves deciduous, 5″ to 8″ long, 3″ to 4½″ wide; *shape* broadly obovate to oblong-obovate; *margin* deeply crenate to coarsely dentate, often with large glandular-tipped teeth; *apex* acute or slightly obtuse; *base* cuneate; *surfaces* dark green and lustrous above, pale green to silvery white and pubescent below.

F‌ɪɢ. 134. *Quercus michauxii.* Swamp chestnut oak. *1.* Twig × 1¼. *2.* Acorn × 1. *3.* Leaf × ½. *4.* Bark.

Fruit solitary or paired, sessile or nearly so; *nut* 1″ to 1½″ long, ovoid to oblong, enclosed for not more than a third of its length in a thick bowl-shaped cup, with distinct, somewhat wedge-shaped scales; about 100 (55–195) nuts to the pound.
Twigs moderately stout, reddish brown to orange-brown; *terminal buds* ¼″ long, acute, covered with thin, red, puberulous scales, pale on the margin; *lateral buds* similar.
Bark irregularly furrowed or scaly, ashy gray, tinged with red; freshly cut surfaces reddish brown.

GENERAL DESCRIPTION

Swamp chestnut oak (commonly called cow or basket oak) is probably the most important species of this group. It is a well-formed tree with a straight massive trunk and narrow crown, averaging 60 to 80 ft in height and 2 to 3 ft in diameter (max. 130° by 9° ft). This oak, at least in the lower Mississippi Valley, is somewhat irregular in occurrence, but when present locally, it is frequently abundant.

Swamp chestnut oak is found on the best, relatively well-drained, loamy ridges and silty clay and loamy terraces in bottomlands. Principal associates are cherrybark, Shumard, white, and Delta post oaks and blackgum; other bottomland hardwoods are also present.

The quality of the wood is second only to that of the best white oaks, and for this reason the tree has suffered excessive cutting in many localities; the name "basket oak" undoubtedly originated through the production of basket splints.

RANGE

The Atlantic and Gulf Coastal Plains and Mississippi River Valley (map, Plate 45).

1. *Quercus michauxii.*   2. *Quercus prinus.*

PLATE 45

Quercus prinus L. [Quercus montana Willd.]   Chestnut oak; rock oak

BOTANICAL FEATURES

Leaves deciduous, 4″ to 8″ long 1½″ to 3″ wide; *shape* obovate to elliptical, or nearly lanceolate; *margin* coarsely crenate, or repandcrenate; *apex* rounded; *base* cuneate; *surfaces* yellowish green and lustrous above, paler and often finely pubescent below.

Fruit solitary or paired, stalked; *nut* 1″ to 1½″ long (commonly smaller), ovoid to ellipsoidal, very lustrous, enclosed at the base, or more often from one-half to one-third of its length in a thin cup with somewhat fused scales; inner surface of the cup only moderately curved vertically; about 75 (55–100) nuts to the pound.

Twigs orange to reddish brown; *terminal buds* ¼″ long, usually acute or acuminate, covered with bright chestnut-brown scales; *lateral buds* similar.

Bark brown to nearly black, on older trees very deeply and coarsely furrowed.

GENERAL DESCRIPTION

Chestnut oak is a medium-sized tree 50 to 60 ft high and about 2 ft in diameter (max. 100 by 7° ft). It is found typically on poor dry upland

Fig. 135. *Quercus prinus*. Chestnut oak. *1*. Twig × 1¼. *2*. Leaf × ½. *3*. Acorn cup showing thin flat sides × 1. *4*. Acorn × 1. *5*. Bark.

rocky sites where it may form pure stands. On somewhat better soils, common associates include white and pitch pines, eastern redcedar, white, scarlet, and black oaks, sweetgum, red maple, and numerous other hardwoods.

Chestnut oak is a prolific sprouter, and much of the new growth on cutover land is of sprout origin. Best growth is made in well-drained coves and other moist sites. The bark of chestnut oak contains about 11 percent tannin.

RANGE

Appalachian region and Ohio River Valley (map, Plate 45).

Quercus bicolor Willd.   Swamp white oak

Distinguishing characteristics. *Leaves* deciduous, obovate, shallowly lobed or coarsely toothed. *Fruit* about 1″ long, usually paired, borne on slender peduncles 1″ to 4″ long. *Twigs* straw-brown, dull, terminal buds ¹⁄₁₆″ to ⅛″ long, orange-brown, essentially glabrous. *Bark* on the upper limbs, peeling off in ragged, papery scales; deeply furrowed below into flat scaly ridges or blocky, dark brown.

General description. Swamp white oak is a medium-sized tree 60 to 70 ft high and 2 to 3 ft in diameter (max. 100 by 7 ft), often with a poorly pruned bole and irregular crown. This species is not abundant except locally where it occurs along stream banks, on moist flats, or in swamps. When present at all, the supply may be large, and even though the quality of the timber is often inferior, it is harvested and used with that of the other white oaks.

Range. Northern half of the eastern United States.

Quercus muehlenbergii Engelm. Chinkapin oak

Distinguishing characteristics. *Leaves* deciduous, obovate to oblong-lanceolate, coarsely serrate with glandular-tipped teeth. *Fruit* sessile or short stalked, about ½" long, with a thin bowl-shaped cup. *Twigs* slender, orange-brown, terminal buds ⅛" long, orange-brown. *Bark* ashy gray, more or less rough and flaky.

Fig. 136. *Quercus bicolor.* Swamp white oak. *1.* Buds × 1¼. *2.* Leaf × ½. *3.* Acorn × 1. *4.* Bark.

General description. This oak is rare over most of its range and hence is of little commercial value. It is usually a small to medium-sized tree found on dry limestone outcrops and soils with an alkaline reaction. In the Ohio and Mississippi Valleys, chinkapin oak is found on moist soils in the higher bottoms; here it averages 60 to 80 ft in height and 2 to 3 ft in diameter (max. 160 by 6° ft).

Range. Eastern United States except for the Atlantic Coastal Plain and most of the immediate Gulf Coast.

Fig. 137. *Quercus muehlenbergii*. Chinkapin oak. *1.* Twig
× 1¼. *2.* Acorn × 1. *3.* Leaf × ½. *4.* Bark.

THE WESTERN WHITE OAKS

Quercus garryana Dougl.   Oregon white oak

BOTANICAL FEATURES

Leaves 4″ to 6″ long, 2″ to 5″ wide; *shape* oblong to obovate; *margin* divided into
5 to 7 rounded lobes separated by moderately deep sinuses, often more or less revolute; *surfaces* lustrous dark green and glabrous above, pale green and with orange-
brown pubescence below; *petiole* about ¾″ long, stout, pubescent.
Fruit solitary or paired, sessile or short-stalked; *nut* 1″ to 1¼″ long, ovoid to obovoid,
light brown, enclosed only at the base in a shallow bowl-like cup with pubescent or
tomentose free-tipped scales; about 100 nuts to the pound.
Twigs stout, orange-red, densely pubescent during the first winter; *buds* ¼″ to ½″
long, covered with rusty-brown tomentum.
Bark smooth on young stems; on old trunks broken up into thin, gray-brown or gray
scaly ridges, separated by narrow, shallow fissures.

GENERAL DESCRIPTION

This, the only oak indigenous to the Pacific Northwest, is a medium-sized
tree seldom more than 50 to 70 ft high and 2 to 3 ft in diameter (max.
120* by 8* ft). The bole, even under forest conditions, is usually short
and rather crooked. It rises above a well-developed lateral root system
and merges into a wide-spreading, round-topped crown. Oregon white

Fig. 138. *Quercus garryana.* Oregon white oak. *1.* Twig × 1¼. *2.* Leaf × ½. *3.* Acorn × 1.

Fig. 139. Bark of Oregon white oak.

oak grows on almost any kind of soil, commonly on hot, dry, grassy but rocky slopes in a region whose rainfall averages 35 in. annually. Best development is attained on the alluvial soils of Washington and in Oregon. Here, limited pure stands are found, but the tree usually occurs as an individual or in small groves mixed with such species as Douglas-fir, ponderosa and digger pines, California black oak, and Pacific madrone. Oregon white oak is a component of five forest types (127).

Large crops of seed are produced every few years, but reproduction by this means is usually poor, owing to the inability of the germinating seeds to penetrate the heavy sods upon which they are so frequently disseminated. Stump sprouts and root suckers are vigorous, and these afford the best means of natural regeneration. Growth is slow. Trees 3 ft in diameter may be 250 years old, but a life span of 500 years may be attained. This oak is usually rated as intolerant, and eventually dies when overtopped by Douglas-fir.

RANGE

West Coast (map, Plate 46).

PLATE 46. *Quercus garryana.*

Quercus lobata Née   California white oak; valley oak

Distinguishing characteristics. *Leaves* about 3″ long, oblong to obovate, 7- to 11-lobed, both surfaces finely pubescent. *Acorns* 1″ to 2¼″ long, elongated-conic, one-third enclosed in a deep bowl-like cup, the cup scales free at their tips and forming a fringe about the cup. *Twigs* slender, pubescent. *Bark* with the appearance of alligator leather.

General description. This white oak is largely restricted to low valley sites in western California. It is the largest of California oaks and attains a height of 90 to 125 ft or more and a d.b.h. of 3 to 5 ft (max. 10 ft). Through the central portion of the state it forms nearly pure open groves. The bole is usually short, but massive, and merges into a large widespread hemispherical to subglobose crown. Best development is reached on deep rich loams, although the tree also occurs on poor, dry, sandy, and gravelly sites.

DISTINGUISHING CHARACTERISTICS OF IMPORTANT SPECIES

Species	Leaves	Fruit
Q. rubra, northern red oak	oblong-obovate, 7- to 11-lobed, with narrow, regular sinuses; glabrous except for inconspicuous axillary tufts below	variable, but mostly subglobose, about 1″ long; nut usually enclosed only at the base by a flat, thick, saucer-like cup
Q. velutina, black oak	obovate to ovate, 5- to 7-lobed, with sinuses of varying depth; more or less scurfy and yellowish to copper-colored below; axillary tufts white to rufous	ovoid-oblong, about ⅝″ long, nut ⅓ to ¼ enclosed in a bowl-like cup; cup scales dull (not shiny), free at the tips
Q. shumardii, Shumard oak	obovate to oval, 7- to 9-lobed, with many bristle tips and moderately deep sinuses; glabrous except for axillary tufts below	oblong-ovoid, tapering toward the apex, about 1″ long; nut enclosed only at the base by a flat, thick, saucerlike cup
Q. falcata, southern red oak	polymorphic; lower crown leaves usually 3-lobed at apex; middle and upper crown foliage 5- to 7- (often falcate) lobed; grayish or rusty tomentose below	subglobose, about ½″ long; nut enclosed only at the base by a flat, saucerlike cup
Q. falcata var. *pagodaefolia,* cherrybark oak	more or less uniformly 5- to 11-lobed, the lobes pointing outward	same
Q. coccinea, scarlet oak	ovate to oval, deeply 5- to 9-lobed, the sinuses nearly circular; glabrous except for axillary tufts below	depressed-globose, about ⅝″ long, usually with several concentric rings below the apex; nut ½ enclosed in a bowl-like cup with shiny, appressed scales
Q. palustris, pin oak	same as *Q. coccinea* except the sinuses broadly U-shaped or squarish	hemispherical, about ½″ long; nut enclosed only at the base by a flat, saucerlike cup with free-tipped scales
Q. nuttallii, Nuttall oak	same except with yellowish axillary pubescence below	oblong-ovoid, about 1″ long; nut ⅓ enclosed in a bowl-like cup

This tree grows with greater rapidity than any other California oak and usually attains large size in a comparatively short time. The oldest trees are commonly defective, heart rot being quite prevalent, and hence are of little value except for fuel. Ring counts of large stumps indicate that an age of more than 200 to 250 years is rarely attained.

Range. Low valleys of western California from the Sierra Nevada Mountains to the coast ranges; as far north as the Trinity River Valley and as far south as Kern and Los Angeles counties.

Quercus rubra L. [Quercus borealis Michx. f.]   Northern red oak

BOTANICAL FEATURES

Leaves deciduous; 5″ to 8″ long, 4″ to 5″ wide; *shape* oblong to obovate; *margin* with 7 to 11 often toothed lobes separated by regular sinuses extending about halfway to the midrib; *apex* acute to acuminate; *base* obtuse to broadly cuneate; *surfaces* somewhat lustrous, or dull above, glabrous below except for occasional often inconspicuous axillary tufts.

Fruit solitary or paired; *nut* ¾″ to 1″ long; variable in shape, but usually subglobose, enclosed at the base in a flat, thick, saucerlike cup; *cup scales* pubescent, their tips appreciably darkened; [1] about 105 (75–150) nuts (for size see Fig. 140, *4*) to the pound.

Twigs moderately stout, greenish brown to reddish brown, glabrous; *terminal buds* ¼″ long, ovoid, pointed, terete, covered by numerous reddish-brown, more or less hairy scales; *lateral buds* similar, but smaller.

Bark smooth on young stems, greenish brown; ultimately brown to nearly black and broken up into wide, flat-topped ridges, separated by shallow fissures; on very old trees more narrowly ridged or corrugated.

GENERAL DESCRIPTION

This species, probably the most important and widespread of northern oaks, is a medium-sized to large tree 60 to 80 ft high and 2 to 3 ft in diameter (max. 160 by 8* ft). Although developing a short massive trunk with an extensive crown in the open, this tree when grown in the forest produces a tall, straight, columnar bole which supports a small rounded head. The root system, although deep like that of many other oaks, is often lacking in a well-developed and persistent taproot which, in heavier soils, makes slow headway after the first few years.

Northern red oak may be found on sandy loam soils in mixture with other northern hardwoods and with white pine. Best development, however, is usually made on richer sites with such associates as basswood, black cherry, ashes, hickories, other oaks, yellow-poplar, and sweetgum.

[1] Figure 140, *3, 4*, shows the variation to be expected in acorns from different trees. Previously, trees bearing the shallow-cupped type were designated as a separate variety. Since intergradations are found, and the two forms do not appear to breed true, there seems to be no good reason for continuing to keep them separate.

FIG. 140. *Quercus rubra*. Northern red oak. *1*. Twig × 1¼. *2*. Acorns at end of first season × 2. *3* and *4*. Mature acorns (*4* the more common type) × 1. *5*. Leaf × ½. *6*. Bark of young tree. *7*. Bark of old tree.

Northern red oak is listed as a component in more than 20 forest cover types (127), and therefore the number of associated species is very large. On a tolerance scale, this oak, like many others, is intermediate.

Good seed crops occur at 2- to 5-year intervals. Unlike most white oaks, germination of red oak acorns does not take place until the following spring, and many of the acorns are destroyed by insect parasites. Growth of seedlings is fast, and on the best soils nursery stock sometimes attains a height of nearly 3 ft the first season. This oak is also a prolific sprouter and quickly restocks cutover areas by this means. Although not so long-lived as white oak, the life span of this species may embrace two to three centuries.

Northern red oak is widely used as an ornamental because of comparative ease in transplanting, the autumnal coloration of the leaves, and the symmetrical form of the tree.

RANGE

Eastern United States except for the south Atlantic and Gulf Coastal Plains (map, Plate 47).

1. *Quercus rubra.*   2. *Quercus velutina.*

PLATE 47

Quercus velutina Lam.   Black oak

BOTANICAL FEATURES

Leaves deciduous; 5″ to 7″ long, 3″ to 5″ wide; *shape* obovate to ovate; *margin* with 5 to 7 often toothed lobes separated by sinuses of variable depth; *apex* acute to acuminate; *base* broadly cuneate to nearly truncate; *surfaces* exceedingly lustrous and dark green above, yellow-green to coppery colored below, and more or less scurfy, pubescent with conspicuous axillary tufts.

FIG. 141. *Quercus velutina.* Black oak. *1.* Twig × 1¼. *2* and *3.* Leaves showing variation in depth of sinuses (*2* most common) × ½. *4.* Acorns showing variation × 1. *5.* Bark.

Fruit solitary or paired; *nut* ½″ to ¾″ long, ovoid to hemispherical, often striate, light red-brown, one-fourth to one-third enclosed in a deep bowl-like cup; *cup scales* loosely imbricated above the middle, dull chestnut-brown, tomentose; *flesh* yellow; about 250 (125–400) nuts to the pound.

Twigs stout, reddish brown, glabrous; *terminal buds* ¼″ to ½″ long, ovoid, sharp-pointed, angular, covered with numerous, hoary tomentose scales; *lateral buds* similar but smaller.

Bark thick, nearly black on old stems, deeply furrowed vertically, and with many horizontal breaks; inner bark bright orange or yellow.

GENERAL DESCRIPTION

Black oak, a tree 50 to 60 ft high and 2 to 3 ft in diameter (max. 150 by 7* ft), is one of the commonest of eastern upland oaks. Although making its best growth on moist, rich, well-drained soils, where it approaches red oak in stature, it is sensitive to competition on such sites and is oftener found on poor, dry, sandy, or heavy glacial clay hillsides. Black oak is featured by a deep taproot, a somewhat tapering, often limby bole, and an irregularly rounded crown. It possesses intermediate tolerance, and although pure stands may occur, this oak is usually found in mixture with a large number of other species. These include pignut and red hickories, post, scarlet, southern red, blackjack, and chestnut oaks, and less often white and red oaks. In the South it is found in the shortleaf pine belt and occasionally in the bottoms, where it occupies the highest and best-drained areas in company with loblolly pine, southern red oak, and sweetgum.

Black oak is a persistent sprouter; good seed years may occur at 2- to 3-year intervals. Growth is slower than in red oak; trees over 200 years old are rarely found.

RANGE

Eastern United States (map, Plate 47).

Quercus shumardii Buckl.   Shumard oak

BOTANICAL FEATURES

Leaves deciduous; 6" to 8" long, 4" to 5" wide; *shape* obovate to oval; *margin* with 7 to 9 lobes often again divided, with many bristle tips, and separated by moderately deep sinuses; *apex* acute to acuminate; *base* obtuse to nearly truncate; *surfaces* dark green and lustrous above, paler and glabrous below, except for axillary tufts.

Fruit solitary or in pairs; *nut* ¾" to 1¼" long, oblong-ovoid, slightly tapering toward the apex, enclosed at the base in a thick, shallow, saucer-shaped cup; *cup scales* appressed, pale pubescent or nearly glabrous.

Twigs slender to moderately stout, gray to grayish brown, glabrous; *terminal buds* ¼" long, ovoid, pointed, usually angled, covered by gray to gray-brown, downy, or nearly glabrous scales; *lateral buds* similar but smaller.

Bark on old trees very thick, broken into pale to whitish scaly ridges by deep, much darker-colored furrows; sometimes like that of *Q. velutina* or *Q. nigra*.

Fig. 142. *Quercus shumardii.* Shumard oak. *1.* Twig × 1¼. *2.* Acorn × 1. *3.* Leaf × ½. *4.* Bark. (*Photograph by U.S. Forest Service.*)

GENERAL DESCRIPTION

This species, one of the largest of the southern red oaks, not infrequently attains a height of 100 to 125 ft and a diameter of 4 to 5 ft (max. 180 by 8 ft). A long, clear, symmetrical bole rises above a slightly buttressed base and moderately shallow root system, while the crown is usually open and wide-spreading. The tree never occurs in pure stands but rather as an occasional individual or in small groves in mixture with other hardwoods, particularly swamp chestnut, cherrybark, and Delta post oaks, black tupelo, white ash, and hickories. This oak will grow on a number of soil types, but it is mostly a bottomland species and reaches its greatest size on deep, moist but well-drained soils on ridges and hummocky flats, and along river courses. Shumard oak is intolerant, and full light is needed for satisfactory reproduction (127). Its seeming sparse distribution is somewhat puzzling. It grows to large size in the Coastal Plain and Mississippi Valley regions, but is nowhere abundant. This may be a matter of recognition, since certain of its features are similar to those of some other oaks.

It has been stated that the wood of this species is mechanically superior to that of many other *Erythrobalanus* oaks. However, it is mixed with other red oak timbers and is not sold as Shumard oak; the name "Shumard" has been applied by botanists and foresters only to separate this species from the other "red oaks."

Eastern United States (map, Plate 48).

| 1. *Quercus shumardii.* | 2. *Quercus falcata.* |

PLATE 48

Quercus falcata Michx.   Southern red oak

BOTANICAL FEATURES

Leaves deciduous; 5″ to 9″ (rarely 12″) long, 4″ to 5″ wide; *shape* obovate to ovate; *margin* (1) shallowly 3-lobed at the apex; (2) more or less deeply 5- to 7-lobed, often falcate, the terminal lobe sometimes much longer than the laterals; *apex* acuminate or falcate; *base* rounded to broadly cuneate; *surfaces* dark lustrous green above, grayish green tomentose below, turning rusty upon drying.
Fruit solitary or paired; *nut* ½″ long, subglobose, orange-brown, sometimes striate, more or less stellate pubescent, enclosed one-third or less in a thin, shallow cup; *cup scales* reddish brown, appressed, pubescent except on the margins; about 595 (390–785) nuts to the pound.
Twigs dark red, pubescent, or nearly glabrous; *terminal buds* ⅛″ to ¼″ long, ovoid, acute with reddish-brown, puberulous scales; *lateral buds* similar but smaller.
Bark dark brown to nearly black, thick, the rough ridges separated by deep, narrow fissures; inner bark only slightly yellow (otherwise similar to that of *Q. velutina*).

GENERAL DESCRIPTION

This species is one of the commonest of upland southern oaks and is particularly characteristic of the drier, poorer soils of the Piedmont region. It is less frequently found in the coastal pine belt and is rare in the bottomlands of the Mississippi Delta. Southern red oak is a medium-sized tree (max. 122* by 7* ft) with a deep root system, a short trunk, and an

FIG. 143. *Quercus falcata*. Southern red oak. *1*. Twig × 1¼. *2*. Acorns × 1. *3*. Leaf × ½. *4*. Bark.

FIG. 144. Trilobed leaf of southern red oak.

extensive rounded crown which even under forest conditions is composed of large branches. This oak is similar in its silvical features to black oak, and is found with it and other dry-soil oaks and hickories, black tupelo, sweetgum, southern magnolia, and shortleaf and Virginia pines.

RANGE

Atlantic and Gulf Coastal Plains, the Piedmont, and lower Mississippi Valley (map, Plate 48).

Quercus falcata var. pagodaefolia Ell.   Cherrybark oak

Comparative botanical features. *Leaves* more uniformly lobed than those of the species, with the margins of the lobes more nearly at right angles to the midrib. *Bark* smooth, soon with narrow, flaky, or scaly ridges; otherwise similar to that of the species.

This oak is a more massive, better-formed tree than the southern red oak and often reachs heights of 100 to 130 ft and diameters of 3 to 5 ft (max. diameter 7* ft), which classes it among the largest of southern oaks. The tree is found in a number of different bottomland types, but it

Fig. 145. *Quercus falcata* var. *pagodaefolia.* Cherrybark oak.
1. Leaf × ½. *2.* Acorn × 1. *3.* Bark.

develops best on loamy ridges, where its associates include swamp chestnut oak, wetland hickories, white ash, and sweetgum. On higher ground, including the rich well-drained soil of old fields, to white ash and sweetgum may be added American beech, southern magnolia, black tupelo, yellow-poplar, and others.

Cherrybark oak is relatively intolerant and is usually dominant or co-dominant in the stand. It is especially plentiful in the lower Mississippi Valley, and on account of its fast growth, clear bole, and the superior quality of the wood it has been rated as the best red oak of this region (288).

RANGE

Atlantic and Gulf Coastal Plains and lower Mississippi Valley (map, Plate 49).

1. *Quercus falcata* var. *pagodaefolia.*

2. *Quercus coccinea.*

PLATE 49

Quercus coccinea Muenchh.   Scarlet oak

BOTANICAL FEATURES

Leaves deciduous; 4″ to 7″ long, 3″ to 5″ wide; *shape* ovate, obovate, or oval; *margin* deeply 5- to 9-lobed, with wide nearly circular sinuses; *apex* acute to acuminate; *base* truncate to broadly cuneate; *surfaces* bright lustrous green above, paler and glabrous below except for axillary tufts.

Fruit solitary or paired; *nut* ½″ to 1″ long, oval to hemispherical, or depressed-globose, reddish brown, rarely striate, often with concentric rings near the apex, one-third to one-half enclosed in a deep bowl-like cup; *cup scales* appressed, reddish brown, lustrous; *flesh* nearly white; about 280 (155–405) nuts to the pound.

Twigs slender, reddish brown, glabrous; *terminal buds* ⅛″ to ¼″ long, ovoid, often angled, covered by dark reddish-brown, pubescent scales, often lighter on the margins; *lateral buds* similar but smaller.

Bark on mature trees dark brown to nearly black, broken up into irregular ridges separated by shallow fissures of varying width; often flaky on the upper branches; otherwise similar to that of *Q. velutina.*

GENERAL DESCRIPTION

Scarlet oak is a medium-sized tree 70 to 80 ft high and 2 to 3 ft in diameter (max. 102* by 5* ft). It is generally found on dry, sandy soils and often forms a considerable part of the oak forests in the states east of the Appalachians. In this region it may grow in nearly pure stands or in mixture with other oaks and with hickories, also with pitch, shortleaf, and Virginia pines.

Scarlet oak is intolerant, and makes rapid growth especially on the better sites, from which it is usually excluded by more tolerant species. This oak is often used as an ornamental on account of its general hardiness and brilliant autumnal leaf coloration.

RANGE

Eastern United States except for the south Atlantic and Gulf Coastal Plains (map, Plate 49).

FIG. 146. *Quercus coccinea.* Scarlet oak. *1.* Twig × 1¼. *2.* Leaf × ½. *3.* Acorn × 1. *4.* Top of acorn showing concentric rings × 3. *5.* Bark.

Quercus palustris Muenchh.   Pin oak

Leaves deciduous; 3" to 5" long,[1] 2" to 5" wide; *shape* obovate to broadly oval; *margin* 5-, less commonly 7- to 9-lobed, with irregular wide to narrow often angled sinuses extending two-thirds or more to the midrib; *apex* acute to acuminate; *base* truncate to broadly cuneate; *surfaces* bright green and lustrous above, paler below and glabrous except for axillary tufts.

Fruit solitary or clustered; *nut* ½" long, nearly hemispherical, light brown, often striate, enclosed only at the base in a thin, saucerlike cup; *cup scales* appressed, red-brown, puberulous, dark-margined; about 410 (320–540) nuts to the pound.

Twigs slender, lustrous, reddish brown; *terminal buds* ⅛" long, ovoid, acute, with reddish-brown scales; *lateral buds* similar but smaller.

Bark grayish brown, smooth for many years, eventually with low, scaly ridges separated by shallow fissures.

GENERAL DESCRIPTION

Pin oak is a medium-sized tree 70 to 80 ft high and 2 to 3 ft in diameter (max. 135* by 5 ft). The root system is shallower than in many of the

[1] In the South often larger.

Fig. 147. *Quercus palustris.* Pin oak. *1.* Twig × 1¼. *2.* Leaf × ½. *3.* Acorn × 1. *4.* Bark.

other oaks and supports a trunk more or less studded with small tough branchlets which do not prune readily; these are also characteristic of the larger limbs, hence perhaps the common name "pin oak." The crown of open-grown trees is broadly pyramidal, with slightly drooping lower branches; together with the deeply cut leaves, this presents a very pleasing appearance, especially in the fall when autumnal coloration is at its height. These features recommend pin oak as an ornamental or street tree.

Pin oak makes good growth on wet clay flats, where water may stand for several weeks during late winter and spring. It is also found on better-drained soils in the bottoms, but here its intolerance gives other species an advantage. Common associates include sweetgum, overcup and bur oaks, elms, green ash, and red maple.

RANGE

Eastern United States except for Atlantic and Gulf Coastal Plains (map, Plate 50).

PLATE 50. *Quercus palustris.*

Quercus ellipsoidalis E. J. Hill   Northern pin oak; jack oak

Distinguishing characteristics. Very similar to those of pin oak except for the ellipsoidal acorn one-third to one-half enclosed in a deep bowl-shaped cup.
General description. This oak is more commonly found on dry upland soils than is the preceding species and also occupies a very small range in comparison with other native oaks.
Range. Southeastern Minnesota, east to north central Wisconsin, central Michigan, and extreme northwestern Ohio; northern Indiana, northern Illinois, and eastern Iowa [according to Rosendahl and Butters (304) also reaching Manitoba].

Quercus nuttallii Palmer   Nuttall oak

BOTANICAL FEATURES

Leaves deciduous; 4″ to 8″ long, 2″ to 5″ wide; *shape* obovate; *margin* usually 5- to 7- (rarely 9-) lobed, lobes rather broad, separated by deep sinuses; *apex* acute to acuminate; *base* truncate to broadly cuneate; *surfaces* dull, dark green above, paler below, glabrous except for axillary tufts.

Fruit solitary or clustered; *nut* ¾″ to 1¼″ long, oblong-ovoid, reddish brown, often striate, one-fourth to one-half enclosed in a stalked, deep, thick cup; *cup scales* appressed, or free at the rim; about 104 nuts to the pound.

Twigs moderately slender, gray-brown to reddish brown, glabrous; *terminal buds* nearly ¼″ long, ovoid, slightly angled, with numerous gray-brown, glabrous or slightly downy scales (similar to those of *Q. shumardii*).

Bark dark gray-brown, smooth; on older trees broken into broad flat ridges divided by narrow lighter-colored fissures (similar to that of pin oak).

Fig. 148. Acorn of Nuttall oak × ¾.

GENERAL DESCRIPTION

When Thomas Nuttall explored the Arkansas bottomlands more than a century ago, he listed among other species *Q. coccinea*, scarlet oak. Not until 1927 was it discovered that what he presumed to be this tree was probably the species which now bears his name (275).

Nuttall oak is a medium-sized tree attaining, however, in virgin stands a height of 100 to 120 ft and a diameter of nearly 4* ft. It is commercially important and, moreover, is one of the few noteworthy species found on poorly drained clay flats in the first river bottoms. Reproduction is consistently good, and second-growth trees reach merchantable size (2 ft in diameter) in about 70 years. The common associates include sweetgum, American elm, green ash, red maple, and overcup, willow, and water oaks.

RANGE

The Mississippi Valley from southeastern Missouri south to Louisiana, eastward to central Alabama; also along lower Louisiana-Texas border and adjacent southeastern Texas (map, Plate 51).

PLATE 51. *Quercus nuttallii.*

Quercus marilandica Muenchh.   Blackjack oak

Distinguishing characteristics. *Leaves* very variable but typically obovate, and shallowly three-lobed at the apex; lustrous above, tawny pubescent below. *Acorn* ¾″ long, oblong, one-half enclosed in a thick bowl-shaped cup with loose, reddish-brown scales. *Twigs* stout, somewhat scurfy-pubescent; *buds* often more than ¼″ long, angled, similar to those of *Q. velutina* but usually more reddish brown. *Bark* black, very rough and "blocky."

General description. Blackjack oak is a small, poorly formed tree characteristic of dry, sterile soils where it is associated in open mixtures with such species as post, black, and southern red oaks, mockernut hickory, and eastern redcedar. It is not common in the North, but very abundant southward, and in the Southwest comprises a large part of the forest growth on the poorest of sites. Although of value chiefly as a cover crop, this oak is utilized locally when of sufficient size.

Range. Long Island (New York) through New Jersey, central Pennsylvania, Ohio, southern Michigan, north central Illinois and southern Iowa to southeastern Nebraska; south through west central Oklahoma to eastern Texas; in the East, south to central Florida.

Fig. 149. *Quercus marilandica.* Blackjack oak. *1.* Twig × 1¼. *2.* Acorns × 1. *3.* Leaf × ½. *4.* Bark.

Quercus laevis Walt. [*Quercus catesbaei* Michx.]   Turkey oak

Distinguishing characteristics. *Leaves* very variable in size and shape, commonly much dissected and with spreading, falcate lobes; lustrous above, glabrous below except for axillary tufts. *Acorn* 1″ long, oval, one-third enclosed in a thin bowl-shaped cup. *Twigs* stout, usually glabrous. *Buds* up to ½″ long, narrow and tapering, rusty pubescent above the middle. *Bark* rough, on old trees nearly black.

General description. Turkey oak is a small tree found in the coastal pine belt of the South, where it occurs on dry sandy soils. The variable leaves are very distinctive and are not readily mistaken for those of other associated species. Turkey oak is especially common near the coast in South Carolina and Georgia, while in Florida it is plentiful on the sandy uplands of the interior.

Range. The Coastal Plain from southeastern Virginia to central Florida and west to extreme eastern Louisiana.

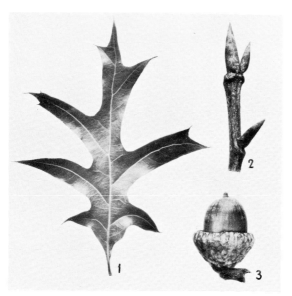

Fig. 150. *Quercus laevis.* Turkey oak. *1.* Leaf × ½. *2.* Twig × 1¼. *3.* Acorn × 1.

THE WILLOW OAKS

DISTINGUISHING CHARACTERISTICS OF IMPORTANT SPECIES

Species	Leaves	Fruit
Q. *phellos,* willow oak	deciduous, mostly linear-lanceolate	about ½″ long; nut greenish brown, hemispherical, enclosed at the base by a saucer-shaped cup
Q. *nigra,* water oak	deciduous, very variable, spatulate, obovate, oblong or linear, pinnatifid-lobed or 3-lobed at the apex	about ½″ long; nut black or nearly so; subglobose; cup similar to above
Q. *laurifolia,* laurel oak	finally deciduous, but persistent until early spring, elliptical to oblong-ovate	similar to that of Q. *nigra*

Species	Leaves	Fruit
Q. virginiana,[a] live oak	persistent, mostly elliptical to obovate	about ¾″ long; nut black, ellipsoidal, maturing in one season (all those above require two seasons), ⅓ enclosed in a turbinate cup

[a] Formerly included with the white oaks. Williams (377), after a critical examination of the wood, asserts that it belongs to the *Erythrobalanus* group; however, it may be questioned whether this species should be included with the willow oaks.

Quercus phellos L.   Willow oak

BOTANICAL FEATURES

Leaves deciduous; 2″ to 5″ long, ⅛″ to 1″ wide; *shape* linear to linear-lanceolate, occasionally oblanceolate; *margin* entire, repand, or rarely few-lobed; *apex* and *base* acute; *surfaces* glabrous above, glabrous or rarely hoary tomentose below.
Fruit solitary or paired; *nut* ½″ or less in length, subglobose, more or less stellate-pubescent, light yellowish or greenish brown, enclosed at the base in a thin saucerlike

Fig. 151. *Quercus phellos*. Willow oak. *1.* Twig × 1¼. *2.* Leaf × ½. *3.* Acorns × 1. *4.* Bark.

cup; *cup scales* thin, hoary tomentose, with a somewhat greenish-red tinge; 595 to 695 nuts to the pound.

Twigs slender, glabrous, red to reddish brown; *terminal buds* ⅛″ long, ovoid, sharp-pointed, covered by chestnut-brown scales paler on the margin; *lateral buds* similar but smaller.

Bark smooth and steel-gray to reddish brown on young stems, ultimately breaking up into thick rough ridges separated by deep, irregular fissures and becoming nearly black on mature trees.

GENERAL DESCRIPTION

Willow oak is a medium-sized to large tree, 80 to 100 ft high and 3 to 4 ft in diameter (max. 130 by 6* ft), although much smaller in the northern part of its range. Open-grown trees are very distinctive with their dense oblong to oval crowns and bright green willowlike leaves. In the forest, the crown, although less developed, is still more or less full or rounded, and the slender lower branches do not prune readily. Numerous spurlike branchlets throughout make this tree similar in appearance to pin oak, which it is often called in some sections of the South.

Willow oak is a bottomland tree commonly found on poorly drained, loamy, or clay flats with such species as laurel, cherrybark, Nuttall, overcup, and swamp chestnut oaks, sweetgum, American elm, cedar elm, green ash, and water hickory. As an ornamental, willow oak has few if any superiors throughout the southern part of its range, and in many southern cities it is the most widely planted shade and street tree.

RANGE

Atlantic and Gulf Coastal Plains and Mississippi River Valley (map, Plate 52).

1. *Quercus phellos.*   2. *Quercus nigra.*

PLATE 52

Quercus nigra L.   Water oak

Leaves deciduous, but many remain green and attached to the tree until late winter; *size* very variable, but usually 2″ to 4″ long, and 1″ to 2″ wide; *shape* spatulate, obovate, and oblong, or sometimes long and narrow (like willow oak); *margin* very variable, usually (1) entire, but sometimes (2) 3-lobed at the apex, or (3) variously pinnatifid-lobed; *apex* acute to obtuse; *base* mostly acute to cuneate (all the above types on the same or on separate trees); *surfaces* glabrous except for occasional axillary tufts below.

Fruit solitary or paired; *nut* ½″ long, hemispherical, black or nearly so, often striate, minutely tomentose, or glabrous, enclosed at the base by a thin, saucerlike cup; *cup scales* appressed, tomentose except on the often darker margins; *flesh* bright orange; 280 to 635 nuts to the pound.

Twigs slender, dull red, glabrous; *terminal buds* ⅛″ to ¼″ long, ovoid, sharp-pointed, angular, with reddish-brown scales; *lateral buds* similar but smaller.

Fig. 152. *Quercus nigra.* Water oak. *1.* Twig × 1¼. *2.* Leaves showing variation in shape × ½. *3.* Acorns showing variation in shape and surface appearance of nut × 1. *4.* Bark. (*Photograph by R. A. Cockrell.*)

Bark gray-black, relatively close, often with irregular patches, eventually with rough, wide, scaly ridges.

GENERAL DESCRIPTION

In the forest, water oak is a medium-sized tree 60 to 70 ft high and 2 to 3 ft in diameter (max. 125 by 6° ft) with a tall, slender bole and a somewhat symmetrical, rounded crown of ascending branches.

This tree is a bottomland species although also found on moist uplands; between these limits it is exceedingly cosmopolitan, occurring in most bottomland types with the exception of permanent swamps. Best development is made on the better-drained loamy or clay ridges in the bottoms, in company with sweetgum, although, because of the diversity in site, the number of associates is very large. On old fields in the bottomlands, especially in the lower Mississippi delta, second-growth water oak is one of the commonest of trees and together with cherrybark oak often comprises nearly 80 to 90 percent of the stand; growth is fast, and trees 50 to 70 years old are merchantable. This species is a favorite ornamental in many southern cities.

RANGE

Atlantic and Gulf Coastal Plains and Mississippi River Valley (see map, Plate 52).

Quercus laurifolia Michx.   Laurel oak

BOTANICAL FEATURES

Leaves semi-evergreen, deciduous during early spring a few weeks before the new leaves appear; 2½" to 4" long, ½" to 1" wide; *shape* elliptical to oblong-obovate;

Fig. 153. *Quercus laurifolia.* Laurel oak. *1.* Acorns showing variability in shape × 1. *2.* Leaf × ½.

margin entire to repand, sometimes irregularly lobed; *apex* acute, or occasionally 3-lobed; *base* cuneate; *surfaces* lustrous green above, paler below, with a more or less conspicuous yellow midrib.

Fruit sessile or subsessile, usually solitary; *nut* ovoid to hemispherical, dark brown to nearly black, ½″ long, one-fourth or less enclosed in a thin, saucerlike cup; *cup scales* red-brown, pale pubescent, appressed.

Twigs slender, dark red, glabrous; *terminal buds* ⅟₁₀″ to ⅛″ long, ovoid to oval, acute, covered by lustrous, red-brown scales; *lateral buds* similar but smaller.

Bark dark brown and moderately smooth on young stems but ultimately black and divided by deep furrows into broad flattened ridges.

GENERAL DESCRIPTION

Laurel oak may be 60 to 70 ft high and 2 to 3 ft in diameter (max. 100 by 7* ft), but it is usually much smaller, and is found on sandy soils near streams along the southern Coastal Plain. Common associates include willow, live, and Nuttall oaks, sweetgum, baldcypress, and loblolly, slash, and longleaf pines. Laurel oak usually occurs as a scattered tree and is not very abundant except in Florida. This species is widely used in the South as an ornamental tree but is shorter-lived (72) than its associate, the willow oak.

RANGE

Atlantic and Gulf Coastal Plains (map, Plate 53).

PLATE 53. *Quercus laurifolia.*

Quercus imbricaria Michx.   Shingle oak

Distinguishing characteristics. *Leaves* deciduous, oblong to elliptical, margin entire to slightly repand, dark green and shiny above, pale to brown and pubescent below. *Fruit* typically sub-globose, about ⅝″ long, the nut enclosed one-third to one-half in a thin bowl-shaped cup with appressed red-brown scales. *Twigs* slender, dark green to greenish brown, buds ovoid, pointed. *Bark* gray-brown, close, eventually with broad low ridges separated by shallow furrows.

General description. The scientific name given to this tree by the explorer-botanist Michaux indicates the use to which he found it put by the early pioneers, namely, the production of split shingles or shakes. Shingle oak, or, as it is often called, "northern

Fig. 154. *Quercus imbricaria.* Shingle oak.
1. Twig × 1¼. 2. Leaf × ½. 3. Acorn × 1.

laurel oak," is a medium-sized tree 50 to 60 ft high and 2 to 3 ft in diameter (max. 80° by 5° ft). It is especially characteristic of the lower Ohio Valley, where it reaches its best development on moist soils along streams or on hillsides in mixture with such species as pin and overcup oaks, elms, and hickories.

Range. The Appalachian region and Ohio River and central Mississippi River Valleys.

Quercus virginiana Mill.   Live oak [1]

BOTANICAL FEATURES

Leaves persistent until the following spring; 2″ to 5″ long, ½″ to 2½″ wide; *shape* oblong, elliptical or obovate; *margin* usually entire and revolute (sometimes sparingly toothed); *apex* obtuse; *base* cuneate or acute; *surfaces* dark glossy green above, paler and often pubescent below.

Fruit usually in clusters of 3 to 5 on a peduncle of varying length; matures in one season; *nut* about ¾″ long, dark brown to nearly black, ellipsoidal, one-third enclosed in a turbinate cup; *seed* sweet; about 390 (335–510) nuts to the pound.

Bark dark reddish brown, slightly furrowed, with small surface scales.

[1] Formerly included in the white oak group. There are several varieties of live oak, but these are often not clearly defined. One of the most common is *Q. virginiana* var. *maritima* (Michx.) Sarg., sand live oak, which has leaves with reticulate venation and strongly revolute margins.

Fig. 155. *Quercus virginiana.* Live oak. *1.* Leaves × ½. *2.* Acorns × 1. *3.* Bark.

GENERAL DESCRIPTION

This species is generally considered to be the only important "live oak" of eastern North America, although several of the willow oak group hold their living leaves so late in the spring that they are almost evergreen. Live oak is usually a medium-sized tree 40 to 50 ft high and 3 to 4 ft in diameter. The short, enlarged, buttressed trunk, sometimes 6 to 8 ft through (max. 11° ft), divides into three or four wide-spreading, horizontal branches; the crown is close, round-topped, and in the largest open-grown trees may be upward of 125 to 150 ft across.

Live oak is a sand-plain species found on a variety of sites from dry to wet. It is remarkably resistant to salt spray and is a dominant tree in the immediate coastal forests and on dunes of islands and outer banks. On dry sand barrens, live oak may exist as a dwarf tree bearing fertile acorns when only a foot tall.

On moist locations, some common associates are southern magnolia, sweetgum, American holly, laurel and water oaks, and hickories.

Live oak is extremely difficult to kill. When a tree is cut or girdled, numerous sprouts spring up from the root collar and surface roots. When these sprouts are cut, many more appear.

When grown ornamentally, especially on rich soils, growth is fast, and one tree in Georgia reported by Coker and Totten (72) attained a diameter of about 4½ ft in less than 70 years. Although very large trees are supposed to be many centuries old, studies have shown that the largest specimens now standing are about 200 to 300 years of age (332).

Certain individual trees yield acorns much sweeter and more edible than others, and it is said that the Indians produced an oil somewhat comparable to olive oil from them.

The wood is exceedingly strong and one of the heaviest of native woods. It was formerly utilized in building frigates and other naval vessels. The United States Navy still owns live oak forests which were acquired during the era of "wooden ships and iron men."

RANGE

Atlantic and Gulf Coastal Plains (map, Plate 54).

PLATE 54. *Quercus virginiana.*

THE WESTERN RED OAKS

There are some 18 or more species of red oak indigenous to the western and southwestern United States. None is important as a timber species, but eight of them occur in sufficient size and abundance to warrant brief mention. Two of these, the California black oak and the blue oak, are deciduous; the leaves of the others are persistent and often hollylike.

California black oak, *Quercus kelloggii* Newb., is a wide-crowned tree of moderate proportions found on dry sandy and gravelly soils of canyon floors, benches, and mountain slopes. Although sometimes attaining a height of 80 ft, the bole is usually short, often crooked, and in old trees, highly defective. Its yellow-green, 5- to 7-lobed leaves, 1-inch ellipsoidal acorns with deep bowl-like cups, and gray to black deeply fissured bark are its principal dendrological features. The tree is typical of the Transition Zone in California. Its most common associates include Douglas-fir, Digger and ponderosa pines, Pacific dogwood, and canyon live oak. At elevations above 4,000 ft it is also found with sugar pine, incense-cedar, giant sequoia, and white fir. Geographically, the tree extends from the McKenzie River basin in central Oregon south over the Cascade and Siskiyou Mountains, thence down the Coast Ranges and western slopes of the Sierra to southern California near the Mexican border. *Altitudinal distribution:* 1,500 to 9,000 ft.

Blue oak, *Quercus douglasii* Hook. and Arn.[1] differs from most other red oaks in that its fruits mature in one rather than in two seasons. Its blue-green, oblong to oval 3-in. leaves with entire, sinuate and/or toothed to lobed margins are most distinctive, as are its elongated acorns with shallow, bowl-like cups. This tree is restricted to low valleys and foothills of the Coast Ranges and Sierra in California, where it forms pure

[1] Previously included in the white oak group, the anatomy of its wood, however, clearly indicates that this species is an *erythrobalanus* oak.

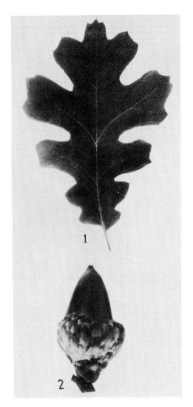

Fig. 156. *Quercus kelloggii*. California black oak. *1*. Leaf × ¾. *2*. Acorn × 1.

groves or mixed forests with Digger pine and several other oaks. Mature trees may exceed a height of 80 ft and a diameter of 30 in., but they are usually much smaller.

Canyon live oak, *Quercus chrysolepis* Liebm., is the second-largest oak in California, at least in terms of diameter and crown spread. At the time of its measurement some years ago, one famous old tree in the Hupa Valley was 95 ft tall, had a diameter

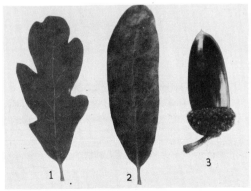

Fig. 157. *Quercus douglasii*. Blue oak. *1* and *2*. Leaves × 1. *3*. Acorn × 1.

of more than 6 ft, and featured a crown with a spread of more than 125 ft. The leaves of the canyon live oak, which persist for three or four years, are thick, polymorphic, and turn a dark blue-green in their second season. Large ovoid acorns, 1½ in. or more in length, with thick, shallow cups covered with golden tomentum, are most distinctive. This tree frequents cool canyon walls and mountain slopes, and on such sites attains its maximum development. Growth is never rapid, maturity being reached in about 300 years. Its principal forest associates include several other oaks, incense-cedar, and ponderosa pine. Two shrubby varieties are (1) *Q. c.* var. *vaccinifolia* Kellogg, and *Q. c.* var. *palmeri* (Engelm.) Sarg. The former features finely toothed leaves while those of the latter [also arborescent (212)], are nearly orbicular and spinescent. Canyon live oak extends from southwestern California south to Baja California and east to central and southern Arizona and southwestern New Mexico. *Altitudinal distribution:* 1,000 to 9,000 ft in the north; 7,500 to 9,000 ft in the south.

Interior live oak, *Quercus wislizenii* A.DC., is commonly shrubby, but may be a tree of some 50 to 60 ft in height and 12 to 24 in. in diameter. It has short (1¼ in.) oblong-elliptical hollylike leaves which persist for two seasons, and the acorn comprises a 1-in. nut deeply encased in a bowl-like cup. The largest trees develop short, thick boles and irregular but wide-spreading crowns. It is most common on dry river bottoms, washes, and slopes where the soil is dry but rich. It is sometimes found in pure groves, but is much more commonly noted in association with Digger pine. This tree occurs from Mt. Shasta south along the Sierra and Coast Ranges to Baja California at elevations of from sea level to 5,000 ft.

California live oak, *Quercus agrifolia* Née, also designated as a holly-leaved oak, closely resembles the previous species in both form and general appearance. Its leaves, however, are somewhat larger and persist for only one year. Trees are found on dry loams and gravelly soils in open valleys and shallow canyons, and on slopes in the coastal regions of southern California and Baja California from sea level to 4,500 ft. Heights of 60 to 90 ft and diameters of 24 to 36 in. or more are not uncommon. This species is quite gregarious and forms pure, open, but extensive stands. In mixed forests, California sycamore, white alder, numerous other oaks, and bigcone Douglas-fir are common associates. When fully exposed to the ocean, it seldom develops beyond shrubby proportions.

Fig. 158. Leaves and acorn of canyon live oak × 1.

FIG. 159. Leaf of interior live oak × 1.

Emory oak, *Quercus emoryi* Torr., is probably the most common arborescent oak of southern Arizona and New Mexico. Its oblong-lanceolate, repand-sinuate, 2- to 3-in. leaves, oblong-ovoid acorn,[1] and alligator-leatherlike bark are its principal diagnostic features. Under the most favorable conditions for growth this species attains a height of from 40 to 60 ft and diameters of as many inches. It is commonly encountered as a massive shrub, however, and as such is often browsed by both horses and cattle. Geographically, Emory oak is restricted to western Texas, southern Arizona and New Mexico, and northern Mexico.

Arizona oak, *Quercus arizonica* Sarg., was at one time regarded as a white oak, and the Check List (212) and "Standardized Plant Names" (197) still refer to this tree as Arizona white oak, which is both misleading and inaccurate. This southwestern tree with persistent, spinose, blue-green leaves and plated bark is common to moist benches and canyon walls in the Southwest. Under favorable growing conditions it attains a height of 40 to 60 ft and a diameter of 24 to 36 in., and develops a short trunk which supports a massive round-topped crown. It is usually dwarfed at timberline, and like

[1] This species, like the blue oak which matures its fruit in a single season, should not be regarded as belonging to the *leucobalanus* oaks.

FIG. 160. Leaves of southwestern evergreen oaks × ½. 1. *Q. emoryi*. 2. *Q. arizonica*. 3. *Q. oblongifolia*.

the previous species provides browse for both cattle and horses. Arizona oak ranges through southern New Mexico and Arizona and northern Mexico between elevations of from 5,000 to 10,000 ft.

Mexican blue oak, *Quercus oblongifolia* Torr. is a small tree rarely attaining a height of more than 30 ft and a d.b.h. of as many inches. It occurs in association with *Q. arizonica* and *Q. emoryi,* previously described, and its foliage, like that of those two species, is a source of forage for range stock. It is somewhat more restricted altitudinally, however, and rarely occurs at elevations of over 6,000 ft. This southwestern tree ranges through western Texas, southeastern New Mexico, southern Arizona and northern Mexico.

II. FLORIFERAE

A. APETALAE

Ulmaceae: The Elm family

The Elm family comprises about 15 genera and more than 150 species of trees and shrubs, widely distributed throughout the temperate regions of both hemispheres, with a few species in the tropics. Five genera are represented in this country, but only two include trees sufficiently common to be of interest to foresters.[1]

BOTANICAL FEATURES OF THE FAMILY

Leaves deciduous (rarely persistent), alternate, simple, stipulate, penniveined, usually serrate, often inequilateral at the base.
Flowers perfect or imperfect (species polygamo-monoecious); *calyx* 4- to 9-lobed or parted; *corolla,* none; *stamens* 4 to 6; *ovary* usually 1-celled with a single ovule; *styles* 2.
Fruit a samara, drupe, or nut.

CONSPECTUS OF IMPORTANT NATIVE GENERA

Genus	Leaves	Flowers	Fruit
Ulmus	doubly serrate (American species)	perfect	samara
Celtis	entire or singly serrate	perfect and imperfect	drupe

[1] *Trema,* a tropical genus, is found with two species in southern Florida; *Momisia,* with two species, ranges from Florida to Texas; and *Planera aquatica* Gmel., the planertree (monotypic), waterelm (SPN), is a small tree with elmlike but crenate-serrate leaves and a prickly drupe, restricted to the swamplands of the southern Coastal Plain.

ULMUS L.   Elm

This genus includes some of the most useful and well-known forest and ornamental trees of the Northern Hemisphere. The 18 to 20 species are scattered throughout eastern North America, Europe, and Asia, and in many regions are important constituents of hardwood forests. The wood is important commercially, and the tough bark fibers were sometimes used by primitive peoples for making rope and coarse cloth; the inner mucilaginous bark of certain species is used in medicine, or occasionally in an emergency as food. Many of the elms are highly regarded as shade and ornamental trees, and some of them are perhaps unsurpassed in form and general usefulness for this purpose. However, their future use must be evaluated in terms of the rapid spread of the lethal Dutch elm disease. Several foreign species have been introduced for ornamental planting, and probably the commonest is Scotch elm, *U. glabra* Huds.; the bark of this tree remains fairly smooth even on large trunks. A common grafted variety, Camperdown elm, *U. glabra* var. *camperdownii* Rehd., is the familiar "umbrella elm" often seen in parks. In certain sections, *U. parvifolia* Jacq., Chinese elm, is a common small-leaved ornamental. Of the six native species, three are of considerable importance and will be described in detail.

BOTANICAL FEATURES OF THE GENUS

Leaves alternate, simple, usually doubly serrate, short-petioled, 2-ranked. **Flowers** perfect, appearing before the leaves unfold, or in some species

DISTINGUISHING CHARACTERISTICS OF IMPORTANT SPECIES

Species	Flowers	Fruit	Twigs
U. americana, American elm	in long-pedicelled fascicles	about ½″ long, deeply notched at apex, ciliate on margin	brown, glabrous or sparingly pubescent, buds brown, acute but not sharp
U. rubra, slippery elm	in short-pedicelled fascicles	about ¾″ long, emarginate at apex, pubescent only on outside of seed cavity	ashy gray, scabrous; buds nearly black
U. thomasii, rock elm	in racemose cymes	about 1″ long, rounded at apex, generally pubescent, ciliate; outside of seed cavity indistinct	reddish brown, glabrous or puberulous, at length corky; buds brown, sharp-pointed

autumnal; borne on slender pedicels in fascicles or cymes (sometimes racemose); ovary flattened, surmounted by a deeply 2-lobed style.

Fruit maturing in the late spring, or in some species autumnal; a flattened, oblong to suborbicular samara; seed cavity encircled by a thin, membranous, or papery wing, which is often notched above, and subtended below by the persistent remnants of the calyx; *seed* exalbuminous.

Twigs slender to stout, in some species corky, slightly zigzag; *pith* terete, homogeneous; *terminal buds* lacking; *lateral buds* medium-sized, with the scales imbricate in 2 ranks; *leaf scars* 2-ranked, small, semicircular; *bundle scars* conspicuous, depressed, 3 or more; *stipule scars* small, at times indistinct.

Ulmus americana L.   American elm; white elm (Tr)

BOTANICAL FEATURES

Leaves 4″ to 6″ long, 1″ to 3″ wide; *shape* oblong-obovate to elliptical; *margin* coarsely doubly serrate; *apex* acuminate; *base* conspicuously inequilateral; *surfaces* glabrous or slightly scabrous above; usually pubescent below.

Flowers vernal, appearing before the leaf buds open, long-pedicelled, in fascicles of 3 or 4.

Fruit maturing in the spring, as the leaves unfold; about ½″ long, oval to oblong-obovate, deeply notched at apex, margin ciliate; about 68,000 (48,000–95,000) to the pound.

Twigs slender, zigzag, brown, glabrous or slightly pubescent; *lateral buds* about ¼″ long, ovoid, acute but not sharp-pointed, smooth or sparingly downy, chestnut-brown.

Bark on older trees typically divided into grayish, flat-topped ridges, separated by roughly diamond-shaped fissures, but sometimes rough and without a definite pattern; the outer bark when sectioned shows irregular, corky, buff-colored patches interspersed with the reddish-brown fibrous tissue.

GENERAL DESCRIPTION

Probably no other North American tree is more easily recognized from a distance or is known by a larger number of persons than is the American elm. When grown in the open, the trunk usually divides near the ground into several erect limbs strongly arched above and terminating in numerous slender, often drooping branchlets, the whole forming a vase-shaped crown of great beauty and symmetry. At times the branches are more wide-spreading and give rise to the so-called "oak form" of this tree. In the forest, the buttressed, columnar trunk, 2 to 4 ft in diameter, may rise to a height of 50 to 60 ft before branching and is topped by a small crown of arching branches (max. 160* by 11 ft).

The root system of American elm is extensive but shallow, and the tree is a common inhabitant of wet flats where standing water may ac-

Fig. 161. *Ulmus americana.* American elm. *1.* Twig × 1¼. *2.* Flower cluster × ¾. *3.* Flower × 4. *4.* Fruit × 1. *5.* Leaf × ½. *6.* Bark. *7.* Section through bark showing alternating brown and white layers.

cumulate in the spring and fall; in such places its associates include the soft maples, some of the swamp oaks, willows, poplars, and black ash. The fastest growth and maximum size, however, are attained on better-drained, rich bottomland soils, in association with sweetgum, basswood, green ash, and other hardwoods. In the western portion of its range,

Fig. 162. Open-grown form of American elm.

American elm is a common tree along water courses in company with boxelder, green ash, and cottonwoods. This elm when planted in the deep dry soils of the Great Plains region (shelterbelts), may send down a taproot 15 to 20 ft to the water table. Since it is a component of no less than 26 forest cover types, the complete list of associates is large (127).

On a tolerance scale, American elm may be rated as intermediate.

Seeds are produced annually (May–June) in extremely large numbers, and they germinate on moist soil within a few days of being released. They may be wind-carried for a quarter of a mile or more, and water-borne over much greater distances. Maturity is reached in about 150 years, but old trees may be twice this age.

American elm, the favorite shade tree of innumerable towns and cities, is being destroyed by Dutch elm disease. This is caused by a fungus carried on the bodies of bark beetles brought to this country presumably

1. *Ulmus americana.*   2. *Ulmus rubra.*

PLATE 55

in a shipment of elm veneer logs from Europe. The entire species may in time disappear unless biological or chemical techniques are devised to stop the spread of the disease. Other native elms are also susceptible to Dutch elm disease.

Eastern United States and Great Plains (map, Plate 55).

Ulmus rubra Mühl. [*Ulmus fulva* Michx.]   Slippery elm; red elm (Tr)

BOTANICAL FEATURES

Leaves 5″ to 7″ long, 2″ to 3″ wide; *shape* elliptical to obovate, or oval; leaf often creased along the midrib; *margin, apex,* and *base* as for the preceding species; *surfaces* very scabrous above, soft pubescent below.

Flowers vernal, appearing before the leaves, in short-pedicelled fascicles.

Fruit maturing when the leaves are about one-half expanded, approximately ¾″ long, suborbicular in shape, emarginate at apex, margin and surface of wing smooth, outer surface of seed cavity pubescent; about 41,000 (35,000–54,000) to the pound.

Twigs stouter than in American elm, ashy gray to brownish gray, scabrous; *lateral* buds dark chestnut-brown to almost black, pubescent; *flower buds* larger, often with an orange tip.

Bark dark reddish brown, and, in contrast to that of both American and rock elms, it does not show buff-colored corky patches or streaks when sectioned with a knife; bark fissures not diamond-shaped in outline, ridges more nearly parallel than in American elm, often coarsely scaly or with vertical plates; inner bark mucilaginous, with a somewhat aromatic flavor.

GENERAL DESCRIPTION

Slippery elm is a medium-sized tree 60 to 70 ft high and 18 to 30 in. in diameter (max. 135 by nearly 7* ft); it resembles American elm in general appearance except for a greater clear length of bole and a tendency of the twigs to be ascending. These features give individuality to slippery elm, and while they are not striking, with a little practice one may learn to identify the tree at some distance by observing them.

This elm makes best growth on moist rich bottomland soils, along streams, and on lower slopes, but is found also on dry soils, especially those of limestone origin. Associates include red and white oaks, butternut, ashes, basswood, hickories, maples, black cherry, and yellow-poplar.

Slippery elm was well known to the early pioneer woodsmen on account of its mucilaginous inner bark, which was chewed to quench the thirst, and when steeped in water produced a common remedy for throat

Fig. 163. *Ulmus rubra.* Slippery elm. *1.* Twig × 1¼. *2.* Leaf × ½. *3.* Fruit × 1. *4.* Bark. *5.* Section through bark showing brownish layers only (compare with that of American elm).

inflammations and fever; the powdered bark was recommended for poultices.

Eastern United States (map, Plate 55).

Ulmus thomasii Sarg. [*Ulmus racemosa* Thom.]   Rock elm; cork elm

BOTANICAL FEATURES

Leaves 2½″ to 4½″ long, 1¼″ to 2¼″ wide; *shape* obovate to elliptical; *margin* coarsely doubly serrate; *apex* acuminate; *base* often nearly equilateral; *surfaces* usually glabrous, often somewhat lustrous above, slightly pubescent below.

FIG. 164. *Ulmus thomasii.* Rock elm. *1.* Fruit × 1. *2.* Corky outgrowths of twig × 1¼. *3.* Leaf × ½. *4.* Racemose flower cluster × ¾. *5.* Twig × 1¼.

Flowers appearing before the leaves, on slender pedicels, in racemose cymes.
Fruit maturing when the leaves are about half grown, ¾″ to 1″ long, oval to obovate, pubescent, more or less rounded at apex, ciliate on the margin, seed cavity indistinct; about 7,000 (5,000–9,000) to the pound.
Twigs light reddish brown, glabrous or slightly puberulous, after a year or two usually developing conspicuous corky ridges; [1] *lateral buds* similar to those of American elm but longer and more sharply pointed, downy-ciliate.
Fruit maturing when the leaves are about half grown, ¾″ to 1″ long, oval to obovate,
Bark somewhat similar to that of American elm but often darker and more deeply and irregularly furrowed, especially on younger trees.

[1] Twigs on old trees often show little or no cork.

Rock elm, so called because of its extremely hard, tough wood, is a medium-sized to large tree which, in virgin stands, attains a height of 100 ft and diameters of 3 to 5 ft. In contrast to the two preceding species, the tall straight trunk extends unbranched for some distance into the narrow oblong crown. Best development is made on moist loamy soils of Lower Michigan and Wisconsin. The tree is also found on rocky plateaus and slopes, especially those of limestone origin. It is intermediate in tolerance and occurs with many other hardwoods, including beech, ashes, maples, basswood, butternut, oaks, hickories, and black cherry. Drastic cutting has greatly reduced the original supply of rock elm timber, which was never very large.

Fig. 165. Bark of rock elm.

RANGE

From the Appalachians through the Ohio and Mississippi Valleys to the Lake States; but not reported or rare in Pennsylvania, West Virginia, Kentucky, parts of Ohio, all but northern Illinois, and Missouri (map, Plate 56).

SOUTHERN ELMS [1]

U. alata Michx. Winged elm. *Leaves* about 2 in. long; *twigs* with two corky wings nearly ½″ wide.[2] This species is usually a small to medium-sized tree often found on dry gravelly uplands from southeastern Virginia to southern Missouri, south to central Florida and eastern Texas.

U. crassifolia Nutt. Cedar elm. This is another small-leaved species found in Mississippi, southern Arkansas, and Texas; the twigs bear two corky wings which are only about half as wide as those of winged elm.

U. serotina Sarg. September elm (red elm). *Leaves* 2 to 4 in. long (larger than those of the first two species); *twigs* with two or three corky wings. September elm occurs only sporadically from eastern Kentucky to southern Illinois, south to northeastern Georgia and eastern Oklahoma.

The last two species differ from other native elms in that they flower in autumn rather than in the spring.

CELTIS L.   Hackberry

The genus *Celtis*, with about 75 species, is found widely distributed throughout the temperate and tropical regions of the world; it is of only minor importance in the production of lumber, but certain species are sometimes used as ornamentals and street trees. The United States has five arborescent species and several varieties, but the group contains a number of forms which have not been well differentiated from one another.

BOTANICAL FEATURES OF THE GENUS

Leaves deciduous (persistent in a few tropical forms), alternate, simple, singly serrate or sometimes entire.

Flowers perfect and imperfect (species polygamo-monoecious) appearing with the leaves; the *staminate* borne below, in fascicles, the *perfect* and *pistillate* flowers above, solitary in the leaf axils; *calyx* 4- to 6-lobed; *stamens* 4 to 6.

Fruit a thick-skinned, thin-fleshed, ovoid or globose drupe; *pit surface* with a netlike pattern.

Twigs slender, zigzag; *pith* terete, very finely chambered at the nodes, homogeneous elsewhere; *terminal buds* lacking; *lateral buds* small, closely appressed; *leaf scars* 2-ranked, oval to crescent-shaped; *bundle scars,* 3; *stipule scars* minute.

---

[1] The first two species are now being cut as substitutes for rock elm (26).

[2] Sometimes sparingly corky, and occasionally completely devoid of cork.

Celtis occidentalis L.   Hackberry; common hackberry (SPN)

BOTANICAL FEATURES

Leaves 2½" to 4" long, 1½" wide; *shape* ovate to ovate-lanceolate; *margin* sharply serrate (often entire below the middle); *apex* acuminate, falcate; *base* inequilaterally cordate; *surfaces* glabrous, or slightly scabrous above; smooth or sparingly hairy below. **Flowers** appearing in May with or soon after the leaves.

Fruit borne on peduncles ½" to ¾" long; ¼" to ⅓" in diameter, subglobose or ovoid, dark red or purple; flesh thin, edible; ripening in September and October, often persistent for several weeks; *pit* conspicuously reticulate; about 4,300 (3,500–5,400) to the pound.

Twigs slender, zigzag, reddish brown, somewhat lustrous; *lateral buds* small, acute, closely appressed.

Bark grayish brown, with characteristic corky warts or ridges, later somewhat scaly.

GENERAL DESCRIPTION

Hackberry is usually a small tree 30 to 40 ft high and about 16 in. in diameter (max. 130 by 5* ft). Best growth is made on rich moist alluvial soils, but especially in the Northeast the tree is commonly found on limestone outcrops. Hackberry occurs as a scattered tree in mixture with other hardwoods. Seedling reproduction is facilitated by birds; and sprouts from young trees often persist.

Fɪɢ. 166. *Celtis occidentalis.* Hackberry. *1.* Twig × 1¼. *2.* Perfect flower × 3. *3.* Fruit × ¾. *4.* Pit showing reticulations × 1. *5.* Leaf × ½. *6.* Bark.

Certain varieties of hackberry are used to some extent as ornamentals and seem to succeed even under adverse conditions of soil and moisture.

Widespread in the eastern half of United States east of the Rocky Mountains; also sporadically in southern Canada (map, Plate 56).

1. *Ulmus thomasii.*   2. *Celtis occidentalis.*

PLATE 56

Celtis laevigata Willd.   Sugarberry; sugar hackberry (SPN)

Sugarberry is a medium-sized tree 60 to 80 ft high and 2 to 4 ft in diameter; it is native to the southern bottomlands. It ranges along the Coastal Plain from Virginia to southern Florida, west to the valley of the Rio Grande, and north in the Mississippi Valley through eastern Oklahoma, Missouri, western Tennessee, and Kentucky to southern Illinois and Indiana. The leaves are narrower than those of hackberry, usually entire, and the fruit is borne on shorter pedicels; the otherwise smooth bark is marked by conspicuous warty excrescences.

Moraceae: The Mulberry family

This is a large family comprising about 70 genera and over 1,500 species of trees, shrubs, and herbs, distributed for the most part in the warmer regions of the world, but with a few forms in the temperate zone. The sap is milky, and in certain genera, notably *Ficus* and *Castilla*, it is a source of rubber. Three genera are represented in this country, and a fourth, *Broussonetia*, papermulberry, has been introduced. They all include small or medium-sized trees of little value as timber producers that are often used ornamentally.

CONDENSED BOTANICAL FEATURES OF THE FAMILY

Leaves deciduous or persistent, alternate, simple.
Flowers imperfect, the species monoecious or diocious.
Fruit a small drupe or achene, usually in multiples.

MORUS L.   Mulberry

Twelve to fifteen species of mulberry are now recognized; two of these are native to the United States, and two others have been naturalized. The fruit, a multiple of drupes, resembles a blackberry and is very attractive to birds.

M. rubra L., red mulberry, is an eastern species with serrate, suborbicular, pubescent, 2 to 3 or more deeply lobed, or unlobed, leaves, 3 to 5 in. long; and an oblong, dark-purple, edible fruit.

M. microphylla Buckl., Texas mulberry, is distributed through New Mexico, Arizona, Texas, and southward into Mexico. The leaves are similar to those of red mulberry but much smaller (1½ in. long), and the fruit is subglobose and nearly black.

M. alba L., white mulberry, a native of Asia, was introduced in colonial times, when attempts were being made to establish the silkworm industry in this country, and is

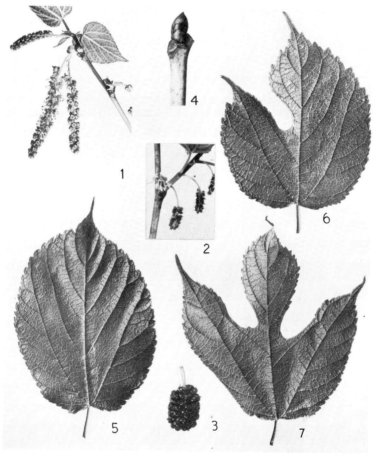

Fig. 167. *Morus rubra.* Red mulberry. *1.* Staminate flowers × ½. *2.* Pistillate flowers × ½. *3.* Fruit × ¾. *4.* Twig × 1¼. *5, 6,* and *7.* Leaves showing variation in lobing × ½.

now naturalized in the East and South. The leaves are lustrous and smaller than those of red mulberry; the fruit is white. *M. alba* f. *tartarica* Seringe, Russian mulberry, was introduced about 1875 by Russian Mennonites and has become widely distributed in the West, where it has been recommended by the Forest Service for planting. It is a tolerant tree, makes fast growth, will grow on sandy or clay soils, and is used in shelter belts or for the production of farm timbers.

M. nigra L., black mulberry, probably a native of Persia, was early introduced in the Pacific and southern states on account of its large, dark-colored juicy fruit.

MACLURA Nutt.   Osage-orange

This genus is monotypic, and the single species, *Maclura pomifera* (Raf.) Schneid. (*Toxylon pomiferum* Raf.), originally restricted to southern Arkansas, southern Oklahoma, and northeastern Texas, is now planted for hedges or as an ornamental throughout the United States. The leaves are 3 to 5 in. long, entire, oblong-lanceolate to ovate, with a narrow, pointed apex, and are dark green and shiny above. The twigs are armed with sharp spines, and the fruit is a peculiar, spherical, green multiple of drupes, about 4 to 5 in. in diameter; when crushed, it exudes a bitter milky juice. The wood is of a characteristic bright orange color and is used for bows, hence the origin of the name "bois d'arc," or bowwood, which is often applied to this species; the wood yields a yellow dye when extracted with hot water.

FICUS L.   Figtree

This is a large group (over 600 species) chiefly tropical, and in this country is restricted to two arborescent species, *F. aurea* Nutt., Florida strangler fig, and *F. laevi-*

FIG. 168. *Maclura pomifera*. Osage-orange. *1*. Leaf × ½. *2*. Twig × 1¼. *3*. Fruit × ½.

gata Vahl., shortleaf fig, both natives of southern Florida. The introduced fig, *F. carica* L., is cultivated for its fruit in the southern states and is sometimes found there as an escape. Rubber may be produced from the latex of *Ficus elastica* Nois., but most of this material is derived from *Hevea brasiliensis* (Muell.) Arg. (Euphorbiaceae), or by synthetic processes.

B. POLYPETALAE

Magnoliaceae: The Magnolia family

This family not only includes some of the most interesting of our modern ˙s, but also claims attention on account of its very ancient lineage in ˙road-leaved group. Fossils of numerous, now extinct, species have ˙ found, some of which extended northward as far as Alaska and ˙land during the latter part of the Cretaceous period.[1] The family comprises 8 to 12 genera and some 210 species of trees or shrubs found in southeast Asia, in the eastern United States southward through Central America, and the West Indies to eastern Brazil. Three genera are represented in the New World. If one considers the least specialized type of floral structure to be the most primitive, then a phylogenetic system might begin with the Magnoliaceae, following the plan of Bentham and Hooker, Hutchinson (181), and others.

BOTANICAL FEATURES OF THE FAMILY

Leaves deciduous or persistent, alternate, simple, stipulate. The stipules enclose the bud and leave conspicuous encircling scars on the twig.
Flowers large, perfect, rarely unisexual, terminal or axillary, solitary; stamens and pistils arranged spirally.
Fruit a conelike aggregate of follicles or samaras.

CONSPECTUS OF NATIVE ARBORESCENT GENERA

Genus	Leaves	Flowers	Fruit
Magnolia	entire, apex acute to obtuse	stamens introrse	an aggregate of semi-fleshy follicles
Liriodendron	lobed, apex truncate to broadly notched	stamens extrorse	an aggregate of samaras

[1] Variously estimated at about 60 million years ago. The Magnoliaceae is not the only family with such a long history. Sweetgum, sycamore, the birches, the oaks, and a number of others have also left their records during this and subsequent periods.

MAGNOLIA L.   Magnolia

The trees and shrubs included in this group are particularly well known on account of their large showy flowers which, in certain species, are nearly a foot or more in diameter. Many ornamental forms have been developed and are widely used to give a tropical aspect to landscape plantings. The genus was named in honor of Pierre Magnol, a celebrated French botanist of the seventeenth century. *Magnolia* numbers some 70 to 80 species, scattered through southern and eastern Asia, Mexico to Venezuela, and the eastern United States. Eight species are native to this country, but only two are important as timber producers.

BOTANICAL FEATURES OF THE GENUS

Leaves deciduous or persistent, unlobed.

Flowers in the native species appearing after the leaves; *sepals* 3; *petals* 6 to 15, in series of 3; *stamens* and *pistils* numerous, spirally arranged.

Fruit a conelike aggregate of spirally placed, 1- to 2-seeded follicles; *seeds* with a scarlet, pulpy outer layer; when mature, suspended by long slender threads. The seeds are distributed to some extent by birds.

Twigs somewhat bitter-tasting, aromatic, moderately stout, straight or slightly zigzag; *pith* homogeneous or inconspicuously diaphragmed, terete; *terminal buds* usually large and conspicuous, with a single outer scale bearing a petiole scar near the base; *lateral buds* smaller; *leaf scars* crescent-shaped to oval; *bundle scars* conspicuous, scattered or in a double row; *stipule scars* conspicuous, encircling the twig.

DISTINGUISHING CHARACTERISTICS OF IMPORTANT SPECIES [1]

Species	Leaves	Flowers	Fruit	Buds
M. acuminata, cucumbertree	deciduous	greenish yellow, about 2″ wide	glabrous	silvery white, silky
M. grandiflora, southern magnolia	persistent	snow-white, about 7″ wide	rusty tomentose	rusty brown, pubescent

[1] Cucumbertree is not considered of importance in forestry by the U.S. Forest Service (127).

Magnolia acuminata L.   Cucumbertree; cucumber magnolia (SPN)

BOTANICAL FEATURES

Leaves deciduous, 6″ to 10″ long, 3″ to 5″ wide; *shape* broadly elliptical to ovate; *margin* entire or repand; *apex* acute to acuminate; *base* broadly cuneate or rounded; *surfaces* glabrous and yellow-green above, glabrous or pubescent below.

Flowers 1½″ to 2″ wide, green to greenish yellow.

Fruit 2″ to 3″ long, cylindrical to ovoid, glabrous, rarely over 1″ in diameter; *seeds* ½″ long, red, after emergence suspended on slender threads; when cleaned, about 4,600 (2,900–6,600) seeds to the pound.

Twigs moderately stout; *terminal buds* ½″ to ¾″ long, silvery silky; *lateral buds* smaller; *leaf scars* horseshoe-shaped; *bundle scars* 5 to 9.

Bark brown, fissured into narrow flaky ridges.

GENERAL DESCRIPTION

Cucumbertree attains heights of 80 to 90 ft and diameters of 3 to 4 ft (max. 125* by nearly 6* ft). It has a straight, clear, slightly buttressed bole, pyramidal crown, a deep but wide-spreading root system, and is usually found on moist, fertile soils of loose texture, with the other hardwoods of the region, such as white and red oaks, hickories, black tupelo, American beech, ashes, and yellow-poplar. Best development is reached at the base of the Appalachians in the Carolinas, Tennessee, and Kentucky, but the tree is nowhere abundant. The wood is commonly mixed and utilized with that of yellow-poplar.

RANGE

The Appalachian region and Ohio and Mississippi River Valleys (map, Plate 57).

1. *Magnolia acuminata.*   2. *Magnolia grandiflora.*

PLATE 57

FIG. 169. *Magnolia acuminata.* Cucumbertree. *1.* Twig × 1¼. *2.* Flower × ½. *3.* Aggregate fruit × ¾. *4.* Leaf × ½. *5.* Bark.

1   2   3   4   5

Magnolia grandiflora L.   Southern magnolia; evergreen magnolia

BOTANICAL FEATURES

Leaves leathery, persistent; 5″ to 8″ long, 2″ to 3″ wide; *shape* narrowly oval to ovate; *margin* entire; *apex* bluntly acute or acuminate; *base* cuneate; *surfaces* bright green and very lustrous above, eventually rusty tomentose below.

Flowers 6″ to 8″ wide, fragrant; with 6, or 9 to 12, large white petals.

Fruit 3″ to 4″ long, ovoid or short cylindrical, 1½″ to 2″ in width; rusty tomentose; about 5,800 cleaned seeds to the pound.

Twigs rusty tomentose; *terminal buds* 1″ to 1½″ long, pale or rusty tomentose; *lateral buds* smaller.

Bark light brown to gray, scaly.

Fig. 170. *Magnolia grandiflora.* Southern magnolia. *1.* Aggregate fruit × ¾. *2.* Flower × ¼. (*Photograph by C. A. Brown.*)

GENERAL DESCRIPTION

Southern magnolia is a medium-sized tree, commonly 60 to 80 ft high and 2 to 3 ft in diameter (max. 135 by 7* ft), with a tall straight bole and somewhat pyramidal crown. It is easily identified in the forest by its persistent shiny leaves, which on older growth are bronze below. This magnolia is a southern bottomland species but will not survive long inundations; it is found on moist but well-drained soils in company with American beech, sweetgum, yellow-poplar, white ash, oaks, and hickories.

Besides the timber produced, southern magnolia is valuable as an

Fig. 171. Bark of southern magnolia.

ornamental on account of its large, showy flowers and evergreen leaves; it is planted for this purpose as far north as New Jersey on the Atlantic Coast and along the Pacific Coast northward to British Columbia.

RANGE

South Atlantic and Gulf Coastal Plains (map, Plate 57). *Altitudinal distribution:* up to 500 ft above sea level.

OTHER NATIVE MAGNOLIAS

Several of the other native species, while of little or no importance as timber producers, are worthy of mention on account of their peculiarities of flower and leaf and because they are in common use as ornamentals throughout the southern states.

M. virginiana L. Sweetbay, sweetbay magnolia (SPN). *Leaves* 4 to 6 in. long, oblong to elliptical, deciduous in the late fall, or persistent until the new leaves appear in the spring. *Flowers* creamy white, cup-shaped, 2 to 3 in. in diameter, very attractive. This species is found in swamps or other moist places along the coast from Massachusetts to Florida; west in the Gulf states to Texas. In the South, where this magnolia may attain a height of 75 ft and a diameter of 3 ft, it furnishes face veneers and furniture parts.

M. macrophylla Michx. Bigleaf magnolia. *Leaves* 20 to 30 in. long, obovate, narrowly cordate at the base. *Flowers* creamy white, 10 to 12 in. or more in diameter. This is a relatively rare tree found in scattered groups through the Piedmont region of North Carolina, south to Florida, and west to Kentucky and Louisiana.

M. tripetala L. Umbrella magnolia. *Leaves* 18 to 20 in. long, obovate, often clustered near the ends of the branches. *Flowers* creamy white, malodorous, 10 to 12 in. in diameter. Rare and local from southern Pennsylvania to southern Alabama, west to central Kentucky and southwestern Arkansas.

M. fraseri Walt. Fraser magnolia. *Leaves* similar in shape to those of *M. macrophylla*, but smaller, 10 to 12 in. long, and more auriculate at the base. *Flowers* fragrant, pale yellow, 10 to 12 in. in diameter. This species is found in the mountains of the Virginias and extreme western Maryland, south to Kentucky, northern Georgia, and west to Alabama.

The two remaining species are similar to certain of those already described. No attempt is made to mention the many ornamental forms, both native and introduced, since these are of interest chiefly to the horticulturist, and descriptions may be found in standard texts on that subject.

LIRIODENDRON L. Yellow-poplar

Fossil remains indicate that this genus, comprising several forms, was once widely distributed over North America and the Old World. At present, however, only two species remain, one, *L. chinense* Sarg. of central China, and the other, *L. tulipifera* L. of the eastern United States. The common name "yellow-poplar" for the American species is misleading since the true poplars are found in the Salicaceae or willow family, a group which is very different from the *Liriodendron*. To avoid repetition, the generic description is omitted.

Liriodendron tulipifera L. Yellow-poplar; tuliptree (SPN)

BOTANICAL FEATURES

Leaves deciduous; 4″ to 6″ in diameter; *shape* nearly orbicular, mostly 4-lobed; *margin* of the lobes entire; *base* and *apex* nearly truncate (or apex often broadly notched); *surfaces* glabrous; *petioles* slender, 5″ to 6″ long; *stipules* large and conspicuous, together encircling the twig.

Flowers appearing in late May or June after the leaves unfold; 1½″ to 2″ wide, cup-shaped; *petals* 6, in 2 rows, light greenish yellow; *sepals* 3; *stamens* and *pistils* numerous, spirally arranged.

Fruit 2½″ to 3″ long, an erect conelike aggregate of samaras, individually 4-angled, terminally winged, and deciduous from the central, more or less persistent axis at maturity (these "cones" are often of value in identifying the larger trees at some distance after the leaves have fallen); *samaras* 1½″ long, 2-seeded, but commonly one-seeded by abortion; about 14,000 (10,000–24,000) to the pound.

Twigs moderately stout, reddish brown, bitter to the taste; *pith* diaphragmed, terete; *terminal buds* about ½″ long, flattened, "duck-billed" in appearance; the scales valvate in pairs, with only the 2 outer ones visible; *lateral buds* much smaller; *leaf scars* circular to oval; *bundle scars* small, scattered; *stipule scars* conspicuous, encircling the twig.

F<small>IG</small>. 172. *Liriodendron tulipifera*. Yellow-poplar. *1*. Twig × 1¼. *2*. Fruit × 1. *3*. Conelike aggregate of fruits × ¾. *4*. Flower × ¾. *5*. Leaf × ½. *6*. Young stem showing characteristic white depressions. *7*. Bark of old tree.

Bark on young trees dark green and smooth, with small white spots; soon breaking up into long, rough, interlacing rounded ridges separated by ashy-gray fissures; inner bark bitter and aromatic.

GENERAL DESCRIPTION

Yellow-poplar is not only one of the most distinctive trees of eastern North America, it is also one of the most valuable timber producers. It probably attains the greatest height (maximum 198 ft) of any eastern broad-leaved tree and may also be the most massive (maximum diameter 12 ft).[1] In the forest this tree presents an unmistakable outline. The tall, clear, almost arrow-straight trunk terminates far above in a small, rather open, oblong crown. The root system is deep and widespreading, and the tree is commonly found on moist, well-drained, loose-textured soils of moderate depth.

Yellow-poplar is intolerant, but on good sites growth in second-growth stands is so fast that young trees outdistance their competition. Such trees in 50 to 60 years may be 120 ft tall and 18 to 24 in. in diameter (127). Maturity is reached in about 200 years, with very old trees attaining the three-century mark. Yellow-poplar is found in some 16 forest types, associated mostly with other hardwoods including oaks and hickories, American beech, sweetgum, maples, sassafras, black cherry, and basswood. Coniferous associates are white pine and hemlock, and in the South, loblolly pine.

Very large seed crops are borne at irregular intervals, and in a good year there may be a seed fall of 200,000 per acre. However, in one study only a few (11 percent) of the seed coats contained seeds; the rest were empty, and even the filled-out seeds germinated poorly. The showy flowers of the tuliptree apparently depend upon honeybees for cross pollination (tuliptree honey is a commercial product), and the lack of their services results in poor seed crops. In cross-pollination experiments, it was possible to increase filled-out seeds up to 90 percent.

Yellow-poplar is a beautiful ornamental tree with its large conspicuous flowers and notched leaves on long petioles that quiver in the slightest breeze. Because of this feature or perhaps certain wood characters, the name "poplar" became attached to this member of the Magnolia family. Although unfortunate, the name is here to stay.

RANGE

Eastern United States (map, Plate 58).

[1] Two reported trees in separate localities are said to be 16 ft in diameter, but this size has not been verified. See also American sycamore.

PLATE 58. *Liriodendron tulipifera.*

Lauraceae: The Laurel family

The Laurel family includes about 45 genera and some 1,900 species of trees and shrubs, which are largely evergreen. Most of them are tropical,[1] although a few extend into the temperate zones.

Many aromatic substances present in the leaves, stems, roots, and fruits of certain species have been investigated and commercially exploited. From "bois de rose" (*Aniba panurensis* Mey.) is obtained linaloa oil, a compound used in the manufacture of expensive perfumes. To *Cinnamomum camphora* Nées is traceable the true camphor of commerce, and cinnamon bark and cassia bark are products of two other Asiatic members of this genus, namely, *C. zeylanicum* Breyn. and *C. cassia* Bl., respectively. A number of commercial oils and drugs, notably oils of anise and oil of sassafras, are also produced by members of this family. The avocado or alligator pear, now so widely cultivated throughout the tropics, is the fruit of *Persea americana* Mill., a small tree originally native to the American tropics but now rapidly becoming naturalized in many other tropical countries.

A few commercial timbers of the Lauraceae find their way into the lumber markets of the world, but most of them are used only locally. *Endiandra palmerstonii* White, the walnut bean or Oriental walnut of eastern Australia, resembles American walnut, *Juglans nigra* L., sufficiently closely (superficially at least) to permit of its substitution for this species. *Ocotea rodioei* (R. Schomb.) Mez., the British Guianan Demerara greenheart, long since has proved its worth in marine construction; this is exported in quantity, particularly to European ports, and small amounts are utilized along the American seacoasts; the gates of the Panama Canal locks were originally fabricated with this wood. The·South African stinkwood, *Ocotea bullata* E. Mey., because of its strength, durability, color, and pleasing figure is also a cabinet wood and building timber of recognized merit.

Five genera have arborescent forms in this country, but these are of only minor importance. *Licaria* is represented by a small tree, *L. triandra* (Sw.) Kosterm., of tropical Florida, and *Nectandra coriacea* (Sw.) Griseb., Jamaica nectandra, with entire, persistent leaves, is native to the same region. *Persea* with three native species is confined to the Atlantic and Gulf Coastal Plains. The most common species is *P. borbonia* (L.) Spreng., redbay. This tree has entire, persistent leaves and is found typically in swampy areas and on pine barrens. *Lindera benzoin* (L.) Bl. [*Benzoin aestivale* Nees], spicebush, is a common shrub of the eastern states; it has deciduous

[1] The forests of the American tropics and those of southeastern Asia support a particularly luxurious growth of lauraceous plants.

entire, aromatic leaves, and small clustered buds. The remaining genera, *Umbellularia* (monotypic) and *Sassafras,* are worthy of a more detailed description.

BOTANICAL FEATURES OF THE FAMILY

Leaves persistent, or deciduous, alternate (rarely opposite), simple, often glandular-punctate, usually aromatic, estipulate.
Flowers perfect and imperfect (some species polygamous), regular; *calyx* 6-parted; *petals* 0; *stamens* in 3 or 4 whorls of 3 each; *pistils* 1, ovary 1-celled and with a solitary ovule.
Fruit a berry or drupe.

Umbellularia californica (Hook. and Arn.) Nutt.   California-laurel; Oregon-myrtle

Distinguishing characteristics. *Leaves* evergreen, lanceolate to elliptical, entire, scented. *Flowers* perfect, yellowish green, in axillary umbels, appearing from January to March before the new leaves. *Fruit* an acrid, yellow-green to purple drupe. *Twigs* yellow-green, pith homogeneous. *Bark* brown, with thin appressed scales.
General description. California-laurel is the only lauraceous species in western

FIG. 173. *Umbellularia californica.* California-laurel. *1.* Leaf × ¾. *2.* Flowers × ¾. *3.* Fruit × 1. *4.* Bark. (*Photos 2 and 4 by W. I. Stein, U.S. Forest Service.*)

North America. On protected bottomland sites in southwestern Oregon it is a large tree 100 to 175 ft in height and 3 to 6 ft in diameter, although elsewhere in its range it is usually a small or medium-sized tree 40 to 80 ft high and 18 to 30 in. in diameter. On dry, shallow, rocky soils it is commonly shrubby, and along the windswept bluffs of the Pacific Ocean it often becomes prostrate and forms a spreading network of thickly matted branches. The bole, even under forest conditions, occasionally divides near the ground into several ascending limbs resulting in a broad, dense, round-topped crown; the root system is usually deep but wide-spreading.

Large burls or smaller excrescences are often formed on the trunks of older trees, and those devoid of defects command a high price in the trade. The smaller ones are often turned into many sorts of fancy articles of woodenware, while the large specimens are shipped to veneer plants where they are carefully cut into thin sheets of intrinsic value and beauty.

The evergreen leaves exhale a strong, camphorlike odor when crushed or bruised. In spite of this, goats are known to forage on them during the winter months when more suitable browse is extremely sparse or wanting.

The aromatic properties of all parts of the tree have been used in primitive medicine (127).

Seeds are produced in abundance after the thirtieth to fortieth year; they mature in one season and germinate within a few weeks after the fruits fall. Seedlings often form dense clumps under partial shade and develop quite rapidly; this species also sprouts from the root collar.

Range. Coos Bay region of southwestern Oregon southward through the coast ranges and lower Sierra to the southern border of California. *Altitudinal distribution:* sea level to 1,500 ft in the North; 2,000 to 6,000 ft in the South.

SASSAFRAS Trew   Sassafras

There are but three species of *Sassafras;* one is found in central China, another in Taiwan, and the third, *S. albidum* (Nutt.) Nées [*S. variifolium* (Salis.) Kuntze], in the eastern United States. The native sassafras is usually a small to medium-sized tree but may reach a maximum of 100 by 6 ft. It is intolerant, and is common as a pioneer tree on abandoned fields and dry slopes. Sassafras has a deeply furrowed, spicy, aromatic bark, green twigs, and leaves which are very variable in shape. On the same tree three different forms of leaves are usually found: (1) entire and somewhat elliptical (typical of older trees), (2) mitten-shaped (either right- or left-handed), and (3) three-lobed. This feature together with the aromatic odor and taste of twigs, bark, and leaves facilitates identification. The flowers are imperfect (species dioecious), and the fruit is a blue drupe.

The wood when cut is mixed with that of black ash. Sassafras may be of greater importance in the future since in certain parts of its range it is, by means of root sprouts (110) as well as seeds, rapidly restocking abandoned farm lands. Sassafras tea may be prepared by boiling the root bark. Oil of sassafras is also used in the preparation of certain soaps.

Saxifragaceae: The Saxifrage family

Although largely herbaceous, this family contains a number of shrubby genera, such as *Philadelphus* and *Hydrangea,* which are widely used as ornamentals. The genus most familiar and important to foresters is *Ribes,* which includes the various species

FIG. 174. *Sassafras albidum*. Sassafras. *1*. Fruit × ¾. *2*. 3-lobed leaf × ½. *3*. Unlobed leaf × ½. *4*. 2-lobed or mitten-shaped leaf × ½. *5*. Twig with lammas shoot × 1¼.

of currant and gooseberry.[1] These shrubs are the alternate hosts for white pine blister rust caused by the fungus *Cronartium ribicola* Fischer, and in certain sections of the East, and also more recently the West, attempts have been made to eradicate them over large areas.

Without describing the various species of *Ribes* in detail, there are a few general features of the group worth mentioning. The leaves are mostly deciduous, simple, usually palmately lobed and maplelike in appearance, but alternate; the flowers are perfect or imperfect (some species dioecious), and are borne in few- to many-flowered racemes; the fruit is a juicy berry with or without bristles on the surface; during the first winter the epidermis on the twigs tends to crack irregularly, giving the twig a somewhat ragged appearance; the buds are covered by several usually loosely fitting scales.

[1] According to some authors the gooseberries are put in a separate family, the Grossulariaceae.

Fig. 175. Flowers of wild black currant, *Ribes americanum*.

Hamamelidaceae: The Witch-hazel family

This family comprises 23 genera and about 100 species of trees and shrubs scattered through the forested regions of eastern North America and Mexico to Central America; South Africa, Madagascar, Australia, Asia, and the Malayan Archipelago.

Commercial storax, a balsam used in the manufacture of soaps, perfumes, and pharmaceutical preparations, is obtained from the resinous exudations of the bark of *Liquidambar orientalis* Mill. of Asia Minor.[1] Burmese storax, a similar but somewhat inferior compound, is traceable to the resinous constituents of *Altingia excelsa* Noroh. and is used locally in the preparation of incense and medicinal compounds. *Altingia, Bucklandia*, and *Liquidambar* are the principal timber-contributing genera of this family.

Three genera are represented in the eastern United States: *Fothergilla* with three or four shrubby species is confined mostly to the Atlantic Coastal Plain from North Carolina southward; *Hamamelis* (two species) is found in the East; and *Liquidambar*, as represented by sweetgum, is an important hardwood of the South.

BOTANICAL FEATURES OF THE FAMILY

Leaves deciduous or persistent, alternate, simple, stipulate.

Flowers perfect, or imperfect (species monoecious); *calyx* 4- or 5-parted; *petals* 4 or 5, sometimes 0; *stamens* 4, 5, or more; *pistils* 1 with a 2-celled ovary enclosing 1 or more ovules in each cell.

Fruit a 2-celled capsule, borne singly, or in multiple heads.

[1] Storax is also prepared in commercial quantities by wounding trees of the native sweetgum (228 and 305), but for economic reasons it will probably not compete with that from abroad, except when the foreign supply is interrupted.

Genus	Leaves	Flowers	Fruit	Buds
Liquidambar	lobed	imperfect	multiple	scaly
Hamamelis	unlobed	perfect	borne singly	naked

LIQUIDAMBAR L.   Sweetgum

The genus *Liquidambar* comprises about six species; only one, *L. styraciflua* L., is native in the New World. The other species are found in Asia. Since there is only one native species, the generic description has been omitted.

Liquidambar styraciflua L.   Sweetgum; American sweetgum (SPN); red gum (Tr)

BOTANICAL FEATURES

Leaves deciduous, 6″ to 7″ in diameter; *shape* orbicular, star-shaped, deeply and palmately 5- to 7-lobed; *margin* finely serrate; *apex* of the lobes acuminate; *base* truncate or slightly cordate; *surfaces* bright green and lustrous above; pubescent in the axils of the veins below; somewhat fragrant when crushed; *petioles* long and slender.

Flowers imperfect (species monoecious), both types in heads; staminate heads in racemes, pistillate terminal and solitary; *staminate* flowers lacking calyx and corolla, stamens indefinite in number; *pistillate* flowers with a minute calyx, no corolla, 4 nonfunctioning stamens, and a 2-celled ovary.

Fruit 1″ to 1½″ in diameter, persistent during the winter; a woody, globose head of 2-celled, beaked capsules; *seeds* 2 in each capsule, about ⅜″ long, terminally winged; about 82,000 (65,000–90,000) to the pound.

Twigs shiny, and green to yellowish brown, slender to stout, somewhat angled, or terete, aromatic, commonly with corky excrescences which sometimes appear the first year; *pith* homogeneous, stellate; *terminal buds* ovate to conical, ¼″ to ½″ long, with several orange-brown scales; *lateral buds* similar but smaller; *leaf scars* crescent-shaped to triangular; *bundle scars* 3, conspicuously annular, white with a dark center.

Bark grayish brown; deeply furrowed into narrow, somewhat rounded, flaky ridges.

GENERAL DESCRIPTION

Sweetgum at its best is a large tree 80 to 120 ft high and 3 to 4 ft in diameter (max. 150 by 5 ft) with a long, straight, often buttressed bole, small oblong or pyramidal crown, and shallow wide-spreading root system. It is a typical southern bottomland species and occurs for the most part on rich, moist, alluvial soils. In the Mississippi delta region, sweet-

FIG. 176. *Liquidambar styraciflua.* Sweetgum. *1.* Twig × 1¼. *2.* Flowers, staminate heads above, pistillate below × ½. *3.* Fruiting head × 1. *4.* Seed × 1. *5.* Leaf × ½. *6.* Bark. (*Photograph by U.S. Forest Service.*)

371

FIG. 177. Sweetgum branchlet showing development of cork × ½.

gum is the commonest and most widely distributed single species and is found on a great variety of sites. It is most common in the first bottoms, where almost pure stands may occur on moist silty clay or silty clay-loam ridges and flats. Sweetgum is also very common on old fields in dense even-aged stands. Its list of associates is large, since the tree is found in some 28 forest-cover types, including not only hardwoods but also southern pines and baldcypress. Some hardwood associates are cherry-bark, Nuttall, pin, willow, and swamp chestnut oaks, cottonwood, beech, southern magnolia, and sycamore; on drier sites northern red oak, mockernut hickory, and yellow-poplar are included.

Seeds are borne in abundance after the twenty-fifth to thirtieth year, and the germination varies from 25 to 75 percent; they are not exacting in their seedbed requirements but should have plenty of moisture. Subsequent growth is fairly rapid at first, but this depends largely upon the site; maturity is reached in 200 to 300 years. Both stump and root sprouts, especially from young trees, may in part restock a cutover stand.

PLATE 59. *Liquidambar styraciflua.*

Sweetgum is intolerant, and plentiful reproduction occurs only on cleared areas; it is also for the same reason a dominant or codominant tree in the forest. This tree resists disease and insects, but is very susceptible to damage by fire. Trees so weakened are then attacked by both fungi and insects.

This species is a desirable ornamental in the milder portions of the North because of the attractive shape and brilliant autumnal coloration of the leaves, and the peculiar corky outgrowths on the twigs. It is hardy at least as far north as central New York and will exist even in dry, heavy clay soils.

Sweetgum is one of the more important commercial hardwoods of the United States, especially in the manufacture of utility and decorative plywood panels.

RANGE

Southern half of eastern United States (map, Plate 59). Also in central and southern Mexico and the highlands of Honduras, Salvador, and Guatemala.

HAMAMELIS L.   Witch-hazel; common witch-hazel (SPN)

Witch-hazel, although of little or no importance commercially, is so common and widely distributed that it deserves mention. The illustrations shown in Fig. 178 are sufficient to indicate the peculiarities of witch-hazel without a detailed description. No more distinctive shrub or small tree can be found in the eastern United States.

Fig. 178. *Hamamelis virginiana.* Witch-hazel. *1.* Flowers × 1. *2.* Fruit and seeds × ¾. *3.* Bud × 2. *4.* Leaf × ½.

The conspicuous flowers with their long, yellow, straplike petals are borne from September to the middle of November and mature the following season into two-valved woody capsules, from which the shining, black, wingless seeds are ejected forcibly to a distance of several feet or more from the tree. The tawny buds, naked except for two small scales, are characteristic of the winter twigs.

Witch-hazel is said to be especially prized by "water diviners," some of whom prefer twigs cut from this tree. An alcoholic extract prepared from the bark or small branches is a well-known rubbing lotion.

Hamamelis virginiana L. is found from New Brunswick to Iowa, south to Georgia and southern Arkansas. A second species, *H. vernalis* Sarg., is a shrub of the Ozark region.

Platanaceae: The Sycamore or Planetree family

This is a monotypic family with the single genus, *Platanus*, comprising 7 to 10 species; 3 are native to this country, one a large tree of the eastern states, the other two being small trees of the West. The foreign species are found in Mexico, and from southeastern Europe to India.

London plane, ×*P. acerifolia* (Ait.) Willd., is presumably a hybrid between *P. occidentalis* L., American sycamore, and *P. orientalis* L., the Oriental plane. London plane is similar in appearance to the native sycamore except that the bark is more olive-green in color and the fruit heads may occur in 2's and 3's rather than singly. This form is commonly used as a street tree in the United States.

PLATANUS L.   Sycamore; planetree

BOTANICAL FEATURES OF THE GENUS

Leaves deciduous, alternate, simple, palmately 3- to 7-lobed; *petioles* enlarged at the base and enclosing the next year's bud; *stipules* foliaceous (leaflike) and very conspicuous.

Flowers imperfect (species monoecious), appearing with the leaves, in separate globose heads; individual flowers minute; *staminate* with 3 to 8 sepals and petals and an equal number of stamens; *pistillate* with 3 to 8 sepals, petals, and carpels.

Fruit a globose head (multiple) of elongated obovoid achenes, each surrounded at the base by a circle of upright brown hairs and usually bearing at the apex a minute curved spur.

Twigs conspicuously zigzag; *pith* homogeneous, terete; *terminal buds* wanting; *lateral buds* divergent, resinous, with a caplike outer scale; *leaf scars* encircling the buds; *bundle scars* several; *stipule scars* encircling the twig.

Platanus occidentalis L.   American sycamore; buttonwood; American planetree (SPN)

Leaves 4″ to 7″ in diameter; *shape* broadly ovate to orbicular, 3- to 5-lobed, sinuses broad and usually shallow; *margin* of lobes sinuately toothed; *apex* acuminate; *base* cordate to truncate; *surfaces* glabrous above, hairy along the veins below; *petioles* stout, 2″ to 3″ long, hollow at the base.

Fruit heads 1″ to 1¼″ in diameter, borne singly on slender stems 3″ to 6″ long; usually persistent on the tree during part of the winter; about 204,000 (151,000–228,000) achenes to the pound.

Twigs moderately slender, dark orange-brown, conspicuously zigzag; *pith* homogeneous, terete; *leaf scars* nearly surrounding the bud; *stipule scars* distinct, encircling the twigs; *terminal buds* lacking; *lateral buds* divergent, resinous, and with a single visible caplike scale.

Bark on young branches brownish; soon characteristically mottled (brown and white) by the exfoliation of the outer bark exposing the lighter creamy-white inner layers, bark on the lower trunk of older trees often entirely brown and scaly.

GENERAL DESCRIPTION

American sycamore is one of the largest (perhaps the greatest in diameter) [1] of eastern hardwood trees and commonly attains a height of over 100 ft. and a diameter of 3 to 8 ft (max. 175 by 11 to 14 ft). Even at a considerable distance this tree can hardly be mistaken for any of the associated species. The mottled bark is very striking in appearance, while the open, spreading crown with its somewhat crooked smaller branches is also characteristic. The root system is superficial, and the tree is one of the commonest of stream-bank and bottomland species. Its associates include American elm, the soft maples, water and Nuttall oaks, river birch, cottonwood, sweetgum, and willows. American sycamore is in-

PLATE 60. *Platanus occidentalis.*

[1] See also yellow-poplar.

2   1   3   6

5

4   7   8

tolerant and occurs only as a scattered tree or in small groves, sometimes of 40 to 100 acres.

Seeds are usually produced each year and are shed irregularly throughout the fall, winter, and early spring. The percentage of germination is low, and little reproduction takes place except on moist, mineral soil in the open. Growth is fast, and sycamore is said to attain an age of 500 to 600 years. Although this species is sometimes planted as an ornamental, the hybrid London plane is the more common.

RANGE

Eastern United States (map, Plate 60).

WESTERN SPECIES

Two western sycamores, occurring in widely separated regions, not infrequently form dense cover along streams or on precipitous slopes and aid materially in controlling erosion.

Platanus wrightii S. Wats., the Arizona sycamore [Arizona planetree (SPN)], is probably the most abundant broad-leaved tree in the Southwest and occurs quite generally along stream banks and canyon walls in southern Arizona and southwestern New Mexico. The tree is readily distinguished by its deeply five- to seven-lobed leaves and heads of achene fruits borne in racemose clusters of two to four.

Platanus racemosa Nutt., the California sycamore [California planetree (SPN)], is a medium-sized, broadly buttressed tree of wide distribution along stream banks in the coast ranges and in the foothills along the west slopes of the Sierra Nevada Mountains in California. It is identified by its narrowly three- to five-lobed leaves with cuneate (rarely cordate) bases and heads of achenes in racemose clusters of two to seven.

Rosaceae: The Rose family

The Rosaceae include about 120 genera and some 3,300 species of trees, shrubs, and herbs, widely scattered throughout the world but more numerous in temperate climates. From the standpoint of forestry, the family is relatively unimportant, but in agriculture it is extremely valuable, since in this group are the apple, pear, plum, cherry, apricot, strawberry, almond, peach, loganberry, raspberry, blackberry, and other valuable plants. The Rosaceae also include a number of highly prized ornamental genera such as *Spiraea, Crataegus, Physocarpus, Amelanchier, Sorbus, Rosa, Kerria, Rhodotypos, Pyracantha, Cydonia,* and *Prunus.*

FIG. 179. *Platanus occidentalis.* Sycamore. *1.* Leaf and foliaceous stipules × ½. *2.* Head of pistillate flowers × ½. *3.* Head of staminate flowers × ½. *4.* Fruiting head × ¾. *5.* Fruit × 1. *6.* Twig × 1¼. *7.* Bark of young tree. *8.* Bark of old tree.

Ten genera are represented by arborescent forms in the United States, but the eastern black cherry, *Prunus serotina* Ehrh., is the only timber-producing species of importance.

Leaves deciduous or persistent, alternate (rarely opposite), simple or compound, mostly stipulate.

Flowers perfect, actinomorphic, 5- (rarely 4-) merous; *pistils* inferior or superior.

Fruit a pome, drupe, capsule, follicle, or achene.

PRUNUS L.   Cherry; peach; plum

The genus *Prunus* includes some 150 species of trees and shrubs which are widely distributed through the cooler regions of the Northern Hemisphere. The peach, *P. persica* Batsch, the plum, *P. domestica* L., the almond, *P. amygdalus* Batsch, the apricot, *P. armeniaca* L., the sweet cherry (mazzard), *P. avium* (L.) L., and the sour cherry, *P. cerasus* L., are all well-known members of this genus.

Between 25 and 30 species of *Prunus* are included in the flora of the United States. Of the some 18 arborescent forms only *P. serotina* is important for timber.

BOTANICAL FEATURES OF THE GENUS

Leaves deciduous or persistent, alternate, simple.

Flowers in terminal or axillary racemes, umbels, or corymbs, appearing with, before, or after the leaves; *calyx* 5-lobed; *petals* 5, white or pink; *stamens* 15 to 20; *pistils* 1; *ovary* 1-celled.

Fruit a thin dry, or thick fleshy, 1-seeded drupe; *pit* bony, smooth or rugose.

Twigs slender or stout, usually bitter to the taste, red to brown, often conspicuously lenticellate; *terminal buds* present, the scales imbricate; *lateral buds* of nearly the same size as the terminals; *leaf scars* semicircular for the most part, with scattered bundle scars (spur growth is common in this genus).

Prunus serotina Ehrh.   Black cherry

BOTANICAL FEATURES

Leaves deciduous, 2″ to 6″ long, 1″ to 1½″ wide; *shape* narrowly oval to oblong-lanceolate; *margin* finely serrate with callous incurved teeth; *base* cuneate; *apex* acuminate or abruptly pointed; *surfaces* dark green and very lustrous above, paler below, and at maturity usually with dense reddish-brown pubescence along the mid-rib near the base of the leaf; *petiole* glandular.

Flowers borne in racemes, appearing when the leaves are from half- to nearly full-grown.

Fruit ⅓″ to ½″ in diameter, depressed globose, almost black when ripe, ripening from June to October, flesh dark purple, edible; pits about 4,800 (3,100–8,100) to the pound.

FIG. 180. *Prunus serotina.* Black cherry. *1.* Twig × 1¼. *2.* Flower cluster × ½. *3.* Fruits × ½. *4.* Leaf × ½. *5.* Bark of young tree. *6.* Bark of old tree.

Twigs with a bitter-almond taste, slender, reddish brown, sometimes covered with a gray epidermis; usually with short spur shoots on older growth; *terminal buds* about ³⁄₁₆″ long, ovate, chestnut brown, with several visible scales; *lateral buds* similar but smaller; *leaf scars* small, semicircular; *bundle scars* 3, often not distinct.

Bark on young stems smooth, reddish brown to nearly black, with conspicuous, narrow, horizontal lenticels; on older trunks exfoliating in small, persistent, platy scales with upturned edges.

GENERAL DESCRIPTION

Black cherry is a medium-sized tree 50 to 60 ft high and 2 to 3 ft in diameter (max. 129 by 7* ft). In the forest it develops a long, straight, clear, cylindrical bole, a narrow oblong crown, and a relatively shallow root system. Best growth is made on rich, deep, moist soils where the tree may occur in pure stands of limited extent, or more commonly mixed with such species as northern red oak, white ash, sugar maple, basswood, white pine, and hemlock. In the northeast this species often reaches commercial proportions in virgin forests of the red spruce–white pine–northern hardwood association on sandy soils. In these and other dense stands, old-growth black cherry is usually a dominant tree because of its intolerance and early rapid growth. Second-growth cherry may grow 3 ft in height and ½ in. in diameter a year for the first 20 years. In other studies, this tree at age 60 was 80 to 100 ft high and 20 to 24 in. in diameter.

PLATE 61. *Prunus serotina.*

Seeds are produced in abundance almost yearly; they are spread by birds and under favorable conditions show a high percentage of germination. Regeneration by sprouts is also good. Black cherry attains an age of 150 to 200 years. Its thin scaly bark allows it to be severely damaged by surface fires.

Eastern United States; also Texas, New Mexico, and Arizona south through Mexico to Guatemala (map, Plate 61).

P. pensylvanica L.   Pin cherry; fire cherry
P. virginiana L.   Common choke cherry

In the Northeast and over a large portion of Canada, *P. pensylvanica* L., pin cherry, is a common species occurring with aspen or burned areas. It is a small tree of no commercial importance and may be distinguished from the preceding species by its thin, yellow-green leaves which are usually narrower, more lanceolate, and less shiny than those of black cherry; the bark is more reddish in color on young stems, the lenticels are lens-shaped, and the flowers are borne in umbels.

Fig. 181. Flower cluster of pin cherry × ¾.

Common choke cherry, *P. virginiana* L., is a shrub or small tree with finely, sharply serrate, obovate leaves and racemose flowers. Together with its several varieties it covers nearly the entire continental United States and also a large area in Canada. This species is very common along hedgerows where the seeds are left by birds. In sections where rabbit damage to other hardwoods and even conifers is extreme, it flourishes untouched, while in certain northern forest plantations it is practically the only species to survive in frost pockets where exceedingly low winter temperatures prevail. Choke cherry sprouts prolifically, and this, together with its general hardiness, seems to ensure its success even under the most extreme conditions. Although usually classed as a forest weed, this species may be useful in erosion control and is used in the plains states in shelter belts.

MALUS Mill. Apple

This genus numbers about 25 species of trees and shrubs scattered through the forests of the Northern Hemisphere. Probably the most important species is *M. pumila* Mill., the common apple. This tree was introduced in colonial times and is now an escape over a large portion of the United States. The leaves are elliptical to ovate, whitish pubescent below and along the petiole; the young twigs and buds are somewhat white tomentose, and the former have a characteristic semisweet taste. There are a number of native species of little or no importance as timber producers.

PYRUS L. Pear

Pyrus comprises about 25 species distributed through Europe, Asia, and northern Africa. The introduced common pear tree, *P. communis* L., is a common escape and bears a superficial resemblance to the apple. The leaves of the pear, however, are thinner, more lustrous, and nearly glabrous; the twigs are less pubescent and are usually armed with thorns.

SORBUS L. Mountain-ash

Of about 80 species, 4 are found in the United States, 2 in the East, and 2 in the West. The common eastern form is *S. americana* Marsh., American mountain-ash.[1] It is a small tree or shrub common to rocky hillsides and is easily recognized by its alternate, odd-pinnately compound leaves with 13 to 17 lanceolate, sharply serrate leaflets and clusters of bright red fruits. *S. aucuparia* L., European mountain-ash or rowan-tree, has been introduced for ornamental purposes and differs from the native species in its leaflets, which are bluntly pointed and pubescent. The rowan-tree has escaped from cultivation in certain sections and is often found growing wild.

AMELANCHIER Med. Serviceberry; shadbush

This genus comprises about 25 species, and one or more of them is found in every state and province of the United States and Canada (193). Of the some 18 species native to the United States, 7 reach tree size. The common eastern form, *A. arborea* (Michx. f.) Fern., downy serviceberry [shadblow serviceberry (SPN)], is usually a small tree with singly serrate, oblong to elliptical leaves and smooth, gray bark often streaked with darker lines; the twigs have a faint bitter-almond taste, and the terminal buds are similar to those of beech, except that they are smaller and fewer-scaled.

CRATAEGUS L. Hawthorn; thornapple

This is a very unstable genus, and many of the species are hybridizing. At least 149 arborescent forms are now recognized in the United States, while some writers list over 200 species for New York state alone.[2] The group is of considerable interest

[1] Also common in some localities is *S. decora* (Sarg.) Schneid.

[2] Some writers estimate that there are perhaps 1,000 species in North America and 90 in the Old World. Lawrence (209) suggests a total of 300 to 1,000 species, with 75 to 200 indigenous to North America.

to the taxonomist, but the identification of closely related forms is not usually attempted by the forester. All are shrubs or small trees with simple serrate or lobed leaves and branches which are armed with thorny modified branchlets. The hawthorns are typical of open pastures, where they are often aggressive and difficult to eradicate. Certain species are used as ornamentals. The accompanying illustration shows the peculiar effects of grazing on pasture trees.

Fig. 182. *Crataegus* spp. Hawthorn. *1*. Pasture trees showing effects of grazing; note small pyramidal one in background. 2. Flowers × ¾. 3. Fruits and seed × ¾. 4. Thorn × 1. 5. Twig × 1½.

SOME WESTERN ROSACEOUS FORMS

Several arborescent forms in the Rosaceae are indigenous to the Pacific Coast. They have little or no commercial value as a group, but the forester should know of their presence and be able to recognize them. The osoberry, *Osmaronia cerasiformis* (Torr. and Gray) Greene, is a large shrub or small tree which is one of the first to bloom in the early spring. It is readily identified by its brittle, ill-smelling twigs, chambered pith, and small plumlike fruits. The Pacific serviceberry or shadbush, *Amelanchier florida* Lindl., extends along the coast from Wrangell, southeastern Alaska, to northern California. This species may be recognized by its blue-black, pomelike fruits, its smooth, gray, and often muscular-appearing stems, and its leaves, which are usually entire below the middle. At least five species of *Cercocarpus* may be found on dry, often precipitous sites in the western states. These are the so-called mountain-mahoganies, large shrubs or small trees with more or less resinous, evergreen leaves and long, feather-tailed achenes. The Oregon crabapple, *Malus diversifolia* (Bong.) Roem., is a small tree of river bottoms and marshy sites. It may be recognized by its yellow, oblong, pomelike fruits, and its leaves which are often glaucous white below. The black hawthorn [Douglas hawthorn (SPN)], *Crataegus douglasii* Lindl., can be identified by its heavy thorns, shiny black or blue-black, pomelike fruits, and dentate-lobed leaves. The Christmasberry or California-holly, *Photinia arbutifolia* Lindl., is an evergreen tree with hollylike leaves and bright red berrylike pomes borne in large terminal panicles. *Prunus subcordata* Benth., the Klamath plum, produces an edible fruit 1½ to 3 in. in length. *Prunus emarginata* Dougl. is a tree of widespread occurrence in both the Rocky Mountain and Pacific regions, featuring elliptical leaves and bright red fruits. It has no commercial value.

Leguminosae: The Pulse or Pea family

The Pulse family includes about 550 genera and some 15,000 species of trees, shrubs, lianas, and herbs, widely scattered throughout the world. It is second only to the Gramineae (Grass family) in its economic importance and also in the number of species included. Among the herbaceous forms of mention are such important food and forage plants as clover, vetch, dal, bean, pea, and alfalfa. These as well as other leguminaceous plants have root nodules containing nitrogen-fixing bacteria of great value in soil building. The Leguminosae also produce some of the finest of cabinet timbers as well as a great many minor forest products such as tannins, gums, resins, dyes, and drugs.

The Indian rosewood of the trade is supplied by *Dalbergia latifolia* Roxb., while cocobolo, derived from several other species of this genus, is found in the forests of Costa Rica and Nicaragua. The colorful vermilion and padouk (padauk) timbers from southeastern Asia and tropical Africa are traceable to the genus *Pterocarpus*. The African zebrawood is obtained from *Microberlinia brazzavillanensis* Chev. Excellent timbers of cabinet grade are also produced by the genera *Albizia, Peltogyne, Acacia, Cassia,* and *Castanospermum.*

Logwood dye is obtained from the wood of *Haematoxylon campechianum* L., a small tree native to the West Indies and Central America. This dye, known also as hematoxylin, is widely used by botanists and wood technologists in staining thin wood sections, and other tissues, and also is important in the textile industry.

Caragana arborescens Lam., the Siberian peashrub with yellow flowers and even-pinnate leaves, has been introduced and is used for shelter-belt planting in the plains states.

Twenty arborescent genera with approximately forty species are included in the native America flora. *Gleditsia* and *Robinia,* however, are the only important timber-contributing genera.

Leaves deciduous or persistent, mostly alternate (rarely opposite), compound or occasionally simple, stipulate; petiole or rachis often swollen at either or both ends.

Flowers perfect and/or imperfect (many species dioecious or monecious); actinomorphic or zygomorphic; *stamens* 10 to many, monadelphous, diadelphous, or separate; *pistils* 1, with an elongated 1-celled ovary.

Fruit a legume.

CONSPECTUS OF IMPORTANT NATIVE GENERA

Genus	Leaves	Flowers	Fruit	Twigs
Gleditsia	1- to 2-pinnate on the same tree	regular, perfect and imperfect	usually large (page 388) and tardily dehiscent; with suborbicular seeds	with branched thorns
Robinia	1-pinnate	papilionate, perfect	usually smaller and dehiscent; with reniform seeds	with short, unbranched stipulate spines

The Leguminosae may be further separated into three subfamilies which are given family rank by some writers.

(Subfamily) Mimosoideae

In this group the leaves are usually large, commonly bi- or tripinnately compound, and the flowers are regular. Five genera are represented in this country with about 15 species, but these are all small trees or shrubs of little importance. This group includes mesquite, *Prosopis juliflora* (Sw.) DC., screwbean mesquite, *Prosopis pubescens* Benth., also Wright acacia, *Acacia wrightii* Benth., and catclaw acacia, *Acacia greggii* A. Gray of the Southwest.

(Subfamily) Caesalpinioideae

The leaves are simple, pinnate or bipinnate, and the flowers show a transition between the regular flowers of the first group and the papilionate in the third (in the bud, the upright or odd petal is enclosed by the others). Five aborescent genera are represented by eleven native species, and one (*Gleditsia*) is a timber producer of some importance.

Eastern redbud, or Judas-tree, *Cercis canadensis* L., is a form with simple, nearly orbicular leaves and conspicuous bright pink flowers which appear before the leaves. It is a small tree and is used considerably as an ornamental, especially with conifers, where it is extremely beautiful in early spring. *Cercis occidentalis* Torr. is a closely related form found in Utah, Nevada, California, and Arizona.

FIG. 183. *Gymnocladus dioicus*. Kentucky coffee-tree. *1.* Twig × 1¼. *2.* Fruit and seed × ½.

Kentucky coffeetree, *Gymnocladus dioicus* (L.) K. Koch, so called because of the similarity in appearance of its seeds to coffee beans, is a medium-sized to large tree with bipinnate leaves from 1 to 3 ft long, imperfect flowers and a short, thick, woody legume. The species is rare locally and ranges through the central hardwood region west of the Appalachians. It is used to some extent as an ornamental, and the wood only occasionally reaches the market.

GLEDITSIA L.   Honeylocust

The genus *Gleditsia* numbers about 12 species of trees scattered through the forests of North and South America, eastern and central Asia, and tropical Africa. The group produces but little timber, although several species are highly prized for ornamental purposes.

This genus is represented in the United States by two species. *G. aquatica* Marsh., waterlocust, is an unimportant bottomland species of the South, while *G. triacanthos* L., the honeylocust, is a tree of secondary commercial importance.

Leaves deciduous, alternate, 1- to 2-pinnately compound, often clustered on 2-year-old twigs, stipulate.

Flowers perfect and imperfect, regular (species polygamous), greenish yellow, borne in axillary spikelike racemes; *calyx* 3- to 5-lobed; *petals* 3 to 5; *stamens* 6 to 10, distinct; *pistils* 1, 1-celled, with 2 to many ovules.

Fruit either (1) an elongated, many-seeded, usually indehiscent legume, or (2) a short, few-seeded, tardily dehiscent legume; *seeds* suborbicular, albuminous.

Twigs stout, conspicuously zigzag, armed with heavy, 3-branched (rarely 2- to many-branched) thorns; *pith* homogeneous; *terminal buds* wanting; *lateral buds* partly submerged, superposed, scaly; *leaf scars* U-shaped; *bundle scars* 3.

Gleditsia triacanthos L.   Honeylocust

BOTANICAL FEATURES

Leaves both pinnate and bipinnately compound, the pinnate with 15 to 30 nearly sessile leaflets, the bipinnate leaves with 4 to 7 pairs of pinnae, 6" to 8" long; *leaflets* 1" to 2" long, ½" to ⅞" wide on pinnate leaves, smaller on bipinnate ones; *shape* ovate, ovate-lanceolate, or elliptical; *margin* crenulate; *apex* acute or rounded; *base* acute or inequilateral; *surfaces* glabrous, dark green, lustrous above; dull yellow-green, glabrous or nearly so below; *rachis* grooved above, pubescent, swollen at the base.

Flowers small, actinomorphic, perfect and imperfect, borne in axillary racemes; *calyx* 3- to 5-lobed; *petals* 3 to 5, greenish white; *stamens* 6 to 10; *pistils* 1, with a subsessile 1-celled ovary.

Fruit a reddish-brown to purplish-brown, strap-shaped, usually twisted legume, 7" to 18" long and about 1" wide; *seeds* oval, dark brown, about ⅛" long; about 2,800 (1,750–4,050) to the pound.

Twigs stout to slender, zigzag, greenish brown to reddish brown, lustrous, with 3-branched (rarely simple or 1-branched) thorns, 2" to 3" long; *terminal buds* wanting; *lateral buds* minute, superposed; *leaf scars* U-shaped, with 3 bundle scars.

Bark on mature trees grayish brown to nearly black, often conspicuously lenticellate, broken up into long, narrow, longitudinal, and superficially scaly ridges which are separated by deep fissures; often with clusters of large many-branched thorns.

GENERAL DESCRIPTION

Honeylocust is a medium-sized tree 70 to 80 ft high and 2 to 3 ft in diameter (max. 140 by 6 ft), with a rather short bole and open, narrow or spreading crown; the root system is wide and deep. Although commonly found on rich, moist bottomlands or on soils of a limestone origin, this species is very hardy and drought resistant when planted elsewhere,

Fig. 184. *Gleditsia triacanthos.* Honeylocust. *1.* Twig × 1¼. *2.* Thorn × 1¼. *3.* Bicompound leaf × ½. *4.* Once-compound leaf × ½. *5.* Bark.

especially in the plains and prairie states, where it has been widely used in windbreaks. When trimmed, honeylocust makes a desirable tall hedge, which soon becomes impassable because of the many forbidding thorns.

Some seeds are produced annually with abundant crops at three- to five-year intervals. They owe their dispersal partly to the persistence of the fruits, which fall irregularly throughout the winter and often roll for a considerable distance over the snow. The seeds show a high percentage of vitality but need hot-water treatment to avoid too large a proportion of delayed germination. Growth is rapid, and maturity is reached in about 120 years, although older trees are sometimes found. Honeylocust is intolerant, and hence it occurs in the open or as a dominant tree in the forest, in mixture with other bottomland hardwoods including Nuttall and willow oaks, sweetgum, green ash, American elm, red maple, and black tupelo.

This species undoubtedly owes its name to the pods, which contain a sweetish substance between the seeds tasting similar to a mixture of

FIG. 185. Fruit and seed of honeylocust × ½.

castor oil and honey. When green, these pods are eagerly eaten by cattle, and the propagation of thornless honeylocust to be planted as a pasture tree has been recommended (66). The thornless *G. triacanthos* f. *inermis* (L.) Zabel is sometimes found growing wild, and in recent years clones of it have been planted by the thousands as street or specimen trees in cities. The form used bears no flowers, or in any case no fruit. Many American elm shade trees killed by the Dutch elm disease are being replaced by the thornless, podless honeylocust; a tree previously rare in cities has become exceedingly common.

RANGE

Eastern United States except for New England and the south Atlantic and Gulf Coastal Plains (map, Plate 62); range much extended through the eastern United States by planting.

1. *Gleditsia triacanthos.*   2. *Robinia pseudoacacia.*

PLATE 62

(Subfamily) Papilionoideae

The leaves are usually pinnately compound and are persistent or deciduous. The flowers are considered more highly developed than those of the two preceding subfamilies and consist of five sepals more or less united, five irregular petals, and ten stamens, nine of which are united to form a tube cleft on the upper side, with the tenth stamen separate (*diadelphous*), or all separate; ovary one to many-celled, superior. A special type of corolla termed "papilionate" is found in this subfamily. One of the petals is larger than the rest, is upright, encloses the others in the bud, and is called the *standard;* the two laterals, *wings,* are modified but little, while the two lower petals are fused to form a trough called the *keel.* Bean and pea are examples of this type.

There are 8 genera with 11 species reaching tree size in the United States, and one (*Robinia*) is of importance.

Cladrastis is represented here by one species, *C. lutea* (Michx. f.) K. Koch, yellowwood, a small southern tree of limited range (chiefly Tennessee, Kentucky, and southern Missouri). The bark resembles beech, but the leaves are compound, the fruit is a legume, and the winter twigs have leaf scars nearly encircling the bud which is short and pubescent. Yellowwood is used as an ornamental both in this country and Europe, sometimes under the name of "virgilia."

ROBINIA L.   Locust

Robinia[1] includes about 20 species of trees and shrubs, all of which are found in the United States and Mexico. Several of these have ornamental value, and *R. pseudoacacia* L. is a timber tree of some importance. Four species reach tree size in the United States.

BOTANICAL FEATURES OF THE GENUS

Leaves deciduous, alternate, pinnately compound, mostly spinose-stipulate.

Flowers perfect, papilionate, borne in racemes which appear after the leaves; *calyx* 5-lobed; *corolla* consisting of a large obcordate standard, 2 obtuse wings, and an incurved, 2-petalate keel; *stamens* 10, diadelphous; *pistils* 1, 1-celled, with many ovules.

Fruit a many-seeded, nearly sessile legume; *seeds* reniform, albuminous.

Twigs moderately stout, angular, somewhat zigzag, reddish brown, usually with stipular spines; *pith* homogeneous; *terminal buds* wanting; *lateral buds* naked, submerged beneath the leaf scar, often superposed; *leaf scars* broadly ovate to somewhat reniform; *bundle scars* 3.

Robinia pseudoacacia L.   Black locust

BOTANICAL FEATURES

Leaves 8″ to 14″ long, pinnately compound with 7 to 19 subopposite or alternate leaflets; *leaflets* 1½″ to 2″ long, ½″ to ¾″ wide; *shape* elliptical, ovate-oblong, or ovate; *margin* entire; *apex* mucronate, or notched; *base* rounded; *surfaces* dull, dark blue-green, glabrous above; paler and glabrous, except for slight pubescence on the midrib, below.

Flowers about 1″ long, white, fragrant.

[1] *Robinia* was named after Jean and Vespasien Robin, herbalists to King Henry IV of France, who grew black locust in the Louvre gardens and did much to popularize the species in that country.

Fruit a flat, brown, oblong-linear, glabrous legume, 2″ to 4″ long and about ½″ wide; *seeds* 4 to 8 in each pod, about ³⁄₁₆″ long, reniform; about 24,000 (16,000–35,000) seeds to the pound.

Twigs (see generic description).

Bark on mature trees reddish brown to nearly black, deeply furrowed into rounded, interlacing, fibrous, superficially scaly ridges. According to Muenscher (265), the inner bark contains a poisonous principle; stock have died from browsing the bark or young shoots, and children have been made ill by chewing them.

GENERAL DESCRIPTION

Black locust is a medium-sized tree 40 to 60 ft high and 1 to 2 ft in diameter (max. 100 by 5* ft), and on good sites it may develop a clear straight bole. However, there are several growth forms of this species, and certain trees are spreading in habit with poorly developed trunks (173). The root system, although often shallow and wide-spreading, may develop several very deep roots, and in the arid Southwest, such vertical roots may be from 20 to 25 ft long (55). The crown is open and irregular. This tree does best on moist, rich, loamy soils or those of limestone origin, but is very cosmopolitan and is found on a wide variety of sites, especially old fields and similar cleared areas.

Abundant seed is produced at irregular intervals, and although slow to germinate, unless previously soaked in hot water, it shows a high percentage of vitality. Black locust is a fast-growing species, especially in youth, when on the best soils it will average 2 to 4 ft in height a year. It is intolerant and is not found in dense woods except as a dominant tree. Some associates are dry-soil oaks, hickories, yellow-poplar, white ash, black walnut, eastern redcedar, and shortleaf and Virginia pines. When cut, this locust sprouts vigorously from stump and roots; in this way it spreads across abandoned fields.

Black locust has been planted extensively for railroad ties and fence posts, but on certain sites the locust borer has severely damaged—even destroyed—whole plantations. Tree vigor is the important factor, and fast-growing trees on the best soils exhibit the greatest resistance (151). Black locust is used for erosion control and is naturally restocking large areas in the South. Like most legumes, this species improves the soil through the agency of nitrogen-fixing bacteria found in nodules on the roots; the leaf litter also contains nitrates and other essential nutrients.

The wood swells or contracts very little with changes in moisture content and therefore finds a special use for such items as insulator pins and "tree nails," the latter used in wooden-ship construction.

There are several forms of this species; one of these (a clone)—shipmast locust, *R. pseudoacacia* var, *rectissima* Raber (290)—is especially valuable because of its tall straight bole.

FIG. 186. *Robinia pseudoacacia*. Black locust. *1*. Twig × 1¼. *2*. Leaf × ½. *3*. Flower cluster × ½. *4*. Fruit × ¾. *5*. Fruit with one valve removed showing seeds × ¾. *6*. Bark.

Black locust was introduced into Germany very early [about 1601 (391)] and has now become in Europe one of the most widely distributed of exotic North American trees; in fact, dealers in the United States have procured considerable quantities of seed from European stock.

RANGE

Originally central Pennsylvania in the Appalachian Mountains, south to northern Georgia and Alabama, west to Indiana; also in southern Illinois, Missouri, Arkansas, and adjacent Oklahoma. Now widely planted and naturalized east of the Rocky Mountains (map, Plate 62).

Zygophyllaceae: The Caltrop family

The Zygophyllaceae number approximately 27 genera and nearly 200 species of tropical and subtropical trees, shrubs, and herbs. A few species of the genus *Guaiacum* L. (or *Guajacum*) are important trees of the American tropics, and one species ranging from Florida southward produces the lignumvitae of commerce.

CONDENSED BOTANICAL FEATURES OF THE FAMILY

Leaves deciduous or persistent, mostly opposite, pinnate or rarely simple. *Flowers* mostly perfect. *Fruit* a capsule.

GUAIACUM L.   Lignumvitae

This genus consists of seven or eight species scattered through the forests of southern Florida, Mexico, Central America, the Antilles, and the Peruvian Andes Mountains. Since only a single species is native to the extreme southern portion of the United States, the generic description is omitted.

Guaiacum sanctum L.   Holywood lignumvitae

Distinguishing characteristics. *Leaves* persistent until the following spring, with three to four pairs of entire, opposite leaflets about 1 in. long. *Flowers* with blue petals. *Fruit* orange in color, opening to release the black seeds which are covered with a scarlet fleshy layer. *Bark* chalky white, marked by numerous warty excrescences when young; later scaly.

General description. Lignumvitae is a small tree 25 to 35 ft high and 2 to 3 ft in diameter. It produces a short crooked bole and a round-topped crown of contorted branches and drooping branchlets. This species produces an exceedingly hard, heavy, oily wood, which is used for self-lubricating propeller bearings in ships.

Range. Florida Keys from Key West eastward on several other islands to the Bahamas; Puerto Rico, Haiti, Cuba, and Yucatan.

Rutaceae: The Rue family

This is a large family of 140 genera and about 1,300 species of trees and shrubs distributed over the warmer and temperate regions of the world. All are characterized by a bitter, aromatic-tasting, volatile oil. The leaves are deciduous or persistent, alternate or opposite, mostly pinnately compound, and the fruit is a capsule, berry, drupaceous, or rarely winged.

The family is of importance in horticulture, and the most noteworthy introduced genus is *Citrus* (orange, lemon, etc.) with a number of species and varieties. A number of tropical genera produce excellent cabinet woods and structural timbers.

There are four native genera containing a number of tree forms. The more common species are Hercules-club (also called toothache tree), *Zanthoxylum clava-herculis* L., a small tree of the South; common prickly-ash, *Z. americanum* Mill.; baretta, *Helietta parvifolia* (A. Gray) Benth., found in southern Texas and northeastern Mexico; the common hoptree, *Ptelea trifoliata* L., with trifoliolate leaves and elmlike fruit, native east of the Great Plains; and sea amyris (torchwood), *Amyris elemifera* L., of southern Florida and the West Indies.

Simaroubaceae: The Quassia family

The Quassia or Bitterwood family with 32 genera and about 200 species is chiefly tropical and subtropical and is represented in this country by only three genera, each with one species; all are small trees which reach only as far north as southern Florida. One of the best-known tropical species is *Quassia amara* L., bitterwood, of northern South America. The wood contains a water-soluble bitter principle which is used commercially in the manufacture of insecticides and in medicines.

Ailanthus altissima (Mill.) Swingle, ailanthus, treeofheaven ailanthus (SPN), or Chinesesumac (187), introduced from eastern Asia, has been used considerably for ornamental purposes. The name "treeofheaven" is rather dubious since the staminate flowers and bruised leaves have an exceedingly disagreeable odor. Since the species is dioecious, this difficulty can be overcome in the first instance by propagating only from pistillate trees. Ailanthus has alternate, pinnate leaves 1 to 3 ft long with 13 to 41 ovate-lanceolate leaflets which are 3 to 5 in. long and glandular-toothed only at the base. The fruit is an oblong, twisted samara 1 to 1½ in. long, with the seed cavity in the center. These samaras are borne in large clusters, and many remain on the tree during the winter. The species is now escaping, makes very fast growth, and is exceedingly hardy, especially in its ability to flourish on poor hard-packed soils, in the smoky atmosphere of industrial cities. Root suckers are plentiful and aggressive, and when once established, the tree can be destroyed only with great difficulty. Stump sprouts are also numerous and sometimes grow in length at the rate of an inch a day; the record season's height growth according to Illick (187) is 12.6 ft.

Meliaceae: The Mahogany family

The Mahogany family, which includes some of the finest known cabinet timbers, consists of about 50 genera and 800 species of trees and shrubs, most of which are tropical. The Spanish-cedar, *Cedrela odorata* L., is a product of the American tropics,

FIG. 187. *Ailanthus altissima.* Ailanthus. *1.* Twig × 1¼. *2.* Fruit × 1. *3.* Leaflet and portion of rachis × ½.

as are also the West Indies mahogany, *Swietenia mahagoni* Jacq., and the Honduran mahogany, *Swietenia macrophylla* King. The West African genera *Khaya, Lovoa,* and *Entandrophragma* produce a number of very beautiful decorative woods which are used by cabinetmakers. In Australia *Dysoxylon, Toona,* and *Owenia* are important timber-producing genera, while in India *Cedrela, Melia, Chukrasia,* and *Amoora* contribute a number of excellent woods.

The Meliaceae are represented in the United States by a single species, the West Indies mahogany, which reaches its northerly limits in southern Florida. The Chinaberry, *Melia azedarach* L., originally a native of the Orient and now widely naturalized in the South, is commonly used as an ornamental and shade tree. It can be recognized by its somewhat globose crown, large bipinnate leaves with serrate leaflet margins, and panicles of purple flowers followed by yellowish drupes.

CONDENSED BOTANICAL FEATURES OF THE FAMILY

Leaves deciduous or persistent, usually alternate and pinnately compound. *Flowers* usually perfect. *Fruit* a capsule, drupe, or berry.

SWIETENIA Jacq.   Mahogany

Swietenia is a small American genus consisting of five or six species scattered through the forests of southern Florida, Mexico, Central America, Venezuela, and Peru. S. *mahagoni* Jacq. and S. *macrophylla* King are the two principal timber species.

CONDENSED BOTANICAL FEATURES OF THE GENUS

Leaves persistent, pinnately compound with opposite leaflets. *Flowers* borne in panicles. *Fruit* a 5-valved capsule, at maturity splitting progressively from base to apex.

Swietenia mahagoni Jacq.   West Indies mahogany

Distinguishing characteristics. *Leaves* with three or four pairs of ovate-lanceolate, entire leaflets. *Fruit* a large, dark brown capsule. *Bark* reddish brown, coarsely scaly. **General description.** This mahogany is a large tropical tree, but in Florida it rarely attains a height of more than 40 to 60 ft or a d.b.h. of 12 to 24 in. Originally this species occurred quite abundantly in the southern tip of the Florida peninsula and neighboring islands, but ruthless cutting in this region has resulted in almost complete extinction of marketable trees.

Anacardiaceae: The Cashew family

This family comprises about 70 genera and nearly 600 species of trees and shrubs found mostly in the warmer regions of the world. Various drugs, dyes, waxes, and tannins are obtained from the juice which is (1) milky, or (2) clear and acrid, turning black upon drying; this feature is utilized in the production of Chinese lacquer, which is obtained from the sap of *Toxicodendron verniciflua* Stokes. Some species have highly colored woods and are valuable as timber producers, while others, such as quebracho wood of South America, one of the heaviest and hardest woods in the world, yield large amounts of tannin. The pistachio nuts of commerce come from the genus *Pistacia*. The family contains a number of plants exceedingly poisonous to man. The fruit husk of a Haitian species, *Anacardium occidentale* L., cashew, contains a caustic which is said to cause severe burns and is used by certain isolated tribes of natives to produce scarred designs on the skin, similar in appearance to tattoos. The nut, however, is edible and is used locally besides being exported. Another well-known tropical species (*Mangifera indica* L.) produces the mango fruit which is sold in the local markets.

CONDENSED BOTANICAL FEATURES OF THE FAMILY

Leaves deciduous or persistent, usually alternate, simple or compound. *Flowers* mostly dioecious or polygamo-dioecious. *Fruit* a drupe or nutlike.

Five genera with about 13 species reach tree size in the United States, but all these are small and of little economic importance. However, certain of them are so common, and in some instances so poisonous to the touch, that they should be recognized by woodsmen and campers generally.

The sumacs are probably the best-known native representatives; four species are found in the eastern half of the country. *Rhus typhina* L., staghorn sumac, is a small tree or large shrub with stout pubescent branches which bear a resemblance to a stag's horns "in the velvet." The leaves are pinnately compound with 11 to 31 leaflets, coarsely serrate on the margin. The fruit is in upright, compact, red, cone-shaped panicles. *R. glabra* L.,[1] smooth sumac, is a shrub with similar characters, except that

[1] Also in the West.

Fig. 188. *Rhus typhina.* Staghorn sumac. *1.* Twig × 1¼. *2.* Fruit × ½. *3.* Leaf × ½.

the branches are glabrous and the fruit is borne in more open clusters. *R. copallina* L., shining sumac (flameleaf sumac), is a small shrub with pinnate leaves, conspicuously winged along the rachis. *R. aromatica* Ait. [*R. canadensis* Marsh.], fragrant sumac, has trifoliolate leaves similar in appearance to those of poison-ivy; they are, however, hairy and have an aromatic odor. The fruit is red and borne in open clusters. This shrub is often found on dry, sterile hillsides.

A similar, but western, species is the skunkbush, *R. trilobata* Nutt., which is very common in the Inland Empire and the Rocky Mountains. The bruised leaves exhale a fetid odor.

All these sumacs contain tannin, which is present in greatest quantity in the leaves and flowers. The amount of tannin in the dried leaflets varies from 39 percent

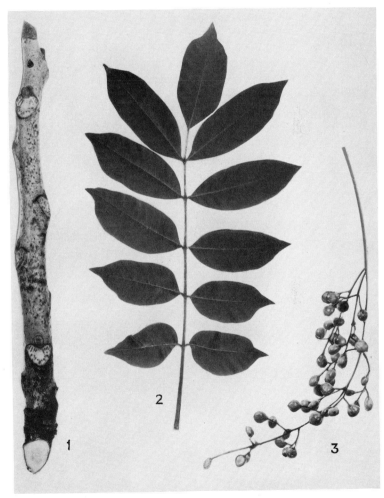

Fig. 189. *Toxicodendron vernix*. Poison-sumac. *1*. Twig × 1¼. *2*. Leaf × ½. *3*. Fruit × ½.

in *R. trilobata* to about 22 percent in *R. aromatica*. For an account of the commercial importance of sumac tannin see Bear and Sievers (27).

The remaining species, unlike those above, have a whitish fruit, and are poisonous. On this basis, some authors put them in a separate genus, *Toxicodendron*. If one considers the genus *Rhus* worldwide, there may not be sufficient reasons for splitting off the poisonous species. One or more species have intermediate characters (47).

Plants of the following taxa contain an oily substance which is exceedingly poisonous and causes a painful dermatitis. Actual contact with the bruised leaves or other portions of the plant is necessary to produce the irritation, which does not, however, begin until several hours after bruising the plant. It is also dangerous to walk through smoke from burning leaves. A few persons are especially susceptible and claim to be affected merely by passing near the offending plant. Since the poison is within the

Fig. 190. *Toxicodendron radicans.* Poison-ivy. *1.* Twig × 1¼. *2.* Leaf × ½. *3.* Fruit × ½.

plant, such cases are probably due to handling clothing or other contaminated articles which have bruised the leaves or twigs. Such articles are dangerous to handle even a year or two after contact with the poison. Some people are more or less resistant to the poison, but resistance may vary from time to time, and only a foolhardy person would needlessly expose himself by rubbing the leaves on his skin. The best practice is to avoid contact with the following species in both summer and winter: *Toxicodendron vernix* (L.) Kuntze,[1] poison-sumac, is a large swamp shrub or small tree of the East with pinnate leaves of 7 to 13 entire leaflets; the fruit is ivory-white in color and borne in open, pendent panicles. The twigs are stout, yellowish brown, and usually mottled; the leaf scars are shield-shaped with numerous bundle scars. *Toxicodendron radicans* (L.) Kuntze [*Rhus toxicodendron* auth. not L.], poison-ivy, is a vine or often small shrub with characteristic trifoliolate leaves and yellowish-white fruit. The twigs and naked buds are brownish, and the leaf scars V- or U-shaped, with several bundle scars; the lenticels are usually conspicuous. *Toxicodendron quercifolium* (Michx.) Greene, poison-oak, is a closely related species of the South. It is more shrublike, and the leaflets are more conspicuously lobed (3 to 7) than in the preceding form. The western poison-oak, *Toxicodendron diversilobum* (Torr. and Gray) Greene, is common on the Pacific Coast.

If any of these species is accidentally bruised, one may paint the contaminated area with a saturated solution of potassium permanganate. Zirconium ointments are also useful and do not stain the skin. Ferric solutions sometimes recommended may cause permanent pigmentation of the skin.

Cotinus, smoke tree, with one native species, is confined to the southern states, and *Metopium*, poisontree, with a single arborescent species, is found in Florida. *Pistacia texana* Swingle is a small tree of the Rio Grande region.

Aquifoliaceae: The Holly family

The Aquifoliaceae include 3 genera and over 300 species of trees and shrubs of wide distribution through the temperate and tropical forests of both hemispheres.

Two genera and about fifteen species of the Aquifoliaceae are found in the United States, but only one genus, *Ilex*, has arborescent forms. *Nemopanthus mucronata* Trel., the mountainholly, a large shrub common to the mountainous regions of the East, is a monotype.

CONDENSED BOTANICAL FEATURES OF THE FAMILY

Leaves often evergreen, but in some species deciduous, alternate, simple. *Flowers* usually imperfect (most species dioecious). *Fruit* a berrylike drupe.

ILEX L.   Holly

The genus *Ilex* consists of about 295 species of evergreen or deciduous trees and shrubs, widely scattered throughout the world and appearing in the floras of every continent with the exception of Australia. *I. aquifolium* L., the English holly, was successfully introduced into this country several years ago and bears fruit more plentifully

---

[1] A black varnish similar to Japanese lacquer has been made by boiling the juice.

than the American species, *I. opaca* Ait. The leafy sprays of both plants are used for Christmas decoration. In the West the climate of the Puget Sound region is favorable to holly culture, and holly farms have paid good dividends. The English holly and many of its varieties are those chiefly favored. Holly culture is also practiced to a certain extent in the Southeast where the native species is used almost exclusively.

The flora of eastern United States includes about 15 species of *Ilex*, 11 of which are arborescent. One of these, *Ilex opaca* Ait., is a timber tree of secondary importance.

CONDENSED BOTANICAL FEATURES OF THE GENUS

Leaves deciduous or persistent, entire or serrate, often spiny-toothed. *Flowers* perfect and imperfect (species dioecious or polygamous). *Fruit* drupaceous.

Ilex opaca Ait.   American holly

Distinguishing characteristics. *Leaves* persistent, leathery, elliptical, entire or spiny-toothed. *Flowers* imperfect (species dioecious), solitary or cymose, small, greenish white. *Fruit* red, [reputedly poisonous when eaten (265)], containing a few ribbed nutlets. *Bark* grayish white with numerous warty excrescences.

General description. This species is the largest of the native hollies and varies from 40 to 50 ft in height by 1 to 2 ft in diameter (max. 100 by 4 ft). The bole is straight and regular but usually short. The tree does best on deep, moist bottomlands but will persist, especially in the North, on dry, gravelly soil. American holly is very tolerant of forest competition and is also quite resistant to salt-water spray; it is used along the coast in exposed places as an ornamental.

Reproduction is facilitated by birds, but the seeds show low fertility and require two or three years to germinate. Growth is slow, and the tree matures in 100 to 150

Fig. 191. Foliage and fruit of American holly × ½.

years. It may be propagated by cuttings and is now raised in this way for decorative purposes. In this connection, the production of fruit can be assured by taking cuttings from pistillate trees only. The branches and leaves are in demand during the Christmas season, and in certain sections the natural stands of this tree have been nearly exterminated. Holly seems to have been a typically southern tree, but during the last few centuries it has moved steadily northward (seeds carried by birds) until it has now reached Clinton County, Pennsylvania, 600 ft above sea level. This is the farthest north (inland) that this species has been reported (Illick, 185).

Since the days of the Greeks, Romans, and Druids, and presumably much earlier, hollies with their evergreen leaves and bright red fruits attracted man's attention and played an important part in primitive magic, medicine, and folklore [see Dengler (99)].

Range. Coastal Plain and part of the lower Piedmont, from Massachusetts south to central Florida (also in southeastern Pennsylvania); west along the Gulf to eastern Texas and north in the Mississippi Valley to southeastern Missouri and western Kentucky (also in central and southern West Virginia, in the mountains).

Aceraceae: The Maple family

The Maple family includes but 2 genera with about 117 species of trees and shrubs. One genus, *Dipteronia* Oliv., comprises two small trees, both of central China; the remaining species are included under the genus *Acer*.

BOTANICAL FEATURES OF THE FAMILY

Leaves deciduous (rarely persistent), opposite, simple or compound, mostly estipulate; the simple leaves usually palmately lobed and long-petioled; the compound leaves pinnate.

Flowers regular; imperfect and perfect (most species polygamous or dioecious); borne in (1) racemes, panicles, corymbs, or fascicles, which appear with or before the leaves, or (2) in lateral fascicles from separate flower buds, which appear before the leaves unfold; *calyx* normally 5-parted; *petals* 5 or 0; *stamens* 4 to 12 (mostly 7 or 8); *pistils* 2-lobed, 2-celled, compressed, winged along the back.

Fruit a double (rarely triple) samara, united at the base, each half long-winged and 1-seeded; *seeds* compressed, exalbuminous. (In *Dipteronia* the wing completely surrounds the seed cavity.)

Twigs moderately stout to slender; *pith* homogeneous, terete; *terminal buds* with either imbricate or valvate scales; *lateral buds* similar but smaller; *leaf scars* more or less U-shaped; *bundle scars* 3, rarely 5 to 7 or more; *stipule scars* rarely present.

ACER L.   Maple

The genus *Acer* consists of about 115 [1] species of trees and shrubs widely scattered through the Northern Hemisphere, but most abundant in the eastern Himalayan Mountains and in central China. Old World maples range southward to the mountains of Java and northern Africa; in the New World they are found from Alaska and Canada to the mountains

DISTINGUISHING CHARACTERISTICS OF PRINCIPAL SPECIES

Species	Leaves	Flowers	Fruit
A. saccharum, sugar maple	about 5″ in diameter, 5-lobed; glabrous below	appearing with the leaves; bright yellow, long-pedicelled, apetalous; species polygamous	autumnal; U-shaped; wings about 1″ long, slightly divergent
A. nigrum, black maple	about 5″ in diameter, mostly 3-lobed; pubescent below	same	same
A. rubrum, red maple	about 4″ in diameter, usually 3-lobed, the sides of the middle lobe mostly converging toward the apex; silvery below	appearing before the leaves; short pedicelled; species polygamous corolla reddish	vernal; wings about ¾″ long, slightly divergent
A. saccharinum, silver maple	about 6″ in diameter, 5-lobed, margins of the middle lobe usually divergent; silvery below	same but apetalous	vernal; wings about 2″ long, extremely divergent
A. negundo, boxelder	3- to 7-pinnately compound	usually appearing with the leaves; species dioecious	autumnal; V-shaped; wings about 1½″ long, slightly convergent at tips
A. macrophyllum, bigleaf maple	about 10″ in diameter, deeply 5-lobed; glabrous below	same, but species polygamous	autumnal; wings about 1½″ long, slightly divergent; outside of seed cavity covered with stout, pale brown hair

[1] According to some authors, 148 species.

of Guatemala. Several species and varieties, both Asiatic and European, are used in this country as ornamentals. These include the Norway maple, *A. platanoides* L., with broad seven-lobed leaves and milky sap; and the sycamore maple, *A. pseudoplatanus* L. For various types of more formal decorations, however, the Chinese maples, including plane-tree maple, *A. truncatum* Bunge, and Amur maple, *A. ginnala* Maxim.; and the Japanese species, *A. palmatum* Thunb. and *A. japonicum* Thunb., are frequently preferred. These have for the most part small, lobed leaves, often red in color.

Of the 13 maples indigenous to the United States, 5 or 6 are important. (To avoid repetition, the botanical features for the genus are omitted; see the family description above.)

Acer saccharum Marsh.   Sugar maple

BOTANICAL FEATURES

Leaves 3" to 5" in diameter; *shape* orbicular, usually palmately 5-lobed (rarely 3-lobed); *margin of lobes* entire or sparingly sinuate-toothed; *apex* acuminate; *base* cordate; *surfaces* glabrous, bright green above, paler below.
Flowers perfect, and staminate (pistil abortive); apetalous, bright yellow, long-pedicelled, appearing with the leaves in crowded, umbel-like corymbs.
Fruit autumnal, borne on slender stems, somewhat horseshoe-shaped with nearly parallel or slightly divergent wings, about 1" long; *seeds* [1] about 6,100 (3,200–9,100) to the pound.
Twigs slender, shiny, and brownish with light-colored lenticels; *pith* white; *terminal buds* ¼" to ⅜" long, acute, sharply pointed, with 4 to 8 pairs of visible scales; *lateral buds* smaller; *leaf scars* V-shaped; *bundle scars* 3.
Bark gray, on older trees deeply furrowed, with long, irregular, thick plates or ridges, sometimes scaly, very variable.

GENERAL DESCRIPTION

Sugar maple commonly attains a height of 60 to 80 ft and a diameter of 2 ft (max. 135 by 6* ft), and under forest conditions develops a clear, straight, full bole; in the open the trunk often branches near the ground and a large dense, rounded, or ovoid crown is produced; the root system is shallow and wide-spreading to deep, depending upon the soil.

Best growth is made on moist, rich, well-drained soils, but the species will persist on more sterile sites. In the Adirondack virgin forest, the common associates are American beech and yellow birch, red spruce, eastern white pine, eastern hemlock, and an occasional black cherry; farther south, sugar maple is found in mixture with the central hard-

[1] Weight of seeds in *Acer* refers to the samaras with more or less of the wings removed.

FIG. 192. *Acer saccharum*. Sugar maple. *1*. Twig × 1¼. *2*. Flower cluster × ½. *3*. Staminate flower × 2. *4*. Perfect flower × 2. *5*. Fruit × ¾. *6*. Leaf × ½. *7*. Bark of old-growth tree.

woods, including basswood, white ash, yellow-poplar, hickories, and oaks. Sugar maple is found in 23 forest-cover types (127).

In good seed years (2- to 5-year intervals), just before the leaves expand, nearly every tree is so covered with flowers that at a distance it appears to be enveloped in a yellow haze. By autumn, enormous quantities of the winged fruits have developed and are released. Seed traps indicate a fall of 8 million of these per acre under some old-growth stands. The following spring countless numbers of seedlings unfold their straplike cotyledons as they emerge from their winter covering of leaves. They prosper even under a heavy forest cover and are extremely tolerant throughout life. Sugar maple also regenerates by stump sprouts and sometimes root suckers. It may attain an age of 200 to 300 years.

Besides its primary importance as a timber producer, sugar maple is used as an ornamental tree and also yields valuable syrup and sugar. Thirty-two gallons of the spring sap may be boiled down to a gallon of syrup or 8 pounds of sugar, but the sugar content of the sap varies widely from tree to tree (210). Individuals are being sought with the highest possible sugar content, to use in tree-breeding programs for the production of high-yielding sugar orchards.

Fig. 193. Open-grown form of sugar maple.

Fig. 194. Bark of sugar maple.

Eastern United States except for the south Atlantic and Gulf Coastal Plains (map, Plate 63).

Acer barbatum Michx.   Florida maple; southern sugar maple

This species is similar to *A. saccharum*, except for its smaller, more undulate-margined leaves, which are blue-green and often tomentose on the lower surface. The tree is also smaller and more spreading in habit than the northern sugar maple, for which it has often been mistaken. It ranges through the Coastal Plain and Piedmont regions from southeastern Virginia to northern Florida, and westward to eastern Texas and southern Arkansas.

Acer nigrum Michx. f.   Black maple

Comparative botanical features. *Leaves* somewhat like those of sugar maple but usually three-lobed, pubescent in varying degrees, and with a drooping habit; base of petiole usually bears two stipules, or stipulelike appendages. *Twigs* commonly stouter, with conspicuous warty lenticels and larger, more hairy buds. *Fruit* often with a slightly larger seed cavity than that of sugar maple. *Bark* more corrugated than that of sugar maple. **General description.** Except for the above differences, these two maples are very similar; in fact, according to some authors, black maple is a

Fig. 195. *Acer nigrum.* Black maple. *1.* Twig × 1¼. *2.* Leaf × ½. *3.* Bark.

variety of sugar maple (var. *nigrum*) rather than a separate species. The silvical features of this form are similar to those already given for sugar maple, except that black maple will grow on the moister soils of river bottoms. Where the ranges of sugar and black maple overlap, frequent hybridization occurs, with the hybrids resembling whichever parent is most abundant locally.

Range. Northeastern United States; Ohio and upper Mississippi River Valleys (map, Plate 63).

1. *Acer saccharum.*   2. *Acer nigrum.*

PLATE 63

Acer rubrum L.   Red maple

BOTANICAL FEATURES

Leaves 2″ to 6″ in diameter; *shape* orbicular, palmately 3- or 5-lobed (usually 3) with acute sinuses, sides of the terminal lobe usually convergent; *margin of lobes* serrate; *surfaces* light green above, at maturity paler and glaucous below.

Flowers perfect, and staminate; appearing in early spring before the leaves, yellow or bright red; short- to long-pedicelled, fascicled; *corolla* present.

Fruit borne in clusters on long slender stems; wings slightly divergent, about ¾″ long, maturing in late spring; *seeds* about 22,800 (12,700–38,200) to the pound.

Twigs slender, dark red, lustrous, odorless or nearly so, dotted with minute lenticels; *terminal buds* obtuse with 2 to 4 pairs of visible, red scales; *lateral* and *collateral buds* smaller than the terminal, slightly stalked; *leaf scars* V-shaped; *bundle scars* 3.

Bark on young trees smooth and light gray, eventually on the older trunks breaking up into long, narrow, scaly plates separated by shallow fissures.

GENERAL DESCRIPTION

Red maple [1] is a medium-sized tree 50 to 70 ft high and 12 to 24 in. in diameter (max. 136* by 5 ft) with a long, fairly clear bole, an irregular

[1] This species and the silver maple are often called the "soft maples" or "swamp maples" in contrast to sugar and black maples which are termed "hard maples."

Fig. 196. *Acer rubrum*. Red maple. *1.* Perfect flowers × ¾. *2.* Staminate flowers × ¾. *3.* Fruit × ¾. *4.* Leaf × ½. *5.* Bark of old tree (on younger trees similar to that of silver maple). *6.* Flower buds × 1¼. *7.* Twig × 1¼.

410

or rounded crown, and a shallow root system. It is characteristic of swampy sites and is associated with such species as black ash, black tupelo, cottonwood, American elm, and the bottomland oaks; however, red maple is often found in drier locations, and in the Northeast is commonly mixed with white pine and the northern hardwoods on moderately moist, sandy loam soils, or even on rocky uplands. Over its extensive north-south range from Newfoundland to southern Florida, and West to the Prairies, it is a most cosmopolitan species, occurring in 54 forest-cover types. Associates, including both hardwoods and softwoods, number more than seventy.

Red maple is one of the first trees to flower in the spring, long before the leaves appear. The fruit matures in early summer and germinates immediately or may hold over until the following spring. Growth is rapid, and maturity is reached in 70 to 80 years, although certain individuals may attain an age of 150 years. Many second-growth stands are of sprout origin, but quality is often poor due to butt rot. On a tolerance scale, this tree is intermediate. This species is said to be the most abundant and widespread tree of eastern North America.

Red maple is used widely as an ornamental and shade tree, and at least in the North it provides a spectacular display after the first fall frosts. Then its leaves turn to a brilliant scarlet against the dark green spruces and pines, and the northern woodlands present an unforgettable sight.

RANGE

Eastern United States (map, Plate 64).

Acer saccharinum L.   Silver maple

BOTANICAL FEATURES

Leaves 6″ to 7″ in diameter; *shape* orbicular, deeply palmately 5-lobed, the sides of the terminal lobe divergent, the lobes often again lobed, sinuses often rounded; *margin of lobes* serrate; *surfaces* pale green above, silvery below at maturity.

Flowers perfect, and staminate; among the first to appear in the spring and long before the leaves unfold; *corolla* lacking, otherwise similar to those of red maple.

Fruit the largest of the northeastern maples, with widely divergent wings 1½″ to 2″ long; often aborted on one side; maturing in late spring, germinating as soon as released; *seeds* about 1,400 (900–1,900) to the pound.

Twigs and *buds* very similar to those of red maple, but often more reddish brown, and with a decidedly fetid odor when bruised.

Bark on young trees silvery gray, later breaking up into long, thin, scaly plates which are unattached at the ends.

Fig. 197. *Acer saccharinum.* Silver maple. *1.* Staminate and perfect flowers, respectively, × 1. *2.* Fruit × ¾. *3.* Leaf × ½. *4.* Twig × 1¼. *5.* Bark.

Silver maple is a medium-sized tree 60 to 80 ft high and 2 to 3 ft in diameter (max. 120 by 7* ft) and usually has a short bole which divides near the ground into several upright branches; the crown is wide-spreading, and the root system shallow. This maple is a characteristic bottom-land species and is not found on dry soils. Young trees recover well even from several weeks of complete inundation (174). Associates are many fewer than in red maple, and besides that species include American elm, cottonwood, sycamore, sweetgum, black willow, and river birch.

Silver maple is a fast-growing tree and reaches maturity in about 125 years. The branches are brittle and often break off during high winds or when loaded with snow or ice; this contributes to early disintegration since wood-destroying fungi readily enter the exposed wood. Several horticultural varieties are used for ornamental planting, including the cut-leaf form, var. *wieri* Pax. Planted trees seem to do well even on dry clay soils.

RANGE

Eastern United States (map, Plate 64).

1. *Acer rubrum.*

2. *Acer saccharinum.*

PLATE 64

Acer negundo L.   Boxelder

Leaves pinnately compound with 3 to 7 (rarely 9) leaflets; *leaflets* short-petioled; *shape* very variable, mostly ovate, oval, obovate, or ovate-lanceolate; *apex* acuminate; *base* cuneate, rounded, or cordate; *margin* coarsely serrate, lobed or occasionally again

Fig. 198. *Acer negundo.* Boxelder. *1.* Twig × 1¼. *2.* Leaf × ½. *3.* Fruit × ¾. *4.* Bark. (*Photograph by R. A. Cockrell.*)

divided; *surfaces* light green, glabrous or slightly pubescent above, pale green, pubescent along the veins below; *rachis* stout, enlarged at the base.

Flowers imperfect (species dioecious), apetalous, yellow-green, the *staminate* fascicled, the *pistillate* in drooping racemes, appearing with or before the leaves.

Fruit borne on slender stems, V-shaped, with slightly convergent wings 1″ to 1½″ long; *seeds* about 11,800 (8,200–15,000) to the pound.

Twigs stout, green to purplish green, lustrous or covered with a glaucous bloom, lenticellate; *pith* terete, white; *terminal buds* ovoid, with about 4 visible, usually bluish white, tomentose scales; *lateral buds* short-stalked, appressed; *leaf scars* V-shaped; *bundle scars* 3 (rarely 5).

Bark thin, light brown, with narrow, rounded, anastomosing ridges separated by shallow fissures; on old trees more deeply furrowed.

GENERAL DESCRIPTION

Boxelder has little if any commercial importance but is one of the commonest and best known of the maples. It is usually a small or medium-sized tree (max. 75 by 6* ft) with an irregular bole, shallow root system, and bushy, spreading crown. Most common on deep, moist soils, it is also found on poorer sites and is perhaps the most aggressive of the maples in maintaining itself in unfavorable locations. The early settlers in the Middle West were acquainted with its hardiness, especially in extremes of climate, and planted it widely as a street tree and around their homesteads. Boxelder, however, is not a decorative tree; and although it makes rapid growth, it is short-lived and usually of poor form. Sprouts usually emerge along the trunk and when these are removed, others in increasing numbers appear.

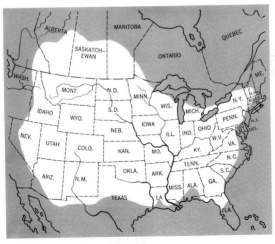

1. *Acer negundo.*   2. *Acer macrophyllum.*

PLATE 65

United States and southwestern Canada (map, Plate 65).

Acer macrophyllum Pursh   Bigleaf maple

BOTANICAL FEATURES

Leaves 8″ to 12″ in diameter; *shape* orbicular or nearly so, usually palmately 5-lobed; *margin of lobes* entire to sinuate or sparingly toothed; *apex* acute; *base* cordate; *surfaces* glabrous, bright green above, pale below; *petioles* frequently lactiferous.
Flowers perfect, and staminate; yellow, scented; in slightly puberulous racemes appearing with the leaves.
Fruit 1¼″ to 2″ long with slightly divergent wings; the portion covering the seed densely pubescent; *seeds* about 3,100 (2,800–3,400) to the pound.
Twigs stout, dark red, or reddish brown to greenish brown, often dotted with rather conspicuous lenticels; *pith* white, homogeneous; *terminal buds* stout, blunt, with 3 to 4 pairs of green- to reddish-colored scales; *lateral buds* small, slightly appressed; *leaf scars* V-shaped to U-shaped, with 5 to 9 bundle scars.
Bark light gray-brown and smooth on young stems, but becoming darker and deeply furrowed on old trunks.

GENERAL DESCRIPTION

Bigleaf maple is one of the few commercial hardwoods on the Pacific Coast. It grows on a variety of soils throughout its range and is usually a small to medium-sized tree some 50 ft tall and 1½ ft in diameter. Best development is made on rich bottomlands, where it attains a height of 100 ft and a d.b.h. of 3 to 4 ft (max. 8* ft). The trees are usually scattered or in small groves in association with both coniferous and other broad-leaved species, of which Douglas-fir, western redcedar, western hemlock, red alder, northern black cottonwood, Oregon white oak, and Pacific madrone should be mentioned. In some sections of southwestern Oregon, however, this maple is the principal forest species, particularly where it invades logged and burned lands.

A rather narrow crown is developed under forest conditions, and the bole is not infrequently free of limbs for one-half to two-thirds of its length. In more or less open situations the trunk usually divides a short distance above the ground into several stout, ascending branches, forming a rather compact ovate to subglobose crown. Regardless of habitat, however, the root system is generally shallow and wide-spreading.

An abundance of seed is produced annually, and natural regeneration by this means is excellent; stump sprouts are also quite vigorous. Growth is rapid during the first 40 to 60 years, but decreases considerably in later life, and maturity is eventually reached between 200 and 300 years.

FIG. 199. *Acer macrophyllum.* Bigleaf maple. *1.* Twig × 1¼. *2.* Raceme of staminate flowers × ¾. *3.* Raceme with perfect and staminate flowers × ¾. *4.* Staminate, pistillate, and perfect flowers, respectively, × 2. *5.* Fruit × ¾. *6.* Leaf × ⅓. *7.* Bark.

Old trees are commonly defective; large burls occasionally develop along their boles. The demand for western maple burls and fancy grained logs has had much to do with increasing the commercial importance of this species.

RANGE

Pacific Coast and Sierra Nevada Mountains (map, Plate 65). *Altitudinal distribution:* Sea level to 1,000 ft in British Columbia; from 3,000 to 7,000 ft in Southern California.

A. pensylvanicum L.   Striped maple
A. spicatum Lam.   Mountain maple

Two very common maples of the northeastern states and Canada are *Acer pensylvanicum* L., striped maple, and *A. spicatum* Lam., mountain maple. Both are small trees or large shrubs found typically in cool moist locations. Striped maple (moosewood) has bright green bark marked by vertical white lines and leaves which are three-lobed and finely doubly serrate. In contrast, the bark of mountain maple is brown, and the leaves three- to five-lobed with coarsely singly serrate margins.

Hippocastanaceae: The Buckeye family

The Hippocastanaceae comprise 3 genera and about 30 species of trees and shrubs scattered through the forests of Mexico, Central America, eastern and western United States, southeastern Europe, eastern Asia, and India. As a group they are of little value for the timber which they produce; but many of them, either because of their showy flowers or handsome foliage, are highly prized for ornamental purposes. One genus, *Aesculus,* is represented in North America.

CONDENSED BOTANICAL FEATURES OF THE FAMILY

Leaves deciduous, opposite, palmately compound. *Flowers* perfect and imperfect. *Fruit* a capsule.

AESCULUS L.   Buckeye; horse-chestnut

The genus *Aesculus* consists of about 16 species of trees or large shrubs widely distributed through the forests of the Northern Hemisphere and into South America. *A. hippocastanum* L., the horse-chestnut, originally a native of the Balkan peninsula, is now widely planted throughout the world as a street and shade tree. It was introduced into the United States many years ago and has become naturalized in certain sections of the East. Horse-chestnut is characterized by palmately compound leaves with seven obovate leaflets, a spiny capsular fruit, and dark brown to nearly black

FIG. 200. Flowers and leaves of horse-chestnut.

sticky buds. Red horse-chestnut, A. ×carnea Hayne,[1] readily recognized while in blossom by its flesh-colored to scarlet flowers, enjoys a widespread ornamental use in the Pacific Northwest. A. parviflora Walt. is a shrubby form of buckeye suitable for formal planting.

Six species and several varieties of the genus Aesculus are included in the arborescent flora of the United States. A. octandra Marsh., however, is the only moderately important species. A single species, A. californica (Spach) Nutt., occurs on the Pacific Coast, but is of little or no commercial significance. The other forms are found in the East.

CONDENSED BOTANICAL FEATURES OF THE GENUS

Leaves palmately 5- to 9-foliolate, with a long petiole; margin serrate. Flowers bell-shaped, conspicuous, borne in upright, many-flowered panicles. Fruit a large, leathery capsule with from 1 to 5 seeds, marked by a conspicuous light-gray hilum.

Aesculus octandra Marsh.   Yellow buckeye

Distinguishing characteristics. Leaves palmately five-foliolate, with nearly elliptical, serrate leaflets. Flowers yellowish white, with the stamens usually shorter than the petals. Fruit mostly smooth. Twigs stout, with large nonresinous terminal buds; leaf scars large, obdeltoid with several bundle scars arranged in a V-shaped pattern. Bark breaking up into fine scales.

General description. The yellow buckeye is a medium-sized to large tree 60 to 90 ft high and 2 to 3 ft in diameter (max. 100 by 5* ft). Best development is made on

[1] (A. hippocastanum ×A. pavia.)

Fig. 201. *Aesculus octandra.* Yellow buckeye. *1.* Twig × 1¼. *2.* Leaf × ½.
3. Fruit × ¾. *4.* Seed × ¾.

deep fertile soils in the mountains of North Carolina and Tennessee, where it occurs in mixture with other hardwoods. In the northern part of its range it is a bottomland species, but farther south it leaves the stream banks and ascends high mountainous slopes, where locally it is sometimes one of the principal species in the stand. Growth is fairly rapid, and maturity is reached in 60 to 80 years.

Range. Extreme southwestern Pennsylvania south along the Appalachians to eastern Tennessee, northern Georgia, and Alabama; west through central Ohio to southern Illinois.

Aesculus glabra Willd.   Ohio buckeye; fetid buckeye

This species is similar in appearance and geographical distribution to the yellow buckeye. It differs, however, in the following features: (1) the leaves are slightly smaller, with leaflets more nearly lanceolate; (2) the bruised foliage and twigs give off a disagreeable odor; (3) the stamens are longer than the corolla; (4) the fruit is somewhat spiny; (5) the bud scales are prominently keeled.

FIG. 202. Bark of yellow buckeye. (*Photograph by U.S. Forest Service.*)

Rhamnaceae: The Buckthorn family

The Rhamnaceae include 45 genera and about 550 species of trees and shrubs (sometimes lianas, rarely herbs) widely scattered through the tropics and warmer regions of the world. *Ceanothus* L., a larger American genus, consists of about 80 shrubby species, many of which are found in the semiarid West. Here they serve as browse for both sheep and cattle, although some species are much more suitable for this purpose than others. The roots, bark, stems, and even leaves of many rhamnaceous plants contain compounds suitable for pharmaceutical purposes. The seeds of several *Ceanothus* species are eaten by Indians, although most of them are quite bitter and are usually shunned even by livestock. The fruits of the common jujube, *Ziziphus jujube* Mill., are edible, and this species is now widely cultivated in many sections of Asia. While there are a few species which produce timbers of commercial rank, the family is not an important timber-contributing group.

Ten genera and about one hundred species of the Rhamnaceae are found in the United States. *Rhamnus,* however, is the only genus with species of special economic interest. Probably the heaviest wood grown in the United States is from leadwood (sp. gr. 1.3), *Krugiodendron ferreum* (Vahl) Urban, found in southern Florida.

CONDENSED BOTANICAL FEATURES OF THE FAMILY

Leaves deciduous or persistent, alternate or subopposite, simple. *Flowers* perfect or perfect and imperfect. *Fruit* drupaceous, winged, or capsular.

RHAMNUS L.   Buckthorn; cascara

Rhamnus comprises 80 to 90 species of trees and shrubs widely scattered through the temperate and tropical forests of both hemispheres. *R. cathartica* L., the European buckthorn, was introduced into the United States for decorative purposes and has been naturalized in many sections of the East, particularly through central New York State.

Twelve species of *Rhamnus* are native to the United States, and five of these are arborescent. *Rhamnus purshiana* DC. is an important tree of the Pacific Coast.

CONDENSED BOTANICAL FEATURES OF THE GENUS

Leaves deciduous or persistent, alternate or subopposite, simple. *Flowers* perfect or perfect and imperfect, axillary. *Fruit* drupaceous.

Rhamnus purshiana DC.   Cascara buckthorn

Distinguishing characteristics.   *Leaves* simple, elliptical to oblong-ovate, finely serrate, and often remotely revolute. *Flowers* axillary in cymes, yellowish green, 5-merous. *Fruit* globose, bluish black, with two or three obovoid nutlets. *Twigs* slender, with naked, hoary tomentose buds; *leaf scars* elevated, narrowly lunate, with a few scattered bundle scars; *pith* homogeneous. *Bark* smooth, or superficially scaly.

General description.   Cascara buckthorn, also known as bearberry, bitter-bark, and chittimwood, is a small tree usually not more than 30 to 40 ft high and 10 to 15 in. in diameter (max. 60° by 3° ft). It is moderately gregarious and often forms small groves on moist bottomlands and burns. It is by no means restricted to such sites, however, and may also be found on gravelly or sandy soils, near sea level or at moderately high elevations. It occurs as an understory species in Douglas-fir forests and is com-

Fig. 203. *Rhamnus purshiana.* Cascara buckthorn. *1.* Twig × 1. *2.* Leaf × ⅗.

monly mixed with grand fir, western hemlock, bigleaf and vine maples, and red alder in many sections of the Pacific Northwest.

The cascara buckthorn is a prolific annual seeder, although the seeds not infrequently remain dormant until the second season after their release. Moist forest litter and mucky soils make the best seedbeds. Growth is extremely rapid on such sites, and maturity is reached in about 50 years.

When the early Spanish missionaries explored northern California, they found that the Indians near the Oregon border were using as a cathartic the intensely bitter bark of this tree, which was christened cascara sagrada, or the "bark holy."

In modern times, Portland, Oregon has become the center for collectors to bring in their annual peel, which may amount to some 5 million pounds (12). The peeled tree dies, but vigorous sprouts seem to ensure a continuing supply of the bark.

Range. Southwestern British Columbia south through western Washington, Oregon, to central California; eastward through northern Washington and Idaho to western Montana. *Commercial range*—Washington and Oregon.

Tiliaceae: The Linden family

The Tiliaceae comprise 41 genera and approximately 400 species of trees, shrubs, and herbs, widely scattered throughout the world, but most abundant in the Southern Hemisphere. Jute, which consists of the bast fibers of several herbaceous species of the genus *Corchorus,* finds use in the production of papers, cordage, and coarse fabrics. *Elaeocarpus, Pentace, Grewia,* and *Tilia* are notable timber-producing groups. Although three genera of this family are found on the North American continent, only one, *Tilia,* is arborescent.

BOTANICAL FEATURES OF THE FAMILY

Leaves deciduous, alternate, simple, stipulate.
Flowers perfect, actinomorphic, borne in cymes or corymbs; *sepals* 5; *petals* 5; *stamens* numerous, in multiples of 5; *pistils* 1, with a 2- to 10-celled ovary.
Fruit a capsule, drupe, berry, or nut; *seeds* albuminous.

TILIA L.   Basswood; linden (SPN)

While not an ancient group geologically, there are, nevertheless, about 30 known fossil species of *Tilia* scattered through the cooler parts of the Northern Hemisphere. The modern genus also includes approximately 30 species [1] widely distributed in eastern North America, Mexico, Europe, central China, and southern Japan. Several exotics are employed ornamentally in both eastern and western United States, par-

[1] Sixty-five species, according to Small (325).

ticularly the European cut-leaf linden, *T. platyphyllos* var. *laciniata* K. Koch, the little-leaf linden, *T. cordata* Mill., and the Japanese linden, *T. japonica* Simonkai. A few of the American basswoods are also suitable for decorative use, while basswood honey is widely known in the eastern part of the country. The name basswood may have originated on account of the strong, tough bark or bast fibers which were used by primitive peoples for cordage of various sorts.

The Check List (212) recognizes but 4 native species of *Tilia*, while some authors have described as many as 18. For a description of southern lindens see "Guide to Southern Trees" by Harrar and Harrar (163).

BOTANICAL FEATURES OF THE GENUS

Leaves mostly ovate to orbicular, serrate; usually unequally cordate at the base; *cotyledons* palmately 5-lobed (this is a very conspicuous feature of young seedlings).
Flowers perfect, pale yellow, fragrant, borne in long-stalked cymes or corymbs, adnate to a pale green, membranous bract.
Fruit a subglobose, woody, nutlike structure containing 1 to 2 albuminous seeds.
Twigs slender to stout, zigzag, glabrous or pubescent; *pith* homogeneous, terete; *terminal buds* wanting; *lateral buds* mucilaginous, stout, more or less inequilateral, usually with 2 or 3 visible scales, divergent; *leaf scars* semicircular; *bundle scars* numerous, scattered, often indistinct; *stipule scars* and *twig scars* rather conspicuous.

Tilia americana L. [*Tilia glabra* Vent.]   American basswood;
American linden (SPN)

BOTANICAL FEATURES

Leaves 5″ to 6″ long, 3″ to 4″ wide; *shape* broadly ovate to suborbicular; *margin* coarsely serrate; *apex* acuminate; *base* unequally cordate to almost truncate; *surfaces* glabrous except for axillary hairs below; *cotyledons* palmately 5-lobed.
Flowers appearing when the leaves are nearly full grown, ½″ long, borne in few-flowered cymes, the stalk long and slender, attached to a narrow leaflike bract 4″ to 5″ long, persisting on the mature fruit.
Fruit ⅓″ to ½″ in diameter, clustered, short-ovoid or subglobose, nutlike, grayish tomentose; *bract* persistent, very characteristic; *seeds* about 5,000 (3,000–8,000) to the pound.
Twigs green to red, zigzag; *pith* terete; *terminal buds* lacking; *lateral buds* inequilateral, mucilaginous, usually with two visible scales; *leaf scars* half-elliptical; *bundle scars* numerous, scattered, not always distinct; *stipule scars* prominent.
Bark on young trees green or grayish green, later gray to brown, breaking up into narrow ridges, somewhat scaly on the surface.

FIG. 204. *Tilia americana*. American basswood. *1*. Leaf × ½. *2*. Bark of old tree, and young sprout, respectively. *3*. Flowers × ½. *4*. Fruits showing persistent leafy bract × ½. *5*. Twig × 1¼.

This is probably the most important of the basswoods and is highly regarded as a timber tree. It varies from 70 to 80 ft in height and 2 to 3 ft in diameter (max. 140 by 5* ft) with a long, clear, cylindrical, sometimes buttressed bole and deep but wide-spreading root system. Best development is reached on moist, deep, loamy soils. Since this tree is found in 16 forest types, the list of associates is lengthy. Some of the more common are eastern hemlock, northern red oak, red and sugar maples, white ash, American elm, and black cherry. American basswood is a very prolific sprouter and quickly regenerates by this means; in fact, the occurrence of a circle of sprouts around a stump or an old decadent tree is so characteristic that basswood can often be identified at some distance by this feature.

PLATE 66. *Tilia americana.*

Seeds are borne almost yearly but require two years or longer for germination unless given special treatment [Meade (248)]. The young seedlings are easily recognized in the forest by their palmately lobed cotyledons, which look quite different from the mature basswood leaves (page 219). Subsequent growth is rather fast, and the tree matures in 90 to 140 years. Basswood is moderately tolerant and will grow under a considerable cover, especially in youth. It is an important soil improver; in a study of the mineral content of the leaves of 24 hardwoods and softwoods, basswood was highest in calcium and magnesium, and also yielded significant amounts of nitrogen, phosphorus, and potassium (127).

In addition to the valuable timber which it produces, American basswood is highly prized in certain localities for its honey. The Iroquois Indians made rope from the bark by soaking it in water for several weeks or months to allow the nonfibrous portions to ret, after which it was twisted into the desired form.

Northern half of eastern United States (map, Plate 66).

Tilia heterophylla Vent.   White basswood; beetree linden (SPN)

Distinguishing characteristics. *Leaves* similar to those of the preceding species except for the lower surface, which is densely whitish or sometimes brownish tomentose. *Flowers* similar to those of *T. americana,* except for their smaller size (¼ in. long) and greater number (10 to 25) in the cluster. *Fruit* slightly smaller; other features like those of the preceding species.

General description. The white basswood is typically a southern species, attaining a height of 60 to 80 ft and a d.b.h. of 18 to 30 in. Its silvical features are similar to those of the preceding species.

Range. Southeastern Indiana, southeast through West Virginia, the upper Piedmont region of the Carolinas, and Georgia to western Florida, and central Alabama; north to central Kentucky.

Cactaceae: The Cactus family

Even though the Cactaceae are not of importance as timber producers, they are often the only woody plants in many parts of the arid West, and hence brief mention of them seems justified. The family includes about 120 genera and over 1,200 species of trees, shrubs, and herbs, the majority xerophytic and indigenous to the Western Hemi-

Fɪɢ. 205. Barrel cactus. (*Photograph by Forrest Shreve.*)

sphere. In point of numbers, best development is reached in Central America and Mexico, although some are found in South America, and several others occur in the western United States and southwestern Canada.

The leaves of most cacti are reduced to spines, so that photosynthesis necessarily takes place in the green portions of the fleshy stems. In several species of *Opuntia*, small awl-shaped leaves are produced, but they are normally fugacious. *Pereskia* and *Pereskiopsis*, two tropical genera, are featured by broad, simple leaves which persist throughout the growing season. The genera *Carnegeia*, *Cephalocereus*, *Cereus*, *Lemaireocereus*, and a few other produce tree forms, some 50 to 60 ft high. The stems are commonly columnar, fluted, profusely branched, and fleshy; one, *Carnegeia gigantea* Britt. and Rose, is particularly common in the Arizona deserts.

Hylocereus undatus Britt. and Rose is the common night-blooming cereus frequently planted in dooryards throughout its range. The prickly pears, *Opuntia* spp., with their green, flattened, spinose, segmentlike stems, are common in many sections, and are frequently used for ornamental planting. *Aporocactus flagelliformis* Lemm., the rattail cactus, and *Schlumbergera truncatus* Schum., are favorite house plants.

The juices of certain species of *Lophophoria* contain alkaloids which when taken internally affect the optic nerve, and the fruits of some of the tunas (*Opuntia* spp.) exhibit powerful diuretic properties. Mexican strawberries are the fruits of *Echinocereus enneacanthus* Engelm., and a mordant for cochineal dye is obtained from the succulent fruits of *Opuntia imbricata* DC. A sweet matrix known locally as cactus candy is made from the pulp of the barrel cactus, *Ferocactus wislizenii* Britt. and Rose. It is a widespread belief that potable water may be obtained from the base of this cactus, but several competent observers state that the water is often highly alkaline (depending upon the season) and contains mucilaginous material which makes it undesirable for this purpose. It might, however, be used in an emergency.

CONDENSED BOTANICAL FEATURES OF THE FAMILY

Leaves reduced to spines; awl-shaped and fugacious; or, in two genera, broad and simple.
Flowers usually perfect, actinomorphic, solitary; *calyx* often petaloid; *corolla* showy, often brilliant red; *stamens* many; *pistil* 1-celled.
Fruit a many-seeded edible berry.

Nyssaceae: The Tupelo family

The Nyssaceae include but 3 genera and about 10 species [1] of trees or shrubs scattered through the forests of eastern and southeastern North America, the Himalaya, Tibet, and the Malayan Archipelago. The three genera, *Nyssa* L., *Davidia* Baill., and *Camptotheca* Decne., are placed in the Cornaceae by several authors. *Nyssa* is the only genus represented on the North American continent.

[1] Sixteen genera and ninety species according to Small (325), who includes the dogwoods in this family. Conversely, the 1953 "Check List" (212) places *Nyssa* in the Cornaceae.

Leaves deciduous, alternate, simple, estipulate.
Flowers perfect or imperfect (species dioecious or polygamo-dioecious), 5-merous.
Fruit a drupe, or samaralike; *seeds* albuminous.

NYSSA L.   Tupelo

The modern genus consists of five arborescent or shrubby species. One of these occurs in central and western China, another from the Himalaya to Java, and the remaining species are in the eastern United States. Fossil leaves, pollen, fruit, and wood of many preglacial *Nyssa* species are widely distributed in Tertiary strata across Europe, Asia, and North America. Large numbers of fruits are found in the brown coal of Brandon, Vermont (119).

Fig. 206. Fruit pits of *Nyssa* spp. *1. N. aquatica.* 2. *N. sylvatica.* 3. *N. sylvatica* var. *biflora.* 4. *N. ogeche.* (All × 1.)

BOTANICAL FEATURES OF THE GENUS

Leaves deciduous, alternate, simple, often crowded toward the tips of the twigs, especially on side branchlets.
Flowers perfect or imperfect (species polygamo-dioecious), appearing with or before the leaves, small, greenish white, borne in capitate clusters, racemes, or solitary.

DISTINGUISHING CHARACTERISTICS OF IMPORTANT SPECIES

Species	Leaves	Fruit	Twigs
N. aquatica, water tupelo	about 7" long, oblong-obovate, sometimes irregularly toothed	about 1" long, reddish purple; the pit prominently ribbed	stout; buds globose, ⅛" or less in diameter
N. sylvatica, black tupelo	about 4" long, obovate, rarely toothed	about ½" long, blue-black; the pit indistinctly ribbed	slender; buds ovoid, ¼" long, commonly divergent

Fig. 207. *Nyssa aquatica.* Water tupelo. *1.* Twig × 1¼. *2.* Staminate flowers × ¾. *3.* Leaf × ½. *4.* Fruits × ¾. *5.* Pit showing thin wings or ridges × 1½.

Fruit an ovoid or oblong drupe, with a 1-celled, 1-seeded, winged or ridged pit.

Twigs slender to stout, glabrous, greenish brown, olive-brown, or reddish brown; *pith* mostly diaphragmed; *terminal buds* present, covered with several imbricated scales; *lateral buds* similar but smaller; *spur growth* often abundant; *leaf scars* reniform to semicircular; *bundle scars* 3.

Nyssa aquatica L.   Water tupelo

BOTANICAL FEATURES

Leaves 5″ to 7″ long, 2″ to 4″ wide; *shape* oblong-obovate; *margin* entire to repand-toothed; *apex* acute to acuminate; *base* cuneate to rounded; *surfaces* dark green and lustrous above, paler and more or less downy below.

Flowers appearing in March and April; *staminate* in dense clusters; *pistillate* solitary on long slender peduncles; stamens present, often functioning.

Fruit pendent on slender stalks; about 1″ long, oblong, dark reddish purple; *pit* light brown to whitish and conspicuously ribbed with about 10 thin ridges; *seeds* about 450 to the pound.

Twigs rather stout, reddish brown; pith diaphragmed; *terminal buds* yellowish, usually small and somewhat globose or rounded, 1/16″ to 1/8″ in diameter; *lateral buds* small and inconspicuous; *leaf scars* rounded; *bundle scars* 3, conspicuous.

Bark thin, brownish gray with scaly ridges.

GENERAL DESCRIPTION

Water tupelo is a medium-sized to large tree 80 to 90 ft high and 3 to 4 ft in diameter (max. 110* by nearly 6* ft). The trunk bulges conspicuously at its base but tapers rapidly to a long, clear bole; the crown is rather narrow and usually open. Water tupelo is one of the most characteristic of southern swamp trees and is found on sites which are periodically under water. For a short time during the summer, this tree may be found on dry ground, while in the fall and winter the water is often 3 to 6 ft deep over the same area. Water tupelo occurs in almost pure stands or mixed with baldcypress, which is its almost constant companion. Other associates include overcup and water oaks, black willow, swamp cottonwood, red maple, sweetgum, and slash pine.

This tupelo is a prolific annual seeder, and the heavy seeds are largely

Fig. 208. A water tupelo swamp, showing old-growth trees and high-water mark. (*Photograph by U.S. Forest Service.*)

Fig. 209. Bark of water tupelo. (*Photograph by J. C. Th. Uphof.*)

NYSSACEAE　431

distributed by water. Following the recession of high water, they become lodged in the mud and up to 50 percent of them may germinate. The growth of trees on moist but well-drained bottomlands is rapid, while that of trees standing on extremely swampy sites is much slower. Water tupelo is intolerant, and on the better sites is suppressed by other species.

The timber is commercially important, and the root wood, which is especially light and spongy, is used locally for bottle corks and fish-net floats. Tupelo honey is an important item in a number of localities where the trees are abundant.

Atlantic and Gulf Coastal Plains and Mississippi River Valley (map, Plate 67). Also in Mexico.

1. *Nyssa aquatica.*   2. *Nyssa sylvatica.*

PLATE 67

Nyssa sylvatica Marsh.   Black tupelo; blackgum

Comparative botanical features. Black tupelo differs from the preceding species as follows: (1) the leaves are smaller (2 to 5 in. long, ½ to 3 in. wide), obovate and usually entire; (2) the fruit is smaller (⅓ to ⅔ in. long), with an indistinctly ribbed pit; (3) the twigs are more slender, and the ovoid terminal buds are about ¼ in. long; (4) the bark is "blocky" or with the appearance of alligator hide; (5) the base of the trunk is less swollen.

Black tupelo is a medium-sized tree 50 to 60 ft high and 2 to 3 ft in diameter (max. 130* by 5* ft). Best growth is made on moist alluvial soils with some drainage, but the tree is very cosmopolitan and also grows on relatively dry upland sites. It is found in 29 forest-cover types (127), and its associates include both wet- and dry-soil hardwoods and soft-woods.

Apparently much of the "black tupelo" harvested from southern coastal plain swamps is from *Nyssa sylvatica* var. *biflora* (Walt.) Sarg., swamp tupelo. This variety may be recognized by its narrower, often oblanceolate leaves and fruit pit which has ridges slightly more prominent than those in *N. sylvatica*. Swamp tupelo, as its name indicates, is typical of very wet sites, while the more northern *N. sylvatica* commonly inhabits higher ground and also wet sites. This and other species of *Nyssa* may produce root sprouts which grow vigorously, and form thickets around the base of the tree (119).

Fɪɢ. 210. *Nyssa sylvatica*. Black tupelo. *1*. Twig × 1¼. *2*. Leaf × ½. *3*. Fruit × ¾. *4*. Bark.

The remaining tree species *N. ogeche* Bartr., Ogeechee tupelo, with tomentose flowers and more or less hairy leaves, is found in coastal Georgia and adjacent South Carolina and northern Florida. Thousands of seedlings have been planted in western Florida for future honey production.

Cornaceae: The Dogwood family

This family includes about 10 genera and nearly 100 species of trees, shrubs, and a few herbs widely scattered through the world, but most abundant in the cooler regions of the Northern Hemisphere. From the standpoint of forestry, the family is relatively unimportant, but several cornaceous species and their varieties are valued highly for decorative purposes.

Two genera (*Cornus* and *Garrya* [1]) with about 18 species are found in the United States.

Leaves deciduous, opposite (rarely alternate), simple, estipulate. *Flowers* perfect (rarely also imperfect). *Fruit* drupaceous, 1 or 2-seeded.

CORNUS L.   Dogwood or cornel

Cornus is a genus of small trees and shrubs (rarely herbs) numbering about 45 species. Except for a single Peruvian form, the dogwoods are restricted to the Northern Hemisphere. Probably the best known of the exotic ornamentals is the cornelian cherry, *Cornus mas* L.

Sixteen species of *Cornus* are native to the United States, and eight attain tree size. These are of but minor importance, except as ornamentals, and only two of them will be considered in detail. Several other species, however, are so common and widespread that they deserve mention.

C. alternifolia L. f., alternate-leaf dogwood, pagoda dogwood (SPN), with alternate leaves, greenish-brown twigs, and blue fruit, is a small tree of the East; *C. drummondii* C. A. Meyer, rough-leaf dogwood, is also arborescent and has leaves with scattered, bristly hairs on the upper surface. The commoner shrubby forms include *C. racemosa* Lam. [*C. paniculata* L'Her.], panicled dogwood, with ashy-gray twigs; *C. stolonifera* Michx., red-stemmed dogwood (transcontinental), with smooth, scarlet twigs; *C. amomum* Mill., silky dogwood, with silky leaves and dark red twigs; and *C. rugosa* Lam. [*C. circinata* L'Her.], round-leaf dogwood, with greenish-red, purple-spotted twigs. The bunchberry, *C. canadensis* L., is a small semiherbaceous species common on duff soils in both eastern and western forests. Western dogwood, *Cornus occidentalis* (Torr. and Gray) Colville, is a large shrub or small tree native to the Pacific Northwest. Its hairy-cyme branches serve to distinguish it from other dogwoods of that region.

Leaves usually opposite, with entire or finely toothed margins, and arcuate venation. *Flowers* perfect, usually small, in terminal cymes, panicles, or heads; flower parts in 4's, calyx and corolla present. *Fruit* a red, white, blue, or green drupe, with a 2-celled pit.

Cornus florida L.   Flowering dogwood

Distinguishing characteristics. *Leaves* opposite, oval, arcuately veined. *Flowers* in heads, with four very conspicuous petal-like, notched bracts. *Fruit* a bright red drupe. *Twigs* slender, somewhat angled, purplish with a glaucous bloom; terminal flower buds subglobose, leaf buds acute, and covered with two valvate scales. *Bark* broken up into small blocks.

General description. Flowering dogwood is a small, bushy, tolerant tree which rarely attains a height of more than 40 ft or a diameter of 12 to 18 in. The trunk is

[1] Relegated to the monotypic family Garryaceae by some taxonomists.

Fig. 211. *Cornus florida.* Flowering dogwood. *1.* Twig × 1¼. *2.* Flower bud × 1¼. *3.* Flower cluster showing the white bracts often mistaken for petals × ¼. *4.* Flower × 3. *5.* Cluster of fruits × 1. *6.* Leaf × ½. *7.* Flower clusters. (*Photograph by C. A. Brown.*) *8.* Bark.

short with little taper; from 6 to 10 ft above the ground it usually breaks up into several large wide-spreading limbs resulting in a low dense crown. Best development is reached as an understory species in association with other hardwoods. This tree is usually found on deep, rich, moist soils near stream banks or on moist slopes. Flowering dogwood is a widely used ornamental and makes a striking display when it is in full bloom.

Range. Southern Maine westward through Massachusetts, New York, southern Ontario, and southern Michigan to southeastern Kansas; south to central Florida in the East and to eastern Texas in the West (also mountains of northern Mexico.)

Cornus nuttallii Audubon   Pacific dogwood

Distinguishing characteristics. *Leaves* opposite, ovate to obovate, *veins* arcuate. *Flowers* in heads, with four to six petal-like acute or truncate bracts. *Fruit* a bright red to orange-red drupe. *Twigs* similar to those of the preceding species. *Bark* smooth or with thin scaly plates near the base of the tree.

Fig. 212. *Cornus nuttallii.* Pacific dogwood. *1.* Leaf × ½. *2.* Head of flowers and bracts × ¾.

General description. This species is a small tree, rarely ever attaining a height of more than 60 ft or a diameter of 12 to 20 in. Best development is reached in the Puget Sound basin and in the redwood belt of California where it appears as an understory species in the coniferous forests of these regions. Under forest conditions it develops a slightly tapered stem which extends through the crown, but in more open situations the bole is commonly short and supports a number of spreading limbs forming an ovoid to rounded-conical crown, or it may break up at the ground into several nearly erect stems resulting in a bushy habit. Pacific dogwood is one of North America's finest ornamental trees and is deserving of a more extensive use in this direction than it now enjoys. The tree is peculiar in that it frequently flowers a second time during the late summer while the fruits of the first flowering are turning red. The snowy-white bracts and the brilliant red fruits against a background of lustrous green foliage produce an extremely beautiful effect.

Range. Fraser River Valley and Vancouver Island, British Columbia, south through western Washington and Oregon to the San Bernardino Mountains of southern California; on the west slopes of the Sierra Nevada between 4,000 and 5,000 ft above sea level.

Fig. 213. Bark of Pacific dogwood.

C. SYMPETALAE

Ericaceae: The Heath family

The Heath family numbers 75 to 80 genera and some 2,000 species of trees, shrubs, and herbs widely scattered through the cooler regions of the world, but particularly abundant in southeastern Asia and South Africa. The family is of little consequence as a timber-contributing group, but several genera, particularly *Rhododendron, Azalea, Kalmia,* and *Arctostaphylos,* include species which are highly prized for decorative purposes. In this connection the very beautiful *Rhododendron macrophyllum* D. Don has been chosen as the state flower for Washington. The burls and root wood of briar, *Erica arborea* L., a small southern European tree, are employed in making the bowls of tobacco pipes. Huckleberries (*Gaylussacia* spp.), as well as cranberries and blueberries (*Vaccinium* spp.), are also members of this family. The leaves of several shrubby genera, notably *Kalmia, Leucothoe, Ledum,* and *Menziesia,* contain appreciable amounts of andromedotoxin, a substance which is very poisonous to livestock, particularly sheep.

Certain of the above plants, as well as many others in this family, are of interest to the forester and ecologist on account of their widespread occurrence in bogs, where they often comprise the greater portion of the shrubby flora. When taken from their natural habitat, it is usually found necessary to keep the soil acid, otherwise these shrubs lose their vigor and often die. About thirty-five genera of the Ericaceae, seven of which include arborescent forms, are represented in the United States.

CONDENSED BOTANICAL FEATURES OF THE FAMILY

Leaves deciduous or persistent, alternate (rarely opposite or whorled), simple. *Flowers* perfect, sympetalous. *Fruit* a capsule, berry, or drupe.

ARBUTUS L.   Madrone

This genus includes about 12 species scattered through the forests of the Mediterranean basin and North, and Central America. The Pacific madrone, *Arbutus menziesii* Pursh, is an evergreen tree native to far western North America.

Arbutus menziesii Pursh   Pacific madrone

Distinguishing characteristics. *Leaves* oval to oblong, coriaceous, entire, or finely to coarsely serrate on vigorous growth; persistent until the new leaves are fully grown. *Flowers* white; in drooping terminal panicles. *Fruit* an orange-red, berrylike drupe. *Twigs* slender, green, red, or brown; *terminal buds* ovoid, with numerous imbricated scales; *lateral buds* minute; *leaf scars* semicircular, with a single bundle scar. *Bark* very distinctive, dark reddish brown, dividing into thin, scaly plates which are deciduous during summer and fall.

General description. Pacific madrone is a medium-sized tree 80 to 125 ft tall and 2 to 4 ft in diameter. In dense stands it forms a clear, symmetrical bole but is apt to produce a short, crooked trunk in rather open situations. The tree is found on a variety of soils but becomes shrubby on very poor sites. Best development is attained on well-drained soils near sea level. This species is quite gregarious and often forms nearly pure stands, although it occurs in much greater abundance as an understory species in Douglas-fir and redwood forests or in association with Digger pine, ponderosa pine, California black oak, bigleaf maple, tanoak, red alder, and golden chinkapin.

The tree is a prolific annual seeder; the seeds exhibit a high percentage of viability, and germination is especially good in loose moist soils. Madrone appears able to endure dense shade throughout its life, although top light is conducive to more rapid growth.

Range. Coastal British Columbia south through western Washington and Oregon to southern California; in California in both the coast ranges and western Sierra below 4,000-ft elevation.

RHODODENDRON L.   Rhododendron

This group is one of the best known in horticulture and comprises some 800 species found through the cooler and temperate portions of the Northern Hemisphere. About 21 species are native to North America, and many others have been introduced, especially from the Orient, for ornamental use. Those with persistent leaves are commonly called "rhododendrons," while deciduous species are often known as "azaleas"; however, there are intermediate forms, and the group is further complicated by many varieties and hybrids.

Rhododendron maximum L.   Rosebay rhododendron; great rhododendron

Distinguishing characteristics. *Leaves* persistent, leathery, oblong, revolute. *Flowers* in large, showy terminal clusters, white to pink. *Fruit* an elongated sticky capsule with many extremely small seeds.

General description. This species is a very common shrub or small tree in the mountainous regions of the South and often forms extensive, almost impenetrable thickets, sometimes known locally as "rhododendron hells." A very common associate is mountain-laurel, *Kalmia latifolia* L., with somewhat smaller leaves (alternate or irregularly whorled) and abundant white flowers. Together, these two species cover some 3 million acres of the southern Appalachians. When grown ornamentally, these species do not thrive in limy soils, and it is customary to surround them with pulverized peat moss to ensure proper soil conditions.

Range. Mostly in the Appalachians and adjacent territory from southern New York to northern Georgia; also in Nova Scotia, Ontario, and Maine.

Fig. 214. *Rhododendron maximum.* Rosebay rhododendron. *1.* Flower bud × 1. *2.* Fruits × ¾. *3.* Flowers × ½. (*Photograph by D. M. Brown.*)

OXYDENDRUM DC.   Sourwood

This is a monotypic genus with the single species, sourwood, *O. arboreum* (L.) DC., a small tree of the East ranging from southern Indiana and Pennsylvania southward. *Leaves* sour-tasting, deciduous, elliptical, and serrulate. *Flowers* small, white, bell-shaped, in delicate, one-sided racemes. *Fruit* a five-angled grayish capsule. *Leaf scars* rounded, each with a single bundle scar. *Bark* longitudinally furrowed, often blocky on the largest trees.

Sourwood is a small tree of the southern states commonly found in mixture with other hardwoods. Although of little commercial use, the flowers are sought by honey-bees, and the tree makes a suitable ornamental except on limy soils.

Ebenaceae: The Ebony family

The modern Ebenaceae embrace 5 or 6 genera and about 325 species of trees and shrubs widely scattered through the tropical and warmer forested regions of both hemispheres. However, previous to the ice age, ebenaceous plants flourished in Greenland and near the Arctic Circle in both Asia and North America. The present floras of tropical Africa and those of the Indo-Malayan region are featured by many members of this family. While true ebony wood is produced by *Diospyros ebenum* Koenig, a number of other species from the genera *Maba*, *Euclea*, and *Royena* also produce black or brownish-black timbers which are distributed under the name of ebony.

CONDENSED BOTANICAL FEATURES OF THE FAMILY

Leaves mostly deciduous, alternate, simple. *Flowers* perfect and imperfect (species usually dioecious or polygamous). *Fruit* a berry.

DIOSPYROS L.   Persimmon; ebony

This is the largest genus of the Ebenaceae and includes about 240 species widely scattered through eastern and southwestern Asia, the Mediterranean region, Indo-Malaya, and North America. The very beautiful Macassar ebony (*Diospyros* spp.) comes from the Celebes Islands; *D. ebenum* Koenig, the true ebony, is largely produced in Ceylon; and *D. melanoxylon* Roxb., is a black Indian ebony.

Two species, *D. virginiana* L. and *D. texana* Scheele, are the only members of this family found in the United States. Only the former is of any importance as a timber species.

CONDENSED BOTANICAL FEATURES OF THE GENUS

Leaves deciduous or persistent, entire. *Flowers* regular (species dioecious or polygamous). *Fruit* globose, oblong, or pyriform, with 1 to 10 seeds, and subtended by the enlarged woody calyx.

Diospyros virginiana L.   Common persimmon

Distinguishing characteristics. *Leaves* oblong-ovate to elliptical or oval, with a somewhat metallic luster, entire, venation slightly arcuate. *Flowers* greenish yellow, somewhat urn-shaped or tubular, less than 1 in. long (species polygamous). *Fruit* a subglobose berry, about 1½ in. in diameter, orange-colored, tinged with purple when ripe, with large seeds and subtended by the persistent woody calyx. *Twigs* moderately slender, grayish brown, glabrous or pubescent; *terminal buds* lacking, the laterals covered by two overlapping scales; *leaf scars* lunate with a single bundle

Fig. 215. *Diospyros virginiana.* Common persimmon. *1.* Bark. *2.*
Seed × ¾. *3.* Fruit × ¾. *4.* Leaf × ½. *5.* Buds × 3.

scar; *pith* homogeneous or diaphragmed in the same twig. *Bark* broken up into small
conspicuous blocks.

General description. Common persimmon is ordinarily a small to medium-sized
tree, averaging 30 to 50 ft in height and 12 in. in diameter (max. 130 by 7 ft). The
bole is usually short with a shallow, or in youth moderately deep, root system and a
characteristic round-topped crown. The tree is tolerant and is often found on moist
bottomlands, where it occurs as a scattered tree with other hardwoods; on old fields
it may form thickets, and it is also very common along roadsides.

The fruit is exceedingly astringent when green, but edible when ripe, and is sold
locally. Probably the distribution of persimmon depends largely upon the widespread
use of the fruit for food, since the seeds are large and not readily disseminated by
other means. Several varieties have been developed for fruit production (125).

Range. Southern Connecticut (New Haven) and Long Island; south to southern
Florida; west through central Pennsylvania, southern Ohio, southern Indiana, and
central Illinois to southeastern Iowa; south through eastern Kansas to eastern Texas.

Oleaceae: The Olive family

The Olive family numbers 22 to 30 genera and more than 400 species of
trees and shrubs distributed mostly through the temperate and tropical
forests of the Northern Hemisphere. The genera *Fraxinus* and *Olea* are
noted for the many fine timbers which they produce, and *Olea europaea*

L. furnishes the olives and olive oil of the trade. While originally a native of the Mediterranean basin, the olive is now widely cultivated throughout the warmer regions of the world, and several varieties are grown in California. Among the shrubby members of this family commonly used for decorative purposes, mention should be made of *Syringa* (lilac), *Forsythia* (goldenbell), *Ligustrum* (privet), and *Jasminum* (jasmine). *Chionanthus virginicus* L., the native fringetree, and several ashes (*Fraxinus*) are also suitable for ornamental use.

Four genera are represented by native arborescent species in the United States, but only one, *Fraxinus*, is an important timber producer (381).

BOTANICAL FEATURES OF THE FAMILY

Leaves deciduous or persistent, opposite or rarely alternate, simple or pinnately compound, estipulate.

Flowers perfect and/or imperfect, actinomorphic; *calyx* 4-lobed or wanting; *corolla* 4- or rarely 5- to 16-lobed, or wanting; *stamens* 2 (rarely 3 to 5), adnate to the corolla and alternating with its lobes, rudimentary or wanting in the pistillate flowers; *pistils* 1, superior, the ovary 2- (rarely 3-) celled, with 2 ovules in each cell, surmounted by a single style and a 2-lobed stigma, rudimentary or wanting in the staminate flowers.

Fruit a samara, capsule, berry, or drupe.

FRAXINUS L.   Ash

The genus *Fraxinus* includes about 65 species of trees, rarely shrubs, largely restricted to temperate regions of the Northern Hemisphere, but extending into the tropical forests of Java and also Cuba. *F. excelsior* L., one of Europe's best-known timber trees, is often planted in this country as a street and shade tree. *F. ornus* L., also a native of both Europe and Asia, is commonly used ornamentally in the Pacific Northwest; this species produces the "manna" of commerce, a medicinal substance used in the preparation of laxatives. A white wax is obtained from scale insects which feed on *F. chinensis* Roxb. Numerous other species produce timbers of intrinsic value. A beautiful veneer stock, which is sold in this country under the name of Tamo, is traceable to the Japanese species *F. mandshurica* Rupr. and *F. sieboldiana* Blume, the Manchurian and Japanese Siebold ashes, respectively.

The arborescent flora of the United States contains some sixteen species of this genus [twelve, according to Miller (256)]. Five species may attain commercial size and abundance.

Species	Leaves	Flowers	Fruit	Twigs
F. americana, white ash	with about 7 serrate to entire, petioluled leaflets, essentially glabrous below	imperfect; species dioecious	lanceolate to oblanceolate; wing often extending along the seed cavity	terete, glabrous; leaf scars notched
F. pennsylvanica, green ash	with about 7 sharply serrate, petioluled leaflets,[a] glabrous to pubescent below and on rachis	same	narrowly lanceolate; wing narrowed or lacking along the outside of the seed cavity	terete, glabrous to velvety-pubescent, leaf scar truncate to shallowly notched

[a] Often entire below the middle.

BOTANICAL FEATURES OF THE GENUS

Leaves deciduous, opposite, odd-pinnately compound (rarely reduced to a single leaflet),[1] the leaflets serrate or entire.
Flowers perfect, and/or imperfect, appearing in the early spring before or with the unfolding of the leaves; *calyx* 4-lobed or wanting; *corolla* with 2–6 petals, or absent (the latter in all North American species except *F. cuspidata*); *stamens* 2–4; *pistils* 1, with a 2-celled ovary.
Fruit a 1-seeded samara with an elongated terminal wing; *seed* elongated, albuminous.
Twigs slender to stout, glabrous or pubescent; *pith* homogeneous, terete between the nodes; *terminal buds* present, with 1 to 3 pairs of scales; *lateral buds* similar to the terminal buds but smaller; *leaf scars* suborbicular to semicircular, sometimes notched on the upper edge; *bundle scars* numerous, arranged in an open U- or V-shaped line, or sometimes an ellipse.

Fraxinus americana L.   White ash

BOTANICAL FEATURES

Leaves 8″ to 12″ long; with 5 to 9 (mostly 7, and rarely 11 or 13) petioluled leaflets; *leaflets* 3″ to 5″ long, 1½″ to 3″ wide; *shape* ovate to oblong lanceolate, or elliptical to oval; *apex* acute to acuminate; *base* rounded to acute; *margin* serrate, remotely

[1] In seedlings, the first leaves are simple; see p. 219.

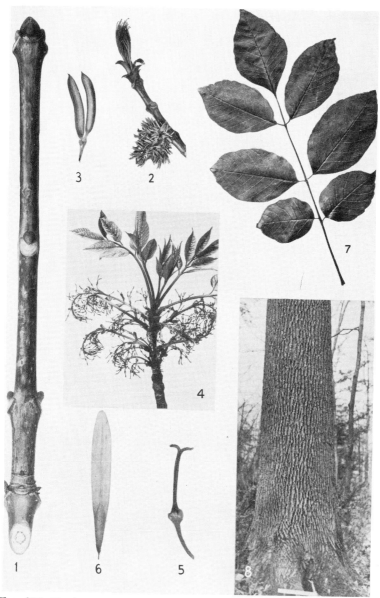

Fig. 216. *Fraxinus americana.* White ash. *1.* Twig × 1¼. *2.* Clusters of staminate flowers × ½. *3.* Staminate flower × 4. *4.* Clusters of pistillate flowers × ½. *5.* Pistillate flower × 4. *6.* Fruit × 1. *7.* Leaf × ⅓. *8.* Bark.

crenate-serrate, or entire; *surfaces* dark green, glabrous above; pale green, glabrous, or sparingly pubescent below; *rachis* slightly grooved, glabrous.

Flowers imperfect, (species dioecious), apetalous, both sexes appearing in glabrous panicles before or with leaves; *calyx* 4-parted, minute.

Fruit a lanceolate to oblanceolate samara, 1″ to 2″ long, and about ¼″ wide; *wing* usually rounded or slightly emarginate (rarely pointed) at the apex, not greatly narrowed at the seed cavity; *seeds* about 10,000 (5,500–18,200) to the pound.

Twigs stout, glabrous, dark green to gray-green, occasionally purplish, lustrous, lenticellate; *terminal buds* broadly ovoid, obtuse, covered with 4 to 6 brownish scales; *lateral buds* somewhat triangular, the first pair at the same level as the terminal bud; *superposed buds* occasionally present on vigorous shoots; *leaf scars* semiorbicular, usually notched at the top; *bundle scars* numerous and arranged in a broadly U-shaped line, sometimes nearly closed at the top.

Bark ashy gray, or on young stems sometimes with an orange tinge, later finely furrowed into close diamond-shaped areas separated by narrow interlacing ridges; on very old trees slightly scaly along the ridges.

GENERAL DESCRIPTION

White ash, the most abundant and important of American ashes, is a tree 70 to 80 ft high and 2 to 3 ft in diameter (max. 125 by 7* ft). The bole is long, straight, clear, and cylindrical and terminates below in a root system which is deep in porous soils but shallow and spreading on rocky sites; the crown is somewhat open. This tree is intermediate in tolerance except in the seedling stage, when it is often found in considerable numbers under forest cover. White ash commonly occurs on deep, moist, fertile upland soils in association with such species as basswood, yellow-poplar, black cherry, American beech, oaks, hickories, and red maple; in the South it may be found on loamy ridges in the bottoms accompanied by the hickories, swamp chestnut, willow, and cherrybark

1. *Fraxinus americana.*

2. *Fraxinus pennsylvanica.*

PLATE 68

oaks, loblolly pine, and sweetgum, or elsewhere on well-drained slopes and coves; toward the northern limits of its range, white ash associates with white pine and the beech-birch-maple-hemlock mixture, occurring here mostly as a scattered tree. This ash is a component of some 24 forest-cover types.

Although some seed may be produced each year, good crops develop only at 3- to 5-year intervals; the germination varies from 40 to 60 per-cent. On good sites, growth at first is rapid, and a height of 6 ft may be attained by the end of the third season. Sprouts from young trees are vigorous, often growing 5 ft or more in height the first year.

RANGE

Eastern United States (map, Plate 68).

Fraxinus pennsylvanica Marsh.[1]   Green ash

BOTANICAL FEATURES

Leaves 6″ to 9″ long, with 7 to 9 petioluled leaflets; *leaflets* 3″ to 4″ long, 1″ to 1½″ wide; *shape* lanceolate to ovate-lanceolate, or elliptical; *margin* serrate, sometimes entire below the middle; *apex* acute to acuminate; *base* acute to unequally obtuse; *surfaces* yellow-green above; paler and glabrous to silky pubescent below; *rachis* moderately stout, grooved, glabrous to pubescent.
Flowers imperfect (species dioecious), apetalous, both sexes borne in glabrous to tomentose panicles which appear after the leaves have begun to unfold; calyx re-motely lobed or cup-shaped.
Fruit a narrowly lanceolate samara, 1″ to 2″ long, ¼″ or less wide; wing pointed or slightly emarginate at the apex, abruptly narrowed along the slender seed cavity; *seeds* about 17,300 (11,000–24,600) to the pound.
Twigs stout to moderately slender, flattened at the nodes, gray to greenish brown, glabrous to velvety pubescent; *terminal buds* conical to ovate, rusty brown, pubescent; *lateral buds* reniform to triangular; *leaf scars* semicircular, shallowly notched to straight along the upper edge; *bundle scars* forming a U- or V-shaped line.
Bark similar to that of white ash but not so deeply furrowed.

GENERAL DESCRIPTION

Green ash is the most widely distributed of American ashes. It is a small to medium-sized tree 30 to 50 ft high and 20 in. in diameter (max. 105* by 4* ft) with a broad irregular crown, short, usually poorly formed

[1] Previously *F. pennsylvanica* Marsh. was designated as red ash, and a variety, *F. pennsylvanica* var. *lanceolata* (Borkh.) Sarg., was recognized as green ash. The 1953 Check List (212) did not recognize the variety and transferred the name green ash to the species.

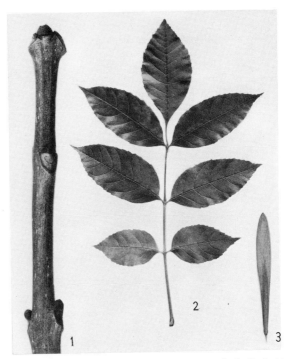

Fig. 217. *Fraxinus pennsylvanica*. Green ash. *1*. Twig ×
¼. *2*. Leaf × ⅓. *3*. Fruit × 1.

trunk, and a superficial fibrous root system. It is common, especially
through the Middle West, as a scattered tree along stream banks and
the borders of swamps. Best development appears to be reached east of
the Appalachians. Green ash has been widely planted throughout the
plains states and adjacent Canada. It is exceedingly hardy to climatic
extremes; although naturally a moist bottomland or stream-bank tree, it
will, when once established, persist on dry sterile soils (55) and has
been used successfully in shelter belts. Under forest competition, green
ash is intolerant to moderately tolerant. Its associates include boxelder,
the bottomland oaks and hickories, sweetgum, cottonwood, willows, red
maple, and—farther north—quaking aspen.

RANGE

Eastern United States and Great Plains (map, Plate 68).

Fraxinus nigra Marsh.   Black ash

Distinguishing characteristics.   *Leaves* with 7 to 13 oblong to oblong-lanceolate, serrate, sessile leaflets. *Flowers* perfect and imperfect (species is polygamous or dioecious), soon naked as the minute calyx falls away, borne in panicles before the leaves. *Fruit* an oblong-elliptical samara with a wide wing and indistinct seminal cavity. *Twigs* stout, grayish; terminal buds ovate-conical, dark brown to nearly black, laterals rounded, the first pair borne some distance below the terminal. *Bark* grayish, relatively smooth, later shallowly furrowed or scaly.

Fig. 218. *Fraxinus nigra.* Black ash. *1.* Twig × 1¼. *2.* Leaf × ⅓. *3.* Fruit × 1. *4.* Bark.

General description.   Black ash, a typically northern tree, varies from 40 to 50 ft in height, with a diameter of about 18 in. (max. 90 by 4 ft). The bole is inclined to be poorly shaped, supports a small open crown, and terminates below in a very shallow, fibrous root system. This species occurs as a scattered tree along stream banks or the borders of swamps where it is associated with such trees as northern white-cedar, balsam fir, red maple, and sometimes yellow birch; farther south, American elm, black tupelo, and other swamp hardwoods are included. Black ash is intolerant and is not found under heavy forest cover. In a few localities it is abundant and of some importance, although the wood is of a much poorer quality than that of the other northern ashes. From early times black ash has furnished material for pack baskets fabricated by the Indians of the Northeast. The growth rings in this species are very narrow, and splints are made by pounding the green wood until it separates along the early wood pores.

Range. Southeastern Canada and the northern half of the eastern United States.

Fraxinus quadrangulata Michx.   Blue ash

Distinguishing characteristics. *Leaves* with 7 to 11 lanceolate to oblong-ovate, serrate, petioluled leaflets. *Flowers* perfect, soon naked as the calyx falls away, borne in panicles as the leaves unfold. *Fruit* similar to that of black ash. *Twigs* stout, 4-angled and 4-winged between the node, thus unlike those of any other ash described in this text; terminal buds broadly ovoid, reddish brown. *Bark* on mature trees, with long, loose, scaly plates, giving a shaggy appearance to the trunk.

Fig. 219. *Fraxinus quadrangulata*. Blue ash. *1*. Twig showing corky wings × 1¼. *2*. Fruit × 1.

General description. Blue ash is a medium-sized tree (max. 120 by 4 ft) which occurs especially on dry limestone uplands through the Ohio and Upper Mississippi Valleys. Here its associates include chinkapin and other oaks, hickories, and redbud. This ash occurs as a scattered tree and is relatively rare in comparison with white ash, which often accompanies it on the better soils. The inner bark contains a mucilaginous substance which turns blue upon exposure to the air. A blue dye prepared by macerating the bark in water was used by the pioneers for dyeing cloth. Blue ash has been planted to some extent in the prairie region. Its silvical features are similar to those of the other upland ashes.

Range. Ohio and upper Mississippi River Valleys.

Fraxinus latifolia Benth.   Oregon ash

Distinguishing characteristics. *Leaves* pinnate, with five to nine ovate, obovate, or elliptical, sessile or petioluled, serrulate leaflets, usually tomentose below. *Flowers,* paniculate, appearing with the leaves (species dioecious). *Fruit* an oblong to elliptical samara, 1 to 1½ in. long. *Twigs* stout, densely tomentose, with conical terminal buds and small, ovoid lateral buds; *leaf scars* suborbicular, the bundle scars arranged in a U-shaped line. *Bark* dark gray to gray-brown, with an interwoven pattern similar to that of white ash.

General description. Oregon ash is a timber tree of secondary importance. Ordinarily it attains a height of 60 to 80 ft and a d.b.h. of 24 to 36 in., although it is capable of attaining nearly twice these dimensions under the most favorable conditions. A clear, symmetrical bole supporting a narrow, compact crown features forest-grown trees. The root system is moderately shallow but wide-spreading, and the trees are unusually windfirm. This species prefers a moist, rich alluvium or a bottom-land site with plenty of moisture; however, trees on moist, sandy, gravelly, or even rocky soils grow quite vigorously. Nearly pure fringes or strips of this ash occur along the banks of water courses and margins of swamps, but it probably occurs more abundantly in mixture with other species. In the northern part of its range it is chiefly associated with bigleaf maple, red alder, numerous willows, Oregon white oak, grand fir, black cottonwood, and Douglas-fir. To the south, however, these species are largely replaced by Digger and ponderosa pines, white alder, California-laurel, California sycamore, and California black oak.

Seed is produced after the thirtieth year, and heavy crops are released every three to five years thereafter. Seedling trees can endure moderate shading when there is an abundance of soil moisture, although they require considerably more light after passing the sapling stage. However, trees which have been suppressed for protracted lengths of time are able to resume a normal rate of growth soon after being released. The growth rate is moderately rapid for the first 60 to 100 years, after which it decreases gradually, and maturity is ultimately reached in about 200 to 250 years. Natural regeneration is also accomplished by sprouts from the root collar.

Range. Southern coastal British Columbia south along the coast through the Puget Sound basin to San Francisco Bay, and south to southern California along the lower western slopes of the Sierra. *Altitudinal distribution:* sea level to about 3,000 ft.

Bignoniaceae: The Trumpet Creeper family

The Bignoniaceae comprise about 100 genera and 750 species of trees, shrubs, vines, and herbs, the majority of which are tropical. *Cybistax donnell-smithii* (Rose) Siebert, a native of Mexico and Central America, is a beautiful wood which enters the American markets under the names of prima vera or white mahogany. A number of other

---

Fig. 220. *Fraxinus latifolia.* Oregon ash. *1.* Twig × 1¼. *2.* Leaf × ½. *3.* Staminate flowers × 1. *4.* Fruit × 1. *5.* Bark.

very fine timbers are traceable to the Indo-Malayan species of the genus *Stereospermum*. The sausage-tree, *Kigelia africana* Benth., a tropical species, so named because of its peculiar sausage-shaped fruits suspended on long slender stems, has been successfully propagated in southern Florida.

Three genera with arborescent forms are native to this country, but only one (*Catalpa*) is of sufficient importance to be described.

Leaves mostly deciduous, opposite or whorled (rarely alternate), simple or compound. *Flowers* perfect, usually large and showy. *Fruit* a capsule or rarely berrylike.

CATALPA Scop.   Catalpa

Catalpa consists of 7 to 10 species distributed through the forests of eastern Asia, eastern North America, and the West Indies.

Two species of *Catalpa* are included in the arborescent flora of the United States. *C. bignonioides* Walt., southern catalpa, is a small tree native to the southern and Gulf states. While it produces wood of very little value, the tree is used ornamentally because of its large and showy panicles of white or purple-tinted flowers. The other species, *C. speciosa* Warder, is a small to medium-sized tree of secondary importance.

Leaves deciduous, opposite, or whorled in 3's, simple, long-petioled. *Flowers* large and showy in many-flowered panicles or corymbs; *corolla* tubular, lipped. *Fruit* a large capsule with many flat seeds, bearded at the ends.

Catalpa speciosa Warder   Northern catalpa; hardy catalpa

Distinguishing characteristics. *Leaves* large, ovate to oval, mostly entire, cordate. *Flowers* white, sometimes with inconspicuous purple spots. *Fruit* a long, semipersistent, terete capsule with many flattened seeds fringed at each end. *Twigs* usually stout, terminal bud lacking; *leaf scars* orbicular, raised with a depressed center; *bundle scars* numerous in a closed oval.

General description. Northern catalpa attains a maximum height of 120 ft and a diameter of 5° ft but is usually much smaller. The bole is well formed if grown under proper conditions of soil, moisture, and side shading, but otherwise is liable to be crooked. The species is naturally an inhabitant of bottomlands, occurs as a scattered tree, and is exceedingly reactive to soil conditions. On rich moist soils a growth of 2½ ft in height and a diameter increase of ½ in. per year may be attained, but on poorer locations the growth is much less. The seasoned timber is very durable when used for posts or ties, although the living trees are subject to heart rot. Catalpa is intolerant, but natural pruning does not take place readily, and best results are obtained in rather dense, pure stands. This species has been widely planted through the Middle West, and it is said that on the proper soil this catalpa will produce more good fence posts in a short time than any other native tree.

Range. Southern Indiana and southern Illinois, western Kentucky and western Tennessee, southeastern Missouri, and northeastern Arkansas (elsewhere through the eastern United States, naturalized through cultivation).

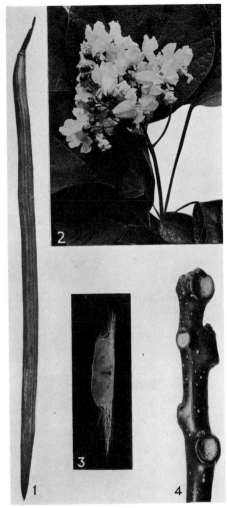

FIG. 221. *Catalpa speciosa.* Northern catalpa. *1.* Fruit × ⅓. *2.* Flowers × ½. *3.* Seed × ¾. *4.* Twig × 1¼.

Glossary

Abortive. Barren or defective.

Accessory. An adjunct, or additional part.

Achene. A small, dry, one-celled, one-seeded, unwinged (but occasionally plumose) fruit.

Acicular. Needlelike.

Actinomorphic. Said of flowers having radial symmetry.

Acuminate. Long, tapering; attenuated.

Acute. The shape of an acute angle but not attenuated.

Adhesion. The union or fusion of unlike parts.

Adnate. Descriptive of unlike parts which are fused together.

Aggregate. A cluster of ripened ovaries traceable to separate pistils of the same flower and inserted on a common receptacle.

Albumen. Nutritive substances surrounding the embryo of seeds.

Albuminous. Having albumen.

Ament. See Catkin.

Anastomosing. Interlacing.

Androgynous. Having both staminate and pistillate flowers in the same inflorescence.

Anemophilous. Descriptive of flowers pollinated by wind.

Anther. The pollen-bearing portion of the stamen.

Anthesis. The act of opening of a flower.

Apetalous. Without petals.

Apiculate. Abruptly pointed.

Apophysis. That part of a cone scale which is exposed when the cone is closed.

Appressed. Flattened against.

Arborescent. Treelike.

Arcuate. Descriptive of the curved leaf veins in *Cornus, Ceanothus,* etc.

Aril. A fleshly appendage growing from the point of attachment of the seed.

Articulate. Jointed; having joints or nodes.

Asepalous. Without sepals.

Attenuate. Long, tapering; acuminate.

Auriculate. With earlike appendages.

Axil. Upper angle between an attached organ and its stem.

Axile. Situated on the axis.

Axillary. Situated in the axil.

Axis. The central line of any organ (i.e., the axis of a cone).

Baccate. Berrylike.

Bast. Fibrous constituents of the bark of many species.

Berry. A simple fleshy fruit, with the seeds embedded in the pulpy mass.

Bi- or Bis-. Prefix denoting two, double, or twice.

Bifid. Two-cleft, split into two portions.

Bilabiate. Two-lipped.

Bipinnate. Twice pinnate.

Bisexual. Having both sex organs on the same individual; a hermaphrodite.

Blade. Lamina; the expanded portion of a leaf.

Boss. A raised projection, usually pointed.

Bract. A modified leaf subtending a flower or belonging to an inflorescence.

Bracteole. Same as bractlet.

Bractlet. A secondary bract.

Bud. An embryonic axis with its appendages.

Calcicole. Descriptive of a plant restricted to, or growing best on, lime soils.

Calyx. The outer floral envelope.

Capitate. Shaped like a head; or in dense headlike clusters.

Capsule. A simple, dry fruit, the product of a compound pistil splitting along two or more lines of suture.

Carpel. A simple pistil; one unit of a compound pistil; in conifers the cone scale.

Catkin. A flexible, usually inverted scaly spike bearing apetalous, unisexual flowers.

Ciliate. Descriptive of a margin fringed with hair.

Cleft. Divided into lobes separated by narrow or acute sinuses which extend more than halfway to the midrib.

Clone. A group of individuals propagated asexually from a single original.

Coalescence. Union of like parts or organs.

Cohesion. Union of like parts.

Collateral. Descriptive of accessory buds arranged on either side of lateral buds.

Complete. Descriptive of a flower having sepals, petals, stamens, and one or more pistils.

Compressed. Flattened.

Cone. An inflorescence or fruit with overlapping scales.

Conifer. A gymnosperm of the order Coniferales.

Connate. United.

Cordate. Heart-shaped.

Coriaceous. Leatherlike.

Corolla. The inner floral envelope, composed of separate or connate petals.

Corymb. An indeterminate inflorescence consisting of a central rachis bearing a number of branched, pedicelled flowers; the lower pedicels much longer than the upper, resulting in a flat or more or less round-topped cluster.

Cove. A small sheltered valley between mountains, especially where two or more streams join and there is an outwash deposit of rich alluvial soil.

Crenate. Descriptive of a margin with rounded to blunt teeth.

Crenulate. Finely crenate.

Cruciform. Cross-shaped.

Cultivar. A cultivated variety.

Cuneate. Wedge-shaped.

Cuspidate. Tipped with a sharp, rigid point.

Cyme. A determinate inflorescence consisting of a central rachis bearing a number of pedicelled flowers.

Cymose. Cymelike.

d.b.h. Diameter breast-high (4½ ft from the ground).

Deciduous. Not persistent; said of leaves falling in autumn or of floral parts falling after anthesis.

Decompound. More than once divided or compounded.

Decurrent. Said of a leaf or leaf scar, part of which extends in a ridge down the twig below the point of insertion.

Decussate. Alternating in pairs at right angles, and scalelike and overlapping.

Dehiscent. Said of the opening of an anther or fruit by valves or slits.

Deliquescent. Descriptive of a tree lacking a main axis. American elm is an extreme example, with its arching habit and drooping branches.

Deltoid. Triangular; the shape of the Greek letter Δ.

Dentate. Said of a margin with sharp teeth pointing outward.

Denticulate. Minutely or finely dentate.

Depressed. Flattened from above.

Determinate. Descriptive of an inflorescence in which the terminal flower blooms slightly in advance of its nearest associates.

Diadelphous. Descriptive of stamens formed into two groups through the union of their filaments.

Dichotomous. Branching by constant forking in pairs.

Dicotyledonous. Having two cotyledons.

Dimorphous. Occurring in two forms.

Dioecious. Unisexual, with staminate and pistillate (ovulate) flowers on separate plants.

Dorsal. Said of the back or outer face of an organ.

Drupaceous. Drupelike.

Drupe. A simple one-seeded fleshy fruit, the outer wall fleshy, the inner wall bony.

Drupelet. A tiny drupe.

Echinate. Armed with prickles.

Eglandular. Without glands.

Ellipsoid. The geometric figure obtained by rotating an ellipse on its longer axis.

Elliptical. Resembling an ellipse.

Emarginate. Having a shallow notch at the extremity.

Entire. Wholly without teeth or other divisions such as lobes.

Entomophilous. Descriptive of flowers dependent upon insects for pollination.

Erose. Irregularly toothed or eroded.

Estipulate. Without stipules.

Exalbuminous. Without albumen.

Excurrent. Descriptive of a tree with a main axis or trunk extending to the top of the crown: e.g. pine, spruce, and fir.

Exserted. Extending beyond.

Extrorse. Facing or operating outward.

Falcate. Sickle- or scythe-shaped.

Fascicled. In clusters or bundles.

Filament. That part of the stamen which supports the anther.

Fluted. Regularly marked by alternating ridges and groovelike depressions.

Foliaceous. Leaflike in appearance and texture.

Follicle. A single carpellate dry fruit dehiscing along one line of suture.

Fruit. The seed-bearing product of a plant.

Fugacious. Soon falling or fading; not permanent.

Fusiform. Spindle-shaped.

Glabrate. Nearly glabrous or becoming glabrous.

Glabrous. Smooth, devoid of pubescence or hair.

Glandular. Furnished with glands, or of the nature of a gland.

Glaucous. Covered with a white waxy substance or bloom.

Globose. Spherical, globular.

Gymnospermous. Bearing naked seeds.

Hammock. An isolated area of Southern hardwood forest on a well-drained site, surrounded by extensive pines or everglade marshland; also a hardwood forest on deep loamy soils rich in humus.

Head. A spherical or flat-topped inflorescence of sessile or nearly sessile flowers clustered on a common receptacle.

Herbarium. A collection of plant specimens, pressed, dried, mounted on sheets, identified and classified.

Hermaphrodite. Bisexual, stamens and pistil(s) in the same flower.

Hilum. Scar or point of attachment of a seed.

Hirsute. With stiff or bristly hairs.

Hoary. Densely grayish-white pubescent.

Hybrid. A cross, usually between two species.

Imbricate. Overlapping.

Imperfect. Descriptive of flowers with the organs of one sex abortive or wanting.

Incised. Cut sharply and irregularly, more or less deeply.

Incomplete. Said of flowers with one or more accessory or essential whorls wanting.

Indehiscent. Not opening by valves or slits.

Indeterminate. Descriptive of an inflorescence in which the flowers open progressively from the base upward.

Indigenous. Native and orginal to the area.

Inequilateral. Asymmetrical.

Inflated. Bladderlike.

Inflorescence. The mode of floral arrangement.

Inserted. Attached to or growing out of.

Internode. That portion of a stem between two nodes.

Introrse. Facing or opening inward.

Involucral. Belonging to an involucre.

Involucrate. Possessing an involucre.

Involucre. A cluster of bracts subtending a flower or inflorescence.

Irregular. See Zygomorphic.

Keel. A central dorsal ridge; the united petals of a papilionaceous flower.

Laciniate. Cut into lobes separated by deep, narrow, irregular incisions.

Lactiferous. Milky, in reference to the sap of certain species.

Lamina. Blade; the expanded portion of a leaf.

Lanceolate. Lance-shaped.

Layering. Rooting of lower side branches.

Leaflet. A single division of a compound leaf.

Legume. A dry fruit, the product of a simple pistil usually dehiscing along two lines of suture.

Lenticellate. Having lenticels.

Lenticular. Shaped like a double-convex lens.

Ligulate. Strap-shaped, or straplike.

Linear. Long and narrow with margins parallel or nearly so.

Lobe. Any protruding segment of an organ.

Lobed. Divided into lobes.

Lunate. Crescent-shaped.

Lustrous. Glossy, shiny.

Membranous. Thin, more or less flexible, and translucent.

Merous. Having a specified number of parts.

Midrib. The main rib or central vein of a leaf.

Monadelphous. Said of stamens united into a tube by the union of their filaments.

Monoclinic. Said of flowers which are perfect.

Monocotyledonous. Having but one cotyledon.

Monoecious. Having unisexual flowers, with both sexes borne on the same plant.

Mucro. Short, narrow, and abrupt tip of a leaf or cone scale (bristle).

Mucronate. Furnished with a mucro (bristle-tipped).

Multiple. A cluster of ripened ovaries traceable to the pistils of separate flowers and inserted on a common receptacle.

Naked bud. Bud without scales.

Nectar. Sweet secretion of a flower.

Nectar gland. Gland secreting nectar.

Nectariferous. Nectar-producing.

Node. That portion of a stem which normally bears a leaf or leaves.

Nut. An indehiscent, usually one-celled, one-seeded fruit (though usually traceable to a compound ovary) with a bony, woody, leathery, or papery wall and generally partially or wholly encased in an involucre or husk.

Nutlet. Diminutive nut.

Ob-. Latin prefix implying inversion.

Obcordate. Inverted heart-shaped.

Oblanceolate. Inverted lanceolate.

Oblong. Longer than broad, with the margins nearly parallel.

Obovate. Inverted ovate.

Obovoid. Appearing as an inverted egg.

Obtuse. Blunt.

Orbicular. Circular.

Oval. Broadly elliptical with the width greater than one-half of the length.

Ovate. Having the lengthwise outline of an egg, broadest at the base.

Ovoid. Egg-shaped.

Ovulate. Pertaining to the ovule, or possessing ovules.

Ovule. That structure which develops into a seed, after fertilization.

Palmate. Radially disposed.

Panicle. A compound or branched raceme.

Paniculate. Resembling a panicle.

Papilionaceous. Descriptive of the flowers of many legumes having a standard, wings, and keel.

Parted. Divided by sinuses which extend nearly to the midrib.

Pectinate. Comblike; beset with narrow closely inserted segments.

Pedicel. The supporting stalk of a single flower.

Peduncle. A primary flower stalk supporting either a cluster or a single flower.

Peltate. Shield-shaped, and attached by its lower surface to the supporting stalk.

Pendulous. Drooping, hanging, or declined.

Penniveined. Veined in a pinnate manner.

Perennial. Lasting year after year.

Perfect. Said of flowers having both sex organs present and functioning.

Perianth. The floral envelope, of whatever form.

Periderm. A protecting layer containing corky cells. The first periderm may form just beneath the epidermis, or deeper in the primary cortex.

Persistent. Evergreen (leaves); long-continuous.

Petal. The unit of the corolla.

Petaloid. Resembling a petal.

Petiole. The stalk of a leaf.

Petioled. Having a petiole.
Petiolule. The stalk of a leaflet.
Petioluled. Having a petiolule.
Pyriform. Pear-shaped.
Receptacle. That expanded portion of the axis which bears the floral organs.
Recurved. Curved downward or backward.
Reflexed. Abruptly bent downward.
Regular. Actinomorphic; uniform in shape.
Reniform. Kidney-shaped.
Repand. Undulate or wavy.
Resin cyst. Cell or cavity occluded with resin.
Reticulate. Forming a network.
Revolute. Rolled backward or under from margin or apex.
Rib. A prominent vein (leaf) or the extended edge of a fruit husk, fruit, or seed.
Rufous. Reddish brown.
Rugose. Wrinkled (leaf surfaces with sunken veins).
Samara. A winged achenelike fruit.
Samaroid. Samaralike.
Scabrous. With short bristly hairs; rough to the touch.
Scurfy. Covered with small scales.
Seed. The ripened ovule.
Sepal. A unit of the calyx.
Serotinous. Descriptive of fruits that ripen late, or later than those of other species in the same genus; also of cones that remain closed long after the seeds inside are ripe (see jack pine).
Serrate. With sharp teeth pointing forward.
Serrulate. Minutely serrate.
Sessile. Without a stalk of any kind.
Sheath. A tubular envelope.
Simple. Of one piece; not compound.
Sinuate. Deeply or strongly undulate or wavy.
Sinus. A recess, cleft, or gap between two lobes.
Spatulate. Spatula-shaped.
Spike. An inflorescence consisting of a central rachis bearing a number of sessile flowers.
Spikelet. Diminutive spike.
Spine. A sharp, woody outgrowth from the stem.
Spinose. Spinelike or furnished with spines.
Spur. A short, compact branch with little or no internodal development.
Stamen. Pollen-bearing organ of the flower.
Stellate. Star-shaped.
Stem. Main axis of the plant.
Sterigmata. Small woody peglike outgrowths of the twig, bearing leaves or needles. (See spruces.)
Sterile. Unproductive.
Stigma. That part of the pistil which receives the pollen.
Stipulate. Furnished with stipules.
Stipule. A leafy appendage attached to the twig at the base of a petiole; usually in pairs, one on each side.
Stolon. A lower branch or runner which is disposed to root.
Stoma (or stomate). A specialized orifice in the epidermis of leaves, communicating with internal intercellular spaces.

Striate. With fine grooves, ridges, or lines of color.

Strobile. An inflorescence (or cone) featured by imbricated bracts or scales.

Strobilus. Same as strobile.

Style. That part of the pistil which connects the stigma with the ovary.

Subulate. Awl-shaped.

Succulent. Juicy or pulpy.

Superposed. Inserted one over the other.

Suture. Line of dehiscence.

Sympetalous. With partially or wholly fused petals.

Terete. Circular in transverse section.

Ternate. In threes.

Thorn. A sharp modified branch.

Tomentose. Furnished with tomentum.

Tomentum. Dense matter pubescence.

Trichotomous. Three-forked.

Trifoliolate. Having three leaflets.

Tripinnate. Thrice pinnate.

Truncate. As though abruptly cut off transversely and forming an angle of about 180 degrees.

Tubercle. A small tuberlike body, not necessarily subterranean.

Tuberculate. Furnished with knoblike excrescences or tubercles.

Turbinate. Top-shaped.

Umbel. An indeterminate inflorescence consisting of several pedicelled flowers all attached at the same point on the peduncle.

Umbellate. Umbel-like.

Umbo. A boss or protuberance.

Undulate. Wavy, repand.

Unisexual. Having one sex only.

Valvate. Opening by valves, as in a capsule or some leaf buds; meeting at the edges without overlapping.

Valve. One of the pieces into which dehiscent fruits are split.

Ventral. Pertaining to the inner or under surface; the opposite of dorsal.

Vernal. Pertaining to spring.

Verticillate. Whorled.

Villous. With long, silky, straight hairs.

Whorl. Cyclic arrangement of appendages at a node.

Woolly. Clothed with long, matted hairs.

Zygomorphic. Capable of equal division by only one plane of symmetry or none at all.

Official State Trees
of the United States

Compiled by the American Forestry Association, 1965 (281); for an evaluation of State Tree Identification Guides, see Andresen (6).

Year
Official

1949 Alabama—Southern pine *Pinus* spp.

1962 Alaska—Sitka spruce *Picea sitchensis* (Bong.) Carr.

1954 Arizona—palo verde *Cercidium* spp.

1939 Arkansas—pine *Pinus* spp.

1937 California—coast redwood *Sequoia sempervirens* (D. Don.) Endl.

1954 California—giant sequoia *Sequoia gigantea* (Lindl.) Decne.

1939 Colorado—blue spruce *Picea pungens* Engelm.

1947 Connecticut—white oak *Quercus alba* L.

1939 Delaware—American holly *Ilex opaca* Ait.

1960 Dist. of Columbia—scarlet oak *Quercus coccinea* Muenchh.

1953 Florida—Sabal palm *Sabal palmetto* (Walt.) Lodd.

1937 Georgia—live oak *Quercus virginiana* Mill.

1959 Hawaii—candlenut *Aleurites moluccana* Willd.

1935 Idaho—western white pine *Pinus monticola* Dougl.

Year
Official

1908 Illinois—native oak *Quercus* spp.

1931 Indiana—tulip tree *Liriodendron tulipifera* L.

1961 Iowa—oak *Quercus* spp.

1937 Kansas—cottonwood *Populus* spp.

1956 Kentucky—yellow-poplar *Liriodendron tulipifera* L.

1963 Louisiana—baldcypress *Taxodium distichum* (L.) Rich.

1945 Maine—eastern white pine *Pinus strobus* L.

1941 Maryland—white oak *Quercus alba* L.

1941 Massachusetts—American elm *Ulmus americana* L.

1955 Michigan—eastern white pine *Pinus strobus* L.

1953 Minnesota—red pine *Pinus resinosa* Ait.

1938 Mississippi—magnolia *Magnolia grandiflora* L.

1955 Missouri—flowering dogwood *Cornus florida* L.

1949 Montana—ponderosa pine *Pinus ponderosa* Laws.

Year
Official

1937　Nebraska—American elm *Ulmus americana* L.

1953　Nevada—singleleaf pinon *Pinus monophylla* Torr. and Frem.

1947　New Hampshire—white birch *Betula papyrifera* Marsh.

1950　New Jersey—red oak *Quercus rubra* L.

1949　New Mexico—pinon *Pinus edulis* Engelm.

1956　New York—sugar maple *Acer saccharum* Marsh.

1963　North Carolina—pine *Pinus* spp.

1947　North Dakota—American elm *Ulmus americana* L.

1953　Ohio—Ohio buckeye *Aesculus glabra* Willd.

1937　Oklahoma—redbud *Cercis canadensis* L.

1939　Oregon—Douglas-fir *Pseudotsuga menziesii* (Mirb.) France

1931　Pennsylvania—eastern hemlock *Tsuga canadensis* (L.) Carr.

Year
Official

1964　Rhode Island—red maple *Acer rubrum* L.

1939　South Carolina—palmetto *Sabal palmetto* (Walt.) Lodd.

1947　South Dakota—Black Hills spruce *Picea glauca* var. *densata* Bailey

1947　Tennessee—tulip poplar *Liriodendron tulipifera* L.

1919　Texas—pecan *Carya illinoensis* (Wangenh.) K. Koch.

1933　Utah—blue spruce *Picea pungens* Engelm.

1949　Vermont—sugar maple *Acer saccharum* Marsh.

1956　Virginia—flowering dogwood *Cornus florida* L.

1947　Washington—western hemlock *Tsuga heterophylla* (Raf.) Sarg.

1949　West Virginia—sugar maple *Acer saccharum* Marsh.

1949　Wisconsin—sugar maple *Acer saccharum* Marsh.

1947　Wyoming—plains cottonwood *Populus sargentii* Dode

Derivations of Some
Scientific Names[1]

To save space, the derivation of such obvious names as *resinosa, shastensis, tomentosa,* and *virginiana* has been omitted, as well as that of such names as *Robinia,* whose origin is already mentioned in the text.

Abies. The ancient Latin name for the European fir.
Acacia. From the Greek *akakia,* the Egyptian thorn-tree; *akis,* a thorn.
Acer. From the Celtic *ac,* hard; a quality of maple wood.
Aesculus. The ancient name for some European nut-bearing tree.
Ailanthus. Said to be from the Mollucan name *ailanto* (treeofheaven), in reference to its height.
alba. From the Latin *alba,* white.
albicaulis. From *alba,* white, plus *caulis,* stem, i.e., "white-bark."
Alnus. From the old Latin name for the alder.
alternifolia. Referring to the alternate leaves (Greek *phyllon,* leaf) of *Cornus alternifolia.*
altissima. From the Latin *altus,* high, in reference to the height of the tree.
amabilis. From the Latin *amare,* to love, or lovely, in reference to the beautiful appearance of *Abies amabilis.*
aristata. From the Latin *arista,* bristle, or thorn.
aucuparia. From the Latin *aucupari,* to catch birds. In Europe, mountain-ash fruits were used as bait in catching birds.
australis. From the Latin *auster,* the south wind, given to trees with a southern range.
avium. From the Latin *avis,* bird.
banksiana. From the surname Banks.
Betula. The common Latin name of the birch; from the Sanskrit *bhūrja,* to shine, referring to the bark of the birch.

[1] Adapted from Gray's "Manual of Botany," 8th ed. (124), an unpublished manuscript by C. C. Forsaith, and the latter's Glossary of Derivations in "Trees of Northeastern United States" by H. P. Brown (51).

bicolor. From the Latin, meaning two-colored, in reference to the leaves of swamp white oak which are green above and pale below.

borealis. From Boreas, the Greek god of the north wind; boreal, meaning northern, stems from the same origin.

Broussonetia. Named for the naturalist Auguste Broussonet.

candicans. From the Latin *candicare*, meaning whitish; referring perhaps to the paler undersurface of the leaf in Balm-of-Gilead.

Carpinus. The Latin common name for the European hornbeam.

Carya. From the Greek *karya*, the name applied to the walnut tree.

Castanea. From the Greek *kastanea*, or chestnut.

Castanopsis. Meaning chestnutlike.

Catalpa. From the Cherokee Indian name *catawba*, applied to this tree.

Celtis. The name which Pliny gave to the African lotus, and later applied to the hackberry genus because of the sweet fruit of the European hackberry.

cembroides. Cembralike, because of the fancied resemblance of *Pinus cembroides* to *P. cembra* of Europe.

cerasus. The old Latin name of the cherry tree.

Cercis. From the Greek *kerkis*, a shuttle, in fancied resemblance of the legume to that instrument.

Chamaecyparis. From the Greek *chamai*, on the ground, and *kyparissos*, the cypress; meaning low-growing.

chrysophylla. From two Greek words *chrysos*, golden, and *phyllon*, leaf.

cinerea. From the Latin *cineris*, dust, or ashes, in reference to the pale gray color of the bark of butternut.

Cladrastis. From two Greek words *clados*, branch, and *thrastos*, brittle, in reference to the somewhat brittle branches of the yellowwood.

clausa. From the Latin *clausus*, to shut, in refernce to the cones of sand pine, which often remain closed for several years.

coccinea. From the Greek *kakkos*, a seed or berry, in reference to the red autumn coloration of the scarlet oak.

communis. From the Latin, meaning common, or as applied to *Juniperus communis*, in reference to its wide distribution.

concolor. A combination of the Latin *con*, together, and color, meaning of one color.

contorta. From the Latin *con*, together, and *torquere*, to twist, referring perhaps to the twisted branches of the "shore pine" form of lodgepole pine.

cordiformis. From the Latin *cor, cordis*, heart, and *forma*, shaped, in reference perhaps to the shape of the fruit of bitternut hickory.

Cornus. The Latin name for the dogwood, from *cornu*, horn, in reference to the hard wood of this genus.

Crataegus. From the Latin name for the hawthorn, through the Greek *krataigos*, thorn-tree, and *kratos*, strength, because of the strong hard wood.

Cupressus. The classical common name of the Italian cypress, from the Greek *kyparissos*, derived from an ancient Semitic name.

decidua. From the Latin *de*, down, and *cadere*, to fall.

dioicus. From the Latin, meaning two houses, and derived from the Greek *di*, two, and *oikos*, house, in reference to the dioecious (same origin) coffeetree.

Diospyros. From the Greek *dios*, of God, and *pyros*, wheat. Probably the name of some Asiatic species with cherrylike fruit.

distichum. From the Greek *di*, two, and *stichos*, rank, meaning two-ranked.

echinata. The Latin for prickly, from the Greek *echinos*, a hedgehog; in reference to the prickly cone scales of shortleaf pine.

eugenei. The Latinized form of Eugene, the son of Simon-Louis, who discovered the Carolina poplar and named it in his son's honor.

Fagus. From the Greek *phagein*, to eat, in reference to the edible fruit.

florida. From the Latin *flos*, flower, flowery, in refernce to the flowers of flowering dogwood.

floridanum. Latinized form indicating the state of Florida; applied to species found in the South or in that state.

Fraxinus. The Latin common name of the ash tree.

Gleditsia. Named after J. D. Gleditsch, a German botanist of the time of Linnaeus.

Gymnocladus. From the Greek *gymnos*, naked, and *klados*, branch, hence "naked branch." Applied to the coffeetree because of its large stout branches from which the leaves emerge later in the spring than those of many of its associates.

Hamamelis. From the Greek name for the medlar, or some similar tree.

heterophylla. From two Greek words *heteros*, different, and *phyllon*, leaf, therefore meaning varied leaf, in reference to the variation in the leaves of certain species.

hippocastanum. The Latin common name for the horse-chestnut tree, from the Greek *hippos*, horse, and *kastanon*, chestnut.

Ilex. The Latin common name for the holly oak, *Quercus ilex*.

ilicifolia. From the Latin *ilicis*, the genitive of *Ilex*, and *folium*, leaf.

imbricaria. From the Latin, meaning covered with overlapping plates or scales.

incana. A Latin word meaning gray or hoary.

Juglans. From two Latin words *Jovis*, Jupiter, and *Glans*, nut.

Juniperus. The Latin common name for the cedar, from *junio*, young, and *parere*, to produce, hence youth-producing, or evergreen.

laciniosa. From the Latin *lacinia*, shred, flap, or tip, in reference to the bark of shellbark hickory.

laricina. Pertaining to the larch.

Larix. The Latin common name for the larch.

Leitneria. Named after Dr. E. T. Leitner, a German naturalist, who was killed in Florida during the Seminole war.

lenta. From the Latin *lenis*, soft or smooth, pliable; in reference perhaps to the supple branchlets of the black birch.

Libocedrus. From the Greek *libas*, resinous, and the Latin *cedrus*, the common name of the cedar.

Liquidambar. From the Latin *liquidus*, liquid, and the Arabic *ambar*, amber, in reference to the resinous juice containing storax which exudes from the injured bark of the Asiatic and also American species of *Liquidambar*.

Liriodendron. From the Greek *leiron*, lily, and *dendron*, tree, hence "lily-tree," in reference to the showy flowers of *Liriodendron*.

Lithocarpus. From the Greek *lithos*, stone, and *karpos*, seed, hence "stony-seed."

lutea. From the Latin *lutum*, mud or clay (yellowish).

lyrata. From the Greek *lyra*, a lyre, or lute, hence lyre-shaped.

Maclura. Named after William Maclure, an eighteenth-century geologist.

macrocarpa. From the Greek *makros*, large, and *karpos*, seed, in reference to the large acorn of bur oak.

Malus. The Latin name for the apple, from the Greek *melon*, through the Doric *malon*.

mariana. From the Latin for the state of Maryland.

marilandica. Same as mariana.

montana. From the Latin *mons, montis*, mountain.

monticola.   A combination of the above and *colere*, to dwell.

Morus.   From the ancient Greek name *morea*, the mulberry tree.

Myrica.   From the Greek *myrike*, the tamarisk.

negundo.   The Latinized form of the Malayan name for V*itex negundo;* presumably applied to the boxelder because of the similarity of the leaves of the two species.

nigra.   The Latin for dark or black.

Nyssa.   From the Greek *nysa*, nymph, in mythology the nurse of Bacchus. Linnaeus applied the name to water tupelo presumably because of its habitat.

occidentalis.   The Latin for west, from *occidere*, to set as the sun; the name given by Linnaeus to several species of the western world.

octandra.   The Latin for eight-stamened, from the Greek *okto*, eight, and *aner, andr-*, male, stamen.

opaca.   The Latin for dark, dull, or shady (opaque), in reference to the dark green leaves of the holly.

Ostrya.   From the Greek *ostrya*, the common name of a tree with hard wood.

ovalis.   Same as ovata, or pertaining to an egg.

ovata.   From the Latin *ovum*, egg, hence egg-shaped.

Oxydendrum.   From the Greek *oxys*, sour or sharp, and *dendron,* tree, in reference to the sour-tasting leaves of this tree.

palustris.   The Latin, meaning "of the swamp," from *palus*, swamp.

papyrifera.   From the Egyptian name for the reed from which paper was made, through the Greek *papuros*, or *papyros*, and the Latin *ferre*, to bear.

phellos.   The Greek word *phellos*, cork; the Latin common name of the cork oak.

Picea.   The Latin common name for the pine, spruce, or fir, from the Greek *pissa*, pitch, or *peuke*, the Greek name for the fir.

Pinus.   The Latin name for the pine, from the Sanskrit *pitu*, through the Greek *pitus*.

Platanus.   The Latin common name for the sycamore, or planetree, from the Greek *platanos*, broad.

plicata.   From the Latin *plicare*, to fold, perhaps in reference to the overlapping or "folded" leaves of western redcedar.

pomifera.   The Latin for apple-bearing, from *pomum*, the apple, and *ferre*, to bear.

ponderosa.   From the Latin *pondus*, a weight, hence of great weight.

Populus.   The Latin common name for this group of trees.

prinus.   From the Greek *prinos*, the name for some evergreen tree.

procera.   The Latin for tall, or high.

Prunus.   From the Greek *prunos*, plum or cherry.

pseudoacacia.   From the Greek *pseudo*, false, and acacia (which see).

Pseudotsuga.   Meaning false hemlock.

pumila.   The Latin for dwarf.

pungens.   From the Latin *pungere*, to sting or prick, hence either prickly or pungent; in reference to the needles of blue spruce which are sharp-pointed and have a pungent taste.

Quercus.   The Latin common name of the oak.

regia.   From the Latin *rex*, or *regis*, a king.

Rhamnus.   From the Greek *rhamnos*, the common name of the buckthorn.

Rhododendron.   From the Greek *rodon*, rose, and *dendron*, tree.

Rhus.   From *rhous*, the Greek common name of the sumac through the Greek *reo*, to flow.

rubens.   From the Latin *rubere*, to be red.

rubra.   The Latin word for red.

saccharinum.   Considered by some to be a misspelling of saccharum (which see).

saccharum. The Latin word for sweet or sugar, through the Sanskrit *śarkarā,* and the Greek *sakcharon.*

Salix. The ancient Latin common name of the willow.

Sassafras. Perhaps derived from the Indian name of the tree in Florida, or from the Spanish *saxafrax* (*saxifraga*) in reference to its possible medicinal value.

sempervirens. From the Latin *semper,* always, and *vivere,* to live, hence "always living," in reference either to the great age of the redwood or to its evergreen foliage.

serotina. From the Latin *serus,* late, in reference to the tardily opening cones of pond pine, the autumn flowering of the red elm, and the late appearance of flowers and fruit in black cherry.

sitchensis. The Latin form of *sitka,* the Indian name for an island in Alaska.

Sorbus. The Latin common name for this genus.

speciosa. From the Latin *species,* form, or appearance, and *osus,* full of, in reference to the showy flowers of the catalpa.

spicatum. From the Latin *spica,* a spike or ear of grain, in reference to the pointed inflorescence of mountain maple.

stellata. The Latin for covered with stars, from *stella,* star, and the Sanskrit *star;* in reference to the starlike tufts of pubescence on the leaves of the post oak.

strobus. From the Greek *strobos,* or *strobilos,* cone.

styraciflua. The Latin word meaning styrax-flowing, in reference to the resinous exudation of the bark of the sweetgum.

sylvestris. (Also sylvatica) from the Latin *silva,* forest, hence "of the forest."

tacamahaca. From the Aztec *tecomahiyac* in reference to the resin of *Bursera tomentosa;* applied to the balsam poplar because of its sticky buds.

taeda. The Latin word meaning a torch of pine wood, in reference to the pine knot torches from the loblolly pine (also other hard pines).

taxifolia. From *Taxus,* yew, and *folium,* leaf, hence with yewlike leaves.

Taxodium. Taxus-like.

Taxus. From the Greek *taxos,* common name of the yew.

Thuja. From the Greek *thyia,* the common name of an aromatic African tree; from *thyo,* perfume.

thyoides. Thuja-like.

Tilia. The Latin common name of the linden (basswood).

Toxicodendron. From the Greek *toxikon,* poison, and *dendron,* tree.

Toxylon. From the Greek *toxon,* bow, and *xylon,* wood, hence bow-wood.

triacanthos. From the Greek *treis,* three, and *akantha,* a spine, in reference to the three-branched thorns of honeylocust.

trichocarpa. From the Greek *thrix,* a hair, and *karpos,* fruit, presumably in reference to the hairy fruit of the black cottonwood.

Tsuga. The Latinized form of the Japanese common name of a hemlock.

tulipifera. Meaning "tulip-bearing" in reference to the flowers of tuliptree.

typhina. Meaning "cat-tail-like," in reference perhaps to the hairy branchlets of staghorn sumac.

Ulmus. The ancient Latin name of the elm.

velutina. From the Latin *velutum,* velvety, and *vellus,* a fleece.

vernix. The Latin for varnish; a black varnish may be made from poison-sumac as well as from the Asiatic species.

vitellina. From the Latin *vitellus,* egg yolk, in reference to the yellow twigs of yellowstem white willow.

Zanthoxylum. From the Greek *zanthos,* yellow, and *xylon,* wood.

Synopsis of Some
Important References

During the last decade or two, the time devoted to dendrology in the nation's schools and colleges of forestry has been reduced, in some cases drastically (156). For those who wish to study the topic further, we have marked with an asterisk some of the "Selected References" in the next section which we and others have found significant; we now give a synopsis of certain ones of them.

1. Abrams, L. "An Illustrated Flora of the Pacific States." 4 vols. Stanford Univ. Press, Calif. 1923 to 1960. This monumental flora includes keys, botanical descriptions, habitat, and geographical distribution, and is illustrated with line drawings.

2. Alston, R. E., and B. L. Turner. "Biochemical Systematics." 404 pp. Prentice-Hall, Inc., Englewood Cliffs, N.J. 1963. An introduction to problems in plant taxonomy is followed by summaries of biochemical research and the ways in which it may be useful in constructing phylogenetic systems.

3. Bailey, L. H. "The Standard Cyclopedia of Horticulture," 2d ed. 3 vols., 3,639 pp. 4,000 engravings, over 100 full-page photo-reproductions, some in color. The Macmillan Company, New York. 1942. This comprehensive work covers the identification and culture of thousands of trees, shrubs, vines, and herbaceous plants used in horticulture. For the forester, or plantsman, it is an almost inexhaustible source of information to answer the many questions often asked by clients.

4. Bakuzis, E. V., and H. L. Hansen. "Balsam Fir." 445 pp. Univ. of Minnesota Press, Minneapolis, Minn. 1965. A monograph based on a review of some 2,300 references, 1,393 of which are cited, the final date for listing references was July 1, 1963. This is the source book for anyone interested in balsam fir or the forests in which it is found.

5. Benson, L., R. A. Darrow, and others. A Manual of Southwestern Desert Trees and Shrubs. 409 pp., illustr. with line drawings, photo halftones, and color plates. *Biol. Bull. 6*, Univ. of Arizona, Tucson. 1944. Keys to genera and species precede dendrological notes; detailed range maps further enhance the value of this publication.

6. Braun, E. L. "Deciduous Forests of Eastern North America." 596 pp., illustr. with photo halftones. McGraw-Hill Book Company, New York. 1950. A comprehensive ecological study of forest types, it follows the development of climax forests following glaciation and the effect of man on today's forests. Maps showing soil types and extent of glaciation are included.

7. ————. "The Woody Plants of Ohio." 362 pp., illustr. with line drawings. Ohio State Univ. Press, Columbus, Ohio. 1961. Keys, botanical descriptions, habitat notes, and distribution (maps) by counties are featured for each species covered. Also included is a list of herbaria in Ohio.

8. Brown, H. P. "Trees of the Northeastern United States." 490 pp., illustr. with line drawings. The Christopher Publishing House, Boston, Mass. 1938. The author describes 152 native and naturalized species with regard to habit, leaves, flowers, fruit, winter characters, habitat, range, and uses. Separate keys to leaves, fruits, and twigs are included.

9. Collingwood, G. H., and W. D. Brush. "Knowing Your Trees." 349 pp., 900 photographic halftones. American Forestry Assoc., Washington, D.C. 1966. Besides the usual dendrological features, the writers include interesting notes on the discovery and pioneer uses of the various species, also a description of the wood and its utilization. Range maps and the numerous illustrations of open-grown specimens, leaves, flowers, fruit, and bark have made this one of the most popular of tree books.

10. Core, E. L., and N. P. Ammons. "Woody Plants in Winter." 218 pp. The Boxwood Press, Pittsburgh, Pa. 1958. Keys, exceptionally clear line drawings, short descriptions, and ranges comprise this useful handbook to northeastern species in winter.

11. Dallimore, W., and A. B. Jackson. "A Handbook of Coniferae and Ginkgoaceae." 5th ed. by S. G. Harrison. St. Martins Press, New York. 1967. 727 pp., illustr. with line drawings and photographic halftones. The world's conifers as then known are listed and described, making this a standard reference work for students, foresters, and gardeners. Keys to species hardy in the climate of Britain are included.

12. Deam, C. C., and T. E. Shaw. "Trees of Indiana." 330 pp., photo illustrated, with herbarium mounts. The Bookwalter Co., Indianapolis. 1953. In addition to dendrological descriptions and keys, range maps showing distribution by counties are included.

13. Den Ouden, P., and B. K. Boom. "Manual of Cultivated Conifers Hardy in the Cold- and Warm-Temperate Zone." 526 pp. Martinus Nijhoff, The Hague, Holland. 1965. Illustrated with many photographic halftones, this comprehensive large-format work lists 303 species, 208 varieties, and 1,935 cultivars, together with their distinguishing characteristics. It is especially valuable for students in landscape architecture.

14. Eifert, V. S. "Tall Trees and Far Horizons." 301 pp. Dodd, Mead & Company, Inc., New York. 1965. These narratives of the adventures and discoveries of early botanists in America include such names as John Bartram, Peter Kalm, Thomas Nuttall, David Douglas, and Henry David Thoreau. The stories give a human dimension to some of the most famous explorer-botanists of their time.

15. Fernald, M. L. "Gray's Manual of Botany," 8th ed. 1,632 pp., illustr. with occasional line drawings. American Book Company, New York. 1950. This monumental work, first published more than a century ago, now contains descriptions

and keys to more than 8,000 species, varieties, forms, and named hybrids. Meanings and pronunciations of scientific names are included, as are abbreviated distributions by states.

16. Fowells, H. A., and others. Silvics of Forest Trees of the United States. 762 pp. *U.S. Dept. Agr. Hdbk.* 271, 1965. For over a decade, the several experiment stations of the U.S. Forest Service have been preparing silvical leaflets on local tree species. These have been reviewed and published in a single volume. Besides the silvics of 127 species, generic descriptions are given, also large-scale range maps prepared by Dr. E. L. Little, Jr., Dendrologist of the Forest Service. Depending upon its importance, each description is followed by 50 to 100 or more references. Photographic halftones of leaves, fruits, and forests appear throughout. This book should be in every forester's library.

17. Fry, W., and J. R. White. "Bigtrees," 114 pp., illustr. with photo halftones. Stanford Univ. Press, Calif. 1930. A delightful narrative of the life history of the giant sequoia, including its encounters with lightning.

18. Hough, R. B. "Handbook of the Trees of the Northern States and Canada." 470 pp., illustr. with photo halftones. Publ. by the author, Lowville, N.Y. 1907. The herbarium-type arrangements of foliage and fruit are photographed upon a grid of 1-in. squares to show relative sizes. Each tree is featured by a page-length photograph of the bark; range maps are also shown.

19. Kelsey, H. P., and W. A. Dayton. "Standardized Plant Names," 2d ed. J. H. McFarland, Harrisburg, Pa. 1942. An effort to bring order out of chaos which has had various responses from those who use "common" names. See Introduction.

20. Little, E. L., Jr. Check List of Native and Naturalized Trees of the United States. 472 pp. *U.S. Dept. Agr. Hdbk.* 41, 1953. The official list of scientific and common names used by the Forest Service. Range descriptions are included. This book should be in every forester's library.

21. MacDonald, D. A. "Native Trees of Canada." 293 pp., illustr. with line drawings and photographic halftones. *Dominion Forest Service. Bull.* 61, Ottawa, 1949. Besides dendrological and silvical descriptions, there are range maps showing where the species are found in Canada and the adjacent areas of the United States.

22. Michaux, F. A., and T. Nuttall. "The North American Sylva." 5 vols. Rice and Hart, Philadelphia, Pa. 1857–1859. A superb early work by these prominent botanist-explorers describing the trees of North America. It also notes their uses "in the arts and their introduction into commerce." The full-page color plates are an outstanding feature.

23. Rehder, A. "Manual of Cultivated Trees and Shrubs," 2d ed. 996 pp. The Macmillan Company, New York. 1940. A comprehensive manual covering more than 2,550 species in addition to many varieties. It features keys, botanical descriptions, ranges, and zone hardiness.

24. Sargent, Charles S. "The Silva of North America." 14 vols. Exquisitely illustrated by the line drawings of French artist Charles E. Faxon. Houghton Mifflin Company, Boston. 1890–1902. These monumental volumes by America's most illustrious dendrologist, founder and director of the Arnold Arboretum, have been the basis for most other books written on North American trees. Long out of print, it can be found in libraries and should be known by everyone with a serious interest in the descriptions of trees.

25. ———. "Manual of the Trees of North America," 2d ed. 910 pp., with 783 illustrations of leaves, flowers, and fruit. Houghton Mifflin Company, Boston. 1922. Reprinted in 2 vols., paperback, Dover Publications, Inc., New York. 1965. Here is an updated condensation of the "Silva" representing the author's continuous study of North American trees over a period of 44 years.

26. Small, J. K. "Manual of the Southeastern Flora." 1,554 pp., illustr. with line drawings of flower parts. Publ. by the author, 1933. In the separation of species and genera there are "lumpers" and "splitters." Students with a conservative background in taxonomy will be fascinated to see how Dr. Small rearranged certain groups. As an example, the native maples are split into five genera, *Acer, Saccharodendron, Argentacer, Rufacer,* and *Negundo.*

27. Steyermark, J. A. "Flora of Missouri." 1,725 pp. Iowa State Univ. Press, Ames, Iowa. 1963. Copiously illustrated and keyed, and giving distribution maps by counties, this book describes some 2,400 species of flowering plants and ferns. It is not only a manual for the central states but also for other regions where the same species are found.

28. Sudworth, G. B. "Check List of Forest Trees of the United States." *U.S. Dept. Agr. Misc. Cir.* 92, 1927. See Introduction.

29. U.S. Dept. Agr. Trees. 944 pp. *Yearbook of Agriculture,* 1949. Here is a veritable treasure house on trees and forests. The dendrology section (available separately as No. 2156) by Dr. E. L. Little, Jr., gives short descriptions, line drawings of leaves and fruits, and range maps for 165 native species. This is followed by a similar section entitled "Fifty Trees from Foreign Lands."

30. U.S. Dept. Agr. Forest Service. Woody Plant Seed Manual. 416 pp. *Misc. Publ.* 654, 1948. Subjects include seeds—their development, production, dispersal, source, collection, extraction, storage, and number per pound; dormancy, germination, and testing. Illustrated with line drawings and photographic halftones of seeds (enlarged) and seedlings, which often look quite different from the adult plant. This book should be in every forester's library.

31. Vines, R. A. "Trees, Shrubs and Woody Vines of the Southwest." 1,104 pp., illustr. Univ. of Texas Press, Austin, 1960. Produced in large format, this manual includes not only the usual identification features but also notes on propagation, medicinal uses, importance to wildlife, appearance and uses of the wood, range, and value to horticulture.

Selected References

*1. Abrams, L. "An Illustrated Flora of the Pacific States." 4 vols. Stanford Univ. Press, Palo Alto, Calif. 1923–1960.

*2. Alston, R. E., and B. L. Turner. "Biochemical Systematics." Prentice-Hall, Inc., Englewood Cliffs, N.J. 1963.

*3. Anderson, E. "Introgressive Hybridization." John Wiley & Sons, Inc., New York. 1949.

4. Anderson, J. P. "Flora of Alaska." Iowa State Univ. Press, Ames, Iowa. 1959.

5. ———. "Trees and Shrubs; Food, Medicinal, and Poisonous Plants of British Columbia." Dept. Ed., Victoria, B.C. 1925.

*6. Andresen, J. W. An Evaluation of State Tree Identification Guides of the United States. *Jour. For.* **59**:349–355, 1961.

7. ———. The Taxonomic Status of *Pinus chiapensis. Phytologia* **10**:417–421, 1964.

8. Anonymous. The Dawn-redwood. *Amer. For.* **54**:353, 1948.

9. Anonymous. The Properties of Australian Timbers. 3. *Pinus radiata* D. Don (*P. insignis* Dougl.) Insignis, Monterey, or Remarkable Pine. *Div. For. Prods. Australia Tech. Paper* 28, 1938.

10. Anonymous. "Science Seeks New Trees for the Forests of the Future." Undated publication, Inst. For. Genetics, Placerville, Calif.

11. Anonymous. South Dakota Trees, Flowers, and Shrubs. Unnumbered and undated circular, Dept. Agr., Pierre, S.D.

12. Arnst, A. Cascara: A Crop from West Coast Tree Farms. *Jour. For.* **43**:805–811, 1945.

13. Ashe, W. W. Loblolly or North Carolina Pine. *N.C. Geo. Econ. Survey Bull.* 24, 1915.

14. ———. Note on Magnolia and Other Woody Plants. *Torreya* **31**:37–41, 1931.

15. Aughanbaugh, J. E. Recovery of the Chestnut in Pennsylvania. *Pa. Dept. For. Waters Cir.* 1, 1930.

16. ———. Replacement of the Chestnut in Pennsylvania. *Pa. Dept. For. Waters Bull.* 54, 1935.

17. Bailey, L. H. "The Cultivated Conifers." The Macmillan Company, New York. 1933.

18. ———. "How Plants Get Their Names." Dover Publications, Inc., New York. 1963.

*19. ———. "The Standard Cyclopedia of Horticulture," vols. I, II, and III. The Macmillan Company, New York. 1942.

20. Baker, F. S. Aspen in the Central Rocky Mountain Region. *U.S. Dept. Agr. Bull.* 1291, 1925.

21. ———. A Revised Tolerance Table. *Jour. For.* 47:179–181, 1949.

°22. Bakuzis, E. V., and H. L. Hansen. "Balsam Fir." Univ. of Minnesota Press, Minneapolis, Minn. 1965.

°23. Baldwin, H. I. "Forest Tree Seed of the North Temperate Regions with Special Reference to North America." Chronica Botanica Co., Waltham, Mass. 1942.

24. Bandekow, R. J. Present and Potential Sources of Tannin in the United States. *Jour. For.* 45:729–734, 1947.

°25. Bannister, B. Dendrochronology. Reprinted from "Science in Archaeology." Basic Books Inc., New York. 1963.

26. Baudendistal, M. E. and B. H. Paul. Southern Hard Elms as Substitutes for Rock Elm. *South. Lumb.* 169(2128):211–215, 1944.

27. Bear, J. E., and A. F. Sievers. Sumac, Its Collection and Culture as a Source of Tannin. *U.S. Dept. Agr. Prod. Res. Rep.* 8, 1957.

28. Bell, L. E., and D. P. White. "Technical Manual for Christmas Tree Farmers." Allied Chemical Corp., New York. 1966.

29. Benson, L. "Plant Classification." D. C. Heath and Company, Boston, Mass. 1957.

°30. ———. "Plant Taxonomy." The Ronald Press Company, New York. 1962.

°31. ——— and R. A. Darrow. "The Trees and Shrubs of the Southwestern Deserts." Univ. of Arizona Press, Tucson, and University of New Mexico Press, Albuquerque, 1954.

°32. Bentham, G., and J. D. Hooker. "Genera Plantarum." London. 1862–1883.

°33. Berry, E. W. "Tree Ancestors." The Williams & Wilkins Company, Baltimore. 1923.

34. Bieberdorf, F. W., and others. Vegetation as a Measure Indicator of Air Pollution, I. The Pine (Pinus Taeda). *Bull. Torrey Bot. Club* 85:197–200, 1958.

35. Billings, W. D. Nevada Trees. *Agr. Ext. Serv. Bull.* 94, 2d ed., Univ. of Nevada, 1954.

36. Bishop, G. N., and W. H. Duncan. A New White Oak from Georgia: Its Associates and Habitat. *Jour. For.* 39:730, 1941.

37. ——— and T. C. Nelson. A Winter Key to the Hickories of Georgia. *S.E. For. Exp. Sta. Res. Note* 89, U.S. Dept. Agr., 1955.

38. Blackburn, B. "Trees and Shrubs in Eastern North America: Key to Broadleaved Species." Oxford Univ. Press, New York. 1952.

°39. Blakeslee, A. F., and C. D. Jarvis. "Trees in Winter." The Macmillan Company, New York. 1913. (Abridged ed., 1931.)

40. Bode, I. T., and G. B. MacDonald. "A Handbook of the Native Trees of Iowa." Iowa State College, Ames, Iowa. 1928.

41. Bowers, N. A. "Cone-bearing Trees of the Pacific Coast." Pacific Books, Palo Alto, Calif. 5th printing, 1956.

°42. Braun, E. L. "Deciduous Forests of Eastern North America." McGraw-Hill Book Company, New York. 1950.

°43. ———. "The Woody Plants of Ohio." Ohio State Univ. Press, Columbus. 1961.

44. Britton, N. L. "North American Trees." Henry Holt and Company, Inc., New York. 1908.

°45. ——— and A. Brown. "Illustrated Flora of the Northeastern United States and Adjacent Canada." Revised by H. A. Gleason, New York Bot. Gard., New York, 1952. Issued in 3 vols. by Hafner Press, New York. 1963.

46. Brizicky, G. K. The Genera of Anacardiaceae in the Southeastern United States. *Jour. Arnold Arb.* **43**:359–375, 1962.

47. ———. Taxonomic and Nomenclatural Notes on the Genus Rhus (Anacardiaceae). *Jour. Arnold Arb.* **44**:60–80, 1963.

48. Brooks, A. B. West Virginia Trees. *West Va. Agr. Exp. Sta. Bull.* 175, Morgantown, W.Va., 1920.

49. Brooks, M. G. Effect of Black Walnut Trees and Their Products on Other Vegetation. *West Va. Agr. Exp. Sta. Bull.* 347, Morgantown, W.Va., 1951.

*50. Brown, C. A. Louisiana Trees and Shrubs. *La. For. Comm. Bull.* 1, 1945.

*51. Brown, H. P. "Trees of the Northeastern United States." The Christopher Publishing House, Boston, Mass. 1938.

52. Buchholz, J. T. Cone Formation in *Sequoia gigantea.* I. The Relation of Stem Size and Tissue Development to Cone Formation. II. The History of the Seed Cone. *Amer. Jour. Bot.* **25**:296–305, 1938.

53. ———. The Generic Segregation of the Sequoias. *Amer. Jour. Bot.* **26**:535–538, 1939.

54. ———. The Ozark White Cedar. *Bot. Gaz.* **90**:326–332, 1930.

55. Bunger, M. T., and H. J. Thomson. Root Development as a Factor in the Success or Failure of Windbreak Trees in the Southern High Plains. *Jour. For.* **36**:790–803, 1938.

56. Burleigh, T. D. The Relation of Birds to the Establishment of Longleaf Pine Seedlings in Southern Mississippi. *U.S. For. Serv., So. For. Exp. Sta. Occ. Paper* 75, 1938.

57. Burton, C. L. Variation in Characteristics of Black Locust Seeds from Two Regions. *Jour. For.* **30**:29–33, 1932.

58. Buswell, W. M. Native Trees and Palms of South Florida. *Bull. Univ. Fla.* 19, no. 6, 1945.

59. Camp, W. H. A Biogeographic and Paragenetic Analysis of the American Beech. *Yearbook Amer. Phil. Soc.* 166–169, 1950.

*60. ———. Biosystematy. *Brittonia* **7**:113–127, 1951.

*61. Canadian Dominion Forest Service. "Native Trees of Canada." King's Printer, Ottawa, Canada. 1949.

62. Chamberlain, C. J. The Age and Size of Plants. *Sci. Month.* **35**:481–491, 1932.

63. ———. The Gymnosperms. *Bot. Rev.* **1**:183–209, 1935.

64. ———. "Gymnosperms: Structure and Evolution." Reprinted by Dover Publications, Inc., New York. 1966.

65. Chang, Ying-Pe. Bark Structure of North American Conifers. *U.S. Dept. Agr. Tech. Bull.* 1095, 1954.

66. Chase, S. B. Propagation of Thornless Honeylocust. *Jour. For.* **45**:715–722, 1947.

67. Cheyney, E. G. The Roots of a Jack Pine Tree. *Jour. For.* **30**:929–932, 1932.

68. Clapper, R. B. A Promising New Forest-type Chestnut Tree. *Jour. For.* **61**:921–922, 1963.

69. Clark, R. M., and J. W. Andresen. Forest Trees of the Lake States. *Prof. Ser. Bull.* 53, Michigan State Univ., East Lansing, 1961.

70. Clepper, H. E. Hemlock. *Pa. Dept. For. Waters Bull.* 52, 1934.

*71. Clute, W. N. "The Common Names of Plants and Their Meanings," 2d ed. W. N. Clute & Co., Indianapolis, Ind. 1942.

*72. Coker, W. C., and H. R. Totten. "Trees of the Southeastern States," 3d ed. Univ. of North Carolina Press, Chapel Hill, N.C. 1945.

73. Collier, H. O. J. Aspirin. *Sci. Amer.* **209:**97–108, 1963.

*74. Collingwood, G. H., and W. D. Brush. "Knowing Your Trees." Amer. Forestry Assoc., Washington, D.C. 1966.

75. Cook, D. B. European Larch Reproduction in Eastern New York. *Jour. For.* **37:**891–893, 1939.

76. Cook, L. F. "The Giant Sequoias of California." U.S. Government Printing Office, Washington. 1942.

77. Cooke, G. B. "The Planting and Growing of Cork Oak Trees in the United States." Crown Cork and Seal Co., Baltimore, Md. 1946.

*78. Core, E. L., and N. P. Ammons. "Woody Plants in Winter." The Boxwood Press, Pittsburgh, Pa. 1958.

79. Critchfield, W. B. Geographic Variation in *Pinus contorta. Maria Moors Cabot Found. Publ.* 3, 1957.

80. ———— and E. L. Little, Jr. Geographic Distribution of the Pines of the World. *U.S. Dept. Agr. Misc. Publ.* 991, 1966.

81. Crocker, W. Harvesting, Storage, and Stratification of Seeds in Relation to Nursery Practice. *Flor. Rev.* **65:**43–46, 1930.

82. Cronemiller, F. P. El Sabino, the National Tree of Mexico. *Jour. For.* **55:**461–463, 1957.

83. Cunningham, F. E. A Seed Key for Five Northeastern Birches. *Jour. For.* **55:**844, 1957.

83*a.* Currey, D. R. An Ancient Bristlecone Pine Stand in Eastern Nevada. *Ecology* **46:** 564, 1965.

84. Dadswell, H. E., and H. D. Ingle. The Wood Anatomy of New Guinea Nothofagus Bl. *Australian Jour. Bot.* **2:**141–153, 1954.

*85. Dallimore, W., and A. B. Jackson. "A Handbook of Coniferae and Ginkgoaceae." 5th ed. S. G. Harrison, St. Martin's Press, New York. 1967.

86. Davies, P. A. Leaf Position in *Ailanthus altissima* in Relation to the Fibonacci Series. *Amer. Jour. Bot.* **26:**67–73, 1939.

87. Davis, E. F. The Toxic Principle of *Juglans nigra* as Identified with Synthetic Juglone, and Its Toxic Effects on Tomato and Alfalfa Plants. *Amer. Jour. Bot.* **15:**620, 1928.

88. Davison, J. "Conifers, Junipers and Yews: Gymnosperms of British Columbia." T. Fisher Unwin, London. 1927.

89. Day, M. W. The Root System of Red Pine Saplings. *Jour. For.* **39:**468–472, 1941.

90. Day, R. C. Douglas of "Douglas Fir." *Can. For. Outdoors* **26:**15, 1930.

91. Dayton, W. A. Geography of Commercially Important United States Trees. *Jour. For.* **51:**276–279, 1953.

92. ————. Important Western Browse Plants. *U.S. Dept. Agr. Misc. Publ.* 101, 1931.

*93. ————.What Is Dendrology? *Jour. For.* **43:**719–722, 1945.

*94. ———— and Others. "Range Plant Handbook." U.S. Dept. Agr. 1937.

*95. Deam, C. C., and T. E. Shaw. Trees of Indiana. *Dept. Cons. Ind. Publ.* 13a, 1953.

96. Dean, B. E. "Trees and Shrubs in the Heart of Dixie." Coxe Publishing Company, Birmingham, Ala. 1961.

97. Decker, J. P. Shade-Tolerance: A Revised Semantic Analysis. *For. Sci.* **5:**93, 1959.

98. ————. Tolerance Is a Good Technical Term. *Jour. For.* **50:**40–41, 1952.

*99. Dengler, H. W. The History of Holly in Murals. *Holly Soc. Amer. Bull.* 7, 1954.

100. ———. Say it with Holly. *Amer. For. Mag.* **72**:1–3, 1966.

100a. ———. Bayberries and Bayberry Candles. *Amer. For. Mag.* **73**:5–7, 1967.

*101. Den Ouden, P., and B. K. Boom. "Manual of Cultivated Conifers Hardy in the Cold- and Warm-Temperate Zone." Martinus Nijhoff, The Hague. 1965.

102. DeVall, W. B. A Bark Character for the Identification of Certain Florida Pines. *Proc. Fla. Acad. Sci.* **7**:101–103, 1945.

103. DeVilmorin, R. "International Code of Nomenclature for Cultivated Plants." Amer. Hort. Council, Arnold Arb., Jamaica Plain, Mass. 1958.

104. Dickson, A. Growing Christmas Trees in the Northeast. *Jour. For.* **63**:855–857, 1965.

*105. Diller, J. D., and R. B. Clapper. A Progress Report on Attempts to Bring Back the Chestnut Tree in the Eastern United States, 1954–1964. *Jour. For.* **63**:186–188, 1965.

106. Doi, T., and K. Morikawa. Anatomical Study of the Leaves of the Genus *Pinus. Jour. Dept. Agr.*, vol. 2, no. 6, Kyushu Imperial University, Fukuoka, Japan, 1929.

107. Dorman, K. W., and I. H. Sims. Loblolly Pine Bibliography. *S.E. For. Exp. Sta. Paper* 6, U.S. Dept. Agr., 1949.

*108. Douglass, A. E. Crossdating in Dendrochronology. *Jour. For.* **39**:825–831, 1941.

109. ———. The Secret of the Southwest Solved by Talkative Tree Rings. *Natl. Geograph. Mag.* **56**:736–770, 1929.

110. Duncan, W. H. Root Systems of Woody Plants of Old Fields of Indiana. *Ecology* **16**:554–567, 1935.

111. Dyal, S. C. A Key to the Species of Oaks of Eastern North America Based On Foliage and Twig Characters. *Rhodora* **38**:53–63, 1936.

*112. Eifert, V. S. "Tall Trees and Far Horizons." Dodd, Mead & Company, Inc., New York. 1965.

*113. Eliot, W. A. "Forest Trees of the Pacific Coast." Binfords, Portland, Ore. 1948.

114. Emerson, A. I., and C. M. Weed. "Our Trees: How to Know Them," 5th ed. Doubleday & Company, Inc., Garden City, N.Y. 1959.

115. Engler, A., and L. Diels. "Syllabus der Pflanzenfamilien," 12th ed. Gebrüder Borntraeger, Berlin-Nikolassee. 1954–64.

116. ——— and E. Gilg. "Syllabus der Pflanzenfamilien," 10th ed. Gebrüder Borntraeger, Berlin. 1924.

*117. ——— and K. Prantl. "Die naturlichen Pflanzenfamilien," 1st ed. 1887–1909; 2nd ed. in preparation, Breslau.

118. Ericson, J. E. Field Identification of Whitebark and Limber Pines based upon Needle Resin Canals. *Jour. For.* **62**:576–577, 1964.

119. Eyde, R. H. Morphological and Paleobotanical Studies of the Nyssaceae, I. A Survey of the Modern Species and Their Fruits. *Jour. Arnold Arb.* **44**:1–52, 1963.

120. ———. Typification of *Nyassa Aquatica* L. *Taxon* **13**:129–131, 1964.

*121. Eyre, F. H. "Forest Cover Types of North America." Soc. Amer. Foresters, Washington, D.C. 1954.

122. Farmer, R. E., Jr. Aspen Root Sucker Formation and Apical Dominance. *For. Sci.* **8**:403–410, 1962.

123. ———. Vegetative Propagation of Aspen by Greenwood Cuttings. *Jour. For.* **61**:385–386, 1963.

*124.   Fernald, M. L. "Gray's Manual of Botany," 8th ed. American Book Company, New York. 1950.

125.   Fletcher, W. F. The Native Persimmon. *U.S. Dept. Agr. Farm. Bull.* 685, new ed., 1935.

126.   Fowells, H. A. Cork Oak Planting Tests in California. *Jour. For.* 47:357–365, 1949.

*127.   ———. "Silvics of Forest Trees of the United States." *U.S. Dept. Agr. Hdbk.* 271, 1965.

128.   Fritz, E. The Role of Fire in the Redwood Region. *Calif. Agr. Exp. Sta. Cir.* 323, 1932.

*129.   ———. The Story as Told by a Fallen Redwood. Unnumbered, undated leaflet of Save-the-Redwood League, Berkeley, Calif.

*130.   Fry, W., and J. R. White. "Bigtrees," 2d ed. Stanford Univ. Press, Stanford, Calif. 1938.

131.   Fulling, E. H. Identification by Leaf Structure of the Species of *Abies* Cultivated in the United States. *Bull. Torrey Bot. Club.* 61:497–524, 1934.

132.   Garin, G. I. Longleaf Pines can form Vigorous Sprouts. *Jour. For.* 56:430, 1958.

*133.   Gates, F. C., and Others. "Trees in Kansas." Vol. 47, no. 186-A, Kansas State Bd. Agr., Topeka, Kans. 1928.

134.   Gerry, E., and Others. A Naval Stores Handbook. *U.S. Dept. Agr. Misc. Publ.* 209, 1935.

135.   Ghent, A. W., and J. B. Thomas. Regularity in Distribution of Supernumerary Needles on the Terminal Growth of Young Jack Pine Trees. *For. Sci.* 6:331–333, 1960.

136.   Gilky, H. M., and P. L. Packard. "Winter Twigs; Northwestern Oregon and Western Washington." Oregon State Univ. Press, Corvallis. 1962.

137.   Gillett, C. A. An Identification Key for Trees and Shrubs in North Dakota. *N.D. Extension Cir.* 4, 1928.

138.   Gleason, H. A. The Genus *Monochaetum* in South America. *Amer. Jour. Bot.* 16:508, 1929.

*139.   ——— and A. Cronquist. "Manual of Vascular Plants of Northeastern United States and Adjacent Canada." D. Van Nostrand Company, Inc., Princeton, N.J. 1963.

140.   Glock, W. S. The Language of Tree Rings. *Sci. Month.* 38:501–510, 1934.

*141.   Graham, S. A., R. P. Harrison, Jr., and C. E. Westell, Jr. "Aspens: Phoenix Trees of the Great Lakes Region." Univ. of Michigan Press, Ann Arbor. 1963.

*142.   Graves, A. H. "Illustrated Guide to Trees and Shrubs," rev. ed. Harper & Row, Publishers, Incorporated, New York. 1956.

143.   ———. Some Outstanding New Chestnut Hybrids, I. *Bull. Torrey Bot. Club* 87:192–204, 1960. Also part II, *ibid.* 89:161–172, 1962.

144.   Graves, G. "Trees, Shrubs, and Vines for the Northeastern United States." Oxford Univ. Press, New York. 1945.

145.   Green, C. H. "Trees of the South." Univ. of North Carolina Press, Chapel Hill, N.C. 1939.

146.   Griffith, B. G. "Pocket Guide to the Trees and Shrubs of British Columbia." Victoria, B.C., Forest Branch. 1934.

147.   Grimm, W. C. "The Book of Trees," 2d ed. The Stackpole Company, Harrisburg, Pa. 1962.

*148.   ———. "Recognizing Native Shrubs." The Stackpole Company, Harrisburg, Pa. 1966.

149.   Haddow, W. R. Distribution and Occurrence of White Pine (*Pinus strobus*

L.) and Red Pine (*Pinus resinosa* Ait.) at the Northern Limit of Their Range in Ontario. *Jour. Arnold Arb.* **29**:217–226, 1948.

150. Hall, B. A. The Floral Anatomy of the Genus *Acer. Amer. Jour. Bot.* **38**:793–799, 1951.

151. Hall, R. C. Suggestions for Locust Borer Control. *Cent. States For. Exp. Sta. Note* 5, 1933.

152. Haney, G. P. Shortleaf Pine Bibliography. *S.E. For. Exp. Sta. Paper* 48, U.S. Dept. Agr., 1955.

153. Hanzlik, E. J. "Trees and Forests of Western United States." Durham Printing Co., Portland, Ore. 1927.

154. Harlow, W. M. The Effect of Site on the Structure and Growth of White Cedar *Thuya occidentalis* L. *Ecology* **8**:453–470, 1927.

*155. ———. "Fruit Key and Twig Key to Trees and Shrubs." Reprinted by Dover Publications, Inc., New York, 1959.

156. ———. How Much Dendrology? *Jour. For.* **63**:129–130, 1965.

*157. ———. Identification of the Pines of the United States, Native and Introduced, by Needle Structure. *State Univ. Coll. For. Tech. Bull.* 32, Syracuse, N.Y., 1931.

158. ———. Poisonivy and Poisonsumac, *State Univ. Coll. For. Bull.*, Syracuse, N.Y., 1949.

*159. ———. "Trees of the Eastern and Central United States and Canada." Reprinted by Dover Publications, Inc., New York. 1957.

160. ———, W. A. Côté, Jr., and A. C. Day. The Opening Mechanism of Pine Cone Scales. *Jour. For.* **62**:538–540, 1962.

161. Harper, R. M. Economic Botany of Alabama. *Univ. Ala. Monog.* 9, 1928.

*162. Harrar, E. S. "Hough's Encyclopedia of American Woods," vols. 1–6. Robt. Speller and Sons, Publishers, New York. 1958–68.

*163. ——— and J. G. Harrar. "Guide to Southern Trees." Reprinted by Dover Publications, Inc., New York. 1962.

164. Harrington, H. D. The Woody Plants of Iowa in Winter Condition. Univ. Iowa, *Stud. Nat. History* **16**:1–116, 1934.

165. Harris, A. S. Sitka Spruce, Alaska's New State Tree. *Amer. For. Mag.* **70**:32–35, 1964.

166. Harrison, S. G. Nomenclature for Cultivated Plants. *Taxon* **12**:259–260, 1963.

*167. Harvey, A. G. "Douglas of the Fir: a Biography of David Douglas, Botanist." Harvard Univ. Press, Cambridge, Mass. 1947.

*168. Haury, E. W. HH-39 Recollections of a Dramatic Moment in Southwestern Archaeology. *Tree-Ring Bull.* **24**:11–14, 1962.

169. Hayes, D. W., and G. A. Garrison. Key to Important Woody Plants of Eastern Oregon and Washington. *U.S. Dept. Agr. Hdbk.* 148, 1960.

*170. Heller, R. C., G. E. Doverspike and R. C. Aldrich. Identification of Tree Species on Large-Scale Panchromatic and Color Aerial Photographs. *U.S. Dept. Agr. Hdbk.* 261, July, 1964.

171. Henry, A., and M. G. Flood. The Douglas Firs: A Botanical and Silvicultural Description of the Various Species of Pseudotsuga. *Proc. Royal Irish Acad.* **35**:67–92, 1920.

172. Hoag, O. G. "Trees and Shrubs for the Northern Plains." N. Dakota Inst. Regional Studies, Fargo, 1965.

173. Hopp, H. Growth-form Variation in Black Locust and Its Importance in Farm Planting. *Jour. For.* **39**:40–46, 1941.

174. Hosner, J. F. Relative Tolerance to Complete Inundation of Fourteen Bottomland Tree Species. *For. Sci.* **6**:246–251, 1960.

175. ———— and S. G. Boyce. Tolerance to Water Saturated Soil of Various Bottomland Hardwoods. *For. Sci.* **8**:180–186, 1962.

*176. Hottes, A. C. "The Book of Shrubs," 6th ed. Dodd, Mead & Company, Inc., New York. 1952.

*177. Hough, R. B. "Handbook of the Trees of the Northern States and Canada." Reprinted by The Macmillan Company, New York. 1955.

178. Howes, F. N. "Vegetable Gums and Resins." Chronica Botanica Co., Waltham, Mass. 1949.

*179. Hu, H. H. How Metasequoia, the "Living Fossil," was Discovered in China. *Jour. N.Y. Bot. Gard.* **49**:201–207, 1948.

180. Hui-Lin Li. Metasequoia, a Living Fossil. *Amer. Scientist* **54**:93–109, 1964.

*181. Hutchinson, J. "The Families of Flowering Plants," 2d ed., 2 vols. Oxford Univ. Press, New York. 1959.

182. ————. "The Genera of Flowering Plants," vol. 1 (Angiospermae): Dicotyledones. Oxford Univ. Press, New York. 1964.

*183. Hyland, F., and F. H. Steinmetz. "The Woody Plants of Maine: Their Occurrence and Distribution." Univ. of Maine Press, Orono, Maine. 1944.

*184. Illick, J. S. Pennsylvania Trees. *Pa. Dept. For. Waters Bull.* 11, 1928, Harrisburg, Pa.

185. ————. "Tree Habits: How to Know the Hardwoods." Amer. Nat. Assoc., Washington, D.C. 1924.

186. ———— and J. E. Aughanbaugh. Pitch Pine in Pennsylvania. *Pa. Dept. For. Waters Res. Bull.* 2, 1930, Harrisburg, Pa.

187. ———— and E. F. Brouse. The Ailanthus Tree in Pennsylvania. *Pa. Dept. For. Waters Bull.* 38, 1926, Harrisburg, Pa.

188. Jeffers, J. N. R., and T. M. Black. An Analysis of Variability in *Pinus contorta*. *Forestry* **36**:199–218, 1963.

*189. Jepson, W. L. "The Silva of California." Univ. of California Press, Berkeley, Calif. 1910.

190. ————. "The Trees of California," 2d ed. Cunningham, Curtis and Welch, San Francisco. 1923.

191. Johanssen, D. Något om Vedens inflytande på utbyte och Kvalitet vid sulfat- och sulfitmassekokning. *Svenska Skogsvardsföreningens Tidskrift*, Årg. 33, Häfte 1, April, 1935.

192. Johnson, A. M. "Taxonomy of the Flowering Plants." Century Company, New York. 1931.

193. Jones, G. N. "American Species of Amelanchier." Univ. of Illinois Press, Urbana, Ill. 1946.

194. ————. Flora of Illinois. *Amer. Mid. Natur. Monog.* 7, 1963, Univ. of Notre Dame, South Bend, Ind.

195. Kearney, T. H., and R. H. Peebles. "Arizona Flora," 2d ed. Univ. of California Press, Berkeley. 1960.

196. Keen, F. P. Longevity of Ponderosa Pine. *Jour. For.* **38**:597, 1940.

*197. Kelsey, H. P., and W. A. Dayton. "Standardized Plant Names," 2d ed. American Joint Committee on Horticultural Nomenclature. J. H. McFarland Co., Harrisburg, Pa. 1942.

*198. Kingsbury, J. M. "Poisonous Plants of the United States and Canada." Prentice-Hall, Inc., Englewood Cliffs, N.J. 1964.

199. Kirkwood, J. E. "Forest Distribution in the Northern Rocky Mountains." Montana State Univ. Press, Missoula, Mont. 1922.

*200. ————. "Northern Rocky Mountain Trees and Shrubs." Stanford Univ. Press, Stanford, Calif. 1930.

201. Klaehn, F. U. Some Interesting Aspects of Flower Morphology and Flower Ecology of Various Forest Trees. *Proc. Fifth Northeastern Forest Tree Improvement Conference*, 71–76, 1958.

202. Korstian, C. F., and W. D. Brush. Southern White Cedar. *U.S. Dept. Agr. Bull.* 251, 1931.

203. Küchler, A. W. Potential Natural Vegetation of the Conterminous United States. Spec. Publ. 36, Amer. Geogr. Soc., New York, 1964.

204. Kuprianova, L. A. On a Hitherto Undescribed Family Belonging to the Amentiferae. *Taxon.* 12:12–13, 1963.

205. Kurz, H., and R. K. Godfrey, "Trees of Northern Florida." Univ. of Florida Press, Gainesville. 1962.

206. Langdon, O. G. Range of South Florida Slash Pine. *Jour. For.* 61:384–385, 1963.

*207. Lanjouw, J. "International Code of Botanical Nomenclature." 10th Inter. Botan. Congress, Edinburgh, 1964. Inter. Bur. Plant Taxonomy, Utrecht, Netherlands. 1966.

208. Larsen, H. S. Effects of Soaking in Water on Acorn Germination of Four Southern Oaks. *For. Sci.* 9:236–241, 1963.

*209. Lawrence, G. H. M. "Taxonomy of Vascular Plants." The Macmillan Company, New York. 1951.

210. Leaf, A. L., and K. G. Watterston. Chemical Analysis of Sugar Maple Sap and Foliage as Related to Sap and Sugar Yields. *For Sci.* 10:288–292, 1964.

211. Lenhart, D. Y. Initial Root Development of Longleaf Pine. *Jour. For.* 32:459–461, 1934.

*212. Little, E. L., Jr. Check List of Native and Naturalized Trees of the U.S. (including Alaska). *U.S. Dept. Agr. Hdbk.* 41, 1953.

213. ———. Designating Hybrid Forest Trees. *Taxon* 9:225–231, 1960.

214. ———. Mexican Beech, a Variety of Fagus grandifolia. *Castanea* 30:167–170, 1965.

215. ———. Miscellaneous Notes on Nomenclature of United States Trees. *Amer. Mid. Nat.* 33:505–507, 1945.

216. ———. Notes on Nomenclature of Trees. *Phytologia* 2:460–463, 1948.

217. ———. Notes on Tropical Dendrology. *U.S. For. Ser.* (mimeo), 1955.

*218. ———. Southwestern Trees. *U.S. Dept. Agr. Hdbk.* 9, 1950.

*219. ———. To Know the Trees. Yearbook of Agriculture, U.S. Dept. Agr., 1949. (Reprinted separately, no. 2156.)

220. ——— and J. D. Diller. Clapper Chestnut, a Hybrid Forest Tree. *Jour. For.* 62:109–110, 1964.

*221. ——— and K. W. Dorman. Slash Pine (*Pinus elliottii*), including South Florida Slash Pine. *S.E. For. Exp. Sta. Paper* 36, U.S. Dept. Agr., 1954.

222. ——— and F. I. Righter. Botanical Descriptions of Forty Artificial Pine Hybrids. *U.S. Dept. Agr. Tech. Bull.* 1345, 1965.

223. ——— and F. H. Wadsworth. Common Trees of Puerto Rico and the Virgin Islands. *U.S. Dept. Agr. Hdbk.* 249, 1964.

224. Little, S., and F. Mergen. External and Internal Changes Associated with Basal-Crook Formation in Pitch and Shortleaf Pines. *For. Sci.* 12:268–275, 1966.

225. Longyear, B. O. "Evergreens of Colorado." Bull. Colo. Agr. Coll. Fort Collins, Colo., 1925.

*226. ———. "Trees and Shrubs of the Rocky Mountain Region." G. P. Putnam's Sons, New York. 1927.

227. Lundell, C. L., and Collaborators. "Flora of Texas," vol. 3. Texas Research Foundation, Renner, Tex. 1961.
228. Mahood, S. A., and E. Gerry. The Production of American Storax. Drug. Circ., 100 William St., New York. 1921.
228a. Major, R. T. The Ginkgo, The Most Ancient Living Tree. Sci. 157:1270–1273. 1967.
229. Manning, W. E. The Genus Juglans in Mexico and Central America. Jour. Arnold Arb. 38:120–150, 1957.
230. ———. A Key to the Hickories North of Virginia with Notes on the Two Pignuts, Carya glabra and Carya ovalis. Rhodora 52:188–199, 1950.
231. ———. The Morphology of the Flowers of the Juglandaceae, II. The Pistillate Flowers and Fruit. Amer. Jour. Bot. 27:839–852, 1940.
232. ———. The Morphology of the Flowers of the Juglandaceae, III. The Staminate Flowers. Amer. Jour. Bot. 35:606–621, 1948.
233. Marco, H. F. The Identification of the Spruces (Picea) by Needle Structure. Unpublished thesis, N.Y. State Coll. For., Syracuse, N.Y., 1932.
°234. Martin, A. C., H. S. Zim, and A. L. Nelson. "American Wildlife and Plants." Dover Publications, Inc., New York.
235. Martinez, M. Picea chihuahana Sobretiro do los. An. Inst. Biol. Univ. Nac. Mexico 19:393–405, 1948.
236. ———. "Los Pinaceas del Estado de Mexico." Toluca, Mexico. 1953.
237. ———. "Los Pinos Mexicanos," 2d ed. Ediciones Botas, Mexico. 1948.
238. Mason, H. L. The Alaska Cedar in California. Madrono 6:90, 1941.
239. Massey, A. B. Antagonism of the Walnuts (Juglans nigra L. and J. cinerea L.) in Certain Plant Associations. Phytopathology 15:773–784, 1925.
240. Mattoon, W. R. Life History of Shortleaf Pine. U.S. Dept. Agr. Bull. 244, 1915.
241. ———. Longleaf Pine. U.S. Dept. Agr. Bull. 1061, 1925.
242. ———. The Southern Cypress. U.S. Dept. Agr. Bull. 272, 1915.
243. McCarthy, E. F. Yellow Poplar: Characteristics, Growth and Management. U.S. Dept. Agr. Bull. 356, 1933.
°244. McGinnes, W. G. Dendrochronology. Jour. For. 61:5–11, 1963.
245. McIntyre, A. C., and C. D. Jeffries. The Effect of Black Locust on Soil Nitrogen and Growth of Catalpa. Jour. For. 30:22–28, 1932.
°246. McMinn, H. E., and E. Maino. "An Illustrated Manual of Pacific Coast Trees," 2d ed. Univ. of California Press, Berkeley, Calif. 1946. (Reprinted 1956.)
°247. McNair, J. B. "Studies in Plant Chemistry Including Chemical Taxonomy, Ontogeny, Phylogeny, etc." Publ. by the author. Los Angeles, Calif. 1965.
248. Meade, F. M. A Silvicultural Study of the Seed of Basswood with Special Reference to Hastening the Germination. Unpublished thesis, State Univ. Coll. For., Syracuse, N.Y., 1933.
249. Meehan, T. Historical Notes on the Arbor Vitae. Proc. Acad. Nat. Sci. Philadelphia 34:110–111, 1882.
250. Mergen, F. Distribution of Reaction Wood in Eastern Hemlock as a Function of its Terminal Growth. For. Sci. 4:98–109, 1958.
251. ———. Ecotypic variation in Pinus strobus L. Ecology 44:716–727, 1963.
252. ——— and H. Rossoll. How to Root and Graft Slash Pine. S.E. For. Exp. Sta. Paper 46, U.S. Dept. Agr., 1954.
°253. Meyer, A. B., and F. H. Eyre. "Forestry Terminology: A Glossary of Technical Terms Used in Forestry," 3d ed. Society of American Foresters, Washington, D.C. 1958.

254. Michaux, F. A. "North American Sylva," vols. 1, 2, and 3. D. Rice and A. N. Hart, Philadelphia. 1857.

255. Millard, N. D., and W. L. Keene. Native Trees of the Intermountain Region. U.S. For. Serv., Ogden, Utah. 1934.

256. Miller, G. N. The Genus *Fraxinus*, The Ashes, in North America, North of Mexico. *Cornell Univ. Agr. Exp. Sta. Memoir* 335, Ithaca, N.Y. 1955.

257. Mills, E. A. A Note on Jeffrey Pine and Yellow Pine. *Jour. For.* 30:93–94, 1932.

°258. ———. "The Story of a Thousand Year Pine." Houghton Mifflin Company, Boston. 1914.

259. ———. "Wild Life on the Rockies." Houghton Mifflin Company, Boston. 1909.

°260. Mirov, N. T. "Composition of Gum Turpentines of Pines." *U.S. Dept. Agr. Tech. Bull.* 1329, 1961.

°261. Molisch, H. "The Longevity of Plants." Trans. by E. H. Fulling, N.Y. Bot. Gard., New York. 1938.

262. Morgenstern, E. K., and J. L. Farrar. Introgressive Hybridization in Red Spruce and Black Spruce. *Univer. Toronto Faculty, For. Tech. Rep.* 4, 1964.

263. Mowery, H. Ornamental Trees. *Agr. Ext. Serv. Bull.* 95, Gainesville, Fla., 1938.

°264. Muenscher, W. C. "Keys to Woody Plants," 6th ed. Comstock Publishing Associates, a division of Cornell Univ. Press, Ithaca, N.Y. 1950.

°265. ———. "Poisonous Plants of the United States," rev. ed. The Macmillan Company, New York. 1951.

266. Munz, P. A., and D. D. Keck. "A California Flora." Univ. of California Press, Berkeley. 1959.

267. Murphy, L. S. The Red Spruce: Its Growth and Management. *U.S. Dept. Agr. Bull.* 544, 1917.

268. Namkoong, G. Female Flowers on One-Year-Old Pitch Pine. *For. Sci.* 6:163, 1960.

269. Neumann, F. P. Scale Movements of Jack Pine Cones. Unpublished thesis, Univ. of Minnesota, 1961.

270. Nichols, G. E. The Hemlock–White Pine–Northern Hardwood Region of Eastern North America. *Ecology* 16:403–422, 1935.

271. Nuttall, T. "North American Sylva," vols. 1 and 2. D. Rice and A. N. Hart, Philadelphia. 1859.

272. Ogden, E. C., F. H. Steinmetz, and F. Hyland. Check-list of the Vascular Plants of Maine. *Bull. Josselyn Bot. Soc.* 8, Orono, Maine, 1948.

°273. Otis, C. H. "Michigan Trees." Univ. of Michigan Press, Ann Arbor, Mich. 1931.

274. Palmer, E. J. Hybrid Oaks of North America. *Jour. Arnold Arb.* 29:1–48, 1948.

275. ———. On Nuttall's Trail through Arkansas. *Jour. Arnold Arb.* 8:24–55, 1927.

°276. Peattie, D. C. "A Natural History of Trees of Eastern and Central North America." Houghton Mifflin Company, Boston. 1950.

277. ———. A Natural History of Western Trees. Houghton Mifflin Company, Boston. 1953.

278. Peck, M. E. "A Manual of the Higher Plants of Oregon," 2d ed. Binfords and Mort, Portland. 1961.

°279. Perry, G. S. The Common Trees and Shrubs of Pennsylvania. *Pa. Dept. For. Waters Bull.* 33, 1932, Harrisburg, Pa.

280. Pessin, L. J. Annual Ring Formation in *Pinus palustris* Seedlings. *Amer. Jour. Bot.* 21:599–603, 1934.

*281. Pierce, R. M. Trees for the States. *Amer. For. Mag.* **71**:4–5, 1965.

282. Pierpont, D. W. Hachinoki: The Art of Dwarfing Trees. *Amer. For.* **41**:113–115, 1935.

283. Piper, C. V., and R. K. Beattie. "Flora of the Northwest Coast." Press of the New Era, Lancaster, Pa. 1915.

*284. Pomeroy, K. B., and D. Dixon. These are the Champs. *Amer. For. Mag.* **72**: 15–35, 1966.

285. Pool, R. J. "Flowers and Flowering Plants." McGraw-Hill Book Company, New York. 1941.

285a. ———. Handbook of Nebraska Trees. *Univ. Neb. Bull.* 7, 1929.

*286. Preston, R. J., Jr. "North American Trees," 2d ed. Iowa State College Press, Ames, Iowa. 1961.

287. ———. "Rocky Mountain Trees," 2d ed. Iowa State College Press, Ames, Iowa. 1947.

288. Putnam, J. A., and H. Bull. The Trees of the Bottomlands of the Mississippi River Delta Region. U.S. Dept. Agr. unnumbered (mimeographed) publication, 1932.

289. Quin, V. "Leaves: Their Place in Life and Legend." Frederick A. Stokes Company, Philadelphia. 1937.

290. Raber, O. Shipmast Locust: A Valuable Undescribed Variety of *Robinia pseudoacacia*. *U.S. Dept. Agr. Cir.* 379, 1936.

291. Rafinesque, C. S. "A Life of Travels." Philadelphia, 1836. Reprinted by Chronica Botanica Co., Waltham, Mass. 1944.

*292. Randall, C. E., and D. P. Edgerton. Famous Trees. *U.S. Dept. Agr. Misc. Publ.* 295, 1938.

293. Reed, A. H. "The New Story of the Kauri." Reed Publications, Wellington, New Zealand.

*294. Rehder, A. "Manual of Cultivated Trees and Shrubs," 2d ed. The Macmillan Company, New York. 1940.

295. Reines, M., and J. T. Greene. Early Cone Production in Loblolly Pine. *Jour. For.* **56**:855, 1958.

296. Rice, H. P. A Rough-barked American Beech. *Jour. For.* **46**:48, 1948.

297. Rigg, G. B., and E. S. Harrar. The Root Systems of Trees Growing in Sphagnum. *Amer. Jour. Bot.* **18**:391–397, 1931.

298. Righter, F. I. Bisexual Flowers among the Pines. *Jour. For.* **30**:873, 1932.

299. Roberts, M. McM. "Public Gardens and Arboretums of the United States." Holt, Rinehart and Winston, Inc., New York. 1962.

300. Robinson, F. B. The Great Ginkgo. *Amer. For.* **54**:146, 1948.

301. Roe, A. L., and K. N. Boe. Ponderosa Pine Bibliography. *Northern Rocky Mt. For. Exp. Sta. Paper* 22, U.S. Dept. Agr., 1950.

*302. Rogers, W. E. "Tree Flowers of Forest, Park, and Street." Reprinted by Dover Publications, Inc., New York. 1965.

303. Rollins, R. C. On the Basis of Biological Classification. *Taxon* **14**:1–6, 1965.

*304. Rosendahl, C. O. "Trees and Shrubs of the Upper Midwest." Univ. of Minnesota Press, Minneapolis, 1955.

305. Ross, C. R. Sweetgum from the Sweetgum. *Amer. For.* **53**:404–405, 1947.

306. ——— and H. Hayes. Trees to Know in Oregon. *Ore. State Bd. For. Ext. Bull.* 697, 1950.

307. Rowley, G. D. The Naming of Hybrids. *Taxon* **13**:64–65, 1964.

308. Ryan, W. A. "Some Geographic and Economic Aspects of the Cork Oak." Crown Cork and Seal Co., Baltimore, Md. 1948.

*309. Rydberg, P. A. "Flora of the Rocky Mountains and Adjacent Plains," 2d ed. Published by the author, New York. 1922.

310. St. John, H. "Flora of Southeastern Washington and of Adjacent Idaho," 3d ed. Outdoor Pictures, Escondido, Calif. 1963.

311. ——— and R. W. Krauss. The Taxonomic Position and the Scientific Name of the Big Tree Known as *Sequoia gigantea*. *Pacific Sci*. 8:341–358, 1954.

*312. Sargent, C. S. "Manual of the Trees of North America," 2d ed. Reprinted by Dover Publications, Inc., New York. 1961.

*313. ———. "The Silva of North America." 14 vols. Houghton Mifflin Company, Boston. 1890–1902.

*314. Schulman, E. Bristlecone Pine, Oldest Known Living Thing. *Natl. Geograph. Mag*. 113:355–372, 1958.

315. ———. "Dendroclimatic Changes in Semiarid America." *Univ. of Arizona Press*, Tucson. 1956.

316. ———. Longevity under Adversity in Conifers. *Science* 119:396–399, 1954.

317. ———. Tree Ring Hydrology of the Colorado River Basin. *Lab. Tree-Ring Res. Bull*. 2, Univ. of Arizona, Tucson, Arizona, 1945.

*318. Scott, C. A., F. C. Gates, and Others. "Trees in Kansas," vol. 47, no. 186–A. Kansas State Bd. Agr., Topeka, Kansas. 1928.

*319. Scott, C. W. "Pinus radiata." Food and Agriculture Organization of the U.N., Rome. 1960.

320. Seton, E. T. "The Forester's Manual." Doubleday & Company, Inc., Garden City, N.Y. 1912.

321. Settergren, C., and R. E. McDermott. Trees of Missouri. *Missouri Univ. Agr. Exp. Sta*. B767, 1962.

322. Shantz, H. L., and R. Zon. Natural Vegetation. *Atlas of Amer. Agriculture*, pt. 1, sec. E, U.S. Dept. Agr., 1924.

*323. Shaw, G. R. The Genus Pinus. *Arnold Arb. Publ*. 5, Jamaica Plain, Mass., 1914.

324. Shimek, B. "Keys to the Woody Plants of Iowa." Published by the author, 1930.

*325. Small, J. K. "Manual of the Southeastern Flora." Published by the author, New York. 1933.

326. Smith, N. F. Michigan Trees Worth Knowing. Mich. Dept. Conservation, Lansing, 1961.

327. Snyder, E. B. "Glossary for Tree Improvement Workers." Society of American Foresters, Washington, D.C. 1959.

*328. Sokal, R. R., and P. H. A. Sneath. "Principles of Numerical Taxonomy." W. H. Freeman and Company, San Francisco. 1963.

329. Spaeth, J. N. A Physiological Study of Dormancy in *Tilia* Seed. *Cornell Univ. Exp. Sta. Mem*. 169, Ithaca, N.Y., 1934.

329a. Squillace, A. E. Geographic Variation in Slash Pine. *For. Sci. Monograph* 10, Soc. Amer. Foresters, Washington, D.C., 1966.

330. Starker, T. J. Giant Growers of the Globe. *Amer. For*. 41:266, 1935.

331. Stearn, W. T. The Self-taught Botanists who saved the Kew Garden. *Taxon* 14:293–298, 1965.

332. Stephens, E. L. How Old Are the Live Oaks? *Amer. For*. 37:739–742, 1931.

333. Sterling, C. Some Features in the Morphology of Metasequoia. *Amer. Jour. Bot*. 36:461–471, 1949.

*334. Steyermark, J. A. "Flora of Missouri." Iowa State Univ. Press, Ames, Iowa. 1963.

335. Stone, E. L., Jr., and M. H. Stone. "Dormant" versus Adventitious Buds. *Science* **98**:62, 1943.

336. ——— and ———. Root Collar Sprouts in Pine. *Jour. For.* **52**:487–491, 1954.

337. Stout, A. B. The Clon in Plant Life. *Jour. N.Y. Bot. Gard.* **30**:25–37, 1929.

*338. Strausbaugh, P. D., and E. L. Core. Flora of West Virginia. *West Va. Univ. Bull. Series* 65, No. 3–1, September, 1964.

339. Stuhr, E. T. "Manual of Pacific Coast Drug Plants." The Science Press, Lancaster, Pa. 1933.

340. Stupka, A. "Trees, Shrubs, and Woody Vines of Great Smoky Mountains National Park." Univ. of Tennessee Press, Knoxville. 1964.

*341. Sudworth, G. B. Check List of Forest Trees of the United States. *U.S. Dept. Agr. Misc. Cir.* 92, 1927.

342. ———. The Cypress and Juniper Trees of the Rocky Mountain Region. *U.S. Dept. Agr. Bull.* 207, 1915.

343. ———. Forest Atlas. I. Pines. *U.S. Dept. Agr.* 1913.

*344. ———. Forest Trees of the Pacific Slope. Reprinted by Dover Publications, Inc., New York. 1967.

345. ———. Miscellaneous Conifers of the Rocky Mountain Region. *U.S. Dept. Agr. Bull.* 680, 1918.

346. ———. The Pines of the Rocky Mountain Region. *U.S. Dept. Agr. Bull.* 460, 1917.

347. ———. Poplars, Principal Tree Willows, and Walnuts of the Rocky Mt. Region. *U.S. Dept. Agr. Tech. Bull.* 420, 1934.

348. ———. The Spruce and Balsam Fir Trees of the Rocky Mountain Region. *U.S. Dept. Agr. Bull.* 327, 1916.

349. Sutherland, M. A Microscopical Study of the Structure of the Leaves of the Genus Pinus. *Trans. Proc. New Zealand Inst.* **63**:517–558, 1934.

*350. Swain, T., and Others. "Chemical Plant Taxonomy." Academic Press Inc., New York. 1963.

*351. Taylor, N. "Plant Drugs that Changed the World." Dodd, Mead & Company, Inc., New York. 1965.

352. Taylor, R. F., and E. L. Little, Jr. Pocket Guide to Alaska Trees. *U.S. Dept. Agr. Hdbk.* 5, 1950.

353. Tidestrom, I. Flora of Utah and Nevada. *Contr. U.S. Natl. Herbarium*, vol. 25, 1925.

*354. Tiemann, H. D. What Are the Largest Trees in the World? *Jour. For.* **33**:903–915, 1935.

*355. Trelease, W. "Winter Botany," 3d ed. Reprinted by Dover Publications, Inc., New York. 1967.

356. Tresidder, M. C. "The Trees of Yosemite," 2d ed. Stanford Univ. Press, Stanford, Calif. 1963.

357. U.S. Dept. Agr. Forest Service. American Woods Leaflets covering many species, too numerous to list separately.

358. ———. Woody Plant Seed Manual. *Misc. Publ.* 654, 1948.

359. Uphof, J. C. Th. Die Amerikanischen Nyssa-Arten. *Mitteil. Deutsch Dendrol Gesell.* **43**:2–16, 1931.

360. ———. Dendrologische Notizen aus dem Staate Florida. 4, Die Sumpf-und Wasserwälder; Pflanzenvereien einiger stehender Gewässer. *Mitteil. Deutsch Dendrol Gesell.* **44**:184–207, 1932.

*361. Van Dersal, W. R. Native Woody Plants of the United States: Their Erosion-control and Wildlife Values. *U.S. Dept. Agr. Misc. Publ.* 303, 1938.

°362.   Viertel, A. T. Trees, Shrubs, and Vines. *State Univ. Coll. For. Bull.* 43, Syracuse, N.Y., 1961.

°363.   Vines, R. A. "Trees, Shrubs, and Woody Vines of the Southwest." Univ. of Texas Press, Austin. 1960.

°364.   Wahlenberg, W. G. "Loblolly Pine: Its Use, Ecology, Regeneration, Protection, Growth, and Management." The School of Forestry, Duke Univ., Durham, N.C. 1960.

°365.   ———. "Longleaf Pine." C. L. Pack Found., Washington, D.C. 1946.

366.   Wakeley, P. C. Seed Yield Data for Southern Pines. *Jour. For.* **28**:391–394, 1930.

367.   Walker, L. C., R. L. Green, and J. M. Daniels. Flooding and Drainage Effects on Slash Pine and Loblolly Pine Seedlings. *For. Sci.* **7**:3–15, 1961.

368.   Weatherby, C. A. Botanical Nomenclature since 1867. *Amer. Jour. Bot.* **36**:5–7, 1949.

369.   Weidman, R. H. Evidences of Racial Influence on a 25-year Test of Ponderosa Pine. *Jour. Agr. Res.* **59**:855–887, 1939.

°370.   Werthner, W. B. "Some American Trees." The Macmillan Company, New York. 1935.

°371.   West, E., and L. E. Arnold. "The Native Trees of Florida," rev. ed. Univ of Florida Press, Gainesville, Fla. 1956.

372.   Westing, A. H. Formation and Function of Compression Wood in Gymnosperms. *Bot. Rev.* **31**:381–480, 1965.

373.   ———. Needle Number in Red Pine. *Rhodora* **66**:27–31, 1964.

374.   Whelden, C. M. Studies in the Genus Fraxinus: A Preliminary Key to Winter Twigs for the Sections Melioides and Bumelioides. *Jour. Arnold Arb.* **15**:118–126, 1934.

°375.   White, J. H., and R. C. Hosie. "The Forest Trees of Ontario." King's Printer, Toronto, Canada. 1946.

376.   Wigginton, B. E. "Trees and Shrubs for the Southeast." Univ. of Georgia Press, Athens. 1964.

377.   Williams, S. Secondary Vascular Tissues of the Oaks Indigenous to the United States. I. The Importance of Secondary Xylem in Delimiting Erythrobalanus and Leucobalanus. *Bull. Torrey Bot. Club* **66**:353–365, 1939.

°378.   Wilson, E. H. "America's Greatest Garden: The Arnold Arboretum." Stratford Company, Boston, Mass. 1925.

°379.   ———. "Aristocrats of the Trees." Stratford Company, Boston, Mass. 1930.

380.   ———. "A Naturalist in Western China." Doubleday & Company, Inc., Garden City, N.Y. 1914.

381.   Wilson, K. A., and C. E. Wood, Jr. The Genera of Oleaceae in the Southeastern United States. *Jour. Arnold Arb.* **40**:369–384, 1959.

382.   Winkenwerder, H. A., and F. F. Wangaard. "Short Keys to the Native Trees of Oregon and Washington." Imperial Publ. Co., Seattle, Wash. 1939.

383.   Wise, L. E. Drugs from the Forest. *Amer. For.* **41**:322–324, 1935.

384.   Wolf, C. B., and W. W. Wagener. The New World Cypresses. *Aliso*, vol. 1, Rancho Santa Ana Bot. Gard., Anaheim, Calif., 1948.

385.   Wood, C. E., Jr. The Citation of Some Genera of the Lauraceae. *Jour. Arnold Arb.* **39**:213–15, 1958.

386.   ———. The Genera of the Ericaceae in the Southeastern United States. *Jour. Arnold Arb.* **42**:10–80, 1961.

387.   ———. The Genera of the Woody Ranales in the Southeastern United States. *Jour. Arnold Arb.* **39**:296–346, 1958.

388. Wright, J. W. Notes on Flowering and Fruiting of Northeastern Trees. *N.E. For. Exp. Sta. St. Paper* 60, 1953.

*389. ———. Species Crossability in Spruce in Relation to Distribution and Taxonomy. *For. Sci.* 1:319–349, 1955.

390. Zimmerman, P. W., and A. E. Hitchcock. Selection, Propagation, and Growth of Holly. *Flor. Exch.* 81:19–20, 1933.

391. Zingher, A. Die alteste Robinie (*Robinia pseudoacacia*) in Europa. *Mitteil. Deutsch Dendrol Gesell.* 45:354–355, 1933.

392. Zon, R. Loblolly Pine in Eastern Texas. *U.S. Dept. Agr. Bull.* 64, 1905.

393. ———. A New Explanation of the Tolerance and Intolerance of Trees. *Proc. Soc. Amer. For.* 2:79–94, 1907.

394. Zsilinszky, V. G. "Photographic Interpretation of Tree Species in Ontario." Ontario Dept. Lands and Forests, Toronto, Canada, 1963.

Index

Page references in **boldface** indicate illustrations. Species names not presently accepted as "official" but often seen are indicated by *italics*.